Irish Divorce

D1388386

This is the first history of Irish divorce. Spanning the island of Ireland over three centuries, it places the human experience of marriage breakdown centre stage to explore the impact of a highly restrictive and gendered law and its reform. It considers the accessibility of Irish divorce as it moved from a parliamentary process in Westminster, the Irish parliament and the Northern Ireland parliament to a court-based process. This socio-legal approach allows changing definitions of gendered marital roles and marital cruelty to be assessed. In charting the exceptionalism of Ireland's divorce provision in a European and imperial framework, the study uncovers governmental reluctance to reform Irish divorce law which spans jurisdictions and centuries. This was therefore not only a law dictated by religious strictures but also by a long-lived moral conservatism.

Diane Urquhart is Professor of Gender History at Queen's University Belfast. She has written widely on Irish women's history and gender and is the author of *The Ladies of Londonderry: Women and Political Patronage, 1800–1959* (2007) as well as *Women in Ulster Politics, 1890–1940: A History Not Yet Told* (2000) which was selected as an *Irish Times* Book of the Year. She is the editor of *The Papers of the Ulster Women's Unionist Council and Executive Committee, 1911–40* (2001), co-editor of *Irish Women at War: The Twentieth Century* (2010) and co-author of *The Irish Abortion Journey, 1922–2018* (2019) with Lindsey Earner-Byrne.

Irish Divorce

A History

Diane Urquhart

Queen's University Belfast

CAMBRIDGE
UNIVERSITY PRESS

CAMBRIDGE
UNIVERSITY PRESS

University Printing House, Cambridge CB2 8BS, United Kingdom

One Liberty Plaza, 20th Floor, New York, NY 10006, USA

477 Williamstown Road, Port Melbourne, VIC 3207, Australia

314–321, 3rd Floor, Plot 3, Splendor Forum, Jasola District Centre,
New Delhi – 110025, India

79 Anson Road, #06–04/06, Singapore 079906

Cambridge University Press is part of the University of Cambridge.

It furthers the University's mission by disseminating knowledge in the pursuit of
education, learning, and research at the highest international levels of excellence.

www.cambridge.org
Information on this title: www.cambridge.org/9781108493093
DOI: 10.1017/9781108675536

First published 2020

Printed in the United Kingdom by TJ International Ltd, Padstow Cornwall

A catalogue record for this publication is available from the British Library.

ISBN 978-1-108-49309-3 Hardback
ISBN 978-1-108-71725-0 Paperback

For Alyson

Contents

Figures

Acknowledgements

The support of family and friends has, as ever, been invaluable. Special thanks are due to Martin O'Neill; Betty and Eric Urquhart; Alyson, Patrick and Joel Lattimer; Mary and Brendan O'Neill; Louise, Colm, Sarah and Hannah Alley; Simone, Shaymus and Kitty Kennedy; Julia, Paul, Ada, Sam and Zac O'Neill; Gail McMullan; Caroline Calvert; Ciara Gallagher; Sinead Carty; and Maura Kennedy. Sincere thanks also to Sarah Roddy, Philomena Gorey, Anna Pilz and Nicola Morris. I am grateful to Marianne Elliott, Kevin Bean, Ciaran O'Neill, Niall Carson, John O'Toole, Maria Power, Gill McIntosh, Maedh Harding, Lindsey Earner-Byrne and Michael Robinson who generously passed material onto me in the course of their own research. Lindsey Earner-Byrne also read the book in its entirety and her insights were invaluable. Thanks also to Michael Watson and Liz Friend-Smith at Cambridge University Press who always believed in this book and have been unfailingly supportive. Rita Duffy's evocative painting of a marriage ceremony seemed a perfect match for the book – the missing faces are a striking metaphor for a history which was not popularly known and for an issue which often saw families sever ties with divorcees. My sincere gratitude is therefore due to Rita for her generosity and kindness in letting this work be used for the book's cover. Staff at the various repositories where this research was conducted have been unfailingly helpful and particular thanks are due to George Woodman, the former librarian at Parliament Buildings, Stormont; the Public Record Office of Northern Ireland; Parliamentary Archives at the House of Lords; the British Library; National Archives, Kew; National Archives, Ireland; the National Library of Ireland; Dublin Diocesan Archives; and the Irish College at Rome. My thanks are also due to colleagues and friends at the Institute of Irish Studies of the University of Liverpool: Lauren Arrington, Kevin Bean, Clare Downham, Marianne Elliott, Dorothy Lynch, Viola Segeroth, Peter Shirlow and Frank Shovlin. I also wish to acknowledge and sincerely thank the British Academy for its kind support for this research.

Introduction: The 'Anatomy of a Divorce'

[The] history of divorce is not the least important, and is certainly one of the most typical chapters in the 'History of Freedom,' and its land-marks are those of that history.

The legalisation of divorce in the Republic of Ireland in 1996 was heralded as epoch making, but there was little acknowledgement that this was the third incarnation of Irish divorce. The reform was preceded by early Irish law which allowed divorce and more than two centuries when divorce could be attained by a parliamentary act. As a satirical matrimonial map, produced in early nineteenth-century Cork, attested: '*Cat and Dog Harbour* . . . is the principle port for trade to the *Divorce Island*' which possessed 'a considerable population'. By comparison, 'The chief building . . . the *Fort of Repentance* . . . situated in the *Vale of Tears*, is scarcely ever inhabited' (see Figure I.1).

The history of divorce was, however, late to develop. As Robert Chester notes, 'up to 1965 the study of divorce was both absolutely and proportionately rare.'[1] Geographically specific studies and some comparative work were subsequently produced, often foregrounding the intersectionality of the institutions of state, church and society.[2] That triangulation

---

The quote in the title of this Introduction is from George Macbeth's poetry collection, *Anatomy of a divorce* (London, 1988).

[1] Robert Chester (ed.), *Divorce in Europe* (Leiden, 1977), p. 2.
[2] See, for example, Lawrence Stone, *Road to divorce: England, 1530–1987* (Oxford, 1990); Allen Horstman, *Victorian divorce* (London, 1985); Leah Leneman, *Alienated affections: Scottish experience of divorce and separation* (Edinburgh, 1998); *Debating divorce in Italy; marriage and the making of modern Italians, 1860–1974* (Basingstoke, 2006); Dirk Blasius, *Divorce in Germany, 1794–1945* and *Historical perspectives on divorce law* (Göttingen, 1987); Roderick Phillips, *Family breakdown in late eighteenth-century France: divorces in Rouen, 1792–1803* (Oxford, 1980); Antony Copley, *Sexual moralities in France, 1780–1980: new ideas on the family, divorce and homosexuality* (London, 1989); Barbara Alpern Engel, *Breaking the ties that bound: the politics of marital strife in late imperial Russia* (Ithaca, 2011); Richard H. Chused, *Private acts in public places: a social history of divorce in the formative era of American family law* (Philadelphia, 1994); Kristen Celello, *Making marriage work: a history of marriage and divorce in the twentieth-century United States* (Chapel Hill, 2009); Henry Finlay, *To have and not to hold: a history of attitudes to marriage and divorce in Australia, 1858–1975* (Sydney, 2005). Divorce in countries such as Norway, Denmark, Iceland and Finland is explored in a special edition of the *Scandinavian Journal of History*, vol. 43, no. 1 (2018). Modern comparative analysis was pioneered by Roderick Phillips, *Putting asunder. A history of divorce in Western society* (Cambridge, 1988). Divorce in non-Christian countries has also been examined. See, for example, Harald Fuess, *Divorce in Japan: family, gender, and the state, 1600–2000* (Stanford, 2004).

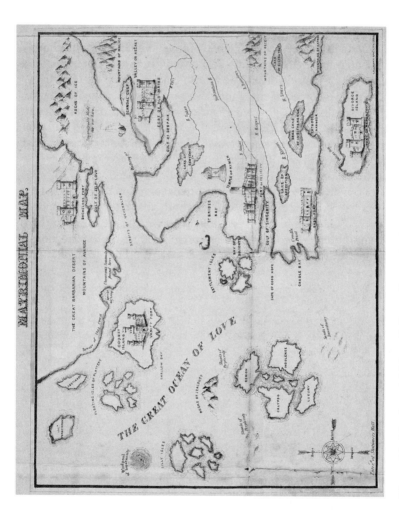

Figure I.1 Matrimonial Map, Callagan Bros., Cork, n.d., c. 1830–40 (image courtesy of the National Library of Ireland, EPH E821).[3]

encapsulates much of Ireland's history of divorce, but the country was often at variance with the progressive liberalisation of family law common to much of Western Europe. Ireland's non-linear liberalism can therefore be compared to post-revolutionary France where the grounds for divorce by mutual consent granted in 1792 were curtailed by the 1804 civil code or Japan following the restrictive civil code of 1898.[4] Little attention, however, was paid to Ireland's divorce provision,[5] a lacuna explained by the late availability of divorce in the Republic of Ireland and a wider neglect of family history which is currently being redressed.[6] Recent examinations of the Irish family challenge notions of the wholesale stability of the rural stem family with its defining features of male inheritance, heir-based marriage, legitimate progeny and intergenerational residence.[7] Rather, with falling and later marriage rates and migratory patterns which often lack European comparators, what is emerging is 'the story of crisis'.[8] Such a trope has recurring resonance in the history of divorce; it conjoins the experience of those in the wealthier classes, who could afford to divorce, with the life stories of other socio-economic groups. There is therefore an irony in the family being cast as a stabilising moral guardian to the extent that it, rather than its individual members, was defended in the 1937 Irish Constitution.[9] Although such constitutional protection was lacking in Northern Ireland, the family was central to its conservative moral terrain. This study therefore seeks to contribute to a more nuanced understanding of the Irish family which variously rallied to defend or disown the minority who sought to divorce.

Divorce was rare in Western Europe until the late-nineteenth century, and material relating to a minority as well as that compiled for legal

---

[4] French divorce law was again reformed in 1884. See Theresa McBride, 'Public authority and private lives: divorce after the French revolution' in *French Historical Studies*, vol. 17, no. 3 (Spring 1992), p. 750; Fuess, *Divorce in Japan*, p. 3.

[5] Fine exceptions are David Fitzpatrick, 'Divorce and separation in modern Irish history' in *Past and Present*, no. 114 (February 1987), pp. 172–96 and John Bergin, 'Irish private divorce bills and acts of the 18th century' in James Kelly, John McCafferty and Charles Ivar McGrath (eds.), *People, politics and power* (Dublin, 2009), pp. 94–121.

[6] See, for example, M. E. Daly, 'The Irish family since the Famine: continuity and change', *Irish Journal of Feminist Studies*, vol. 3, no. 2 (1999), pp. 1–21; Finola Kennedy, *Cottage to crèche. Family change in Ireland* (Dublin, 2001).

[7] D. Birdwell, 'The early twentieth-century stem family: a case study from Co. Kerry' in M. Silverman and P. H. Gulliver (eds.), *Approaching the past: historical anthropology through Irish case studies* (New York, 1992), p. 205.

[8] Lindsey Earner-Byrne, 'The family in Ireland, 1800–2015', in Thomas Bartlett (ed.), *Cambridge History of Ireland*, vol. 4 (4 vols., Cambridge, 2018), p. 626.

[9] Kennedy, *Cottage to crèche*, p. 123. See article 41.1.1, Constitution of Ireland (Dublin, 1937).

purposes needs to be carefully considered[10]: 'Not only were the divorcing minority often unique for their relative prosperity . . . but their willingness to expose their differences to public scrutiny also set them apart at a time when the stigma of divorce ran so deeply.'[11] Evidence presented in some divorce cases was fabricated. Money undoubtedly changed hands to encourage damning testimony and witnesses were, on occasion, imprisoned for perjury. A high level of collaboration and collusion between couples seeking to divorce, although strictly ruled against, was commonplace. Legal evidence was also constructed to maximise the odds of winning or defending a case. The demands of the law thus shaped the frame within which a case was presented. However, this study, much inspired by Lawrence Stone's approach which centred human experience within a legal and reformist backdrop, mines first-person writing like memoirs and diaries as well as correspondence to corroborate many of the claims made in the legal record.[12] This also allows the voice of petitioners, respondents and witnesses to be heard amongst the strictures of parliamentary and later court evidence to reveal the often-hidden reality of matrimonial discord. Indeed, 'No other branch of law deals in such a way with the interweaving of characters, the conflict of wills and the general wear and tear of daily life.'[13]

Some Irish divorces established legal precedent and generated considerable comment in their wake. The press coverage of divorce was extensive due to the upper-class nature of many petitioners and the often-salacious nature of the evidence. The long unfettered reportage of divorce also meant that intimate details of marital woes easily transgressed to the public sphere and individual cases were regularly published.[14] Yet, neither this attention nor the longevity of the history of Irish divorce produced a more popular knowledge regarding its availability. As Harry Vere White commented, there was a 'mistaken ... common notion that Irish marriages are absolutely indissoluble'.[15] In addition, popular opinion towards divorce is hard to gauge. This was particularly marked in the earlier period; however,

---

[10] Phillips, *Putting asunder*, p. xiii.

[11] A. James Hammerton, *Cruelty and companionship. Conflict in nineteenth-century married life* (London and New York, 1992), pp. 3–4.

[12] Stone, *Road to divorce*.

[13] John M. Biggs, *The concept of matrimonial cruelty* (London, 1962), p. 3.

[14] The reporting of divorce cases was unregulated in the UK until 1926 and in Ireland until 1929. See Gail Savage, '"They would if they could": class, gender and popular representation of English divorce litigation, 1858–1908', *Journal of Family History*, vol. 36, no. 2 (2011), pp. 173–90.

[15] Harry Vere White, 'Divorce', *Irish Church Quarterly*, vol. 6, no. 33 (April 1913), p. 94. White was later dean of the Anglican Christ Church Cathedral, Dublin, 1918–21 and Bishop of Limerick, Ardfert and Aghadoe, 1921–33. Montgomery Hyde also noted the

even in the nineteenth century, it was the likelihood of reform which excited the most comment. Those publicising their views tended to reside firmly in pro- or anti-divorce camps; more moderate opine often remained unheard. Despite the polarisation, there was rarely a monolithic response to divorce from state, church or society. Indeed, the belief that the Catholic Church was the sole moral compass guiding Irish divorce provision is one of several popularly held assumptions that this study questions.

The grounds for divorce were also subjectively applied: spousal behaviour may be unacceptable to one person but not to another. Alleged marital misdemeanours therefore should be considered in relation to the other spousal party. The law of divorce also augmented as the mores of acceptable conduct within marriage altered and its history illuminates this often–cloaked aspect of marital life. Gender roles changed little up to the 1970s, but there were important shifts in attitudes relating to spousal behaviour. As Carolyn Conley highlights, the acceptability of domestic violence and unrestrained physical chastisement of wives lessened as men, gradually and unsteadily, became seen as the protectors of women.[16] The definition of marital cruelty also augmented, which allowed more women to seek protection, recompense and freedom. Views of divorced women similarly altered although often in contradictory ways. Frequently socially outcast, women's need for financial spousal support to fund a divorce and economically survive thereafter became acknowledged. This was embodied in the parliamentary position of the Lady's Friend who determined financial provision for wives being divorced.

To chart Ireland's engagement with divorce and the testing process of divorce law reform, the book's chronology stretches from the eighteenth century to as close to the present day as the annual release of divorce statistics allows. However, early Irish Brehon law allowed remarriage, divorce at will (*imscar*) and on the basis of mutual consent (known as 'blameless divorce'), but there were

---

misapprehension that in 'Ireland there was no divorce on any ground' (H. Montgomery Hyde, *A tangled web: sex scandals in British politics and society* [London, 1986], p. 18); Wood and O'Shea aver parliamentary divorce 'was never used' in Ireland (Kieran Wood and Paul O'Shea, *Divorce in Ireland. The options. The issues. The law* [Dublin, 1997], p. 11).

[16] See Carolyn A. Conley, *Melancholy accidents: the meaning of violence in post-famine Ireland* (Lanham and Oxford, 1999). Single motherhood, rape within marriage and illegitimacy would also be legally and culturally redefined in late twentieth-century Ireland (Earner-Byrne, 'The family in Ireland', p. 653).

various grounds for divorce.[17] These, like the later grounds, encompassed both property and propriety and were gender specific.[18] Numerous grounds existed whereby a wife could legally divorce her husband and retain all or part of her bride-price (*coibche*), property she brought to the marriage, obtain damages for injury and remain in the marital home: if her husband was adulterous; homosexual; failed to support her; slandered her or was indiscreet in discussing their marital relations; was leprous; hit her and left a mark; tricked her into marriage by the use of magic; was in holy orders; infertile; impotent or too corpulent for intercourse. Women could lose their bride-price or be fined for attempting to poison a spouse, failing to produce a 'bed blanket' on marriage which raised suspicions of virginity, allowing the deliberate destruction of wool or leaving a marriage too swiftly or without due cause although the length of time was unspecified.[19] A man could divorce a woman on the grounds of adultery, persistent theft, inducing an abortion on herself, shaming a husband's honour, smothering a child or being without milk through sickness, requirements which stress both the maternal function and the need for heirs. If infertility was the cause of a divorce, the equivalent of the bride-price would be returned by the party deemed at fault. The division of property was dependent on the grounds of the divorce and what each party brought to the union as well as the amount of household work performed. Yet, in an early example of class dictating access to divorce, this was a preserve of the wealthy and this social complexion strongly re-emerged in the modern history of divorce.[20]

The gendered grounds for divorce, the sexual double standard and the idea of female perseverance also survived in various forms, but whether these were inherited from the early Irish Brehon model or the canon/common law hybrid of the English legal system is difficult to decipher. The Brehon grounds were transcribed in the seventh century as part of the 'conversion to Christianity, with its emphasis on the authority of the

---

[17] Mutual consent developed in Roman law and was much contested in modern European divorce reform debates. See Chester, *Divorce in Europe.*

[18] On early Irish divorce see Fergus Kelly (ed.), *Marriage disputes. A fragmentary Old Irish Law-Text* (Early Irish Law Series, vol. 6, Dublin, 2014); Fergus Kelly, *A guide to early Irish law* (Dublin, 1998 reprint of 1988 edition), pp. 73–4 and Art Cosgrove (ed.), *Marriage in Ireland* (Dublin, 1985), pp. 8–10. Fines could also be levied to ally marital disputes (Kelly, *Marriage disputes*, p. 4).

[19] Kelly, *Marriage disputes*, p. 10 and p. 90. A father may have to assist his daughter with the payment of fines and would resume responsibility for her after her divorce (ibid., p. 4). As a commodity, the destruction of wool was deemed harmful to the economic interests of the household. See Clare Downham, *Medieval Ireland* (Cambridge, 2018), p. 197.

[20] Jennifer F. Spreng, *Abortion and divorce law in Ireland* (Jefferson, NC, 2004), p. 23.

written word and its own legal system'.[21] The eighth-century *Cáin Lánamna*, for example, is 'The Law of Couples'. This tract on marriage and divorce did not denote the grounds for divorce but focused on property when a union, depicted as 'a situation that could result in children', ended.[22] A gradual move to Anglo-Norman law evolved by the fourteenth century, but Gaelic forms of divorce only ended in the early seventeenth century.

The church was involved in divorce from the fourth century when Constantine sought to align church and state. Yet, church control was not absolute; it co-existed, and sometimes fused, with the civil regulation of marriage.[23] This was evident in legislation and marital cases heard in both the ecclesiastical and temporal (non-church) courts. Roman (civil) law was also highly influential in the early church.[24] As Roman law developed, divorce for causes such as adultery or a plot to murder gave both husbands and wives the right to divorce. Mutual consent as a ground for divorce subsequently emerged and remained in place until Justinian's tenth-century rebuke. Divorce was, however, controversial within the early church, and marriage became a matter of increasing ecclesiastical concern in continental Europe from the sixth century onwards. From the end of the ninth century to the first half of the eleventh century, the church established marital laws, developing from decretals, the papal rulings superseding Roman laws that were 'binding on all Christians'.[25] Canon law was subsequently introduced to England in the eleventh century. Although some of the early church councils permitted divorce for adultery, the anti-divorce stance of St Augustine triumphed at the 1545–63 Council of Trent: marriage was confirmed as a sacrament and was therefore indissoluble; only a non-legitimate marriage could be annulled.[26] Canon 7, for example, reasserted the teaching of St Paul and prohibited divorce:

[T]he marriage bond cannot be dissolved because of adultery on the part of one of the spouses and that neither of the two, not even the innocent one ... can contract

---

[21] From the ninth to the sixteenth centuries, 'glosses and commentary were written' (Charlene M. Eska, 'Varieties of early Irish legal literature and the *Cáin Lánamna* fragments', *Viator*, no. 1 [2009], p. 3 and p. 5). See also Charlene M. Eska, *Cáin Lánamna: An old Irish tract on marriage/divorce law* (Leiden, 2009).

[22] Ibid., p. 10.

[23] Kitchin, *History of divorce*, p. 31. Ecclesiastical courts were established from 1085.

[24] William G. Brooke, 'Rights of married women in England and Ireland', *The Irish Law Times and Solicitors' Journal*, vol. 7 (31 May 1873), p. 280.

[25] Kitchin, *History of divorce*, p. 60.

[26] Brooke, 'Rights of married women', p. 280. Marriage was a sacrament from the thirteenth century. The decrees of the Council of Trent only applied to countries which acknowledged papal supremacy. England was thus excluded.

another marriage during the lifetime of the other; and that the husband who dismisses an adulterous wife and marries again and the wife who dismisses an adulterous husband and marries again are both guilty of adultery.[27]

The popular movement against canon law enshrined in the sixteenth-century Reformation had a minimal impact on the law of divorce. However, outside of the Catholic Church, marriage ceased to be a sacrament; it was a secular and contractual union which could be dissolved.[28] In 1553 *Reformatio Legum Ecclesiasticarum*, the Reform of the Ecclesiastical Laws, would have heralded significant divorce reform, providing a system of Anglican law as an alternative to medieval canon law and recommending that 'in cases of adultery, malicious desertion, long absence, or capital enmities, the marriage ... should be dissolved, with liberty to the injured party to marry again, except in the case of capital enmities'. Edward VI's demise before its enactment left marriage as an indissoluble contract; only separation was permitted which forbade remarriage.[29] The 1646 Westminster Confession of Faith, following the teaching of St Matthew, however, permitted Presbyterian divorce and remarriage on the grounds of adultery or wilful desertion, but this was a seemingly rare occurrence.[30]

Separation, nullity, bigamy, spousal murder, fake pregnancy, procuring foundlings, impotence, desertion and migration all featured in Ireland's history of marriage and its dissolution.[31] Indeed, migration motivated by marital disharmony was so commonplace that it was referred to as Irish-style divorce by the mid-twentieth century.[32] Private deeds of separation were also used to end marriages.[33] Controversial and

---

[27] John McAreavey, *The canon law of marriage and the family* (Dublin, 1997), p. 44.

[28] Luther, for example, refuted marriage as a sacrament in 1517 (Stone, *Road to divorce*, pp. 3–5).

[29] Brooke, 'Rights of married women', p. 280. See also Arthur Browne, *A compendious view of the ecclesiastical law of Ireland* ... (2nd ed., Dublin, 1805).

[30] Sources are rare, but divorces secured in the Presbytery could be deemed bigamous and church ceremonies for second marriages could be denied. See Mary O'Dowd, 'Marriage breakdown in Ireland, c. 1660–1857' in Niamh Howlin and Kevin Costello (eds.), *Law and the family in Ireland, 1800–1950* (London, 2017), p. 12.

[31] See, for example, the 1770s impotency/fake pregnancy case of Grace Maxwell and her spouse Colonel John Maxwell of Co. Monaghan, later governor of the Bahamas. Grace sought to procure a foundling child and, binding herself with increasing amounts of fabric, present it as her own (Public Record Office of Northern Ireland [hereafter PRONI], D1556/17/4). Also see A. P. W. Malcomson, *The pursuit of the heiress. Aristocratic marriage in Ireland, 1750–1820* (Belfast, 1982), pp. 21–2. Women brought other cases of impotency to the ecclesiastical court. See, for example, Margery Walker v. Thomas Walker in the Consistorial and Metropolitan Court of Dublin, 1791 (PRONI, D2107/4/7). For bigamy, see, for example, Earl Annesley's 1796 marriage to Sophia Connor (née Kelly) (PRONI, D1503/3/8/10/9).

[32] Dorine Rohan, *Marriage Irish style* (Cork, 1969).

[33] See, for example, Lord O'Hara's discussion of his daughter's private separation in a letter to Lady O'Hara. The proposed alimony was £100 with half of the jointure given towards

often subject to legal challenge, private separations were never recognised by the ecclesiastical courts and barred the parties from remarriage. Common law's acceptance of these deeds in the eighteenth century decreased early in the following century when distaste for clauses which attempted to ban subsequent legal actions and seemingly encouraged adultery emerged.[34] Private separation deeds were, however, legally recognised as contracts from 1848 but could not be drawn up by women until the Married Women's Property Act of 1882.[35]

Wrongful confinement was another stratagem to control and punish an errant spouse. The mid-eighteenth-century case of Lady Belvedere was the most widely publicised Irish example, described by one legal writer as incomparable to 'all the cases of adultery which have happened of late years'.[36] In 1744, after eight years of marriage, Lord Belvedere suspected his wife, Mary Molesworth, of adultery with his brother, the Hon. Arthur Rochfort. Belvedere sought to avoid the financial toll of divorce by detaining his wife at his second seat, Gaulston Park in Co. Westmeath. At his main Westmeath estate, he erected the so-called jealous wall to obscure views of his brother's house.[37] Mary admitted a two-year affair, a potentially illegitimate child and the possibility of spousal poisoning in a letter, likely written under duress. She also made a plea common to the adulterous wife: 'O my lord, kill me yourself, but do not discover me to my father.' Mary's fear of her father was justified: he left her in an uncle's custody, declaring 'Damn the whore! let him make her a public example.' For twenty years, 'he was never heard to mention her name again ... to the day of his death'; familial support was not therefore guaranteed to those who strayed from the marital bond; only Lord Belvedere's death secured Mary's liberty in 1774.[38]

---

the children's education and maintenance until the age of twenty-one and thereafter divided between the two sons (PRONI, T2812/10/1–27).

[34] Private deeds of separation continued to be executed in the nineteenth and twentieth centuries in both England and Ireland (Stone, *Road to divorce*, p. 181).

[35] Under the 1882 Married Women's Property Act, married women became *feme sole* regarding property and had the ability to contract (Fitzpatrick, 'Divorce and separation', p. 176).

[36] Francis Plowden, *Crim. con. biography*, vol. 1 (8 vols., London, 1830), p. 20. Plowden was also a historian who gained a reputation as a legal and political writer.

[37] Malcomson, *The pursuit of the heiress*, p. 37. Lord Belvedere was formerly Viscount Bellfield. Mary was the eldest daughter of the 3rd Viscount of Swords. She brought £6,000 to the marriage and bore four children. Always professing her innocence, she died in c. 1777.

[38] Plowden, *Crim. con. biography*, p. 25. John Hely-Hutchinson advised a similar containment to Jack [John] Bagwell, c. 1756 (PRONI, T3459/C/2/215). Hely-Hutchinson was a lawyer, member of the Irish parliament and provost of Trinity College Dublin, 1775–94. Wrongful confinement also featured in fiction. See, for example,

Although there were various means to end an unhappy union, some more permanent and satisfactory than others, only *divorce à vinculo matrimonii*, divorce from the bonds of marriage, allowed the parties to remarry whilst a spouse was living.[39] Its history dwells inevitably on marital malcontent and misdemeanours, but that should not obscure the longevity, stability and happiness of countless Irish unions. Yet, it is also clear that many remained in marriage as they lacked the financial, moral and at times legal means to pursue its termination. The multi-tiered and much maligned process of *divorce à vinculo matrimonii* compounded this. It was secured by a parliamentary act from the mid-seventeenth century; the process was still evolving when a pseudonymous tract queried, 'should not some more easy method be thought of, than now is practis'd, for relieving the party injur'd and oppress'd?'[40] The critique continued; in the nineteenth and early twentieth centuries, parliamentary divorce was described as 'cumbrous'[41] and 'of great peculiarity'.[42]

The first stage in securing a parliamentary divorce normally required a husband to bring a criminal conversation action against his wife's lover in the common law courts. Popularly abbreviated to crim. con., this suit developed in the late-seventeenth century although its roots lie in thirteenth-century cases for trespass and ravishment.[43] Trespass was the strongest inheritance from these origins as husbands were compensated for damage caused to their legal property: their wives. As spousal property, wives were barred from bringing these suits, proffering a defence or presenting evidence. The latter was permitted following the Evidence Further Amendment Act of 1869; however, although seemingly progressive, Judge Baron Dowse, sitting in the first Irish criminal conversation suit where he heard a wife give evidence in 1880, described placing a woman 'into the witness box to declare her own shame and by her own evidence carry the case in favour of her husband ... the most painful case he ever had the misfortune to try'.[44]

Maria Edgeworth, *Castle Rackrent* (first published 1800, reprinted London, 1992) which features a seven-year imprisonment for Lady Rackrent.

[39] *Divorce à vinculo matrimonii* was also known as *divortium plenum* and *divortium perfectum*.

[40] 'Castamore', *Conjugium languens: or, the natural, civil, and religious mischiefs arising from conjugal infidelity and impunity* (London, 1700), pp. 27–8.

[41] Kitchin, *History of divorce*, p. 182.

[42] John Fraser Macqueen, *A practical treatise on the appellate jurisdiction of the House of Lords and Privy Council together with the practice on parliamentary divorce* (London, 1842), p. 194.

[43] Laura Hanft Korobkin, *Criminal conversations. Sentimentality and 19th-century legal stories of adultery* (New York, 1998), p. 16.

[44] The case was Joynt v. Jackson; £5,000 damages were claimed and £1,000 was awarded. The Joynts divorced in parliament in 1888. Richard Joynt was the editor of the *Ballina Herald*. See Anon., *Authentic report of the crim. con. trial of Joynt v. Jackson, in the Exchequer Court, Dublin, commencing May 10th, 1880* (Dublin, 1880), p. 28.

Criminal conversation was not part of Scottish law although it was possible to sue for damages. There was no equivalent to this action in parts of Europe like France or

Criminal conversation was the most sensationalised and romanticised of the prerequisite suits required to divorce. Proof that a sexual act had occurred was needed and consequently these cases attracted considerable attention. Proceedings were published with increased frequency from the mid-eighteenth century onwards and there was a profitable business, especially between 1760 and 1860, in pamphlets detailing the most salacious cases. One Dublin courtroom was, for example, frequented by 'a famous note-taker' collecting details of a case for publication in 1804.[45] Such publications often printed letters which were presented as evidence as well as servant testimony. This served a dual purpose: to titillate readers with tales of sexual misdemeanours and as a cautionary tale to those who might stray from the marital bond. The seven-volume *Trials for Adultery* thus revealed a zealous determination to deter the 'wavering wanton'.[46]

In early criminal conversation cases, wives were sometimes depicted as seducers. In 1796, for instance, Lady Westmeath was portrayed as a 'neglected beauty' seeking revenge on her spouse; the published proceedings asked 'where could be found a man resolute enough to withstand female beauty when determined to conquer?'[47] However, as part of a nineteenth-century cultural shift which designated men as the protectors of women, adulterous wives became more commonly seen as the victims of predatory men.[48] Celebrated, if verbose, Irish barrister Charles Phillips subsequently proclaimed an adulterous wife as 'a wretched victim ... starting on the sin of a promiscuous prostitution as a consequence of a man's sensual rapine'.[49] This change in emphasis not only denied female agency in straying from the marital bond, but evidence presented in these cases also increasingly accentuated broken

Germany. However, it existed in numerous US states, many of which abolished the procedure in the 1930s. In parts of Canada like Ontario it was not abolished until 1975 and in some US states like North Carolina it is still in existence where a revival in cases was seen from 1997. For married women, a criminal conversation suit did not necessarily mark the end of a marriage. See Stephen Cretney, *Family law in the twentieth century. A history* (Oxford, 2005), pp. 153–5.

[45] Stone, *Road to divorce*, p. 252. The case was Rev. Massy v. Marquis of Headfort where, as discussed later, high damages were awarded.

[46] Anon., *Trials for adultery* ... vol. 1 (7 vols., London, 1779 reprinted New York and London, 1985), p. iii.

[47] George Frederick Nugent, *Crim. con.* ... (Dublin, 1796), p. 9. The Earl of Westmeath asked for £20,000 in damages and £10,000 was awarded. The Westmeaths, as is discussed later, divorced in the Irish parliament in 1796.

[48] Abby L. Sayers, 'Publicizing private life: criminal conversation trials in eighteenth century Britain' (unpublished MA thesis, Auburn University, 2010), p. 92.

[49] The case was Connaughton v. Dillon (Charles Philips [ed.], *The speeches of Charles Philips, Esq. delivered at the Bar, on various public occasions, in Ireland and England* [London, 1817], p. 149).

families and children tainted by the ruin of a mother's reputation. This suggestion of moral contagion was often expressed in mawkish terms to invoke sympathy from a jury. Phillips thus referred to a woman's infidelity reducing her 'husband to widowhood ... smiling infants to anticipated orphanage, and that peaceful, hospitable, confiding family, to helpless, hopeless ... ruin'. The spectacle of children wearing mourning garb as their mother left the marital home underscored an adulterous women's lack of custodial rights: 'poor innocents ... to them her life is something worse than death ... far better, their little feet had followed her in funeral'. As was common to many criminal conversation cases, Phillips expressed pity for the mother to further highlight the damage caused by her paramour; her fine dress adorned her only 'for the sacrifice ... Poor, unfortunate, fallen female! How can she expect mercy from her destroyer? How can she expect that he will revere the character he was careless of preserving?'[50]

Servants provided much of the evidence in criminal conversation suits. In the 1796 case of Westmeath versus Bradshaw, servants testified that furtive London meetings led to a 'very much powdered' sofa, 'rumpled' carpets and 'tumbled' dress. Alleged impropriety in a coach led the defence in this case to inquire of the coachman giving evidence 'if he was so well acquainted with her Ladyship's thighs that he would know them from those of any other Lady'.[51] Juries were also encouraged to consider the significance of the case beyond that of the individual and to defend the institutions of family and Christian society by making substantial awards of damages. As the jury in an 1820 Irish case was cautioned: 'Many a brood of young adulterers might now be hatching ... the verdict ... would crush them in the shell ... and protect the purity of domestic virtue.'[52]

Criminal conversation damages confirmed that not all wives were considered of equal value. Irish awards of damages ranged from a farthing to £20,000.[53] Class was a key consideration in determining

---

[50] Charles Phillips, *The speech of Mr. Phillips, delivered in the Court of Common Pleas, Dublin, in the case of Guthrie v. Sterne, for Adultery* (n.p., 1816), pp. 95–105. Damages in the amount of £5,000 were awarded. The reform of custody rights is discussed in Chapter 5.

[51] Nugent, *Crim. con.*, p. 7.

[52] Damages in the amount of £5,000 were awarded in this case. Anon., *Crim. con. A full, faithful, and impartial report of the trial wherein Sir John M. Doyle, KCB and KTS was plaintiff: and George Peter Brown, Esq. defendant for criminal conversation with the plaintiff's wife ...* (Dublin, 1820). See also *Freeman's Journal*, 23 and 31 May 1820.

[53] In the aforementioned Belvedere case, Lord Belvedere secured £20,000 criminal conversation damages from his brother, Arthur Rochfort, in 1759. Rochfort was subsequently imprisoned for debt in King's Bench prison (Anon., *Crim. con. actions*, pp. 80–3). The Belvedere damages were the largest Staves found in her eighteenth-century study of this suit (Susan Staves, 'Money for honor: Damages for criminal conversation', *Studies in 18th-Century Culture*, vol. 11 [1982], p. 284). Lord Cloncurry was awarded the same amount

awards; a woman from respectable stock would merit higher damages as the loss of both monetary wealth and consortium was measured. Fidelity was also highly prized as 'a faithful wife's value to her husband is much enhanced if she has made his home happy, attended to his children, and assisted him in life'. Her opposite, leading 'a loose life before marriage', was much devalued.[54] One farthing was, for instance, awarded for the allegedly 'unscrupulous and lying adventuress' at the centre of the Lynch versus Macan-Lynch trial of 1890.[55] Nominal amounts could also be awarded when a husband was considered negligent. Dublin's Rev. Vanston was accused of cruelty in an 1897 case he brought against a man his wife married after divorcing in the Dakota Territory in the United States. A three-day trial saw a farthing awarded on the ground that Vanston should have kept better control of his spousal 'property'.[56] London lacemaker Thomas Pollard, however, hoping to divorce his wife for adultery with Captain Wentworth Doyle, the son of an Irish Protestant clergyman, in 1843, only asked for £100 damages in his criminal conversation suit, as this brought him a stage closer to parliamentary divorce.[57] However, Ireland's use of the criminal conversation suit was increasingly at legal odds with the rest of the United Kingdom. The suit was abolished in England, which included Wales in its jurisdiction, as part of a wide-reaching matrimonial reform in 1857, although some of its pecuniary function remained in the damages that could be awarded by court until the 1970s. By comparison, criminal conversation survived in Northern Ireland until 1939, and the suit remained in the Republic of Ireland until 1981 where it was far from a nineteenth-century relic: six cases were brought in the decade preceding its abolition.[58]

The second suit required for parliamentary divorce was a separation, *divorce à mensâ et thoro*, divorce from bed and board. From the twelfth century, the ecclesiastical courts of the Anglican Church, usually the

---

against baronet Sir J. B. Piers in 1808. There are only twenty-four cases of damages of more than £10,000 being awarded in Britain in the period 1680–1857 (Sayers, 'Publicizing private life', p. 15).

[54] Henry Edwin Fenn, *Thirty-five years in the Divorce Court* (London, 1911), pp. 219–23.

[55] Lynch, 'a poor man' residing in America, claimed £5,000 against Master of Dublin's Rotunda Lying-in Hospital Macan-Lynch. The damages were applauded in court and Macan-Lynch was claimed to have no 'stain on his character', *Irish Times*, 2 July 1890.

[56] James Roberts, *Divorce bills in the Imperial Parliament* (Dublin, 1906), pp. 92–3. The Vanstons divorced in 1897.

[57] *Freeman's Journal*, 13 May 1843. Doyle admitted adultery and offered to pay damages. Irish lawyer Isaac Jackman's 1781 play *The divorce, a farce* included a faked criminal conversation case for Sir Harry Trifle to fund a divorce.

[58] The Northern Irish action for damages remained until 1978. Criminal conversation's reform in Northern Ireland and in the Republic of Ireland is discussed in Chapters 7 and 10, respectively.

consistory courts which were organised on a diocesan basis and were a level above the lower archdeacon's courts, granted this fault-based form of separation. This allowed the parties to live apart, but not to remarry.[59] Its ground for both men and women was cruelty or adultery. Additional female grounds were adultery with the rape of a party outside of the marital union and unnatural practices such as sodomy or bestiality.[60] Evidence was submitted in writing for these hearings which were heard by ecclesiastical lawyers rather than by juries. Although sources are scare, there is evidence that non-Anglicans and Catholics used the ecclesiastical courts.[61] Irish Quaker Benjamin Fayle, for example, separated in the consistorial court in the 1780s. The Irish rate of separation was also not the lowest in the UK: from 1840 to 1843, for instance, fifty-seven divorces *à mensâ et thoro* were granted in Ireland in comparison to two in Wales. Measured per head of population, the Irish rate was on a par with that of England but below that of Scotland; an aversion to formalise separation or publicise marital discord was clearly not absolute.[62] Yet, whilst separation provided sufficient salvation for some, for others it was a legal halfway house that precluded remarriage during an estranged spouse's lifetime.[63]

[59] Ireland had ecclesiastical Metropolitical (also referred to as Metropolitan) Courts in Armagh and Dublin and twenty-seven consistorial courts which sat approximately once per month (Henry Jefferies, *Priests and prelates of Armagh in the age of the reformations, 1518–58* [Dublin, 1997], p. 108). On *divorce à mensâ et thoro*, see W. Harris Faloon, *The Marriage Law of Ireland* (Dublin, 1881). Property and maintenance issues resulting from *divorce à mensâ et thoro* would most commonly be dealt with by Chancery or Probate. Examples of Irish cases of *divorce à mensâ et thoro* include Hanna v. Hanna brought by a husband on the basis of his wife's adultery in 1873, Balance v. Balance brought by a wife on the basis of her husband's cruelty in 1899 and Ross v. Ross brought by a wife on the basis of her husband's adultery in 1908.

[60] The rape of a separated spouse was illegal, but rape within marriage remained legal in Ireland until the Criminal Law Rape Act of 1990 and in the UK until R. v. R. in 1992. A husband could, however, be tried for sexual assault or aggravated sexual assault (Maebh Harding, 'The definition of marriage in Irish law in the twenty-first century: a comparative analysis, I' (2 vols., unpublished PhD thesis, University College Dublin, 2008), pp. 161–2. The first successful prosecution for marital rape in the Republic of Ireland was in 2002.

[61] O'Dowd, 'Marriage breakdown in Ireland, c. 1660–1857', p. 10.

[62] The Irish separation rate was just below half of English and Scottish rates. Separation figures from the *First Report of the Commissioners appointed by Her Majesty to enquire in the law of divorce, and more particularly into the mode of obtaining divorces à vinculo matrimonii* (1853) in *Irish University Press Series of British Parliamentary Papers. Report from the Commission on the laws of Marriage and Divorce*, vol. 1 (3 vols., Shannon, 1969), p. 89.

[63] Ecclesiastical courts could also annul marriages to enable remarriage, but any children of the first marriage would be declared illegitimate. By the late nineteenth century, nullity was also available as a civil suit, but as in the church process, it was expensive and, in consequence, rare. The grounds for nullity were various and included, for example, bigamy, duress, being within the proscribed degrees of consanguinity, fraud and impotence (see Stone, *Road to divorce*, pp. 191–2).

Ecclesiastical law continued to provide the foundation for separation after the Divorce and Matrimonial Causes Act of 1857 ended the Anglican Church's jurisdiction by establishing a new London court of divorce and matrimonial causes for English petitioners. In Ireland, however, separation remained within the remit of the ecclesiastical courts until the disestablishment of the Church of Ireland in 1869. In the following year, ecclesiastical court jurisdiction was transferred to the Irish High Court, usually Queen's or King's Bench, although, in a replication of the English process, church law continued to underpin the grounds for separation. In contrast to English courts, however, the Irish ecclesiastical courts never granted separation on the ground of desertion, as it was feared that an absent spouse might return to the marital fold and this distinction remained.

The final stage of parliamentary divorce was the introduction of a private bill. Until the Act of Union of 1800, Irish petitioners could present a divorce bill to the British or the Irish parliaments. Indeed, at times, when a bill failed to pass in one parliament, the more determined would-be divorcee would proceed to the other assembly, which was potentially advantageous for Irish petitioners. Prior to the 1782 independence of the Irish parliament, all bills, regardless of subject matter, required Westminster's sanction. Bills were read three times in Dublin before the heads of bills (draft bills usually agreed to at the cabinet level but not yet published) were sent to the lord lieutenant to be forwarded to the Privy Council in Westminster. When the heads were returned, a bill was introduced and examined by committee. After the Act of Union, Irish divorce bills were heard solely in Westminster, primarily in the House of Lords which oversaw private business. The second reading of the bill in that house constituted the trial of the case with parties represented by counsel at the Bar of the Lords and witnesses cross-examined. The practice whereby the whole house would hear a divorce bill continued in the lower and upper houses until 1839 and 1840, respectively. The subsequent appointment of a Select Committee on Divorce Bills, composed of nine members of the law lords and peers holding judicial office who were appointed in each parliamentary session, was indicative of a growing reliance on legal parliamentary expertise. As barrister at Lincoln's Inn and authority on marriage John Fraser Macqueen commented, 'The lay and spiritual peers generally left all to the Lawyers.'[64] The committee was privy to the lords' minutes of evidence and proceedings of the bill and could hear counsel and examine witnesses for both the petitioner and respondent.

---

[64] Anon., *Crim. con. actions and trials and other legal proceedings relating to marriage before the passing of the present Divorce Act* (London, c. 1857), p. 26.

Under modern precedent, the lord chancellor heard the case, but evidence was still delivered at the bar of the house. Committee, report and third readings followed before a bill was sent to the Commons where the first and second readings were essentially formalities. After a successful third Commons' reading, the bill returned to the upper house for royal assent.[65] A parliamentary divorce could take at least nine months to secure or be delayed by years if the whereabouts of an errant spouse was unknown or if funds were insufficient to finance a bill.[66]

Parliamentary divorce was first used in Lord Roos's 1669 English case and by Irish petitioners from 1701.[67] The rarity of parliamentary divorce (averaging four per annum from 1700 to 1857) and high social status of petitioners provide a clear indication of the cost of the procedure. This ranged from £200 to £50,000; although an estimated half of parliamentary divorces cost less than £500,[68] it effectively 'supplied a remedy for the rich, and left the humbler classes, who had no means of defraying the enormous cost of relief, without help or redress'.[69] Indeed, as Fitzpatrick notes of the 325 parliamentary divorces passed by Westminster from 1700 to 1857, 'Two-thirds of the petitioners carried titles or honorifics, most of the residue being professional men or merchants.'[70] The Irish *Freeman's Journal* consequently mused on the possibility of a cheaper and more easily available alternative to be rid of an unwanted spouse: 'There are readier means of procuring ... liberation from the bond of matrimony than by act of parliament. Toxicology supplies the deficiency of the legislation. A decree in the House of Lords is an expensive matter, but poison is dirt cheap.'[71] This was sardonic, but the poisoning of a spouse was a ground for divorce under early Irish law and occurred with some regularity in cases of spousal murder in the modern period.[72]

---

[65] Brooke, 'Rights of married women', p. 280. The report stage gives MPs an opportunity, on the floor of the House of Commons, to consider further amendments to a bill which has been examined in committee.

[66] Exceptionally, divorce could be attained in less than nine months. See, for example, Irish petitioner Rev. Vanston's 1897 bill where all proceedings were completed in five months. Vanston's case is discussed in Chapter 5.

[67] *House of Lords Journal*, 25 March 1701, vol. 16, pp. 633–4. On Lord Roos's case, see Stone, *Road to divorce*, pp. 309–12. Early Irish parliamentary divorce is discussed in Chapter 1.

[68] See Stuart Anderson, 'Legislative divorce; law for the aristocracy' in G. R. Rubin and David Sugarman (eds.), *Law, economy and society, 1750–1914* (Abingdon, 1984), pp. 412–44.

[69] Brooke, 'Rights of married women', p. 281.

[70] Fitzpatrick, 'Divorce and separation', p. 173.

[71] *Freeman's Journal*, 5 September 1847.

[72] See Pauline M. Prior, *Madness and murder. Gender, crime and mental disorder in nineteenth-century Ireland* (Dublin, 2008).

There was also a distinct gender divide; the grounds for divorce provide one of the most striking and long-lived examples of the sexual double standard inherent in early Roman law whereby a wife was regarded as her husband's property. Canon law also categorised a wife as subservient to her spouse and thus a husband's 'evidence was generally preferred to her[s]. . . . She was practically without a remedy.'[73] Adultery on the part of the wife was sufficient for a husband to divorce and was popularly believed to bring a wound which was 'the most painful and incurable that human nature knows'.[74] The editor of the *Belfast News-Letter* thus described wifely adultery as 'the most terrible wrong to which a man can be subjected'.[75] *The Times* expanded the theme:

Undoubtedly the position of the wife is very different from that of the husband, and it cannot be alleged that there is a similarity either of natural feeing or of public opinion in the two cases. A woman may marry a man known to be licentious, without forfeiting her place in society ... a man can do no such thing. The difference is founded in nature, and society cannot do otherwise than recognize it. Parliament, too, must do the same.[76]

These sentiments had transnational reach. As the *Sydney Morning Herald* remarked, '[I]nfidelity on the part of the man being, in the eye of the world, by no means as infamous as that on the part of the wife.'[77] By comparison, a husband's adultery was an insufficient ground for female divorce; a wife was widely believed to have 'no right to inquire into the conduct of her superior, whom she ought to presume to be chaste'.[78] A woman therefore had to prove aggravated adultery, often referred to as double offences, on the part of her husband to divorce: adultery coupled with incest, bigamy or cruelty to the extent that the latter would have entitled the wife to a separation.[79] As in separation suits, rape of a party outside of the marital union and unnatural offences provided 'sufficient evidence of a man's depravity' to constitute lone grounds for female divorce.[80] Adultery with desertion of two years or above without reasonable excuse was introduced as an additional ground for divorce in the

---

[73] Kitchin, *History of divorce*, pp. 1–2 and pp. 77–8.
[74] James Patrick Byrne, *The New Law of Divorce and Matrimonial Causes applicable to Ireland . . . popularly explained* (Dublin, 1859), pp. 16–17.
[75] *Belfast News-Letter*, 12 June 1857.
[76] The paper also noted there were limits to what women should be expected to tolerate within marriage (*The Times*, 20 May 1857).
[77] Henry Finlay, 'Lawmaking in the shadow of the empire; divorce in colonial Australia', *Journal of Family History*, vol. 24, no. 1 (January 1999), cited p. 91.
[78] Kitchin, *History of divorce*, pp. 77–8.
[79] The definition of incest was sexual relations within the seven degrees of consanguinity and thus stretched far beyond children and siblings.
[80] Cretney, *Family law*, p. 169.

Divorce and Matrimonial Causes Act of 1857, but this was not applied in the British Parliament until the late-nineteenth century.

The impetus for double offences was based on concerns for the hereditary transmittal of property and the possibility of a woman concealing spurious issue from her spouse. As Roman jurist Gaius observed, 'maternity is a fact, paternity is a matter of opinion'.[81] Being accessory to the adultery, connivance, collusion or condonation was a peremptory bar to a husband's divorce whilst recrimination, cruelty, desertion, wilful separation and neglect, misconduct and unreasonable delay were discretionary bars. Although the same bars applied to a wife's suit, less weight was attached to condonation, further highlighting the sexual double standard and female forbearance; it was a wife's 'merit ... to bear, and endeavour to reclaim. It is not her duty, til [sic] compelled by the last extremity, to have recourse to legal remedies.'[82] Condonation was also difficult to prove: cohabitation should end immediately on the discovery of an adulterous liaison or following any other marital offence to avoid charges of condonation being levelled in a subsequent divorce. If an errant spouse was forgiven for their misdemeanours, their actions were deemed by law to be condoned and a legal proceeding to end the marriage could not go forward. If a subsequent offence was committed or the same offence was repeated, the first condoned offence was revived.[83]

The impact of the gendered grounds for divorce is patent: just four Englishwomen and no Irish women divorced in the period to 1857.[84] The sexual double standard also meant that the fate of divorced women was often trying. In the 1880s, Francis Plowden, a Catholic lawyer at Doctor's Commons, suggested that an adulterous woman's short period of criminal enjoyment' would be ill repaid by a subsequent life of degradation and avoidance. ... There is a common unwritten consent among women of character to shun those who have forfeited their fidelity which is more forcible than law. Even when the guilty parties marry, an odium will attach, and ... nearly all ... females ... are forced into retirement, or lead a fugitive life.[85]

---

[81] Stone, *Road to divorce*, cited p. 7.   [82] Byrne, *New Law of Divorce*, p. 36.

[83] See, for example, the Houghton and Paine cases in 1903 (Roberts, *Divorce bills*, p. 28).

[84] See the English cases of Jane Addison (1801) and Louise Turton (1830) who divorced on the ground of incestuous adultery, Ann Battersby (1840) on the grounds of adultery and cruelty and Georgina Hall (1850) on the grounds of adultery and bigamy although technically this was an annulment as the parties never cohabited. Parliament rejected an additional four divorce bills brought by women in the period from 1771 to 1809.

[85] Plowden, *Crim. con. biography*, vol. 1, p. iii. Some, like Irish reformer Frances Power Cobbe, believed that adulterous women should be ostracised. See Frances Power Cobbe, *The duties of women. A course of lectures* (Edinburgh, 1881), p. 98.

A decade later, Gladstone, commenting on the moral and political fallout from Irish nationalist leader Charles Stewart Parnell's citation as a co-respondent in the 1890 divorce of one of his Irish Parliamentary Party (IPP) lieutenants, Captain William O'Shea, noted of Katharine O'Shea, 'the Almighty has smitten the woman heavily. Nor will her social punishment be slight.'[86] Other women, after long legal battles, believed that all they could aspire to was invoking legal change. Although parliamentary divorce became more commonplace from the 1770s and a growing level of acceptance was apparent, particularly among episcopal peers,[87] the process of reforming divorce law in Ireland was convoluted, contested and slow.

Those who remained hostile to divorce often sought to formalise its strictures. This included Lord Chancellor Loughborough who made the criminal conversation suit a preliminary step to parliamentary divorce in 1780. His subsequent reaction to the rise in the number of divorce bills coming before the British Parliament, with forty-one bills heard in the 1790s, and the rapid increase in French divorce following its reintroduction on the basis of mutual incompatibility in 1792, was to make an action for criminal conversation and *divorce a mensâ et thoro*, or sufficient explanation for not having brought such suits, part of the standing orders regulating divorce in 1798.[88] Petitioners were also required to attend the House of Lord's second reading of a divorce bill and be prepared for cross-examination regarding collusion and separation. This was in stark contrast to the ecclesiastical court practice to consider only written testimony, and Loughborough's reforms were in part an observation on the inadequacies of such a practice. A further amendment to the standing orders from 1809 demanded that criminal conversation transcripts accompany each divorce bill. The matrimonial state before any 'offence' was committed as well as a husband's fidelity and treatment of his wife were also deliberated to ascertain whether he had contributed to her infidelity. Determining evidence of collusion was central to these proceedings and notes from the judge in the ecclesiastical court were demanded for parliamentary perusal from 1831. Changes in parliamentary process also impacted the content of divorce bills; as the lords moved towards the oral examination of witnesses, preambles to divorce bills became increasingly formulaic. Financial and bastardy clauses also

---

[86] Frank Callanan, *The Parnell split, 1890–91* (Cork, 1992), cited p. 189.
[87] Robert Cecil Mortimer, *Putting asunder. A divorce law for contemporary society* (London, 1966), pp. 84–5.
[88] Loughborough also focused on the date of the separation in relation to the adultery (Stone, *Road to divorce*, p. 333).

declined in popularity although illegitimate issue and the loss of consortium continued to feature.

Despite this formalisation, parliamentary divorce remained fraught with difficulties and had both moral and legal critics. By 1854, Lord St Leonards, former lord chancellor, rightly emphasised the challenge of unearthing the facts in divorce proceedings. Divorce by mutual consent was illegal but entirely possible: parties could be encouraged not to defend either criminal conversation or separation suits; criminal conversation damages could be returned or waived to encourage co-operation in a subsequent divorce and wifely maintenance could be pre-arranged in a private deed of separation. It was therefore often in the interest of all parties to concur with the contents of a bill or overlook a husband's adultery or cruelty which might prejudice the case. Indeed, undefended bills and the non-specification of wifely maintenance augmented from 1780.

The financial and moral corollaries of divorce remained substantial, which explains why the annual number of divorce bills heard in Parliament rarely exceeded double figures. Twelve petitions for divorce were submitted to Westminster in 1799, ten of which were successful. This marked the high point in annual parliamentary divorce proceedings. The bearing of individual lord chancellors also affected both the number of petitioners and divorce success rates. Lord Chancellor Thurlow's aversion to divorce and the infamous rigour of his questioning led to a decline in petitioners approaching Westminster to divorce during his tenure from 1778 to 1792. Lord Chancellor Eldon shared Thurlow's distaste for divorce and gained a deservedly fierce reputation for forceful cross-examination that deterred collusive parties from 1801 to 1827. However, Eldon's influence waned as sympathy for petitioners and the Whig representation in the House of Lords grew; Parliament increasingly relinquished the need to cross-examine petitioners in the 1820s although the practice was revived in the later nineteenth century.[89] As Lord Chancellor Cranworth admitted, the passage of a divorce bill was 'virtually automatic' if it was accompanied by successful separation and criminal conversation suits.[90] However, an unsuccessful criminal conversation action or award of nominal damages did not necessarily preclude divorce; some successful separation cases were found to be collusive by parliament, but this did not halt the divorce proceedings whilst some divorced without a separation.[91]

---

[89] Ibid., pp. 333–5. See also Anderson, 'Legislative divorce', p. 424.
[90] Stone, *Road to divorce*, pp. 324–5.
[91] Lord Ellenborough, for example, divorced despite evidence of collusion and the fact that neither a separation nor a criminal conversation suit was obtained in 1830 (Stone, *Road to divorce*, p. 324, p. 330 and p. 336).

Cranworth oversaw the Divorce and Matrimonial Causes Act of 1857 which moved separation and divorce in England to a court-based process.[92] This transition lacks a neat Irish chronology; Ireland was excluded from the 1857 act and the system of parliamentary divorce thus endured for Irish citizens until 1922. Ireland's retention of the parliamentary system placed it in an increasingly unique position in the British Empire. By 1869, only Irish divorces were routinely heard at Westminster and Ireland was soon being depicted as 'more restricted than any country in the world in so far as their civil law permits no relaxation of the ecclesiastical law'.[93] This history therefore assesses the uniformity of legislative provision within the British Empire, the United Kingdom and post-1922 within Ireland itself. Partition and independence for twenty-six counties of Ireland in 1922 saw the newly created Irish Free State attempt to rewrite its earlier history of divorce to the extent that its existence was, at times, denied. There was no provision for divorce in the new state, a position confirmed by the 1937 constitutional ban. Debates on Irish divorce law reform subsequently became highly politicised; its availability was associated with minority rights and the country's reunification. By comparison, the new six-county Northern Irish state adopted the parliamentary system of divorce until 1939. In both Irish jurisdictions, divorce was often portrayed as endangering the institution of marriage and social stability. Those who sought its reform, seeking to standardise legal provision throughout the UK and the Empire, or end the suffering that such a restricted and partial law engendered, were frequently considered morally bankrupt. A fear of unsettling Ireland by introducing divorce was also apparent in successive administrations from the mid-nineteenth century onwards. As attempts to break the legislative union by both reason and force brought the 'Irish problem' centre stage, it was consequently deemed advisable to allow the admittedly flawed system of parliamentary divorce to continue for Irish petitioners. The trepidation of reform, evident whilst Ireland was under the union, was shared by those who opposed divorce with an increased ferocity in the post-independence era. A sense of Irish moral superiority also prevailed. It was repeatedly claimed that Ireland did not need divorce because 'CHASTITY IS THE INSTINCT OF THE IRISH FEMALE,

---

[92] Scotland developed a court-based system of divorce from the time of the Reformation. The Scottish system of divorce was less biased on the grounds of the sex of the petitioner and cheaper than parliamentary divorce: an undefended Scottish suit could cost £20 in the mid-nineteenth century. From 1841 to 1858, Scotland passed ninety-five divorces, averaging nineteen per annum (Macqueen, *Practical treatise on the appellate jurisdiction*, p. 24).

[93] Lord Guthrie to the *Royal Commission on Divorce ... Minutes of Evidence*, vol. 1 (London, 1912), p. 18. Imperial divorce provision is further discussed in Chapter 3.

the pride of her talents, the power of her beauty, the splendour of her accomplishments, are but so many handmaids of this vestal virtue.'[94] This first history of Irish divorce, however, counters the veracity of such claims; in restoring divorce to the Irish historical narrative, it is clear that both husbands and wives strayed from the marital bond and experienced many of the same travails that tried couples worldwide despite the difficulty and, at times, impossibility of attaining divorce.

[94] Philips, *The speeches of Charles Philips*, p. 153.

1   Divorce in Two Legislatures: Irish Divorce, 1701–1857

Divorce, although often claimed as an anathema in Ireland, spanned the final century of the Irish parliament. Bergin's pioneering work, the first to examine divorce bills in that assembly, revealed that eleven private divorce acts were passed during its lifetime, with 81 per cent brought in the post-1782 period when the Irish parliament was independent. An additional three bills, including a separation bill, were introduced from 1705 but failed to pass.[1] The association between divorce and aristocratic petitioners in Westminster, although not absolute, was evident in the Irish parliament. It was not only those who inherited the family title and estate but also their offspring who sought to divorce. However, the emergent middle classes brought divorce bills to the Irish parliament highlighting that wealth rather than title dictated accessibility to divorce. Cork merchant Joseph Austin, for example, brought the first divorce granted by the Irish parliament in 1730. A preponderance of Irish MPs and their progeny as well as legal professionals were similarly apparent, which intimates that a familiarity with parliamentary and legal processes further aided the initiation of divorce proceedings. In 1747, for instance, George Lowther, MP for Ratoath in the Irish parliament from 1739, divorced Judith Ussher, daughter of the former Carrick representative in that assembly, and barristers James Waddell and Matthias Finucane divorced in 1767 and 1793, respectively.[2]

Male petitioners brought all divorce bills in the Irish parliament, a complexion which is comparable to the almost exclusively male preserve of divorce in Westminster. A religious profile is also easy to determine and dovetails with class. All divorces in the Irish parliament were brought by

---

[1] John Harrison of Tipperary gentry stock and the son of an MP in the Irish parliament brought the first unsuccessful bill. Harrison married sixteen-year-old actress Anne Boden. She was adulterous, but he failed to secure a divorce in Westminster probably because he did not have a divorce *a mensâ et thoro*, although he secured the latter in 1716 (Bergin, 'Irish private divorce bills', pp. 94–5 and p. 105). See their divorce decree by Theophilus Bolton, Archbishop of Dublin, 11 February 1716 (NLI, MS 29,806/77). See also James Kelly, 'The private bill legislation of the Irish parliament, 1692–1800', *Parliamentary History*, vol. 33, issue 1 (February 2014), pp. 73–96.

[2] Bergin, 'Irish private divorce bills', pp. 98–9, p. 100, p. 104, p. 106 and p. 112.

Anglicans, the wealthiest section of Irish society and, in some instances, by Anglican clergymen like Richard Gibbings of Cork who divorced clergy-man's daughter Alice Hyde in 1782.[3] For those of other faiths, divorce was difficult to secure. Quaker merchant Benjamin Fayle tried unsuccessfully to divorce his wife, Sarah Ridgeway, in the Irish parliament in 1787 and 1789. Fayle's bills were brought on the basis of wifely adultery and cohabitation with a servant but lacked a criminal conversation suit in 1787. He secured this in the following year, but the second bill also failed, which, as Bergin suggests, raises the possibility of religious discrimination. However, both parties entered bigamous marriages in the late 1780s; Fayle was now adul-terous and, like his spouse, was guilty of a matrimonial offence.[4] This was censured by Lord Earlsfort who deemed Fayle 'obnoxious to the law against bigamy ... [and] had otherwise misdemeaned himself'. He was therefore 'unworthy' of the relief that parliament could afford.[5]

As the Fayle case highlighted, adultery with servants was a common, although often falsified, ground for divorce. Women were particularly vulnerable to the fake testimony which money could procure, but they could, and did, challenge financial settlements; £5,000 was, for example, awarded to George Lowther in a criminal conversation suit brought against his coachman, but petitioners tried to defend his wife in the Irish parliament in 1747. She claimed to have been held against her will when a 'pretended adultery' was alleged in 1745, and she was forced to alter her marriage settlement from £500 jointure a year to 100 guineas. This produced some sympathetic amendments to the bill; she was granted £113 maintenance per annum whilst her husband and mother-in-law were alive, £200 a year thereafter and her two children were not bastardised.[6] In Austin's 1730 divorce, his wife, Mary Mitchell, the daughter of a Cork merchant, also contested the bill as maintenance of £350 was at odds with her £1,000 dowry. This served little purpose; the bill passed without amendment. The rationale for her maintenance, that 'she may not be left to starve, or be tempted by her necessity to become a common prostitute', emphasised the enormity of her potential moral fall and financial vulnerability as an adulterous woman.[7] In addition, not all

---

[3] Ibid., p. 99, p. 107 and p. 113.

[4] In the first bill, Sarah Fayle petitioned for part of her fortune to be returned (ibid., p. 99, p. 103 and p. 106).

[5] *Freeman's Journal*, 17 March 1789. Earlsfort was an Irish barrister, judge and Lord Chief Justice of the King's Bench for Ireland, 1784–98.

[6] This was the first Irish case where a parliamentary agent was employed to bring the measure on behalf of the petitioner, which became commonplace thereafter. Alleged impropriety with a servant also provided the grounds for James Waddell's divorce in 1767 (Bergin, 'Irish private divorce bills', pp. 98–9, pp. 103–4, p. 106 and p. 112).

[7] Ibid., p. 97, p. 103, p. 105 and p. 112.

female respondents were represented in parliament; Sarah Fayle was unrepresented at two unsuccessful divorce hearings in 1787 and 1789, and lack of representation for Anne O'Brien delayed, but did not defeat, the bill brought by her spouse, Matthias Finucane, in 1793.[8] The O'Brien-Finucane case encouraged MPs like Colonel John Blaquiere, the former Irish chief secretary, to appeal for divorce bills, especially the examination of witnesses, to be conducted with solemnity in the Irish parliament as the 'character' of women was 'at stake'. There were also calls for witnesses to be placed under oath, but this was not common practice, although witnesses could choose to take a voluntary oath at the bar of the house.[9]

Other women did not lack representation or agency; they provoked divorce and were sometimes collusive to the proceedings. Collusion was a prevailing concern in parliamentary divorce hearings and later in court; if proven, it could be a peremptory bar, but there was considerable variation in the application of collusive charges. In 1793, Armar Lowry-Corry, the 1st Earl Belmore of Castle Coole in Co. Fermanagh, divorced his second wife, Lady Harriet Hobart, the eldest daughter of the 2nd Earl of Buckinghamshire. This was an advantageous match for Belmore; Harriet brought £20,000 to the marriage whilst a minor in 1780 and her father's position as Irish lord lieutenant secured her bridegroom a peerage as Baron Belmore. Yet, her 'total aversion' and 'visible disgust' towards her spouse was described by many in their separation trial, the record of which was reproduced in pamphlet form.[10] Her adultery, allegedly 'instigated no doubt by the devil', with William Kerr, Lord Ancram, later the 6th Marquess of Lothian, led Belmore to such 'distraction' that he 'almost entirely secluded himself from society'. A private deed of separation was drawn up after several years of non-cohabitation and six weeks after the birth of a daughter in 1781. This bestowed £1,000 a year on Harriet, but she wanted to divorce. Her husband was at first reluctant to concede, so she provoked him by living openly with Kerr, taking the name of Lady Ancram and bearing another child in 1791. The subsequent divorce bill was collusive as its terms, including her jointure of £2,000 a year, were pre-agreed. The wealth of the parties also complicated the parliamentary proceedings; the divorce cost £4,187 with separation and criminal conversation suits secured in London, heavy legal representation in the Irish lords and

---

[8] Ibid., p. 100 and p. 104.
[9] The Recorder of Dublin, for example, swore in some witnesses (*Freeman's Journal*, 30 April 1793).
[10] Armar Lowry-Corry (Earl Belmore), *The trial of Viscountess Belmore (formerly Lady Henrietta Hobart, daughter to John Earl of Buckinghamshire) for adultery with the Earl of Ancram* (London, 1793), p. 7 and p. 23. This sold for one shilling and sixpence.

witnesses brought from France who required interpreters in parliament, but a divorce was secured in 1793.[11]

The Belmore case attracted more interest than any other Irish divorce up to the mid-1790s but was eclipsed by George Nugent, the 7th Earl of Westmeath's divorce in 1796. This was not only due to the rank of the parties but also Westmeath's motivation; he wanted to marry another. He married Anne Jeffereyes, eldest daughter of James St John Jeffereyes of Blarney Castle, Co. Cork, and niece of John FitzGibbon, the 1st Earl of Clare and lord chancellor of Ireland, in 1784, but it was purported that Westmeath planned to get rid of his adulterous wife and remarry in 1795. Even with 'Lady W.'s. guilt, of which ... there is no doubt', many hoped 'that the divorce may not be confirmed in the House of Lords. ... It is commonly said that he was not very nice as to living with her after her conduct was evident to him, till this fancy of [marrying] Lady E. came into his mind, they are a miserable set altogether.'[12] This case saw the highest Irish criminal conversation damages awarded to date in the Court of the Exchequer: £10,000 was granted although Westmeath sought twice that amount against baronet's son and Irish MP, the Hon. Augustus Cavendish-Bradshaw, described by the solicitor general as 'honourable ... only on account of his rank'. Servant testimony confirmed that the countess was often alone with Bradshaw and 'appearances of the sofa being in much disorder, with marks of hair powder and dirt of shoes upon it'. She was also alleged to have slept away from home, but Bradshaw's counsel disputed proof of adultery and questioned the reliability of testimony from servants 'who might be actuated by motives of malice or hopes of rewards'. Unconvinced, the jury found in Westmeath's favour.[13] The Westmeaths divorced in the Irish parliament in the same year. A £400 annuity for Anne was £200 less than she would have received from her jointure, but she married Bradshaw within weeks of the divorce; Westmeath remarried a year later.[14] Multiple transcripts of the

---

[11] See PRONI, D3077/B/5/8/3A; D3007/B/5/8/3A and D623/A/136/24; Malcomson, *The pursuit of the heiress*, p. 37 and Bergin, 'Irish private divorce bills', p. 100, pp. 103–4, p. 107 and p. 113. Collusion also featured in the last divorce and final act passed by the Irish parliament: Alexander Montgomery, a captain in the Monaghan militia, divorced Mary (née Chute, of Protestant landed stock) in 1800. They married in 1781 when Mary was age seventeen, but the birth of an illegitimate child in 1799 led to a private deed of separation. The latter hinted to collusion but, as in the Belmore case, did not halt the divorce. Mary's married lover, Thomas Balfour, died in 1800. Mary remarried in 1802, but that union failed by 1806; it seems that her mother had to financially support her (Bergin, 'Irish private divorce bills', p. 102 and p. 107).

[12] Lady Anne Roden to Lady Harriet Skeffington, 26 March 1795 (PRONI, D562/2579).

[13] Anon., *Crim. con. actions*, pp. 54–60.

[14] Charles Annesley also remarried within weeks of divorcing his wife of fourteen years, Sarah Carter, in the Irish parliament in 1800. Sarah's fate is unknown (Bergin, 'Irish private divorce bills', p. 102).

Westmeath case were published,[15] and it was satirised by Dr John Walcott, writing as the pseudonymous 'Peter Pindar' in *Lord Auckland's triumph or the death of crim. con: a pair of prophetic odes*: 'Lady Westmeaths no more shall rise, Victims of fascinating eyes.'[16] This was overly optimistic; many in a similar predicament would later find themselves subject to public scrutiny and moral censure.

The legitimacy of children was another parliamentary divorce preoccupation. Few were as fortunate as Judith Lowther whose progeny were not illegitimatised in her 1847 divorce. Indeed, in 1751 George Frend, a Limerick landed soldier, divorced Elizabeth Vanluen, daughter of a Dublin physician and sister of the marriage reformer Laetitia Pilkington. This case was based on Elizabeth's adultery which produced illegitimate issue whilst her spouse was abroad for thirteen years. After Elizabeth married in 1734 whilst apparently a minor and without the consent or knowledge of guardians or relations, a son was born in the following year before Frend was posted abroad in 1736. The divorce bill successfully requested that the children born during this absence be bastardised.[17] Such a clause was not unusual in Westminster divorce bills; until the mid-1760s, many included bastardy clauses for children conceived a year or more after a separation or conceived whilst a husband was abroad. However, these clauses became rarer; after 1829, only one bill passed with such a proviso as the English lords, reflecting a growing concern for child welfare, became increasingly sensitive to the impact of illegitimating children who could not defend themselves.[18]

There were also attempts to divorce in the British Parliament when the Irish parliament refused a bill and vice versa. Indeed, the first bill brought to the Irish parliament by John Harrison in 1705 had earlier failed in Westminster. The English lords also considered the case of Arthur Judge of Co. Westmeath in 1708. The Judge case was brought on the grounds of his wife Maria Pier's adultery after fourteen years of marriage, but no bill was presented. Judge petitioned the lords in the following year and later presented an affidavit from his wife confirming her agreement to have the marriage 'made void by an act of parliament' but again no bill followed. Judge then petitioned the Irish lords in 1710 and 1711; the first attempt stalled and the second was rejected outright. Like the Fayle cases of 1787 and 1789, bigamous remarriage was resorted to by both parties which

---

[15] Ibid., p. 100, p. 107, p. 109 and p. 114.
[16] Peter Pindar, *Lord Auckland's triumph or the death of crim. con: a pair of prophetic odes* (London, 1800), p. 30. Three decades later another Westmeath matrimonial dispute excited even higher levels of public interest. See Chapter 2.
[17] Bergin, 'Irish private divorce bills', p. 98 and p. 112.
[18] This was also apparent in custody rulings (Stone, *Road to divorce*, pp. 326–8).

negated the prospect of introducing a successful divorce bill to either Westminster or the Irish parliament.[19]

The case of William Townsend Mullins of the Kerry gentry similarly bestrode both parliaments, revealing not only the complexity of marriage settlements but also considerable financial resources. Mullins divorced Frances-Elizabeth Sage, a daughter of the former governor of Patna in the West Indies, in the English House of Lords in 1796 but, in a move which the lord chancellor declared of 'abundant caution', he also successfully petitioned the Irish parliament to divorce in 1798. To secure an Irish estate settled on his marriage, a divorce was initiated; however, it essentially secured the marriage settlement. It was also a rearrangement which worked against the financial interests of his wife who brought a £17,000 dowry to the marriage: her £1,000 a year jointure was replaced by an annuity of £541.[20]

The fallout of divorce was not solely financial. As Bergin notes, many male petitioners and those named as co-respondents subsequently retained or secured election to both the Irish and Westminster parliaments. Husbands, as the wronged parties in these cases, were clearly able to maintain status post-divorce: Austin, for example, was elected mayor of Cork in the same year as his 1730 divorce; George Lowther divorced in 1747 but remained a member of the Irish parliament until his death in 1792.[21] The reaction to paramours was, at times, less magnanimous: Lady Westmeath's lover's prospects for promotion were seemingly damaged by her high-profile 1796 divorce. Some female divorcees also married the men named in relation to their infidelity. Indeed, *Bon Ton Magazine* went as far as to claim that divorced women gained 'éclat to their name, especially when they wing the bird and fix him in their snare'.[22] However, the female rate of remarriage was lower than that of their former spouses, and some paramours, like that of Frances-Elizabeth Mullins, married other women. Therefore, a suggestion that 'the consequences of adultery, illegitimacy and even bigamy' were slight overlooks stigma, problematic second unions and the fact that bigamy could bar divorce bills.[23]

Divorce also fractured familial relations. Wives normally lost custody of children, and, as in Mullins's case, marriage settlements were significantly reduced. The sexual double standard was also in evidence. Although it is doubtful that a divorce occurred between the Rev.

---

[19] Bergin, 'Irish private divorce bills', pp. 96–7, p. 105 and p. 108.
[20] Ibid., p. 101, p. 104, p. 107 and p. 114.   [21] Ibid., p. 97, p. 103 and p. 112.
[22] E. A. Y., *Annals of fashionable gallantry: a collection of remarkable trials for crim. con., divorce, adultery, seduction, cruelty* ... (London, 1830), cited p. 51.
[23] Bergin, 'Irish private divorce bills', p. 109.

Matthew Pilkington and his wife, Laetitia, their 1737 Dublin separation, caused by allegations of adultery which she contested, led Jonathan Swift to cut them from his society. To Swift, Matthew Pilkington was 'the falsest rogue', but his wife was 'the most profligate whore in either kingdom'. The split plunged her into debtor's prison and the limelight. Both parties published accounts of their marital woes which amounted to 'pamphlet warfare'. Laetitia's three-volume memoirs, issued between 1748 and 1754, detailed the impossibility of regaining reputation. She was doubtless considering her own alleged fall and that, more convincingly proven, of her sister Elizabeth Vanluen who was divorced in the Irish parliament in 1751. Laetitia also offered an overly sanguine 'warning' to female readers: '[B]y my fall they may stand the more secure.'[24]

Like gender mores, the fate of divorced women changed little in the late eighteenth and early nineteenth centuries. Sarah Fayle, party to two unsuccessful attempts to divorce in the Irish parliament, was disowned by the Society of Friends in 1782 due to her alleged intemperance, debts and keeping of 'unsuitable' company even before her case came before parliament for the first time in 1787.[25] By 1798, the press alleged that she was 'common to the officers of the garrison'.[26] Lord Paget's adulterous liaison, which led to a criminal conversation action in 1809 and a divorce in the following year, with Lady Charlotte Cadogan, the wife of the Rt Hon. Henry Wellesley and sister-in-law of the Duke of Wellington, however, did not prevent Paget's appointment as Irish lord lieutenant in 1828. By comparison, even after Charlotte's marriage to Paget, she was 'snubbed by the wife of the Irish under-secretary, who refused to receive her'.[27]

Popular criticism of Irish divorce was more muted. John Forbes, MP for Drogheda, urged 'very great precaution' in passing divorce bills as he feared 'for the dignity of Parliament' in 1793, but this was a rare critique of a practice which rarely aroused popular opposition.[28] Whilst the comic operas *The divorce: or, fashionable folly* and *The farce, the divorce* showed in Dublin theatres, Irish press coverage of parliamentary divorce was perfunctory and sporadic. Reportage of divorce bills increased from the 1790s but remained far from exhaustive and often lacked editorial comment. The identity of parties of a higher social standing was obscured,

---

[24] Laetitia moved to London and wrote to support herself. Matthew remarried and cut the children of his first marriage from his will a month after Laetitia's death in 1750 (Laetitia Pilkington, *Memoirs of Mrs Laetitia Pilkington, 1712–50* [with introduction by Iris Barry] [London, 1928 reprint of first ed. 1748–54], p. 9, p. 18, p. 25, p. 124 and p. 151).

[25] Bergin, 'Irish private divorce bills', p. 99, p. 103 and p. 106.

[26] *Freeman's Journal*, 17 March 1789.   [27] Stone, *Road to divorce*, p. 344.

[28] *Freeman's Journal*, 9 March 1793.

with only the initials of names given and terms like 'carnal knowledge' were similarly masked.[29] This self-censorship was inspired less by a concern for the modesty of the parties than by a fear of litigation. In the 1790s, however, there was some consternation that Ireland was adopting English vices and facing a moral decline: 'there is a change in our manners. . . . Adulteries until of late were scarily known on this side of St. George's channel.' The press also claimed a corruption of upper-class manners, their 'bodies enervated by foreign vices and luxury'.[30] Others did not blame imported immorality but the search for fortune and aggrandisement which dictated the aristocratic match.[31] More than a decade later, with two divorces heard in the Irish lords in one parliamentary session for the first time in 1793, fears re-emerged that 'the unimpeached chastity of our fair country women', which rendered divorce 'almost unknown in Ireland . . . for centuries', was under threat. However, the *Freeman's Journal* would not aver whether this represented 'a growing dissoluteness of manners in the female sex, or . . . the profligate pursuits and subsequent defects of the male'.[32] Yet, the impact of moving Irish divorce to Westminster and the site of the alleged moral corruption was lost in the debates concerning the Act of Union of 1800. Any concerns were seemingly tempered by the fact that Westminster heard Irish bills for divorce in the pre-union period and that the Irish parliamentary divorce process was very close to that of the British Parliament.

Until the Act of Union, Irish petitioners were uniquely placed; they could divorce in either the Dublin or Westminster parliament. Although bringing a private bill to each entailed considerable expense, greater outlay was entailed in travelling to London with legal counsel and at least two witnesses required to confirm adultery. Westminster granted the first divorce to an Irish petitioner, Sir John Dillon of Lismullen in Co. Meath, in 1701. As was later apparent in the Irish parliament, Dillon was willing to divorce in either assembly to be free of his adulterous spouse. Although an Irish knight and a member of the Irish parliament, Dillon was one of the first commoners to seek divorce. He married Mary Boyle, daughter of Lord Blessington and granddaughter of two Dublin archbishops, in 1694, settling a £500 jointure on her. She bore two daughters but eloped in 1695, living thereafter in what was alleged to be 'lewd and open Adultery', possibly with James, 4th Earl of Annesley, who

---

[29] See, for example, the *Freeman's Journal*'s coverage of Lord Belmore's divorce in the Irish parliament, 7 March 1793.

[30] *Freeman's Journal*, 15 December 1781. *Finns Leinster Journal* also suggested 'Our people of fashion are getting fast in the British tou of divorces', 6 September 1783.

[31] Anon. letter to the *Freeman's Journal*, 14 March 1769.

[32] *Freeman's Journal*, 13 April 1793.

was involved in a duel with Dillon in the same year. Dillon tried unsuccessfully to reduce her dower and free himself from her debts in the Irish Privy Council, but its English counterpart rejected the bill in 1697.[33] In 1699, Mary bore an illegitimate child and 'for aught the Petitioner knows, she may have had more'.[34] This and Dillon's earlier lack of success in the Privy Council likely encouraged his approach to Westminster in 1701, where he successfully divorced, bastardised all issue from the date of Mary's elopement and discharged 'his estate from her jointure, debts and demands'.[35] She did not oppose what she saw as a 'very prejudicial' bill but petitioned the lords for 'competent maintenance' until the bill was read. Dillon was subsequently ordered to pay her legal fees to allow her to present a defence. This stands as the earliest example of a husband providing such financial support. Mary reportedly still found 'it difficult to get any to appear for her', although it is unclear whether this was due to the rarity of divorce at this juncture, moral disdain or more pragmatic concerns over payment. Her inheritance was also questioned. Although the bill passed and she received £200 towards her debts, the £200 per annum she was to receive on Dillon's death was halved.[36] Post-divorce, Mary may have been cast out from her family and likely moved to England while her former spouse remarried.[37] This early Irish divorce encapsulated many of the traits that would later become commonplace: a law shaped by the sexual double standard and moral censure of divorced women. It also highlighted that even in the early eighteenth century, there was an acceptance that women who were 'guilty' of a matrimonial offence required some level of financial support. This laid the foundation for the House of Commons' position of the 'Lady's Friend', whereby an MP with an interest in private bill legislation would be appointed to determine suitable financial provision for wives being divorced in the British Parliament.[38]

Irish divorce petitioners' quandary of whether a case should be presented to the Dublin or London assembly gained more prominence in the mid-eighteenth century. This was first raised in 1753 when Irish resident,

---

[33] Bergin, 'Irish private divorce bills', p. 95 and p. 110. Dillon sat in the Irish parliament as member for Kells from 1692 to 1693 and Meath from 1695 to 1699 and 1703 to 1708.

[34] *House of Lords Journal*, 25 March 1701, vol. 16, pp. 633–4.

[35] Frederick Clifford, *A history of private bill legislation*, vol. 1 (2 vols., London, 1968 new impression of London, 1885 edition), pp. 412–3. Clifford, a Middle Temple barrister, was also a journalist and legal commentator. His *History of private bill legislation* was the key text until O. C. Williams, *Historical development of private bill procedure* (London, 1948).

[36] *House of Lords Journal*, 9 April 1701, vol. 16, p. 646; 14 April 1701, p. 651; and 29 April 1701, p. 664.

[37] Bergin, 'Irish private divorce bills', p. 104.

[38] The Lady's Friend is further discussed in Chapter 3.

barrister at Middle Temple and later Irish MP Samuel Low petitioned the English Lords to introduce a bill allowing Irish residents to divorce in Westminster. Low married in England but resided in Ireland from where his wife eloped, allegedly committing adultery in Wales and Yorkshire. Low was permitted to bring his case to Westminster and successfully divorced.[39] Thirteen Irish petitioners followed Low to present divorce bills to Westminster in the eighteenth century. This comprised 10.9 per cent of all divorces heard, and Roberts was therefore correct to infer that the Irish demand for divorce was lower than that in England.[40] Westminster, as the sole venue for parliamentary divorce from 1800, heard sixteen Irish divorces from 1804 to 1856. Although this represented a fractional rise in actual petitioners, proportionally this was a decline to 8.4 per cent of all divorces heard, a fall caused by the augmented costs of travel to London.

The class composition of Irish petitioners to Westminster was equivalent to the Irish parliamentary profile: of seventy divorce petitions presented to Westminster between 1803 and 1827, six were of Irish gentry stock including Rev. Massy, son of an Irish baronet, who divorced in 1808, and Stepney St George, captain of the 52nd Light Infantry and son of an Irish landed family, who divorced in 1826.[41] Others were upper-middle-class merchants like Andrew Jameson of the Irish whiskey family who divorced in 1826; Robert Green, a Dublin merchant, who divorced in 1775; and Stephen Popham, later a member of the Irish parliament and Woodmason, a Dublin banker, who both divorced in 1798.[42] There were also a number of Irish military divorces.[43] Major general in Portuguese service, Sir John Milley Doyle's divorce cost £7,500 in 1822 but, like Stepney St George, he had aristocratic connections. Doyle, for example, used his personal acquaintance with Irish peer Lord Donoughmore to have his case presented to the lords. Corresponding with the latter, he asked 'when I proposed being in London, as it was his wish to bring his divorce bill, which I was to take charge of in the House of Lords, as soon

[39] See *Journal of the House of Lords*, vol. 28, p. 50. The location of the adultery was also cited in the legal advice offered in the nineteenth-century McClintock case discussed in Chapter 3.

[40] Roberts, *Divorce bills*, p. 9.

[41] In his 1804 criminal conversation suit, Rev. Massy accused the Marquis of Headfort of committing the 'offence' while he performed 'Divine Service on the Sabbath Day'. The defence was based on Rev. Massy's 'general carelessness, and the lady's open declaration of her attachment to the defendant'; £10,000 was awarded with the timing of the adultery contributing to the high damages (Fenn, *Thirty-five years*, pp. 220–1).

[42] *Calendar of the Journals of the House of Lords*, from 10 May 1768 to 21 January 1808, p. 422; Anderson, 'Legislative divorce', pp. 419–20 and p. 429.

[43] See, for example, the Irish divorces of army officer Creagh (1846) and Captain Eustace Hill (1849) (See Roberts, *Divorce bills*).

as possible'.[44] His divorce bill was successfully heard in Westminster five months later.

The earlier aristocratic complexion of divorcees also remained in evidence. Charles Daly's 1768 bill was brought to Westminster because of his wife and cousin Anastasia's adultery with the Rt Hon. Francis Fitzmaurice, popularly known as the Earl of Kerry. Daly was the Galway member of the Irish parliament, described as a gentleman of 'an ancient family and considerable estate'. He married in 1747, but Kerry was alleged to have paid Anastasia 'great attention . . . and was generally near her' from 1763. She was later portrayed as a victim of seduction 'by the Devil' and castigated for being 'unmindful of her conjugal vow, and not having the fear of God before her eyes'.[45] In the following year, Kerry arranged for her to be taken from her home and they were allegedly witnessed by servants 'toying and caressing each other in a very free, indecent, and lewd, manner', leaving 'rumpled and tumbled' couches in their wake. Mrs Daly's maid, from a vantage point 'behind a settee', saw the Earl of Kerry 'after kissing and toying with her for some time, laid her down'.[46] Like Lady Belvedere, Anastasia Daly was forcibly taken by her spouse from Dublin and 'locked up' in Galway.[47] Daly's Westminster divorce bill made no financial provision for her; although counsel for both parties were instructed by the lords to come to some arrangement, their decision was unrecorded.[48] The case also met some opposition from the 'brothers of the mitre' in the upper house which was not uncommon at this juncture, although one correspondent believed the passage of the bill saved Anastasia from 'a drubbing'.[49]

In 1799, John James Hamilton, the 1st Marquess of Abercorn, became the first sitting member of the lords to divorce. This, coupled with the fact that Cecil, his second wife and first cousin, committed adultery with

[44] Doyle, London to Donoughmore, 28 January 1822 (PRONI, T3459/D/41/52). Doyle sought £30,000 damages from George Brown in Dublin in 1820. He was awarded £5,000 and costs, but by 1842 Doyle was in King's Bench prison, his debts including the £7,500 cost to divorce Lady Doyle (Anon., *Crim. Con.* [Dublin, 1820], p. 35; *Freeman's Journal*, 8 June 1842).

[45] Anon., *Trials for adultery*, vol. 1, p. 40. Other witnesses denied 'any criminal correspondence, or that they committed the crime of adultery together', ibid., pp. 1–8 and pp. 17–34.

[46] Plowden, *Crim. con. biography*, vol. 1, pp. 136–7.   [47] Stone, *Road to divorce*, p. 167.

[48] Roberts, *Divorce bills*, p. 104.

[49] A 'drubbing' is a severe thrashing. Lady Bolingbroke's divorce received similar criticism. Elizabeth Griffin to Agar, 25 February 1768 (PRONI, D3719/C/2/1). Anastasia married the Earl of Kerry. Other upper-class Irish petitioners included Edward, Viscount Ligonier who divorced Penelope Pitt in Westminster in 1772. Witnesses were heard, but no defence counsel was presented. The bill passed after amendments were made in the commons. See *Calendar of the Journals of the House of Lords*, from 10 May 1768 to 21 January 1808, p. 415.

Captain Joseph Copley, a brother of Abercorn's first wife, led the case to become 'a sort of historic cause célèbre'.[50] More unusually, pity and a sense of social protocol led Abercorn to encourage the marriage of his wife to Copley, financially support her and allow her access to their children. Cecil lived as part of the Abercorn household from the time of her father's death in 1787; rumours abounded regarding her attachment to Copley; Abercorn's alleged, but denied, role in her being granted the rank of an earl's daughter in 1798; and her pre-marital relationship with Abercorn before his first wife's death.[51] In 1792, age twenty-one, she married Abercorn, a widower in his mid-thirties, and they lived together until 1798. Yet, from 1796 Abercorn observed Copley showing 'too great attention' towards his wife, seeking 'to attend and meet her at various places of public amusement as well as at private and public assemblies and other parties in London'. He warned his wife of his 'uneasiness at such conduct' and insisted that she avoid Copley 'if she expected to live under his protection as his wife'. She promised and Copley was barred from the Abercorn circle. Abercorn's absence to attend to militia duties in 1798, however, saw Copley take, what Abercorn claimed was, 'advantage' and Cecil 'too much favoured and encouraged and accordingly becoming unmindful of her conjugal vow ... [they] had the carnal use and knowledge of each other[']s Bodies and committed the crime of adultery'.[52]

Cecil, believing that she was carrying Copley's child, confessed to her spouse. He reportedly reacted 'very coolly ... and behaved with sufficient temper and liberality', agreeing to let her continue to see their children: 'She meant to return to her back chaise, but Lord Abercorn insisted on her going like the marchioness of Abercorn and taking his coach and servants.'[53] She went to her mother's before living with Copley 'as Husband and Wife'. The *Morning Post* quickly announced the 'Elopement of a Captain in the Guards' with 'the Marchioness of – ', highlighting the open secret of this infidelity in the echelons of high society: 'It was unnecessary ... to name the parties in our Paper. ... The whole Fashionable World knew at once who they were. The measure is said to have been long on the tapis.'[54]

---

[50] Lady Mary Hamilton, typescript, 'John James, 1st Marquess of Abercorn', compiled pre-1909 but amended thereafter (PRONI, D2152/2), p. 35 and *passim*.

[51] Ibid.

[52] Extracts from the *Journal of the House of Lords* re. the Abercorn Divorce Bill, 1799, PRONI, T3691/1.

[53] A. P. W. Malcomson, 'A lost natural leader: John James, first Marquess of Abercorn (1756–1818)', *Proceedings of the Royal Irish Academy*, vol. 88 (September 1988), p. 70. It is claimed that Cecil refused the offer of the family coach (Hamilton typescript, p. 64).

[54] Hamilton typescript, p. 61. A *tapis* is a carpet, tapestry or other covering. The term 'on the tapis' refers to a topic which is under consideration or discussion.

Abercorn brought a criminal conversation case to the court of King's Bench at Westminster against Copley claiming £20,000 damages in 1798. This case underscored the lurid detail required to prove adultery: '[T]here was only one Bed in the Bedchamber in which they slept [and] . . . lay every night naked and alone . . . and did commit the Crime of Adultery together.' Abercorn was awarded £10,018 with costs and separated in the consistory court in 1799. Evidence from servants, including a groom, footman, post-boy, chambermaid and hotel manager, confirmed 'very serious conversation' between the unchaperoned marchioness and Copley in the latter's apartments where 'there was but one bed . . . [and] they slept together' and in a hotel. Sir William Scott, overseeing the separation case, claimed that the marchioness, like Anastasia Daly, lacked 'the fear of God before her Eyes'.[55]

Abercorn's 1799 divorce bill to the lords recounted that his wife's 'Adulterous Behaviour dissolved the Bond of Marriage on her part', depriving him of the 'Comforts of Matrimony, and maybe liable to have Spurious Issue imposed on him to succeed to his Titles[,] Honour[,] Estate and Fortune'. He sought to remarry as if Cecil 'were naturally dead' with any issue from a subsequent union to be legitimate and able to inherit, with his second wife barred from dower or any claims.[56] In compliance with the standing orders, he was present when the bill was read in the House of Lords and was prepared to be cross-examined although as a peer he would not be called to the bar but would be permitted to give evidence from his seat or at the table of the house. Decorum prevented Abercorn's cross-examination, but his speech was remarkable for its lack of invective and candour to those who were his 'peers' in every sense:

I am the first peer of this House who ever stood in so extraordinary a predicament . . . where every question may in itself be an insult. . . . [T]he questions I am liable to are, whether I have connived at the dishonour of my wife . . . been in collusion with her or the author of her ruin, and whether at the time in question she was relieved by my consent from all conjugal ties and duty! . . . [T]o hear such questions from any man would be so revolting to my feelings, my character and my nature, that my only way to reconcile those feelings with your Lordships' resolutions is to anticipate the questions, to answer before I am asked . . . of such base connivance, collusion or consent I am as guiltless and as incapable as any one of your Lordships. I have not seen either of the parties against whom I have been obliged to proceed, since I was aware of the distressing event. . . . As to the base and foolish calumnies which I have read and heard of,

55 Extracts from the *Journal of the House of Lords* re. the Abercorn Divorce Bill, 1799, PRONI, T3691/1.
56 Ibid. Abercorn married Lady Ann Hatton in 1799.

that I would promote the continuance of that connection which . . . I knew too well must only sink deeper and deeper in the misery the unhappy and lamented victim of it . . . I distain to say more than that they are calumnies as base as utterly unfounded. . . . When an unfortunate woman in an agony of mind which I hope never to witness again in a fellow-creature the most indifferent to me, made me her heartbreaking confession, I felt much horror, much surprise, much pity, but no resentment, for God knows, I found no place for it. I believe I did . . . assure her that whatever measure might be due to myself and my family, they should not be vindictive measures, nor such as to involve her deeper in ruin that she had involved herself.

His lack of animosity towards his errant wife, apparent on learning of her infidelity, remained: 'God knows, her cup is bitter enough, without my adding more bitterness.'[57] Abercorn was not renowned for fidelity and this, and a sense of obligation, influenced his decision 'that a woman who had borne his name' should not 'suffer complete social extinction; and by way of rehabilitating her so far as was possible, he did his best to further her marriage with Captain Copley'. Indeed, 'forgiveness for past injuries is offered, together with an annuity to the Lady. . . . If this should be refused, the Captain is threatened . . . with every sort of hostility the law can wage.' Abercorn did not claim the damages awarded in the criminal conversation case and settled £2,000 on his wife.

The *Morning Post* was less magnanimous. Four hundred false invites issued for an Abercorn ball in 1800 led the paper to speculate that the source was 'a certain Lady, who invited every person the Marquis disliked, except herself'.[58] Cecil, informing the children of her situation, also 'held up herself as a warning to them not to mix in the fashionable dissipation of the age, and above all to preserve their honour'. Despite Abercorn's efforts, Cecil's marriage to Copley in the same year as the divorce and the subsequent birth of two children could not restore her reputation. Cecil was excluded from the royal court, and social hostess Lady Holland recalled post-revolutionary France, where the former nobility was devoid of title, by branding Cecil 'ci-devant'. In later life, Cecil resignedly confessed, 'I suffered much . . . but the worst is past now.'[59]

Post-union, Irish divorce bills were presented with some regularity at Westminster, although no Irish bills were heard between 1816 and 1825. The continued wealth of the petitioners facilitated absorption of the

---

[57] Lord Abercorn, 1799, PRONI, D623/A/233/41.

[58] Hamilton typescript, p. 67, p. 68 and p. 79.

[59] Ibid., p. 35 and *passim*. Cecil's marriage to Copley was described as an 'unhappy passion . . . the sacrifice she had made to attain happiness had failed; for the object of her love was not all that she had hoped to find' (Diary of Lady Charlotte Susan Maria Campbell Bury in A. F. Steuart (ed.), *The diary of a lady in waiting*, vol. 2 (2 vols., London, 1908), p. 485. Cecil died in 1819.

increased cost of travelling to London with witnesses and counsel, but it is harder to determine whether more middle-class petitioners could now proceed. Robert Tighe's was the first post-union Irish divorce bill heard at Westminster in 1804, but his finances were boosted by £10,000 in criminal conversation damages awarded by the Court of King's Bench in Dublin in 1800.[60] Lord Cloncurry was similarly unrestricted. His 1811 divorce followed some of the largest criminal conversation damages: an Irish jury awarded £20,000 against Sir John Piers in 1808. Cloncurry's divorce, however, emphasised the problem of presenting personal correspondence as evidence. Married in 1803, his wife's adultery was discovered in 1806 resulting in a duel between Cloncurry and Piers. A letter to Cloncurry in his wife's handwriting, alleged to contain an admission of her adultery, and other correspondence were refused as evidence in House of Lords. Her missive to Lord Cloncurry's agent was, however, accepted as evidence, illuminating the distinction which was made between letters exchanged by the parties divorcing and those written to acquaintances. Parliament also questioned why Lady Cloncurry remained at home for a few months after her adultery was unearthed. The lords' concern was that this could provide evidence of condonation on the part of her husband but, explaining his wife's predicament, Cloncurry showed compassion: 'she was an Englishwoman ... she had no place where she could get protection in Ireland, and ... the person who had seduced her was in the neighbourhood. I wrote to her father with[in] half an hour' of discovering the adultery and a maid was ordered to sleep alongside her whilst she remained in the house.[61] This did not bar the divorce, but the recurring theme of women's adultery being caused by unscrupulous seduction rendered them as victims in need of protection rather than willing participants in extramarital affairs. Furthermore, as legal counsel was abundantly aware, such an interpretation also emphasised the wronged husband.[62]

General William Dyott of Staffordshire, divorcing in 1816 after a decade of marriage, was of a different class to Cloncurry, but his Irish wife Eleanor was a wealthy heiress. Her marriage settlement included freehold properties in Ireland and the West Indies, cattle, slave stock and £6,000 in government securities. With £800 per annum for her own use

---

[60] Tighe's divorce bill passed with amendments in the House of Commons (*Calendar of the Journals of the House of Lords*, from 10 May 1768 to 21 January 1808, p. 495).

[61] Fenn, *Thirty-five years*, p. 221; Roberts, *Divorce bills*, p. 49 and p. 63; and Macqueen, *Practical treatise on the appellate jurisdiction*, p. 609. *The Bold, Bad Baronet*, a BBC drama based on the Cloncurry case, was produced in 1978.

[62] The Irish divorces of Blackford (Blachford) and Garde in 1812 and 1814, respectively, followed.

and the power to raise £10,000 on the estates with her spouse having access to half that amount, her husband admitted to being 'a little hurt that the family house was left to her for her life'. He also averred that she 'had long shown symptoms of unkindness and inattention', but her request in 1814 for a separation in consequence of an alleged adultery 'amazed and hurt' him. Aided by her family, he sought reconciliation, but Eleanor eloped in the same year.[63] In the divorce bill, Dyott sought to secure the children's interest in their mother's property and abolish her annuity and the powers granted to her by the marriage settlement. Eleanor maintained that she would be destitute, denied her fortune and unable to defend the divorce without an annuity. Her husband, however, claimed that money had not been withheld and an advance would be made to allow her defence. General Dyott's adultery was not proven and the bill passed; yet he recorded this as 'the most melancholy event, which deprived my children of a mother and me of a wife'. Eleanor, however, was defiant; she brought an amending bill to the Court of Common Pleas in the following year under her maiden name of Thomson as some text was mistakenly omitted from the 1816 bill. This was amended; she then attempted to have the bill withdrawn. This failed, but her annuity for life was restored with the proviso that if she outlived her spouse she would receive a quarter of the income from the trust estate with the remainder for her children. Her power to grant leases from the estate if she outlived her husband was not revived, but this was of no consequence: the pair never saw each another again and Eleanor died in 1841, predeceasing her husband by six years.[64]

Families not only brokered reconciliations but also, sometimes to the detriment of their kin, gave evidence in parliamentary divorce hearings.[65] In the 1826 divorce of Lord Cornelius Lismore, members of both parties' families gave evidence to the lords. Married in 1808 and resident in Ireland, early marital problems concerned Lady Eleanor Lismore's 'disappointment with her way of life' and wish for a London home which her husband could ill afford.[66] By 1819, she went abroad to improve her health when her husband was called to London, although financial considerations may also have prevented him from accompanying his wife.

[63] Reginald W. Jeffery (ed.), *Dyott's diary, 1781–1845: a selection from the journal of William Dyott, sometime general in the British army and aide-de-coup to His Majesty King George III*, vol. 1 (2 vols., London, 1907), p. 305 and p. 308.

[64] Ibid., p. 313. This bill was followed by the Irish divorces of Moore in 1825 and Saint George in 1826.

[65] In Hawkes's 1842 divorce, his brother-in-law gave evidence as to his sister's elopement and adultery (*The Times*, 8 June 1842).

[66] Elean or brought £38,000 to the marriage in addition to colliery shares worth £50,000. Prior-Wandesforde papers (NLI, MS 35,466 [5]).

Adultery with the Hon. William Bingham ensued, which allegedly resulted in the birth of a child in 1819. A private deed of separation, giving £2,500 maintenance to Eleanor, was brokered in 1822. Often in arrears, it was claimed that she was forced to live 'small style' whilst abroad with staff paid irregularly.[67] A criminal conversation suit followed where only nominal damages were awarded, but this did not preclude divorce. In the UK Parliament, Lady Lismore opposed the divorce due to her husband's conduct which she claimed was 'deficient in kindness and affection'. Lacking evidence, this defence was abandoned. This postponed, but did not defeat, the bill. Evidence of Lord Lismore's brother, Sir George O'Callaghan, 'proved extreme violence on the part of Lady Lismore towards her husband, and that on one occasion she struck him', calling him 'a coward, a wretch, and a liar' in front of their eldest son, age seven, whom she threatened to turn against his father. Lady Lismore was thus portrayed as lacking due respect for spousal authority. O'Callaghan's evidence also noted that their 'quarrels were chiefly about the style of the Irish house and establishment kept by Lord Lismore, which she objected to', claiming they might be 'good enough for the wife of Lord Lismore, but not for the sister of Lord Ormonde', averring to the difference between aristocratic and gentry expectations.[68]

Coverage of this case was more extensive than many earlier bills. *The Times* printed correspondence from Lord and Lady Lismore in full, including the latter's admission of guilt and her pleas for forgiveness to her brother after separating in 1819, which, unlike the Cloncurry case, were accepted as evidence. The letters also revealed the suffering of an errant wife and the stigma of divorce: 'I am as well aware as any one [sic] can possibly be of the misery and disgrace, that will be entailed not only on me, but my poor children ... and God knows there is nothing I would not do to avoid it. I am sincerely penitent, and conscious of my many faults.' Referring to her 'misery', physical 'weakness' and 'agony of mind', she sought atonement: 'There is nothing I would not do to be reconciled to Lord Lismore ... and restore me to him and my children. ... Don't let me and my children be disgraced for ever [sic].' Although her two daughters remained with her, she had not seen her two sons for five months and feared that her youngest daughter 'will grow up to hate me'. Suffering 'more than I have words to express', she was mindful of a divorced mother's fate: she would 'lose all my children, and become an outcast from everything I love'.[69]

---

[67] Ibid.   [68] Macqueen, *Practical treatise on the appellate jurisdiction*, pp. 640–1.
[69] *The Times*, 3 May 1826. After divorcing, Eleanor was known as Lady Butler and lived in Italy. Her maintenance was problematic; in 1831 she asked, 'Would it not be possible to

The Lismore divorce came in the wake of the Queen Caroline affair whereby, on acceding to the throne, George IV tried unsuccessfully to divorce his estranged wife.[70] This provoked an ecclesiastical spat between John MacHale, later Catholic Bishop of Tuam, and the Rev. Dr Manners, Archbishop of Canterbury. Writing under the respective pseudonyms of 'Hierophilos' and 'Bibliophilos', their letters to the Dublin *Weekly Register* were collectively published in 1821. MacHale was critical of Anglican disunion on divorce, evident in the church response to the Queen Caroline affair which he claimed scandalised 'the faithful'. He thus depicted divorce as a matter of 'momentous' imperial importance

involving the best interests of mankind, and ... the safety and honour of the empire. ... The facility of divorce weakens the mutual desire of pleasing; a neglect of reciprocal attention soon creates indifference [that could] ripen into disgust, and rankle into enmity, until the happy couple see no hope of release from a cruel bondage, except in mutual separation, and the prospect of new nuptials.

The suggestion that divorce incentivised adultery became a recurring trope in both clerical and lay debates: 'What an unnatural state of society ... in which ... people marry for the sake of divorce, and divorce for the sake of marriage.' Yet, unlike the late eighteenth-century claim that immorality was an upper-class preserve, the frequency of infidelity was now deemed to 'penetrate ... from the highest regions into the remotest creeks of society. ... If we were to judge from observation, we could not believe that we lived in a Christian country.'[71]

Despite MacHale's claim of a moral decline, popular interest in divorce was more commonly piqued by the private revelations contained in a bill. Conyers's divorce in 1835 was the first Irish bill to be presented in nine years but, described as 'the most extraordinary and aggravated' bill ever considered by the lords, it caused a sensation. The petitioner was the only son of Charles Conyers of Castletown Conyers in Co. Limerick. Married in 1815, the subsequent conduct of his wife was claimed to exhibit 'the grossest violation of common decency and propriety that had ever [been heard] in such a case'. To provide evidence of his wife's adultery, Conyers hid on a landing as five or six armed servants witnessed the adultery from a window in 1832. Trying to protect her lover, Edmund Odell Westropp when

---

oblige him to pay £550 regularly quarterly?' Eleanor Butler to Richard Eaton, 4 January 1831 (NLI, MS 35,469 [6]).

[70] See R. A. Melikan, 'Pains and penalties procedure: how the House of Lords "tried" Queen Caroline', *Parliamentary History*, vol. 20 (2001), pp. 311–32.

[71] MacHale was appointed bishop in 1825. *The letters of Hierophilos on the education of the poor of Ireland; together, with a letter on divorce, to the Archbishop of Canterbury: to which are subjoined, the letters of Bibliophilos* (Dublin, 1821) (British Library, 8282.c43), p. 61 and pp. 65–6.

discovered in a compromising situation, she clung 'so resolutely to him . . . it became necessary to tear her night-dress to tatters off her back, and to reduce her to a state of literal, natural nudity'. Her lover was beaten during the incident and she nursed him for six weeks, living 'in a state of avowed, undisguised adultery'. Conyers received £2,500 in a criminal conversation suit and the divorce bill passed in the UK Parliament.[72]

Other cases of wifely impropriety were only discovered after the death of a lover. Dr Dionysus Lardner, an academic and the editor of *Lardner's Clcopadia*, proceeded to Westminster in 1839 without a criminal conversation suit as the adulterer was deceased. Lardner married Cecilia Flood in Dublin in 1815 and they lived together for four years and had children; however, due to 'the violence of the lady's temper' they informally separated in 1819. Cecilia lived between her father and her father-in-law, before, in 1820, boarding with Mr Murphy, a married customs official in Dublin. An 'improper familiarity' ensued, prompting Murphy's wife to leave and only return on the condition that Cecilia left. Murphy then hired Dublin lodgings where they lived under an assumed name and the pretence that she was his sister; a child was born in 1821. Murphy's deathbed confession of the affair in 1828 led his brother to inform Cecilia's father. He in turn told Lardner's mother and sister when Cecilia was residing with them. Cecelia denied nothing and took the child, then in the care of Mrs Murphy, into her custody. Lardner moved to London in 1827 to follow 'literary occupations' and was not told of the affair or illegitimate child until 1830. His attempts to secure a separation in the Dublin ecclesiastical court were met by a recriminatory suit lodged by his wife, whilst difficulty in finding witnesses and financing the proceeding postponed the case until 1832. Lack of finances also caused a nine-year delay from discovering his wife's adultery and nineteen years from the event itself before divorcing in the UK Parliament.[73]

Although not fulfilling MacHale's claims, divorce became more commonplace in the 1840s when fifty-eight divorce bills were heard in Westminster including, in an augmentation in Irish petitioners from the previous decade, the cases of Hawkes (1842), Borlean (1845), army officer Creagh (1846) and Captain Eustace Hill (1849). Hill's case was one of several military divorces

---

[72] *The Times*, 18 May 1835.

[73] C. Clark and W. Finnelly (eds.), *Reports of cases heard and decided in the House of Lords on appeals and writs of error . . . during the sessions 1838 and 1839*, vol. 6 (Boston, 1873), p. 569 and p. 991. This was one of eight divorces heard during this session. Lardner later gained a dubious reputation as the first man to divorce in the UK Parliament and be cited as a co-respondent: in the 1845 Heaviside divorce; £8,000 in damages were awarded against Lardner in a criminal conversation suit (Anderson, 'Legislative divorce', p. 433). Edward Fitzgerald, MP, divorcing in 1903 was later cited as co-respondent in fellow MP Henry Norman's divorce (see the *Weekly Irish Times*, 7 February 1903).

but attracted considerable attention and verbatim accounts of the cross-examination of witnesses in the Lords were published. Hill, an army man who served as a stipendiary magistrate in Longford from 1827, married Georgiana Keppel, a daughter of the Earl of Abelmarle, in the same year. She bore twelve children, ten of whom survived, before eloping with Captain William Mangan and adopting his name in 1845. Separation and a criminal conversation suit, where £2,200 in damages were given without a trial, ensued. When the divorce bill came before the Lords, the apprehension of the house in having to examine the details of a peer's daughter was encapsulated by Lord Brougham: '[T]his was a very painful case indeed. A calamity of the heaviest character had befallen a noble Lord a member of their Lordships' House, and an old and esteemed friend.' With a valet testifying that Mangan called him into a room to witness the adultery, Brougham thought it 'beyond belief that any gentleman could have committed so gross, so coarse an act . . . of calling his servant into his room when he was in bed even with his wife . . . but that woman was the wife of another man, with whom he was committing an act of adultery'. Brougham, with a deserved reputation for thorough cross-examination, was insistent on this point; although he discounted the valet's evidence, other witnesses corroborated that Georgiana sat the head of Mangan's table and was 'the mistress of the house'.[74]

Yet, not all who began parliamentary divorce proceedings followed these through to their natural conclusion. Some Irish petitioners, like the Rt Hon. George Annesley, Viscount Valencia, withdrew bills from Westminster. Witnesses were examined in 1808, but the bill's second reading was adjourned and, on Annesley's petition, was withdrawn.[75] As in the Dublin parliament, Westminster also denied the legitimacy of some claims. Taaffe twice tried to divorce in Westminster in 1818–19, failing to provide sufficient evidence for the bill to proceed on the first attempt and then prevented by illness from attending the House of Lords. This delayed the second reading of the bill three times before it was abandoned. Major Bland's 1808 bill was delayed at the request of his spouse's counsel who sought extra time to call servant witnesses from Ireland: their testimony proved her spouse's 'extremely culpable' conduct, 'scandalous improprieties' and having a 'Woman in keeping, whom he passed off as his Wife'. The bill failed and thus stands as a rare example of a successful defence proffered by an Irish female respondent.[76]

[74] *Freeman's Journal*, 28 July 1849; *The Times*, 27 July 1849. Brougham favoured increasing access to divorce.

[75] *Calendar of the Journals of the House of Lords*, from 10 May 1768 to 21 January 1808, p. 475.

[76] Taaffe secured £5,000 in a criminal conversation suit against Lord William Fitzgerald in the Dublin Court of Common Pleas (Macqueen, *Practical treatise on the appellate jurisdiction*, p. 605).

Fears of a moral decline, so pithily professed by McHale, were accompanied by a sense of Irish moral superiority. Despite Irish divorces featuring in both Westminster and, until 1800, the Irish parliament's deliberations, infidelity was depicted as neither indigenous 'to Irish soil' nor 'naturalized beneath an Irish climate ... [as] Ireland most obeyed, most loved, most reverenced the nuptial contract'.[77] This was accompanied by boasts of the country 'being more free [sic] from such vices than any other nation in Europe'.[78] However, in the mid-1850s two cases of Irish divorce allowed such plaudits to be dismissed as idealists and drew popular attention to the vulnerability of women under the existing law of divorce and the need for its reform.

---

[77] This was noted in the 1816 Guthrie v. Sterne criminal conversation case (Phillips, *The speech of Mr. Phillips*, p. 89).

[78] This was stated in the 1820 criminal conversation of case of Sir John Milley Doyle (Anon., *Crim. con.*, p. 35).

2 The Failings of the Law: The Cases of Talbot and Westmeath

Described in 1856 as 'the most remarkable affair of its kind that has ever occurred in this kingdom', the divorce of John Talbot of Mount Talbot, a deputy lieutenant and JP in Co. Roscommon, and Mary Anne (née MacCausland), the daughter of a 'gentleman of the highest respectability' of Fruit Hill in Co. Londonderry, was highly publicised. The case also raised popular criticism of Talbot for conspiring to be rid of his wife, the ecclesiastical courts and parliamentary divorce. Various suits in the Talbot case were heard over a four-year period at a collective estimated cost of £10,000; even the divorce hearing took three weeks to proceed as 5,080 questions were asked.[1] The Talbots married in 1845, and one daughter was born who was age seven when they separated in 1852. As Mount Talbot could only be settled on male issue, Talbot treated his wife with 'indifference, coldness, and unkindness, and with a want of liberality', denying her money, proper clothing and a lady's maid. He then claimed that William Mullane, a coachman in his employ, was adulterous with his wife from 1850 and a butler and under steward corroborated the claim. This was fiction: Mary Ann Talbot was 'punched or dragged', held in 'a water closet' and consigned to the 'custody' of two male servants, Finnerty and Halloran. The latter made some form of physical and likely sexual attack on her: she was rendered 'out of her mind and a lunatic'.[2] Church of Ireland rector at the Mount Talbot estate Rev. McClelland subsequently found Mary Anne 'excited and in a very distracted state ... she neither admitted or denied her guilt'; yet when he accompanied her to Dublin, she allegedly made a lucid confession.

Talbot began separation proceedings on the following day, issuing a writ against Mullane who left the country, possibly for America. A separation, brought on the ground of her alleged adultery, passed in the ecclesiastical court. Talbot was awarded £2,000 and legal costs of

---

[1] Anon., *Divorce in 1857: the Talbot case. Letters by 'Cujus' containing full particulars of the case with observations on the present unsatisfactory state of the law* (London, 1857), p. iii and p. 123.
[2] Ibid., p. 3 and p. 9.

£51.11.2 in a criminal conversation suit against Mullane. However, the separation was appealed in Dublin's High Court of Delegates, composed of three common law judges and three canon lawyers, appointed on the request of the lord chancellor in 1855.[3] Mary Anne Talbot was defended by Irish solicitor general William Keogh, MP, who was highly critical of the clerical involvement, eking out a confession from a woman professed as sane but known to be 'insane, delirious' and suicidal, making 'repeated attempts to destroy herself' by trying to throw herself out a window, asking for poison and tearing at her hair and skin. Six witnesses for John Talbot were discounted as perjurers by the Court of Delegates' judge and a seventh was found to have been paid for evidence. Halloran's statement, for example, was procured by Talbot for an alleged £10 a year but was allowed as evidence in the ecclesiastical court. Such was the extent of paid testimony that Keogh presented this as a criminal case: '[T]his is pre-fabrication; there is not a scintilla of evidence to sustain the allegation.' Delivering his defence, Keogh stressed Mary Anne's high birth, repeatedly referring to her as a 'lady' who was denied financial support in marriage and was now 'condemned as a woman who has prostituted herself like the vilest wretch that walks the streets at midnight ... her offspring shall bear the stain of opprobrium on her brow for ever'. Mullane was also reported to be suffering from 'obstinate and virulent gonorrhoea' which Mary Anne did not contract. To Keogh this proved 'a nefarious plot ... so demonical as only to be conceived by ... polluted conspirators'.[4] Yet, the Court of Delegates, after a month's deliberation, upheld the ecclesiastical court's separation ruling.

Mary Anne was placed in an English asylum before being taken into the care of her brother-in-law and barrister at Middle Temple John Tertius Paget in Leicestershire where she remained 'as great a lunatic as any in Bedlam'. Medical reports confirmed her insanity; its correlation to assumed infidelity was described by Dr Conolly, head of Hamwell asylum, as 'common': '[L]adies ... labour under a delusion that they have been guilty of infidelity to their husbands.' Paget championed Mary Anne's case from 1854, publishing a 121-page letter to the Irish lord lieutenant and petitioning the House of Commons two years later to prove her innocence as 'a mother ... torn from her child – a wife, slandered, – maddened by her husband who swore to love and to cherish

---

[3] Stone, *Road to divorce*, p. 183.
[4] Anon., *Talbot v. Talbot. A report of the speech of William Keogh, Esq., MP, Solicitor General for Ireland on behalf of the appellant, before the High Court of Delegates, January 8, 1855* (London, 1855), *passim*. The Dublin ecclesiastical court and Paget put considerable emphasis on the non-transmittal of this venereal disease.

her. ... I cry aloud against laws which obstruct, and Courts which pollute.'[5] The House of Commons, however, also upheld the separation.

Paget paid £2,586.8.8 to defend Mary Anne in the divorce proceedings in 1856. The written evidence of adultery presented in the ecclesiastical suit was discounted by Parliament as Finnerty and Halloran were discredited as witnesses. This countered the normal parliamentary practice for witnesses in preliminary suits to be examined and their testimony compared.[6] Lord St Leonards, however, was not willing to question the legitimacy of the claim of adultery, averring that 'criminal intercourse must be supposed to have taken place'.[7] In consequence, the non-transmittal of Mullane's venereal disease was not fully considered as a defence. Familial concerns for the potentially damaging impact of the case on their 'connection and prospects' also disadvantaged Mary Anne. In Paget's view, this explained why only thirty-six questions were asked by her counsel in the House of Lords: such 'inaction must have been the result of restraint imposed ... virtually instructed to allow the case "to proceed" ... with as much privacy and quietness as possible'.[8] Although much of the evidence was conflicting, the divorce bill passed. In the UK Parliament, Rev. Abram Sergent, vicar of Derrygarth and Prebendary of Cashel, gave evidence which, later handing himself into the resident magistrate at Clonmel, he admitted was false. This led to a short imprisonment, but he was released into the care of friends on the ground of insanity and the divorce was not challenged. This case was therefore a masquerade, highlighting the role of collusion, false testimony, wrongful confinement and women's legal vulnerability regardless of their social standing.

The Talbot divorce attracted considerable legal attention. Robert Phillimore, MP, convinced of Mary Anne's innocence, denounced it as a 'foul conspiracy ... concocted by unscrupulous men'.[9] Numerous publications followed: Keogh's 1855 defence speech to the Court of Delegates; Paget's *Talbot v Talbot ... A report of judgment delivered by Dr Radcliffe in Consistorial Court in Dublin, 2 May 1854*, and *Talbot v. Talbot ... on the second reading of Talbot's divorce bill, May 22, 1856*. Post-divorce, the lengthy, anonymously authored *Divorce in 1857* was produced to vindicate Mary Anne and promote the reform of divorce law.[10] Paget also fuelled press condemnation in an attempt to clear Mary

---

[5] Thomas Tertius Paget, *A letter to his Excellency the Lord Lieutenant of Ireland in the Judgement of the High Court of Delegates in the case of Talbot v. Talbot* (London, 1856), p. 1.
[6] Roberts, *Divorce bills*, pp. 82–6.   [7] Anon., *Talbot v. Talbot*, p. 151.
[8] Anon., *Divorce in 1857*, p. 117 and p. 125.
[9] Anon., *Talbot v. Talbot*, p. 226. Paget also wrote to the *Freeman's Journal*, 20 July 1857.
[10] Anon., *Divorce in 1857*, p. iv.

Anne's name, which formed part of a wider mid-century panic regarding the wrongful confinement of 'unwanted wives' and the sane in private asylums.[11] Further censure questioned the legitimacy of divorce law: 'An insane person has been confined for six months without any legal authority ... any gentleman who wishes to get rid of his wife, may have her placed in seclusion, under a false name, whilst he procures a divorce.' Others found it incredulous that the House of Lords could believe that 'a lady who received a proper and religious education, prostituted herself with a dirty groom, in rooms with doors unlocked, in outhouses and stables' and that a clergyman who claimed to witness her adulterous acts at first hand permitted 'his unmarried daughters afterwards to visit the woman ... so abandoned and so polluted'. The acceptance of Mary Anne's confession and 'statements of Irish servants of the lowest class' which led the Lords to believe her 'to be more reckless and shameless than most abandoned prostitutes in our cities' was also doubted.[12] As a divorce would not have been possible without a separation in the ecclesiastical court, the need for trial by jury rather than written evidence and the abolition of these courts was called for in the aftermath of the Talbot case. Indeed, some proclaimed both the ecclesiastical courts and parliamentary divorce 'doomed' with this case as 'the coup de grâce, because [of] its hideous features'.[13]

Paget decreed Mary Anne a martyr and asked that no other innocent women be 'sacrificed to the ... injustice of the Ecclesiastical Courts. If that pestilence is stayed, the blood of the victim will not have been scattered on the threshing floor in vain.'[14] Although the English ecclesiastical courts would soon be abolished in consequence of the Divorce and Matrimonial Causes Act of 1857, Ireland waited another fifteen years for this reform. The Talbot case was also the last Irish divorce to pass in the pre-reform era which moved divorce hearings to court for English residents, but the system of parliamentary divorce continued for Irish petitioners into the twentieth century. The Talbot divorce therefore drew more popular attention to the failings of both the procedures for separation and parliamentary divorce, but to suggest that it inexorably led to

---

[11] There were 'lunacy panics' in 1858–9 and 1876–7 (Peter McCandless, '"Liberty and lunacy": the Victorians and wrongful confinement', *Journal of Social History*, vol. 11, no. 3 [1978], p. 366).

[12] Anon., *Crim. con. actions*, cited pp. 21–2 and p. 32. *The Leader* and *The Globe* also sided with Mary Anne Talbot.

[13] Anon., *Talbot v. Talbot*, p. 227. The case was also sympathetically considered in 1890 when Mrs Talbot was depicted as a 'deeply injured woman' (Anon., *Crim. con. actions*, p. 11). Nuala O'Faolain used the Talbot divorce as a backdrop to *My dream of you* (London, 2002).

[14] Paget, *A letter to his Excellency*, p. 89.

reform would be hyperbole: divorce law reform already loomed on the parliamentary agenda. Moreover, although Paget averred that support for Mary Anne amounted to a 'victory, public opinion has already reversed the decision of the three law lords', this could not aid the quarry of this case: Mary Anne remained in the care of her family, where 'her condition ultimately became one of harmless imbecility' as she repeatedly called out for her child.[15]

Mary Anne Talbot's mental incapacity prohibited her from personally defending her case or commenting on the injustices of matrimonial law, but some women who lacked the grounds for divorce publicised their marital woes in an effort to prompt reform. In 1857, the *Narrative of the Case of the Marchioness of Westmeath* was published in London to coincide with Parliament's consideration of the Divorce and Matrimonial Causes Bill.[16] Stone considered the Westmeath case in detail, deeming the author of the *Narrative*, Emily, 1st Marchioness of Westmeath, 'obstinate, petty, vindictive and fanatical about the injustices done to married women'.[17] The Westmeath case was one of the most protracted and highly publicised marital wrangles of the nineteenth century, but an alternative portrait of the Marchioness of Westmeath can be drawn: she was the author of a feminist lambaste railing against the realities of the sexual double standard.

In 1812, age twenty-two, Lady Emily Cecil, second daughter of the 1st Marquess of Salisbury, married George Nugent, Lord Devlin, son and heir of the 7th Earl of Westmeath, in her family's private chapel at Hatfield House, Herefordshire. The Nugent family seat was Clonyn Castle in Co. Westmeath and George had a second residence at Blackrock in Dublin, but the estates were encumbered largely due to the costs of his father's divorce in the Dublin parliament in 1796.[18] Marriage into the Cecil family was hugely advantageous and the marriage settlement epitomised the difference in the families' standing: Emily received a £15,000 portion settled on any younger children resulting from the marriage and pin money of £500 per annum. A jointure of

---

[15] Anon., *Divorce in 1857*, p. 46 and p. 55. Paget described Mary Anne's condition as one of 'great depression ... a terror hanging over her ... subject to paroxysm of the most acute distress', p. 55. Talbot married Gertrude Bayly in 1858. She bore a son, but Talbot died, age forty, in the following year.

[16] The Marchioness of Westmeath (Emily Anne Bennett Elizabeth Nugent), *A narrative of the case of the Marchioness of Westmeath* (London, 1857) (British Library, 6497.c.13). Lord Devlin was promoted from Irish Earl to Irish Marquess of Westmeath by the Tory government in 1822 and was elected an Irish life peer in the Lords in 1831.

[17] Lawrence Stone, *Broken lives. Separation and divorce in England, 1660–1857* (Oxford, 1993), p. 298.

[18] The 1796 Westmeath divorce is also discussed in Chapter 1.

£3,000 per annum, to be paid from the Nugent estates, was also settled but proved difficult to fulfil. Stone rightly suggests that the disparity between the families' statuses indicates that this marriage was grounded in mutual affection but Emily's mother, the daughter of Irish peer Lord Hillsborough, later the Marquess of Downshire, may also have favoured an Irish match.[19]

At the time of their marriage, George had an illegitimate child by an Irish mistress and, although her brother informed Emily of this, financially supporting this second family caused discord. A legitimate daughter, Rosa, was born in 1814, but George's mistress bore another illegitimate child and his support of them, whilst refusing to hire a wet nurse for his legitimate daughter, was another cause of conjugal conflict.[20] As Emily wrote in 1815:

[I]f you do not entirely get rid of the whole of that infamous gang ... it is impossible for us to live together without making ourselves miserable. ... I cannot endure such a want of sincerity towards me. I must have all or nothing. You know my opinion in regard to your conduct before marriage; and God knows that that discovery was sufficiently afflicting to me, without having further to discover all that has since passed in that respect; but let us make an end to it; you have been the dupe of two wretches, the very dregs of mankind, and you and I have very nearly become the victims of our enemies, high and low, and this ought to be a lesson for us never to disguise any thing [sic].[21]

Emily was also subjected to domestic abuse and a reconciliation was brokered in 1815 by neighbour and friend Henry Wood, who sided with Emily in this and future legal challenges.[22] This agreement limited financial support for George's mistress but was only upheld for a few years. Emily was also denied money from 1816 to 1817, writing: 'You took possession of my pin-money, would turn me out of doors if I dared to insist upon having it. You beat me ... and all this time, when I was undergoing all the privations ... for want of money, you could find money for a prostitute.' She hankered after the social niceties of English aristocratic life and accused her husband of removing her from 'all my

[19] Stone, *Broken lives*, pp. 285–6. George inherited the Westmeath title and estates in 1814.
[20] In Westmeath's 1827 Court of Arches case, Nicholl believed that this was proof of 'contrivance ... deception ... concealment' on Lord Westmeath's part (Marchioness of Westmeath, *Narrative*, cited p. 17). There was no Irish equivalent to the Court of Arches.
[21] John Haggard, *Reports of cases argued and determined in the English Ecclesiastical Courts at Doctors' Commons and in the High Court of Delegates*, vol. 2 (4 vols., London, 1830), supplement p. 91.
[22] Wood also acted as a trustee for Emily and brought a case against the Marquess of Westmeath in the Court of King's Bench, 1820. See the pro-Marchioness of Westmeath, Anon., *Reports of some cases, in which the Marquess and Marchioness of Westmeath have been litigant parties* (London, 1825), pp. 30–60.

friends, [and] as good as shut me up in an obscure corner of the world'.[23] Yet, Emily did not lack agency: a deed executed in 1817 determined the grounds for any future separation and provides one of several examples of her sense of social superiority. She agreed to continue cohabitation if a separate annual sum for her use was raised from the Irish estates and if George gave up his mistress. In a reversal of the paternal norm, she also specified that their daughter should reside with her if they separated, but with paternal maintenance. George reneged; in mid-1817 Emily left him, taking Rosa to London.

George freely admitted that he was at fault and considered suicide in the wake of her departure:

> I brought everything on myself. . . . I changed you . . . under your contempt and disregard I cannot live. . . . All I dare hope for, and what I only value in the world, is your regard, that the person . . . whose soul has given over to the loving friend of wretched, wretched me, should not fling me from her mind. . . . I only wish and pray to die when I have secured my impoverished Estate, in the way you wished it, to little Rosa, your flesh and blood. . . . *Thank God, Emily, I did not commit a last act of brutality and madness by taking her away from you.* . . . I have gone through my repentance, but bitterly, bitterly as I have suffered . . . pardon for much *brutality* I have shown you.[24]

He also apologised for threatening to disinherit his daughter in favour of his half-brother and exclude his wife from the family home but made less comment on his attempts to hide encumbered estates whilst continuing to financially support a second family.

Further mediation from Wood and parental pressure from the Salisburys, anxious to avoid the public scandal of a formal separation or divorce, led to the execution of a second deed in 1818. This was ostensibly to prevent Emily from separating in the ecclesiastical courts but gave her considerable leverage: she was allowed to live where and with whom she pleased and George agreed not to pursue restitution of conjugal rights in the ecclesiastical courts which would force her to return to the marital home.[25] Her portion of £15,000 was reversed to Rosa along with much of the Nugent estate if a surviving male heir was not produced and George was unprotected from his wife's debts.[26] In securing custody and alimony as a married woman, Emily was essentially pre-empting matrimonial

---

[23] Haggard, *Reports of cases argued and determined in the English Ecclesiastical Courts*, vol. 2, p. 102.

[24] *Reports of some cases, in which the Marquess and Marchioness of Westmeath have been litigant parties*, cited pp. 60–5.

[25] From 1884, non-adherence to a restitution of conjugal rights order was considered as evidence of desertion even if two years had not elapsed.

[26] *Freeman's Journal*, 27 March 1820.

reform. William Sheldon, a bencher of Gray's Inn and George's legal advisor, later averred, 'he . . . would rather cut off his right hand than put it to such a deed'.[27] The attorney general also branded it as 'viscous' as it allowed separation at the will of one of the parties or by mutual consent rather than by ecclesiastical court ruling. Indeed, Lord Chancellor Eldon saw this case as 'not only important as to the parties, but to the public at large' and others concurred that 'private divorces' endangered 'public policy and morality'.[28]

Emily was, however, too assured in dictating the terms of her marriage. Her boast, 'I now have George completely in my power',[29] deterred him from signing the document until mid-1818 when he claimed it was done 'by surprise, and . . . misrepresentation'. Emily was also pregnant, and George feared that 'her life and that of the child she was carrying, would be in danger if he would not execute the deed'.[30] The Westmeaths subsequently lived together for twelve months and a son was born in 1818. Emily and her counsel claimed they did not cohabit as husband and wife from 1820 but maintained a façade so 'that the separation might not be known to the world'.[31] This constituted condonation and barred Emily from pursuing a divorce.

Despite claims to the contrary from Emily's counsel, both the Court of Exchequer in 1819 and the House of Lords in 1831 decreed the separation deeds worthless due to the pair's reconciliation. The publicity which enveloped the Westmeaths was not, therefore, borne solely from curiosity of aristocratic misdemeanours: many of their legal cases tested the validity of private deeds of separation.[32] Lord Westmeath was, however, partially responsible for giving the case wider resonance. His attempted injunction in the Irish Court of Chancery to prevent £1,300 being raised on Irish lands as an annuity for his wife's maintenance, as agreed in the 1818 deed, went against the counsel of the attorney general, J. S. Copley, later Lord Lyndhurst, who wanted the case to be heard privately: '[I]t was the interest of the parties to bury their disputes in oblivion.' He optimistically predicted that 'the public could be in no way interested'. Emily also wanted the case heard publicly and thus must be held similarly accountable for publicising the case. The attorney general subsequently queried

---

[27] *Reports of some cases, in which the Marquess and Marchioness of Westmeath have been litigant parties*, p. 45.
[28] Ibid., p. 11, p. 19 and p. 22.   [29] Stone, *Broken lives*, cited p. 291.
[30] *Reports of some cases, in which the Marquess and Marchioness of Westmeath have been litigant parties*, p. 16.
[31] Marchioness of Westmeath, *Narrative*, p. 6.
[32] Such deeds were not recognised by ecclesiastical courts, but chancery and common law judges often permitted them (Maeve E. Doggert, *Marriage, wife-beating and the law in Victorian England* [London, 1992], p. 19).

whether their private correspondence needed to be read in court and only agreed to this after both parties consented.[33] Emily's defence argued that Lord Westmeath's charges against her were 'of such an infamous and horrible nature ... that no Judge ... would order the woman so abused to again cohabit with a man who was infamous enough to make them'. Westmeath was portrayed as a 'slanderer and abuser', subjecting his wife to 'the greatest cruelty, violence, and ill-usage ... [he] struck, [and] beat [her] ... she could not, consistent with her personal safety, suffer herself to be under his protection again'.[34] But the case was not decisive. The lord chancellor inferred that it provided an opportunity for a judicial decision on private deeds of separation and postponed judgement to seek the assistance of two equity and two law judges. Their ruling deemed the 1817 deed null and void except in relation to the children's maintenance and education whilst the 1818 deed remained 'in place for a year to enable the parties to try the effect of it at law'.[35] George, however, successfully appealed to the London Consistory Court in 1821 for the restitution of conjugal rights, which, although at odds with the 1818 deed, forced his wife to return home. Emily then sought a separation on the basis of thirty-three charges of cruelty in 1821; twenty-five charges of adultery with five women were levied a year later although they were later dropped due to questionable evidence.[36] The Westmeaths' litany of legal challenges and counter suits continued for another quarter of a century and amounted to 'at least seventeen law suits before eleven or more different tribunals' in the equity, common law and ecclesiastical courts and in the UK Parliament. Five attempted reconciliations also failed.[37]

Alimony and custody, which underpinned the earlier deeds, remained the main points of contention. Both the ecclesiastical courts and chancery ordered George to pay maintenance, yet Emily's £500 per annum pin money was unpaid from 1823 to 1826. She consequently ran up debts and successfully arranged for one of her creditors to sue George in King's Bench for repayment. George's refusal to pay led him to debtors' prison from May to August 1822. Emily also tried to secure custody in chancery

[33] *Reports of some cases, in which the Marquess and Marchioness of Westmeath have been litigant parties*, pp. 8–10 and p. 15. Each would steal the other's correspondence and would pay for evidence.

[34] *Freeman's Journal*, 29 March 1820.

[35] *Reports of some cases, in which the Marquess and Marchioness of Westmeath have been litigant parties*, p. 7 and pp. 21–2.

[36] *Freeman's Journal*, 6 April 1830.

[37] In 1830, for example, Lord Westmeath appealed to the House of Lords to have the 1818 deed removed (Stone, *Broken lives*, p. 315). See also *Reports of some cases, in which the Marquess and Marchioness of Westmeath have been litigant parties* and Elizabeth Nugent (Marchioness of Westmeath), Arches Court of Canterbury, appellant for separation (1834) (PCAP 1/3, National Archives, Kew).

but, despite the earlier deeds granting her custody, was unsuccessful. She was unsupported in this endeavour by her mother who, although claiming to 'protect the interests of her daughter', refused when asked by Lord Chancellor Eldon to care for the children whilst he considered the case: she 'would not be a party in keeping children from their father'.[38] Further motivation lay in her aversion to publicity and fear of her daughter's marriage 'becoming "town-talk" … this feeling became almost a morbid sensibility'.[39] The children were taken to Clonyn and although George agreed to give Rosa back if he could approve her governess, this arrangement collapsed as he became convinced that his wife was turning their daughter against him. In 1820, after the death of their infant son in the previous year, he refused to return Rosa and denied his wife access. Emily immediately brought a writ of *habeas corpus* to the Court of Common Pleas, but Lord Chief Justice Dallas ruled, 'The father, in point of law, was entitled to the custody of the child', underscoring the still inalienable reach of paternal custody.[40] Emily smuggled letters to her daughter but only saw her once by stealth in 1825. Later in the same year she tried to see her again but the child rejected her. There was no reconciliation between mother and daughter after Rosa passed out of minority; she rebuffed her mother's advances and Emily alleged that her daughter was 'brought up to detest her'.[41] This was the cruellest part of the case for Emily; the earlier deeds indicated the importance of maintaining custody. Those deeds and the legal challenges that followed also highlight that she refused to meekly accept the law as it stood regarding custody rights.

One of the most important suits was the ecclesiastical Court of Arches case of 1827 when Emily was granted a separation due to spousal cruelty, alimony and partial costs.[42] Correctly branded as her 'greatest victory', Stone suggests it was won 'on very narrow, and indeed dubious, grounds'.[43] There were, however, witnesses to her abuse. Her personal

---

[38] *Reports of some cases, in which the Marquess and Marchioness of Westmeath have been litigant parties*, cited p. 56.

[39] This formed part of Sir John Nicholl's 1827 judgement (Haggard, *Reports of cases argued and determined in the English Ecclesiastical Courts*, vol. 2, supplement, cited p. 66).

[40] *Reports of some cases, in which the Marquess and Marchioness of Westmeath have been litigant parties*, cited p. 30.

[41] Letter of Lady Westmeath to William Leake, 21 October 1832 in the Marchioness of Westmeath, *Narrative*, cited p. 189. Permanent and forced separation from children provoked despair in many women and extreme actions from a few: in 1799 Elizabeth Lady Webster 'staged a mock funeral with an empty coffin' in an unsuccessful attempt to regain her daughter (Stone, *Road to divorce*, p. 341).

[42] The marquess appealed the verdict. See *The most noble George Thomas John, Marquess of Westmeath, appellant, against the most noble Emily Anne Bennett Elizabeth, Marchioness of Westmeath (his wife), respondent: an appeal from the Arches Court of Canterbury* (London, 1828).

[43] Stone, *Broken lives*, pp. 331–2. George appealed to the Court of Delegates in 1829, refusing to pay her expenses of £1,500 and alimony. Emily sued him for contempt of

maid claimed Emily was 'literally without money for months' and 'as poor as any poor person'. Verbal abuse was also documented; she was called 'a damned bitch, and ... he [was] ... more like a madman than a reasonable being'.[44] Physical violence from 1814 included beatings to the extent that Emily 'carried the marks for a long time' and required medical treatment.[45] George admitted to slapping her and placing a pillow over her face; apprehension of more violence affected her health by 1815.[46] The abuse continued whilst she was pregnant, which Judge Nicholl castigated in the 1827 trial: 'It requires no definition of cruelty to pronounce this to be an act of aggravated cruelty. ... No provocation could justify it or palliate it.'[47] He also interpreted her efforts to conceal the abuse, pretending 'that she had fallen', as indicative of a desire, shared by many women who were subjected to domestic violence, 'to bear her wrongs secretly and in silence'.[48] Granting Emily a separation on the grounds of cruelty and discounting her renewed cohabitation with her spouse from 1818 to 1819 as condonation of her husband's behaviour, Nicholl's judgement countered the English and Irish chanceries, the House of Lords and the London Consistory Court rulings. It was also significant in widening the legal definition of marital cruelty beyond physical violence which endangered life to include non-physical abuse that threatened health.[49] The question of how the upper classes might tolerate such abuse was central to Nicholl's decision and he was not alone in holding such a view. To the Marchioness of Westmeath, writing in 1857, 'superior rank not only is no protection, but an aggravation of the offence, and brings "his order" into disrepute'.[50]

court and he 'claimed immunity from arrest by virtue of his privilege as an Irish peer'. However, it was found that a writ of contempt from a church court 'was not enforceable in law against a peer'. In 1853, some costs were still outstanding and thus Emily sued her spouse for unpaid alimony. He successfully had the amount reduced by the Judicial Committee of the Privy Council to £315 per annum but he had to pay £20,000 in arrears from 1822 to 1833 and costs (ibid.).

[44] Marchioness of Westmeath, *Narrative*, cited p. 13.   [45] Ibid., p. 22 and p. 28.

[46] Ibid., cited pp. 44–7. After another incident, Lady Westmeath feared a strike to her breast 'would end in a cancer' and asked a servant to fashion a 'handkerchief to hide it' at the Duke of Leinster's house (ibid.).

[47] Ibid., p. 17.

[48] The prosecution used fourteen letters dating from 1813 from Lady Westmeath to her spouse, as they made no reference to her abuse.

[49] See Biggs, *Concept of matrimonial cruelty* and Elizabeth Foyster, *Marital violence: an English family history, 1660–1857* (Cambridge, 2005). The widening definition of marital cruelty is further discussed in Chapter 5.

[50] Marchioness of Westmeath, *Narrative*, p. 76. Lord Westmeath appealed unsuccessfully against the 1827 judgement in the Court of Delegates and then in the Commission of Review.

Although both publicised their marital discord, Lord Westmeath's 1828 pamphlet, *A sketch of Lord Westmeath's case*, broke new ground.[51] Written after eleven years of marital litigation, it aimed to vindicate its author. Westmeath's inspiration came from the more voluminous case evidence presented by his wife, running to fifty-three pages compared to his ten, presented to the House of Lords, and more particularly an over-ruling on appeal which allowed much of her evidence to be heard even though it had not been presented to a lower court. To Westmeath this 'disingenuous compilation' had the 'scandalous purpose' of humiliating him, providing 'gossip to the tea-table of every lady who had a lord a member of that House'.[52] Westmeath maintained that his wife's printed evidence amounted to a pamphlet and as such he was justified in answering in print. His rationale would have been more convincing had he only disseminated his printed case notes submitted to the House of Lords, but his forty-seven-page 'answer' was compiled without having to meet the strictures of the House of Lords' rules for evidence.

Westmeath was particularly rankled by the indictment of domestic violence. This was common to many levelled with such a charge as it was at odds with the notion of a husband as a wife's protector which grew as the century progressed.[53] Westmeath admitted to giving his wife 'a *fillip* on the cheek' but professed to be an 'innocent man' who only wanted to provide a 'decent existence for those children both born before my marriage'. He thus portrayed himself as the prey of 'vermin in action ... venom ... malice[,] pure fabrication to degrade me from my caste'.[54] He also depicted Emily's concealment of marital violence as evidence of invention. That his wife, like so many victims of domestic violence, may have been ashamed of being treated in such a way or feared reprisals if she spoke out was not entertained.[55] Non-maintenance of his wife rested more easily with Westmeath; he did not consider her worthy of financial support.[56] Moreover, as evidence of his cruelty towards his wife was levied from servants rewarded for their testimony by Lady Westmeath, which was not unusual in such cases, this was used to undermine their credibility.[57]

---

[51] The Independent Press, Dublin, published the pamphlet (British Library, 1609/4162).

[52] Marquess of Westmeath, *A sketch of Lord Westmeath's case* (Dublin, 1828), p. 6.

[53] See, for example, James Snell, 'Marital cruelty: women and the Nova Scotia divorce court, 1900–39', *Acadiensis*, vol. 18, no. 1 (Autumn 1988), pp. 3–32.

[54] Westmeath, *Sketch*, pp. 9–10, p. 16, pp. 21–2, p. 29, p. 37 and p. 91.

[55] Ibid., p. 12. The latter was inferred in the 1827 Ecclesiastical Court of Arches case where 'making no allusion to those occasional acts of harshness' was deemed 'not discreditable to Lady Westmeath ... by conciliatory conduct, she hoped to soften the violence of her husband's temper' (Marchioness of Westmeath, *Narrative*, cited pp. 15–16).

[56] Westmeath, *Sketch*, pp. 6–7.

[57] Ibid., pp. 12–3. Claims that Emily paid witnesses to lie were unproven. She and her attorney were cleared in 1822 when George sued the witnesses for conspiracy before the

Westmeath suggested that his wife's behaviour countered the strictures of her class and gender; he accused her of having 'entirely forgotten her rank and sex'.[58] Her stance was, however, divined from the social superiority she felt over her spouse. Westmeath also attempted to dehumanise her, citing as evidence her departure from Ireland before the burial of their infant son in 1819 and refusal to reconcile with her mother following her father's death: 'unmoved by this second death bed scene, as she was at the former one, even at those of a child and a father!'[59] The suggestion that she would not live 'with any husband' or bear any more children because 'it spoilt the shape'[60] was deemed a rejection of maternal and wifely function: 'supercilious selfishness ... dictated by caprice [and] ... audacious ... a married woman ruining her husband's *de gaité de coeur* as a passport to a footing of *respectable independence*'.[61] Westmeath was emasculated: 'She wished to leave me, and I wished her not. She had laid her plan, and employed every species of insulting and unworthy device to induce me to leave my house and abandon my children – *to make it appear as my act*. My own servants were taught to insult me.'[62] Westmeath, however, admitted that he had written letters 'in terms of humiliation and self abasement' which his wife appended in 'wanton publication' to her House of Lords' evidence but claimed that they were part of a wider correspondence which he had destroyed and 'if they proved there had been differences, they evidenced also the strongest affection for the person for whose confidence they were written'.[63] This did not deter Westmeath from the same act: he published the following 1817 letter from his wife: 'Frankly speaking, I will never live with a man as his wife, who thought any other woman and her children, had the slightest claim upon him. You and I are not intended for each other, and cannot understand each other.'[64]

Emily made no public response to the *Sketch*. She considered publishing in the mid-1840s but kept her counsel until 1857 when she sought to help reform the 'barbarous' laws relating both to divorce and married women's property. In 'shattered health' she now felt duty bound to publicise her case, which although 'not unexampled ... has few parallels in the sad history of the wrongs of women'.[65] She was also inspired by the 'recipe' of English reformer Caroline Norton who, 'tormented and

---

Commission Court in Dublin. Three witnesses, including George's alleged mistress, Anne Connell, were found guilty. They were fined and sentenced to eighteen months in prison.

[58] Ibid., p. 43.   [59] Ibid., p. 30.   [60] Ibid., p. 45.   [61] Ibid., pp. 46–7.

[62] Ibid., cited pp. 10–11. A housekeeper, for example, defied George's authority claiming she was Emily's employee (Stone, *Broken lives*, p. 309).

[63] Westmeath, *Sketch*, pp. 15–16.   [64] Ibid., cited p. 21.

[65] Marchioness of Westmeath, *Narrative*, p. 3 and p. 104.

restless' in her own marriage, suffered from a want of legal protection.[66] Westmeath and Norton were personally acquainted, co-operating over Thomas Talfourd's unsuccessful 1837 bill to give custody of young children to mothers although the Custody of Children Act enshrining this passed in 1839.[67] In 1855, Norton published *A Letter to the Queen* on the divorce bill then before Parliament, appealing for married women to have a separate legal identity from that of their spouses. Depicting women as naturally inferior to men and therefore in need of the law's protection, Norton was highly critical of condonation barring divorce; this only proved that women 'endured as long as endurance was possible'. Like the Marchioness of Westmeath, Norton was prevented from divorcing her spouse as she was considered to have condoned his actions and could not divorce on the sole ground of cruelty.[68] Norton thus saw her marriage and that of the Westmeaths as examples of the legal partiality against women.[69]

Emily dedicated her tract to the later lord chancellors Lyndhurst and Brougham who in 'making to obtain justice for a suffering class, may be further stimulated, by this Narrative, published with a view to the exposure of such cruelties, legal and personal ... may, I trust, lead to mitigation of persecution against others, by providing a remedy for all' by reforming the law regarding married women's property, custody and marital breakdown.[70] Although Norton claimed that her husband's advertisement to make it known that he would not cover her debts was the first of its kind, Lady Westmeath disputed this: 'I was advertised by Lord Westmeath in the newspapers very early in the business.' Emily also believed that her own well-publicised treatment served as a model 'for the

---

[66] Ibid., p. 104 and p. 127.

[67] Prior to 1839, only illegitimate children could remain with their mothers until the age of seven. The 1839 act allowed mothers to petition the lord chancellor or master of the rolls for custody of children under the age of eight and for access to children thereafter. In 1873, the age for custody was increased to sixteen and adulterous women could apply for custody. From 1886, English mothers could apply to the Chancery division of the High Court or a county court for custody or access regardless of a child's age although equal guardianship was not yet established.

[68] Norton also highlighted that the inaccessibility of divorce as well as the criminal conversation action, especially women's inability of offer a defence, required urgent reform (Caroline Norton, *English laws for women in the nineteenth century* [London, 1854], pp. 1–2 and *passim*).

[69] Caroline Norton, *A letter to the Queen on Lord Chancellor Cranworth's Marriage and Divorce Bill* (London, 1855), p. 4, p. 5, p. 33, p. 48, p. 67 and p. 79. Norton's reputation was damaged by an unsuccessful criminal conversation suit her spouse brought against Prime Minister Lord Melbourne. Four of the sixty-eight clauses of the 1857 divorce act originated from Norton's 1855 *Letter*. See Diane Atkinson, *The criminal conversation of Mrs. Norton* (London, 2012), p. 395.

[70] Marchioness of Westmeath, *Narrative*, p. 2.

course pursued' against Norton.[71] Westmeath's new mistress's use of her former title, Lady Devlin, and his unsuccessful attempt to present her at the viceregal court in Dublin, coupled with the birth of three further illegitimate children, whom he maintained were legitimate, strengthened her zeal.[72] Westmeath referred to this woman as 'Lady Westmeath' whilst *The Times* labelled Emily as the Marchioness Dowager of Westmeath as if she were widowed.[73]

Given the earlier emphasis on custody rights, the trial of being separated from her surviving child unsurprisingly featured prominently in the *Narrative*. An unsuccessful 1821 case to recover custody in the Court of Common Pleas saw Emily's health decline: she was confined to bed with erysipelas, a skin infection causing blisters and lesions. Without alimony when separated from 1819 to 1827, she received £315 per annum thereafter: 'I am supposed to have lived upon air. . . . I was too poor to procure a bit of meat for myself . . . [and] lived for three months . . . upon bread, cheese and barley-water. . . . I paid my servants' wages and board wages from my [£250] allowance as Lady of the Bedchamber' to the Duchess of Clarence from 1818.[74] Emily faced difficulties but still financed the publication of the *Narrative*. Nor was she wholly lacking in supporters. The anonymous preface in a published compendium of reports of the Westmeath's trials expressed 'sympathy and commiseration' towards her, which 'every generous mind must feel'.[75] The Duke of Wellington, a second cousin of Emily's mother and brother-in-law of her sister, also mediated on her behalf with the result that George challenged him to a duel and considered bringing a criminal conversation case against him in 1818.[76] In 1826, Emily was given a rent-free apartment at St James's Palace and the heir to the throne, the Duke of Clarence, successfully approached Wellington to secure a controversial Irish pension of

---

[71] Ibid., pp. 103–4.

[72] Stone, *Broken lives*, p. 342. Westmeath bequeathed £600 per annum jointure to this mistress and £10,000 to his three children by her although the deaths of two of these children pre-dated his own death.

[73] Westmeath, *Narrative*, p. 129, p. 131 and p. 133. Fearing perjury, Emily also refused to attempt to secure a Scottish divorce in 1823–4.

[74] Ibid., cited pp. 107–8. See also Lord Westmeath, *A Reply to the 'Narrative of the case of the Marchioness of Westmeath'* (London: n.p., 1857), p. 40 (British Library, 16417.g.57). Lord Westmeath countered this claim by noting that she refused alimony in the House of Lords in 1821 when the suit for restitution of conjugal rights was pending as to accept could invalidate the deed of 1818.

[75] Anon., *Reports of some cases, in which the Marquess and Marchioness of Westmeath have been litigant parties*, pp. v–vi.

[76] Emily persuaded Wellington to secure places for some of her Irish witnesses, for example, in the Ordnance Office (although one was unable to write English). McGuire, her attorney, was appointed as government solicitor; this served to discredit Wellington (see Stone, *Broken lives*, p. 326).

£385 per annum for her as an 'injured lady ... [and] excellent and ill-used friend' who was 'much in want' in 1829.[77] When the Duchess of Clarence became queen in 1830, she appointed Emily an extra lady of the bed-chamber at £275 per annum in a largely sinecurial post.[78]

Believing the country was on the cusp of divorce law reform, Emily exaggerated the popularity of this cause, referring to it as 'a measure so loudly called for by the voice of the public, for the liberation of her sex from cruelty and oppression'.[79] If she could procure no improvement in her own situation, she hoped that her *Narrative* would bolster reform. Stone questioned the sincerity of her avowed motive, but at the time of writing she not only had little left to lose but also to gain. She was clearly disillusioned: 'I am not sanguine as to any *real* justice being intended' by the proposed reforms regarding married women 'but at any rate, I hope the married women separated from their husbands may have the means secured to them of defending themselves and punishing libels, and may be freed from further interference in business matters'. Unimpressed by the proposed divorce reform, which neither aided accessibility nor equalised the grounds of divorce, Emily suggested that it breached 'any principle of justice'.[80] She concluded her 'sad scene' thus: '[I]f I shall have assisted the spirit of inquiry now aroused, as to the dreadful state of the laws, respect-ing married women in this country in any degree, my object is answered.'

To Stone, this *Narrative* was a vengeful 'diatribe'

against all her enemies, real and imagined, including her husband, her daughter, the members of her own family, and the judges who had sided with her husband. She once more dredged up all the sordid details of her version of the story of her sufferings during her marriage some forty years back, and the injustices she had met with in the lengthy litigation.[81]

Lord Westmeath's reaction, aired during the committee stage of the Divorce and Matrimonial Causes Bill in 1857, was similar. Moving a controversial, self-serving amendment to allow remarriage for any hus-band or wife separated for twenty years or more 'without Condonation or subsequent Cohabitation' proffered him the first opportunity to vent on the *Narrative*. This was striking as Westmeath, although a regular attender at the House of Lords, seldom contributed to its proceedings, especially at length:[82]

---

[77] For example, the Irish lord lieutenant opposed this pension and it was questioned, but not withdrawn, in 1833 (ibid., pp. 335–6).

[78] Ibid., p. 333.   [79] Marchioness of Westmeath, *Narrative*, p. 3.   [80] Ibid., p. 128.

[81] Stone, *Broken lives*, p. 341.

[82] James Grant, for example, offered an unflattering portrait of the 'zealous Tory' Westmeath in the House of Lords in *Random recollections of the Lords and Commons*, vol. 1 (2 vols., London, 1838), p. 86.

[I]t was in the power of any woman who was separated from her husband ... to make her husband's life totally unendurable. This Bill was no sooner bruited ... than a book was put forth of 200 pages, which was surreptitiously published ... bearing the name of the lady who did him the honour to call herself by his ... name. It was sent to all the clubs; and ... a severe, and ... libellous attack had been made upon him in consequence in the columns of a most respectable newspaper ... this book contained the grossest perversion of matters where they related to fact, and some of the most unjustifiable untruths that could be put together to blast and ruin the reputation of the man who was the subject of it. ... Their Lordships might think it a very serious thing for a man sitting in his place to be the subject of accusations which if true, would make him unfit to move in any respectable circle of society, and disqualified to take his seat in their Lordships' House.

The lords were unimpressed, if not unmoved, by Westmeath's protest. Called to order by chair of the committee, Lord Redesdale, for introducing 'matters in which he was personally concerned', Westmeath persevered with characteristic tenacity: 'The Marchioness of Westmeath had named him at full length ... he defied any lawyer to show how he had any means of redress.'[83] He found a partial salve in June of the same year, publishing a ninety-seven-page *Reply* which failed to note that he fired the opening shot in publicising his marital woes three decades earlier. His version 'of the history of our lives' reproduced familial correspondence, much of it extant, from 1819 onwards. He deemed the deeds of 1817 and 1818 'valueless', extracted 'as the price of cohabitation', and denied the charges of cruelty levelled against him.[84] He refuted, 'with good reason' according to Stone, Emily's proclaimed reformist fervour in publicising their affairs, asking whether her pamphlet 'was not rather prompted by the pent-up malice of years':

[I]n defiance of all rules and feelings of shame and delicacy, and in disregard of the anxious desire of relations and friends, that events now almost forgotten, except by those immediately connected with them, should not again be obtruded on public notice. ... It is so unusual and so alien to the habits of this country for a woman to interfere, or come forward actively in the promotion of any measure of legislation, that one is inclined closely to scrutinize the motives of any lady whom does so distinguish herself.[85]

Westmeath alleged that his wife's real object was to be rid of him, citing her emancipatory reproach when she left him in 1819; she had 'a right to live where I think proper, unmolested by you'.[86] By 1846, he referred to himself as her '*quasi* husband', but he claimed to be 'the injured and

---

[83] House of Lords debates, 25 May 1857, vol. 140, cols. 809–12.
[84] Marquess of Westmeath, *Reply*, pp. 5–6.
[85] Ibid., pp. 95–6. See Stone, *Broken lives*, p. 341.
[86] Marquess of Westmeath, *Reply*, cited p. 35 and p. 37.

oppressed party' and criticised Wellington's mediation as intruding on 'the rights which belong to me as a husband'.[87]

George claimed the legal proceedings cost him £30,000; Emily maintained that she spent £12,000 in litigation up to 1831, but the cost was not only financial. Emily's health was permanently damaged and by the 1840s she was 'chronically sick'.[88] She could never be free of her spouse and believed that her family abandoned her, but separation and estrangement from her surviving child was the bitterest blow. Emily died in 1858; George remarried a month later, age 73.[89] The Westmeaths' marital saga underscores the emotional and financial costs of not being able to divorce in the Victorian era. Emily was non-adulterous and thus, even if her spouse wanted to be rid of her, divorce was not an option and claims of condonation barred her from taking that route. The Westmeaths' penchant for self-publicity, however, provides a lens through which the impact of the law of divorce and the need for reform become clear. Some of their multiple legal challenges, particularly the 1827 Court of Arches separation granted to Emily on the basis of spousal cruelty, were significant: Nicholl's focus on verbal as well as physical cruelty which, although not endangering Emily's life, made her live in fear and impacted her health was indicative of the legal shift which was occurring and, in such a highly publicised case, hastened this change.[90] Moreover, the much disputed separation deeds 'made legal history'.[91] The inability of the ecclesiastical courts to overrule decrees passed by Parliament was also highlighted by this case. This, alongside a desire to force Westmeath to pay his wife's legal costs and alimony, prompted Lord Brougham to introduce the Ecclesiastical Court Powers Bill in 1832. The bill was abandoned but others, like the 1844 Ecclesiastical Courts Bill, followed and the English ecclesiastical courts were abolished in 1857. Therefore, the parallels which Lady Westmeath drew between her role in effecting change and Norton's part in reforming custody law in 1839 were not so implausible.

Stone assigned Emily equal responsibility for the breakdown of her marriage; whilst he concurred that the law failed to offer protection to married women, he depicted her as frigid and in possession of 'an iron will . . . extremely obstinate, and never forgot or forgave an injury . . . self-righteousness . . . almost unendurable'.[92] She was certainly determined to

---

[87] Ibid., p. 45 and p. 97.   [88] Stone, *Broken lives*, p. 333 and p. 338.

[89] George sought a divorce on the ground of his second wife's adultery four years later. Claiming English residency, this case passed in the divorce court. In 1864, he married for a third time and this union lasted until his death in 1871. Neither of these unions produced a child so his legitimate heir was Rosa, his daughter with Emily.

[90] Biggs, *Concept of matrimonial cruelty*, p. 38.   [91] Stone, *Broken lives*, p. 344.

[92] Ibid., pp. 297–8. Stone also suggests that she was more interested in 'parties, fashion, power, money and the rights of women than in sex', p. 302.

exert control, a desire which was reinforced when the failings of the law for married women became evident. This attracted some criticism; during the 1825 suit George's counsel noted that his client had 'a foolish notion that he should be master in his own house. The Marchioness, however, had her own notion of the interesting subject. She is a genuine descendent of the great Cecil, the minister and favourite of the glorious virgin queen [Elizabeth I], and inherited from her progenitor a natural propensity to petticoat government.'[93] Yet claims that she was 'a bully' who provoked her spouse's 'outbursts of uncontrolled fury' are difficult to substantiate. Those relating to her 'sluggish libido', 'prudery', 'immaculate chastity' and what she was willing to sexually entertain are even harder to support. Beating her when she refused sexual demands further alienated her from her spouse. This marriage was broken and trust was lost. As Emily wrote: 'You lived three years with me in constant deceit. . . . Last year . . . you . . . broke your most solemn word of honour; and now you dare to tell me that you never thought of anyone but me.'[94] Stone also branded her desire for fidelity within marriage as equating to 'unusual sexual possessiveness' and that she 'was by far the stronger character of the two'. Yet, Emily was not superior in terms of legal status or physical capacity to defend herself from abuse. There can be little surprise that she 'no longer showed much affection' to her spouse after 1814.[95] Westmeath, by comparison, does not evoke much sympathy – his alleged attachment to Emily involved violence and fathering and financing another illegitimate child when he knew this would endanger the marriage.

It is hard to countenance one side of the Westmeath story above the other, but Emily Westmeath is a forgotten divorce law reformer. Her flair for publicity provides one of the best documented, if partial, depictions of how women were affected by marital breakdown and gendered legal restrictions. Yet, wealth and aristocratic standing provided no protection from abuse or a law which treated all married women as spousal property and punished those who endured cruelty and infidelity as condoning the acts. It was therefore understandable that Emily Westmeath ultimately depicted herself, like all married women, as a pauper.[96]

---

[93] Ibid., cited p. 300. Lady Westmeath was also described by various witnesses in the 1827 case as able to express herself 'with warmth and even with bitterness and acrimony . . . but she had considerable self-command, and her natural temper and disposition are . . . good' (Marchioness of Westmeath, *Narrative*, p. 19).

[94] Haggard, *Reports of cases argued and determined in the English Ecclesiastical Courts*, vol. 2, p. 103.

[95] Stone, *Broken lives*, pp. 300–302 and p. 308.

[96] Marchioness of Westmeath, *Narrative*, p. 2.

3 A Non-Inclusive Reform: Ireland and the Divorce and Matrimonial Causes Act of 1857

Parliamentary divorce came under increased scrutiny from the 1840s. To legal commentator John Fraser Macqueen, it was 'a contrivance … of great peculiarity' that was beyond the financial reach of many:

The poor, nay even the moderately opulent, are excluded from the benefit of this truly aristocratic indulgence. … Undue facilities in obtaining divorce are to be deprecated. But an unreasonable stiffness on the other side is contrary to justice. … This cannot be maintained. … Either, then, it is wrong to pass any Divorce Bill, or it is wrong to restrict the remedy to a particular and favoured class.[1]

The engrained gender bias of the grounds for divorce and the 'humiliating burden' of wifely maintenance, decided by the so-called Lady's Friend in the House of Commons, gave Macqueen additional rationale for reform. The latter's origins lay in the parliamentary 'relatives and friends' of women of high station who were divorced and in some husbands 'being willing to agree to almost any condition which would win them their freedom'.[2] However, the Lady's Friend, a post often championed by those of political ambition, determined appropriate maintenance for the divorced wife, but between 1811 and 1830 a change occurred whereby a divorced woman could only be financially maintained by her former spouse if she remained unmarried and chaste, which countered the life-long support common to earlier divorce bills.[3] Moreover, whether or not a husband ceased to be responsible for a divorced wife's debts also required a specific clause in divorce bills and often proved problematic.[4] Pressure was also exerted on some women not to pursue financial support. Lady Lismore, divorced by her spouse in 1826, for example, was advised that it would result in 'the property of her grandchildren … [being] destroyed'.[5]

---

[1] John Fraser Macqueen, *The rights and liabilities of a husband and wife at law and at equity as affected by modern statutes and decisions* (London, 1848), p. 194 and p. 209.

[2] Stone, *Road to divorce*, p. 346.

[3] Macqueen, *Practical treatise on the appellate jurisdiction*, p. 55.   [4] Ibid., pp. 212–19.

[5] Lord Lismore to Mathew Franks, 2 July 1821 (NLI, MS 35,466 [5]). The Lismore case is discussed in Chapter 1.

Other reformers were motivated by a desire to make divorce more testing. In the early 1800s, both Lord Auckland and the archbishop of Canterbury decried the frequency of divorce bills sullying parliamentary business. As the latter remarked, 'very seldom ... could ... their lordships' table [be] pure and clean from the pollution of divorce bills' which were 'now becoming daily more frequent'.[6] Auckland's remedy was to make adultery punishable by fine and imprisonment and ban the remarriage of adulterous spouses to their paramours, making the most serious of four unsuccessful attempts to legislate for this in 1809.[7] In the same year, a new standing order on divorce introduced a clause to prohibit the marriage of an adulterous wife to her lover. This was printed on subsequent divorce bills but was always struck out at the committee stage to prevent prolonging 'the unseemly spectacle of adultery, and inflict bastardy on innocent and helpless offspring'.[8] Despite the concern for child welfare which this shift embodied, the clause was indicative of the distaste with which some viewed divorce and remarriage. It also hints at the strenuous opposition that future divorce law reform would provoke.

The frequency of divorce was certainly more modest than Auckland intimated. Divorce remained uncommon. The 1830 parliamentary session, for instance, heard nine divorce bills, an increase of two from the previous year. Although these did not include any Irish petitioners, the last Irish bill being enacted in 1829, Lord Ellenborough's highly publicised divorce, which passed despite evidence of collusion and without a separation or criminal conversation action, in conjunction with the second divorce granted to a woman, caused unease.[9] Dr Joseph Phillimore, lawyer and MP for Yarmouth, thus asked that the lords be 'discharged from the weight of this duty'. Pre-empting calls for a more accessible procedure, Phillimore also moved an unsuccessful motion for the Royal Commission inquiring into the practice of the English and Welsh ecclesiastical courts to consider the law of divorce. Irish nationalist leader Daniel O'Connell was one of several opponents: he wanted divorce removed from the preserve of the wealthy by an absolute ban; he would not be the last Irish representative to make such a request.[10]

It took another two decades for a Royal Commission to examine the means of obtaining a divorce. The commission's first report in 1853 made

---

[6] House of Lords debates, 8 March 1809, vol. 13, col. 331.

[7] Ibid., cols. 1–2. Auckland first attempted to introduce this legislation in 1771. His 1809 bill passed in the House of Lords but was defeated in the House of Commons.

[8] Clifford, *A history of private bill legislation*, vol. 1, p. 419.

[9] Mr Stock divorced in 1829. Louisa Turton divorced on the grounds of incestuous adultery in 1830.

[10] *Freeman's Journal*, 7 June 1830. Phillimore's motion was defeated 45 to 102 votes.

no reference to Ireland's exclusion from any forthcoming reform, but there was little doubt that a change in the law was desirable. With class and gender bias inherent in the system and unrestrained newspaper coverage, 'Wonder was expressed in many quarters that such a Commission had been so long delayed.'[11] High levels of collusion between the spousal parties provided further incentive for the reformers and the wholesale complexity of obtaining a judicial divorce by a legislative process was openly acknowledged: '[I]t had all the inconveniences which necessarily result from the discussion of such a question in a mixed or popular assembly.'[12] The commission ultimately reported in favour of the creation of a court with jurisdiction to end marriages and was so fixated on its reforming mission that its report verged on propaganda.[13] Divorce reform was under parliamentary consideration from 1854 when a bill embracing the commissioners' recommendations was read for a second time. A subsequent bill in 1856 made less progress, being abandoned after its first House of Commons reading, whilst a third was halted by the sudden dissolution of Parliament in 1857. Lord Chancellor Cranworth was therefore understandably cautious when introducing the fourth divorce bill to Parliament in mid-1857.[14]

Cranworth was never an innovative legislator and *The Times* was justified in suggesting that he 'was afraid to go further' in this bill.[15] He would not, for example, challenge the sexual double standard which underpinned the procedure:

[A]lthough the sin in both cases was the same, the effect of the adultery on the part of the husband was very different from that of adultery on the part of the wife. It was possible for a wife to pardon a husband who had committed adultery; but it was hardly possible for a husband ever really to pardon the adultery of a wife.[16]

This conservatism countered the views of both the Royal Commission and its honorary secretary Macqueen, whose 1842 *Practical Treatise on the Appellate Jurisdiction of the House of Lords* espoused 'no reason for granting to the husband a remedy withheld from the wife ... the protection of his

---

[11] *Report of the Royal Commission on Divorce and Matrimonial Causes* (London, 1912), cited p. v. For a synopsis of the commission's recommendations, see 'The law of divorce' in *The Times*, 23 May 1853.

[12] *First Report of the Commissioners* (1853), vol. 1, pp. 9–10.

[13] Anderson, 'Legislative divorce', p. 444.

[14] Robert Monsey Rolfe, Baron Cranworth and Lord Chancellor, 1852–8. He was succeeded by Lord Campbell, the former head of the 1850s Royal Commission on Divorce. Lord Campbell was John, first Baron Campbell of St Andrews.

[15] *The Times* reprinted in the *Belfast News-Letter*, 23 May 1857. *The Times* earlier noted Cranworth was 'not an ambitious legislator' and correctly anticipated a transfer of the existing parliamentary process to court (*The Times*, 20 May 1857).

[16] House of Commons debates, 19 May 1857, vol. 145, col. 490.

rights as regards spurious progeny ought not to be regarded as the only object of divorce'.[17] The gendered grounds were further denounced during the divorce debates: Lords Lyndhurst, Hutchinson and Harrington and Irish peers Lord Talbot de Malahide and the Earl of Belmore wrote to *The Times* on the subject but failed to amend the bill.[18]

Ireland was excluded from the bill by the House of Commons' removal of its fifth clause which indicated that it would apply to all UK citizens. This replicated the exemption of Ireland from the previous divorce bills, a stance justified by Cranworth on the basis that an Irish court of divorce and matrimonial causes could not be introduced at the same time as an English equivalent.[19] Lord Campbell, head of the 1850s divorce commission, was unconvinced: he called for the establishment of an Irish civil tribunal or a mechanism to allow Irish petitioners to access the new English divorce court.[20] This rallied some Irish opposition; Viscount Dungannon emerged as the most strident critic, denouncing the bill as 'one of the most mischievous ever submitted to Parliament', striking 'at the very root of the best interests of society, civil, moral and religious . . . it would supply additional encouragement to the indulgence of illicit desires'.[21] Unlike the royal commissioners who believed that such 'repeated exposures' of private misdemeanours were 'very much to the detriment of public morals',[22] Dungannon and many other members, Irish and otherwise, remained unconvinced that divorce reform was either necessary or desirable. Indeed, leading lay Catholic spokesman and Limerick MP William Monsell tendered his resignation as president of the soon-to-be abolished Board of Health on the premise that it was incompatible to oppose the government-sponsored divorce bill whilst remaining in its employ.[23] More than a third of those opposing the second reading of the bill were Irish, but there was also a high level of Irish absenteeism which indicates more tacit disapproval as well as

---

[17] Macqueen, *Practical treatise on the appellate jurisdiction*, p. 484 and p. 486.

[18] *The Times*, 2 July 1857. Another letter to the *Times*, published on the same day, saw Lord Lyndhurst and Irish peer Lord Donoughmore appeal for wilful desertion on the part of a husband to provide grounds for female divorce.

[19] See, for example, the Earl of Clancarty's comments, House of Lords debates, 30 June 1854, vol. 134, col. 945.

[20] Ibid., col. 513.

[21] Ibid., cols. 513–14 and 23 June 1857, vol. 146, col. 228. Arthur Hill-Trevor, 3rd Viscount Dungannon, sat in the House of Commons, with some interruptions, from 1830 and was elected a representative peer for Ireland in 1855. He also opposed the 1859 bill to allow marriage to a deceased wife's sister.

[22] House of Commons debates, 19 May 1857, vol. 145, col. 512.

[23] Matthew Potter, *William Monsell of Tervoe 1812–94* (Dublin, 2009), pp. 101–2. Monsell converted to Catholicism in 1850, was MP for Limerick from 1847 to 1874 and a key member of the Irish Catholic Whigs who supported Catholicism, liberalism and unionism.

acquiescence.[24] The Irish opposition was also not denominationally demarcated. Like Monsell, Dundalk MP George Bowyer was 'a consistent defender of Catholic causes in parliament', but the Earl of Wicklow, despite a personal belief that divorce opposed the sacraments, supported the bill due to the need for equality between two countries wedded by the act of union.[25] This invoked Sir Edward Coke's earlier proposition for Ireland that a 'UNION OF LAWS IS THE BEST MEANS FOR THE UNION OF COUNTRIES' but held little sway in the 1857 divorce reform debates.[26]

The Marquess of Westmeath's involvement in one of the most protracted marital wrangles of the century meant that he was more qualified than most to contribute to this debate. Appealing for Ireland's inclusion in the bill, Westmeath was highly sceptical of Cranworth's assurances that Irish reform would come and cited previously unfulfilled Irish legislative promises.[27] Attorney general, MP for Mallow, Cork, and liberal Sir Denham Norreys was similarly committed to the reform and its Irish application: '[I]f it did extend to that country [Ireland], he rejoiced in the fact, and should object to any proposal which would deprive the Irish people of the benefit it would give them.'[28] Yet, few of the Irish contributions to the 1857 divorce debates were distinct; most plied well-worn pro- and anti-reform arguments.

The most obvious potential bar to Irish divorce reform, opposition from Ireland's Catholic majority, was only discussed in the later stages of the bill after an interjection by Loftus Wigram, the Cambridge University representative. As an interested outsider, Wigram proved less restrained than many Irish representatives:

The position of society as regarded this question was very different in England from what it was in Ireland, because in Ireland the proportion of Roman Catholics was large and the feeling which existed in that country against the indissolubility

---

[24] For instance, 36 Irish MPs, comprising two-thirds of the Irish members present, voted against the second reading of the bill which passed by 208 votes to 97. An additional 69 Irish members were absent for this vote (Fitzpatrick, 'Divorce and separation', p. 186).

[25] Boyer converted to Catholicism in 1850 and was elected in 1852. He was an advisor to Cardinal Manning (Michael Lobban, *Dictionary of national biography*, www .oxforddnb.com).

[26] Michael Brown and Seán Patrick Dolan (eds.), *The law and other legalities of Ireland, 1689–1850* (Farnham, 2011), cited p. 29. Coke was an acclaimed seventeenth-century English barrister, judge and jurist. In the nineteenth century, Jeremy Bentham and John Austin also called for 'legal uniformity . . . British legal supremacy and the rise of statute law', ibid., p. 24.

[27] House of Commons debates, 19 May 1857, vol. 145, cols. 522–3. William Forward, the 4th Earl of Wicklow, shared Westmeath's cynicism regarding guarantees to introduce Irish versions of English legislation. The Westmeath's marriage is discussed in Chapter 2.

[28] Ibid., 20 August 1857, vol. 147, cols. 1183–4.

of the marriage tie was most strong ... if marriage was to be made dissoluble in England, was not the same principle to be applied to Ireland?

This provoked a reassertion of Ireland's alleged moral superiority:

Ireland, where the greater proportion of the people were Roman Catholics and the celebration of marriage was considered as a sacrament. They never heard any outcry in Ireland against the indissolubility of marriage. They never heard of internal quarrels in families, of their suffering under a worse than Egyptian bondage. ... The people were convinced that, once married, it was utterly impossible that they could ever be divorced, and to that cause was attributable the happiness of Irish homes. When the Irish peasant girl came to the alter to pledge her troth to her husband she dismissed from her mind the reflection of the possibility of their ever being disunited. ... If they once passed this law they could never go back, but must continue in the same course, however terrible the evils which would flow from it.[29]

Such romanticism was moot; Irish citizens sought divorce but there was never a popular clamour for divorce reform in Ireland or England in the nineteenth century. Some Irish representatives subsequently endeavoured to stall future reform: Joseph Napier, MP for Dublin University, questioned the practicality of moving Irish divorce proceedings to court, querying whether Catholic judges 'would, from conscientious motives, be able to administer the law'.[30] This mustered some support[31] and, with both a Catholic Irish Chief Justice of the Common Pleas and Chief Baron of the Exchequer at the time of the debate, was a legitimate concern. This was later borne out in the new English divorce court where, as Cretney highlights, Catholic lawyers' dislike of divorce work was evident.[32] But no

---

[29] Wexford MP John Hatchell, ibid., 30 July 1857, vol. 147, cols. 755–8. P. O'Brien, King's County MP, was similarly boastful: 'Roman Catholics ... required no such protection for the marriage state' (ibid., 18 August 1857, vol. 147, col. 1837). Isaac Butt, MP for Youghal in Cork, also sought clarification on the jurisdiction of the new court, bringing an unsuccessful late amendment to further confirm that only English and Welsh residents could access the divorce court (ibid., 6 August 1857, vol. 147, cols. 1174–5). Butt was called to the bar in 1838 and became queen's counsel (QC) in 1844. He entered the House of Commons in 1852 and later led the campaign for Irish home rule, establishing the Home Rule Association in 1870. He supported the Bishop of Oxford's unsuccessful call to criminalise adultery.

[30] Ibid., 4 August 1857, vol. 147, col. 1071. Napier was a former Irish attorney general and held the Dublin University seat from 1848 to 1858. He opposed the growing influence of the Catholic Church and was a defender of the Church of Ireland. See, for example, his published response to Irish peer Lord Monteagle, *England or Rome, which shall govern Ireland? A reply to the letter of Lord Monteagle* (Dublin, 1851). Napier was appointed lord chancellor of Ireland in 1858.

[31] See the comments of Lord John Manners, Tory MP for Leicestershire, House of Commons debates, 6 August 1857, vol. 147, cols. 1157–9. Manners later noted that new divorce laws would have to be introduced for Ireland, India and the colonies, ibid., 13 August 1857, col. 1543.

[32] Cretney, *Family law*, p. 198.

consideration was given to the inclusion of an opt-out clause for judges with conscientious objections as was contained in the 1857 act for Anglican clergy who chose not to remarry divorcees.[33]

The government thus sought to widen accessibility to divorce, but this was territorially limited. Its defence of Ireland's exclusion was tentative. Indeed, to Macqueen its motivation was ambiguous: it was either because it 'deemed it unnecessary, or ... objectionable'.[34] A more compelling explanation for governmental consternation can be found in the condition of post-famine Ireland with regional distress continuing into the 1850s. The disquiet surrounding a religiously controversial issue with the potential to rouse the Irish Catholic majority, especially in the wake of protestations over the restoration of the Catholic hierarchy in England and Wales in 1850 which marked the zenith of anti-Catholicism in Victorian Britain, was also imperative.[35] Although a close association was drawn between Catholicism and the indissolubility of the marital bond, with Westmeath's plea for Ireland's inclusion in the 1857 bill described as 'wholly impracticable in view of the implacable opposition to divorce of both the Irish Catholic Church and the Catholic laity', the rationale for Ireland's exclusion from the 1857 reform did not lie in Catholic Church orthodoxy emerging victorious against this modest liberal reform.[36] A distinction also needs to be drawn between the Catholic hierarchy's public and private views of divorce. The Catholic Church's view of marriage as a sacrament was clear and unwavering. Pope Gregory XVI's 1832 encyclicals *Summo Iugiter Studio* and *Mirari Vos* both censured divorce. The former expounded: 'You know how strong by divine law the bond of marriage is. This bond cannot be broken by human authority.'[37] This was buttressed by *Mirari Vos*, citing St Paul and calling for zealous teaching on marital indissolubility:

[F]or those joined in matrimony God has ordained a perpetual companionship for life and a knot of necessity which cannot be loosed except by death. Recalling that

---

[33] In the House of Lords, both the Bishop of Kilmore and the Bishop of London opposed the right of divorcees to remarry. See *Freeman's Journal*, 29 May 1857. The issue of Catholic judges objecting to divorce re-emerged in England in 1920. See Cretney, *Family law*, pp. 198–9.

[34] Sessional papers of the House of Lords, vol. 24 (1861), cols. 5–6 and 14. The Scottish system of divorce remained court based post-1857.

[35] From the seventeenth century, English and Welsh Catholics were led by the Congregation of Propaganda at Rome rather than by bishops. Post-1850, they were divided into twelve dioceses with bishops and the archbishop of Westminster having the highest authority. The Catholic hierarchy never ceased to function in Ireland.

[36] Stone, *Broken lives*, pp. 341–2.

[37] *Summo Iugiter Studio*, 27 May 1832 (www.papalencyclicals.net) focused mainly on mixed marriages.

matrimony is a sacrament and therefore subject to the Church, let them consider and observe the laws of the Church concerning it.[38]

Pius IX's 1846 *Qui Pluribus* augmented the idea of the marital bond in crisis: 'A filthy medley of errors ... creeps in from every side, and as a result of the unbridled licence to think, speak and write ... the sanctity of marriage [is] infringed.'[39] Such pronouncements, however, did not encourage the Irish Catholic hierarchy to front opposition to the 1857 bill. Indeed, by comparison to the protestations of the Catholic Church in England, the response of the Irish Catholic Church was modest.[40]

This is not to suggest a liberal church. In 1854, Catholic submissions to the Ecclesiastical Commission of Ireland on national education, for example, protested against a Sunday school book detailing Henry VIII's marital misdemeanours; the Rt Rev. Denvir questioned whether this was 'proper instruction to give children'.[41] However, little Catholic comment was forthcoming on divorce reform in 1857. With echoes of *Qui Pluribus*, some members of the Irish Catholic hierarchy, including Bishop Walsh, privately expressed a belief that the government sought to 'liberalize and thereby protestantise the Irish Catholics', averring 'It is our duty to oppose these insidious designs.'[42] Paul Cullen, then archbishop of Dublin and Ireland's first cardinal from 1866, was more circumspect. A champion of liberal ultramontanism, which distinguished between theological and political purviews, Cullen would not challenge the government.[43] A circular to the Dublin clergy announcing the novena in preparation for the Assumption in mid-1857 first publicised his views of the pending reform. Citing Matthew, Luke and Canon 7 of the Council of Trent on matrimony, Cullen was unconvinced either of the bill's defeat or its non-application to Ireland. It therefore had the potential to 'shake the convictions of the public mind':

We trust the bill ... will never supplant the old law of the land, handed down from the Catholic times; but even should it be sanctioned by the legislature, we, as

---

[38] *Mirari Vos*, 15 August 1832 (www.papalencyclicals.net) was primarily concerned with liberalism and religious indifference.

[39] *Qui Pluribus*, 9 November 1846 (www.papalencyclicals.net) focused on faith and religion.

[40] The Catholic Church in England has been described as taking 'the lead in sending petitions to Parliament' (Horstman, *Victorian divorce*, p. 50).

[41] *Minutes of evidence before select committee*, vol. 43 (1854), p. 192.

[42] Bishop Walsh, Kilkenny to Cullen, 25 January 1857, Cullen papers, 339/5/I/111 (Dublin Diocesan Archives [hereafter DDA]).

[43] This form of ultramontanism also acknowledged state sovereignty and sought to 'guard the liberty of the church from a state that had become alien to it, and yet retain that state within ... Christendom' (Emile Perreau-Saussine, *Catholicism and democracy* [Princeton and Oxford, 2011], p. 57).

Catholics, can look on it in no other light than as an attempt to repeal and annul the everlasting Gospel of Jesus Christ and the unerring decrees of the Catholic Church.[44]

Like Walsh, Cullen saw the reform as a challenge to Catholicism, but he never sought to mobilise popular opposition. This was indicative of his non-combative approach to government: 'I have held myself aloof from the government without attacking it.'[45] He also introduced regulations to limit clerical political interaction in 1854 which exemplified a distancing from the state which was not unusual in the nineteenth-century church.[46] Seeking further concessions in the wake of the Maynooth grant also meant that it was tactically expedient to avoid censuring the government.[47]

Privately, however, Cullen scrutinised the voting patterns of Catholic MPs in the divorce debates. Attorney General J. D. Fitzgerald subsequently came under suspicion when his vote for amendments which he hoped would defeat the bill was misconstrued as support for the measure.[48] Clarifying this position, Cullen was informed of Fitzgerald's belief that the government was 'determined' to extend divorce reform to Ireland in the coming parliamentary session. This further convinced Cullen that his non-confrontational course was prudent.[49] He also monitored annual reports of public petitions which cited hundreds in circulation in opposition to divorce reform in 1857, but significantly none originated in Ireland which highlights the lack of Irish popular protest.[50]

The Irish Protestant churches shared Cullen's reticence. For the Church of Ireland, this was motivated by a similar desire to maintain cordial governmental relations. In tandem with the Catholic Church in England, some members of the Anglican Church led opposition to the 1857 bill, but the Church of Ireland's response was subdued. A joint Church of England and Ireland petition, with between 9,000 and 10,000 clerical signatories opposing the reform, was submitted to Parliament, but elsewhere caution was apparent. As Church of Ireland primate Lord John Beresford explained, he was unwilling to 'vote on bills which do not directly affect the church', especially if they were government-

---

[44] *Freeman's Journal*, 4 August 1857.
[45] J. H. Whyte, 'Political problems, 1850-60' in Patrick J. Corish (ed.), *A history of Irish Catholicism*, vol. 5, no. 2 (Dublin, 1967), cited p. 21.
[46] Potter, *Monsell*, p. 89.
[47] In 1845, Peel controversially increased the annual grant to the Catholic seminary in Maynooth, Co. Kildare from £8,000 to £26,000 per annum.
[48] G. B. Lyons to Cullen, Irish College, Rome, 17 September 1857, Cullen papers, 339/III/10 (DDA).
[49] See Cullen to William Monsell, 18 May 1861, Cullen papers, 64/16/50 (DDA).
[50] See the 23rd report on Public Petitions, 1857, Cullen papers, 47/1/52/2 (DDA).

sponsored measures: '[T]hey have shown a disposition lately to act with consideration and kindness towards ... the Church establishment over which I preside.'[51] Bereford's assuaging approach was driven by fears of his church's disestablishment: he consequently made no comment on Ireland's exclusion from the divorce bill or the wider implications for both marriage and, most surprisingly, his clergy in relation to the remarriage of divorcees.[52] Therefore, the collective conservatism of the Irish Catholic and Anglican Churches in 1857 was at least partially motivated by a self-interested desire to appease Westminster.

Other faiths shared the disinclination to discuss divorce, seemingly fearful that this would engender an Irish divorce debate and ultimately reform. Despite the Westminster Confession of Faith, nineteenth-century Irish Presbyterian publications emphasised marital indissolubility: '[T]his Church has never considered marriage as a mere civil contract, but a divine institution – a covenant and oath, whereby one man and one woman do pledge their vows in solemn appeal to God, the Judge of all.'[53] This unambiguous stance was again evident, alongside the other Irish dissenting churches, in 1859: '[A]ll Christians will agree that marriage is a Divine institution ... it emanates from God, – it is His command that gives the connection between the sexes that sacred and permanent character which is one of the chief distinctions between man and the lower animals.'[54] However, the annual General Assembly of the Presbyterian Church of Ireland's committee with remit to communicate with the government made no attempt to protect that 'divine institution' in the 1850s.[55] An Irish Methodist newspaper was not produced until 1859, but the British Methodist press aggressively opposed the divorce bill. To *The Watchman and Wesleyan Advertiser*, which enjoyed a wide Irish circulation, divorce was 'the highest social crime' previously 'worthy of death'. The paper thus backed Bishop of Oxford Samuel Wilberforce's call to the House of Lords, which garnered support from Isaac Butt, that '[I]t might not be too much to punish it even now with long imprisonment and civil

[51] Beresford to the Earl of Eglinton, 29 June 1854 (PRONI, T2772/2/6/57). The Church of Ireland's *Irish Ecclesiastical Gazette* similarly made no comment on divorce reform.
[52] The Church of Ireland was disestablished in 1869.
[53] *Presbyterian Marriages. Authentic Report of the Rev. Dr. Cooke's speech, at the special meeting of the General Assembly of the Presbyterian Church in Ireland, May Street Church, Belfast, 10 March 1842* (Belfast, 1842), p. 2.
[54] A Committee of Ministers of Various Denominations, *Grievances of Protestant Dissenters under the recent Irish Marriages Act, and the immoral tendency of that measure stated and exposed* (Belfast, 1859), p. 13.
[55] See *Minutes of the General Assembly of the Presbyterian Church of Ireland, 1850–60* (Belfast, July 1860). The church, for example, sent petitions to Parliament on improving Sabbath observance in 1857, reformatory schools in 1858 and seeking freedom from the jurisdiction of ecclesiastical courts in 1859 (see ibid.).

death.'[56] This did not embolden a response from the annual Irish Methodist conference.[57] The reform similarly excited little public censure in Ireland and some claimed an 'unexampled' apathy.[58] Sergeant Shee's opposition to the bill, for example, formed part of his 1857 electoral manifesto in Kilkenny. Presenting himself as a defender of the Catholic faith, Shee urged his return as issues like divorce were 'to be discussed in a Protestant parliament ... would they not send at least one Roman Catholic to represent them and their interest in parliament?' This met with cheers, but support was insufficient for Shee to retain his seat.[59]

The Irish Catholic and Protestant presses opposed the bill more forcibly than any of the churches, which further evidences that Irish resistance to divorce was not always denominationally bound, but they never encouraged more popular protest. The pro-Protestant *Belfast News-Letter*'s depiction of divorce as an 'objectionable ... anti-Christian statute ... opposed to the Divine Law' was undistinguishable from the stance adopted in pro-Catholic papers like the *Freeman's Journal*. Indeed, such was the *News-Letter*'s disdain for 'cheap and speedy' new court-based divorce, which it suggested would encourage adultery and destroy 'the indissolubility of marriage', that it adopted a rare ecumenical approach: 'The Protestant, quite as much as the Roman Catholic, regards marriage as "a holy estate" ... as a religious, and not merely a social or civil contract.'[60] The *Freeman's Journal* similarly recounted the allegedly 'demoralising effects' of divorce including bribery, wife swap and multiple marriages following the enactment of Prussian consensual divorce in the 1840s.[61] Castigating the English reform as 'the pet of the social latitudinarians', the paper averred that the cost of court action would be prohibitive even to the middling classes; the publicity surrounding parliamentary divorce would shift to court and replacing the 'opprobrious' and 'unjust' criminal conversation action with damages, which could be used to

---

[56] *The Watchman and Wesleyan Advertiser*, 3 June 1857. This was the leading Methodist journal in the mid-nineteenth century. It ceased publication in 1884.

[57] See *Minutes of Irish Methodist Annual Conference* (Cork, 25 June 1857).

[58] *Belfast News-Letter*, 12 June 1857.   [59] *Freeman's Journal*, 11 April 1857.

[60] The *News-Letter* also opposed the speed of the reform and the remarriage of divorcees (*Belfast News-Letter*, 12 June and 5, 21 and 28 August 1857). The *News-Letter* gave front-page coverage to alternative views, like that expressed in *The Times* regarding women's unaltered grounds for divorce and the hope that Parliament might extend these: 'where her wrong is really intolerable, where nature revolts, and society itself requires her to leave her husband ... there ought to be due provision in the law' (*The Times* reprinted in ibid., 23 May 1857).

[61] *Freeman's Journal*, 25 May 1857. The Prussian grounds of divorce included illness and insanity. See Renate Künzel, 'The Federal Republic of Germany' in Chester, *Divorce in Europe*, p. 178.

support children 'out of the dishonour of their mother', was unethical. This reportage was highly selective: the continued existence of parliamentary divorce for Ireland, including the prerequisite criminal conversation suit, was overlooked and the cost of a court-based divorce was overestimated at £400–£500. The moral slur it cast on their English 'neighbours['] relish' for details of divorce bills also conveniently ignored the fact that it and other Irish papers regularly reprinted such articles verbatim from the English press.[62]

The newly established *Catholic Telegraph* provided an ideal platform for Rev. Dr Cahill's invective; his extremism led the more pragmatic Cullen to ban him from preaching in Dublin. To Cahill, the 1857 reform was an 'Easement of Profligate Bill . . . [a] shameless, filthy, adultery bill' to allow 'all the vagabonds of Great Britain to get rid of their old wives' and facilitate multiple marriages. Embracing *Qui Pluribus*, Cahill depicted the reform as part of a wider liberal threat to Catholic moral teaching, but even he shied away from mobilising opposition or commenting on the proposed extension of the divorce bill to Ireland.[63] *Catholic Telegraph* editorials largely concurred with Cahill, portraying the bill as another example of 'mischievous legislation . . . in all Protestant states' to relax Catholic ordinances by increasing state control, causing 'insecurity, uneasiness, and instability in the domestic circle of every class of the community'.[64] The latter was greatly exaggerated but was an assertion that forcibly re-emerged in twentieth-century debates on Irish divorce law reform. With the divorce act's passage in August 1857, the *Telegraph* could only conclude that the '*monstrum horrendum*' of the parliamentary session shamed its creators and would herald an upsurge in domestic strife. Religiously mixed marriages were espoused as especially vulnerable: a 'Protestant husband desirous of being rid of his Catholic wife, or a Protestant lady anxious to sever the bonds which she regrets . . . [with] a Catholic[,] her liege lord' could now be rid of their spouses. In refraining from detailing the 'loathsomely revolting' grounds for divorce, the *Telegraph* failed to inform its audience that no one could divorce at will: the allegorical Catholic wife would have to be proven as adulterous and the Catholic 'lord' found guilty of aggravated adultery or another recognised marital offence.[65]

As Lord Westmeath feared, the promise of Irish divorce reform was unfulfilled, but the government encouraged other areas of the Empire to

---

[62] *Freeman's Journal*, 21 August 1857.
[63] *Catholic Telegraph*, 6 June 1857. See Sheridan Gilley, 'Cahill, Daniel William (1796–1846)', *Oxford dictionary of national biography*, Oxford: Oxford University Press, 2004 (www.oxforddnb.com).
[64] *Catholic Telegraph*, 30 May 1857.   [65] Ibid., 29 August 1857.

apply the rulings of the 1857 divorce act. As early as 1858, Lord Stanley, the secretary of state for the colonies, issued a circular to every Australasian colony enclosing a copy of the act and urging 'the great importance of uniformity of legalisation on this head' to prevent endangering 'public morality' and 'family interests'. Between 1858 and 1873, the six Australian colonies, for example, separately introduced divorce legislation which, whilst not identical and at times facing serious opposition, was based on the English court model.[66] Legislation was also forthcoming for Canada: the North American Act of 1867 moved divorce jurisdiction for Ontario and Quebec, which lacked divorce courts, from Westminster to the Canadian Parliament.[67] New Zealand and India moved to indigenous courts in 1867 and 1869, respectively, and thereafter only Irish divorces were routinely heard at Westminster.[68] Indeed, closer to home, Westminster remained averse to introducing divorce reform for Ireland. This inertia continued for decades as successive administrations proved disinclined to extend the 1857 act to Ireland and few called for its application.

---

[66] Finlay, 'Lawmaking in the shadow of the empire', p. 84. Westminster opposed extending the grounds for divorce in the dominions, refusing, for example, to pass a bill for Victoria which would have equalised the grounds for divorce between the sexes and added desertion as a ground for divorce (ibid., p. 88).

[67] Nova Scotia, New Brunswick and Prince Edward Island introduced court-based divorce in 1761, 1791 and 1837, respectively, and retained this process following the 1867 act. One hundred and forty Canadian parliamentary divorces were passed by 1912 (Kitchin, *History of divorce*, p. 231). Canadian divorce moved to a unified court-based system in 1968. See Phillips, *Putting asunder*, p. 436; see also J. A. Gemmill, *The practice of the Parliament of Canada upon bills of divorce* (Toronto, 1889) and Robert Victor Sinclair, *The rules and practice before the parliament of Canada upon bills of divorce* (Toronto, 1915).

[68] See Henry Rattigan, *The law of divorce applicable to Christians in India (the Indian Divorce Act 1869)* (London, 1897).

4   Divorce in the Post-Reform Era
     of 1857–1922: 'Like Diamonds, Gambling,
     and Picture-Fancying, a Luxury of the Rich'

The divorce bill that passed into law in 1857 was much revised with the 'labours of the pitchfork . . . visible in every page', but its impact was swift and far-reaching.[1] Many of its opponents feared that the number of divorces would significantly augment and the first post-reform year fulfilled that prophesy: 416 divorces were granted by the new London-based Court of Divorce and Matrimonial Causes in 1858.[2] Thereafter, the numbers fell steadily, averaging 202 per annum from 1859 to 1861 and experiencing only moderate growth that shadowed the population increase from 1862. By 1914, there were more than 800 divorces a year and annual rates exceeded 1,000 per annum for the first time in 1918, but this was lower than Western European norms. More striking was the growing number of women and members of the middle classes seeking to divorce in court: women, for example, filed 46 per cent of divorce petitions from 1859 to 1909. This profile was replicated in Canada and America from the 1870s and was indicative of a growing sense of female agency.[3]

The sexual double standard, however, endured in court as the grounds for divorce were not equalised in England until 1923.[4] This was a serious limitation, but the new court-based process was advantageous in comparison to the lengthier, costlier and more socially and gender-biased parliamentary divorce procedure. A parliamentary divorce could take months to pass whilst the cost, estimated at a conservative minimum of £450–£500 in the 1910s, was prohibitive to the majority; the cost of an undefended court-based divorce was approximately £40–£45 if the parties were resident in London. With an unskilled labourer's wage averaging

The quote in the chapter title is from *Belfast News-Letter*, 5 August 1857.

[1] John Fraser Macqueen, *A practical treatise on divorce and matrimonial jurisdiction under the act of 1857 and new orders* (London, 1858), p. v.

[2] The court rejected twenty-nine divorce petitions in 1858 (Cretney, *Family law*, p. 194).

[3] Phillips, *Putting asunder*, p. 421.

[4] Hammerton, *Cruelty and companionship*, cited p. 105. Earl Russell, divorced in America, remarried and was prosecuted for bigamy in England. He tried unsuccessfully to increase and equalise the grounds for divorce and move the procedure from the London court to a county court basis in 1902.

£55–£60 per annum in 1906, court costs were still considerable, which explains the middle-class complexion of many petitioners.[5] Higher court costs would be incurred if the couple and witnesses had to travel to London to access the court or if the suit was defended: a defended case could cost from £70 to £500.

Access to the divorce court was also restricted by residency: permanent residence in England or Wales was required rather than that of a 'casual' or 'traveller' basis at the time of a divorce suit.[6] Consequently, 'for the purposes of the question of the jurisdiction of the [Divorce] Court, Ireland is to be deemed a foreign country'.[7] With 730,335 Irish-born in Britain, comprising 2.9 per cent of the population of England and Wales and 7.2 per cent of the population of Scotland in 1851, many of whom gained a deserved reputation for transience, the effect of this exclusion reached beyond Irish residents.[8] There were also changes affecting the status of a divorced woman whom the 1857 act recognised as *feme sole*, enabling her to exercise control over property acquired after divorce. This was not enacted in Ireland until 1865. The act also gave the courts limited power to make a protection order for a divorced wife which might enable her to exercise some control over her property which Parliament could not provide.[9]

For William Brooke, barrister and most vocal nineteenth-century proponent of Irish divorce law reform, the 'comparative disability' between the English and Irish divorce provision post-1857 was unconstitutional and its impact on women was especially marked. His 1873 report to the Statistical and Social Inquiry Society of Ireland emphasised that 'the relief afforded by law (if relief it may be called) to such women as are afflicted with brutal or faithless husbands' was woefully inadequate: 'Practically . . . in Ireland no matter how infamous or disgusting may be the character and conduct of a husband, his wife can never free herself

---

[5] *Royal Commission on Divorce* (1912), p. 18. Procedural amendments in 1914, 1920 and 1926 made divorce in court more affordable with the provision of financial assistance and the ability to hear cases outside of London (Gail L. Savage, 'The operation of the 1857 Divorce Act, 1860–1910: a research note', *Journal of Social History*, vol. 16, no. 4 [Summer, 1983], p. 103 and Savage, '"They would if they could"', p. 174).

[6] W. G. Brooke, 'Report on the differences in the law of England and Ireland as regards the protection of women', *Report to the Council of the Statistical and Social Inquiry of Ireland*, 21 January 1873, p. 208.

[7] Brooke, 'Rights of married women', p. 280.

[8] David Fitzpatrick, 'A curious middle place: the Irish in Britain, 1871–1921' in S. Gilley and R. Swift (eds.), *The Irish in Britain, 1815–1939* (London, 1989), p. 10. The 1851 figure is from E. Royle, *Modern Britain. A social history, 1750–1997* (2nd ed., London and New York, 1997), p. 72.

[9] Fitzpatrick, 'Divorce and separation', p. 173. In addition, see Savage, 'The operation of the 1857 Divorce Act', p. 103.

during her husband's life from the matrimonial obligation, and if she were to marry any other person, would be liable to a prosecution for bigamy.'[10] Brooke thus called for an assimilation of the laws of both countries to protect women:

[T]o deny to women in this country what is freely given to women in England, is at once ungenerous and unfair – ungenerous, because as a class, women are power-less to insist on their rights, being politically without rights; unfair, because in any theory of a United Kingdom, the helpless class bound to yield obedience to the same laws, should be treated, as regards rights and privileges, on an equal and impartial footing.[11]

Although citing the moderate increase in the number of post-reform court-based divorces to allay fears that reform would increase the number of divorces, Brooke's appeal produced no support to facilitate legislative change. This tellingly indicated the tardy pace of Irish divorce reform which characterised the late nineteenth and early twentieth centuries.[12]

Despite this, and the preclusion of Irish petitioners from the divorce court, Dublin solicitor James Byrne hurriedly wrote a legal guide to 'popularly' explain the 1857 act and obviate the necessity of discussions 'of a most delicate nature' when clients consulted him on matrimonial matters. Published in 1859, with one review noting that 'Every husband and every wife' should read it, Byrne supported divorce reform, believing that it bolstered 'morality and happiness' rather than hastening their decline. A supporter of divorce by mutual consent which the recent Prussian reform facilitated, he regretted that the 'expense, delay, and increased humiliation caused by the ... repeated terrible exposures' of parliamentary divorce remained for Ireland. Byrne was assured that the 'benefits' of the new act, including desertion as a ground for divorce, could be enjoyed by Irish citizens in the alternative venue of Westminster, but neither this nor a parliamentary embrace of the precedents estab-lished in the new divorce court were guaranteed.[13]

Ireland's retention of the parliamentary system of divorce had other legal critics. Macqueen disparaged it as 'satisfactory, except the delay, the expense, and ... the terrible exposure'. Like Byrne, he regarded the

---

[10] The report was funded by Alexander Thom, vice-president for Reports on Questions of Irish Jurisprudence (Brooke, 'Rights of married women', p. 280). Irish bigamy prosecu-tions were rare but see, for example, The People v. Hunt, *Irish Law Times and Solicitors' Journal*, vol. 8 (1946), p. 19; *Irish Times*, 12 December 1945 and The People v. Ballins, *Irish Jurist Reports*, vol. 14 (1964).

[11] Brooke, 'Report on the differences', p. 229.

[12] Brooke, 'Rights of married women', p. 280.

[13] Byrne, *New Law of Divorce*, preface, p. 1, p. 7 and p. 27.

process as 'humiliating' whilst the continued sexual double standard affecting the grounds for both court-based and parliamentary divorce meant that 'however gross, flagrant and persevering', adultery could not be a lone ground for female divorce.[14] Calls for Irish reform were also made in Parliament. Within months of the 1857 act's passage, the attorney general was questioned on extending the new law of divorce to Ireland and the dominions.[15] In a later debate, Lord Campbell candidly acknowledged that 'justice had not been done to Ireland in being excluded from the Divorce Act. ... Ireland would be greatly aggrieved unless steps were taken to assimilate the laws.'[16] The Divorce and Matrimonial Causes Act Amendment Bill of 1858 sought to allow 'Persons abroad ... to institute proceedings' in the divorce court and British Lord Chancellor Chelmsford's response was more revealing than any made during the 1857 debates. Referring to 'some apprehension' in Ireland, 'he certainly did not envy any one [sic] ... who undertook to introduce a Bill on such a subject in reference to the sister country.' No one had to perform the task; the House of Lords struck out the amendment.[17]

The issue of Ireland's divorce provision was not dormant for long. The seemingly innocuous Divorce Court Bill of 1859 sought to improve court transactions but also provided the Earl of Wicklow with an opportunity to emphasise that the disparity between English and Irish divorce provision undermined the act of union: 'Why should there be a union of two countries if, Session after Session, Bills were introduced which applied to only one portion of the empire?' Even the staunchly anti-reformist Viscount Dungannon now claimed that 'it was something like injustice not to give the Protestants in Ireland the same privileges as those of England'. However, conservatism again triumphed as Lord Chancellor Campbell anticipated Irish resistance: '[T]he Irish people would not receive favourably a provision enabling them, if they thought fit, to avail themselves of this Court; and he [Campbell] did not think that it would be wise to establish a similar Court in that country until the experiment had been thoroughly tried in England.' Irish peer the Earl of Clanricarde proffered a pragmatic Irish solution, advising against establishing a new court but 'as quietly as possible to allow the few cases of divorce in Ireland to come to the Court in this country', especially as this would rid Ireland of 'the scandal' of the criminal conversation suit.[18] Wicklow consequently presented a clause

---

[14] Macqueen, *Practical treatise on divorce*, p. 27 and p. 31.
[15] House of Lords debates, 12 February 1858, vol. 148, col. 1261.
[16] Ibid., 29 April 1858, vol. 149, cols. 1923–5.
[17] The amendment was introduced by Lord Redesdale, ibid., 14 June 1858, vol. 150, cols. 1200–1202.
[18] House of Lords debates, 21 July 1859, vol. 155, cols. 141–50.

embodying this which enjoyed some early support in the House of Lords from Earl St Germans, former lord chancellor Cranworth and Irish peers the Duke of Leinster and Viscount Dungannon. Lord Monteagle, however, alluded to cross-denominational Irish resistance and a lack of demand for reform, although this was effectively negated by Lord Donoughmore: '[I]t was precisely one of those matters in which no man liked to be complainant in his own case, and the House would therefore have to wait a long time . . . until they received many petitions on the subject.' There was also already a precedent of Irish citizens attempting to access the new divorce court: three petitions from Ireland were currently before the court and although questions were asked of the court's jurisdiction, 'they had come over to this country, taken houses and paid rates' to claim English residency in an attempt to divorce in court rather than in Parliament.[19]

Prudence ultimately convinced Campbell to abandon support for Wicklow's clause. Central to his decision was scaremongering from 'friends', including Monteagle, warning him 'most strongly' against supporting the bill which would only ostensibly 'raise a tempest which would overwhelm him' and lead to defeat.[20] The comments of the soon to be appointed Irish solicitor general and MP for Cork Rickard Deasy on the incongruity of opening the divorce court to Ireland further reiterated an exaggerated sense of opposition: '[I]t was totally opposed to the feelings of the people.' He also revealed a nationalist distain for the British rule of law: '[I]t made the Irish subject to a foreign tribunal.'[21] The clause was thus removed in the House of Commons with further threats of an Irish 'storm of indignation' accompanied by more sustainable claims that this would be a covert way of bringing Ireland under the provisions of the 1857 act.[22]

Monteagle's and Deasy's efforts did not prevent Irish divorce from regularly featuring in Westminster's debates in the 1860s. Chelmsford, for example, presented a Law of Divorce (Ireland) Bill to extend the 1857 act to Ireland in 1860. Campbell did not actively oppose the bill, but supposing that Catholics would not access the divorce court, he declared it 'useless' for the majority of Ireland's citizens; it was not read a second time.[23] There were also occasional extra-parliamentary calls for Irish

---

[19] Ibid., 28 July 1859, cols. 510–18.   [20] Ibid., 21 July 1859, cols. 141–50.

[21] *Catholic Telegraph*, 30 July and 13 August 1859. Deasy was appointed Irish attorney general in 1860 and called to the bench in 1861. See G. F. R. Barker, 'Deasy, Rickard (1812–1883)', rev. Sinéad Agnew, *Oxford dictionary of national biography* (Oxford, 2004) (www.oxforddnb.com).

[22] House of Commons debates, 1 August 1859, vol. 155, cols. 995–6.

[23] Ibid., 26 April 1860, vol. 158, col. 134.

reform: in 1860 Wicklow presented a petition from Dublin 'praying that the Law relating to Divorce may be so Amended as to allow Irish Suitors to sue for a Divorce in the English Courts'. Campbell subsequently pledged to support any forthcoming bill that would deliver 'justice for Ireland' but judiciously navigated the religious question: whilst Catholics may not avail of the divorce court, 'the Protestant portion of the people were entitled to the full benefit of the new jurisdiction'. Given the recent reception that the bill to attain this end received in the House of Commons, he refused to reopen the subject on behalf of the government. Individual petitions calling for reform were also submitted: Clanricarde presented a petition from Rowan Cashel of Tipperary who lacked the means to pursue a parliamentary divorce in 1860, but there was no immediate relief for Cashel; he only divorced in Parliament in 1866.[24]

Cashel's case was one of several Irish divorces that underscored the personal trials that the lack of legislative uniformity in the UK caused. The 1861 Yelverton case, described as 'a romance in real life which will rank among the most interesting of our *cause celèbres*', was even more complex, invoking Scottish, Irish and English law. Theresa (née Longworth), the Catholic daughter of a Manchester silk merchant, married Anglo-Irish Captain Charles Yelverton, the eldest son of Lord Avonmore, in a clandestine ceremony in Scotland followed by a private Catholic marriage ceremony without banns in Rostrevor, near Newry, in 1857. Captain Yelverton later tried to convince the Irish and Scottish courts that no union had occurred as he married another woman in 1858. The 1861 Dublin hearing of the case followed a successful Scottish suit brought by his first wife seeking financial support and, unlike the divorce act, provoked 'unprecedented' Irish interest; the 'people of Dublin seem capable of thinking and talking about nothing else':

The excitement is not confined to the metropolis. All the provincial papers are full of the proceedings. . . . The editors have not patience to wait for the conclusion of the trial, but given vent to their feelings in comments, lauding the deserted wife, and execrating the man whom she claims as her husband.[25]

Newspapers reproducing verbatim accounts of the cross-examinations were reportedly in short supply and Yelverton's descriptions of attempting to take his future first wife's 'virtue' compelled ladies to leave the courtroom with the details deemed unfit for publication.[26] His object was to prove that the woman who claimed to be his first wife was a consensual

[24] House of Lords debates, 16 March 1860, vol. 157, col. 704 and *Irish Times*, 6 March 1866.
[25] *The Times*, 5 March 1861.   [26] Ibid.

'permanent mistress'.[27] Theresa's counsel received a standing ovation after instructing the jury that they should 'do justice to that injured woman ... you cannot relieve the sorrows of her bursting heart; but you may restore her to ... society'. The Scottish and Irish first marriages were found to be valid and the verdict was applauded both in court and by crowds gathered outside.[28] Yelverton, although not imprisoned for bigamy, then attempted to divorce in court, but the case ended in Parliament, highlighting the divergent divorce laws of England, Scotland and Ireland.[29] This confirmed that the divorce court was 'a court for England alone. ... Ireland and Scotland, for the purposes of jurisdiction, were to be deemed foreign countries equally with France and Spain'.[30]

The logistical horrors of the Yelverton case partially inspired Lord Chancellor Campbell to introduce a Royal Commission to consider extending the jurisdiction of the divorce court in 1861. Irish members included the Earl of Wicklow, Lords Monteagle and Kingsdown and long-serving Irish Lord Chancellor Maziere Brady. From the outset, Campbell claimed, wrongly, that previous attempts to extend the 1857 act to Ireland 'excited great alarm'. The establishment of the commission, however, certainly caused unease: the *Catholic Telegraph* was ever watchful whilst Monteagle averred to the enmity 'both of the Irish people and their representatives to ... such a hateful proposal' and 'warned his countrymen to be prepared for resistance': 'There was more unanimity against it than he ever remembered upon any other subject. ... The manners and morals of that country did not cause any necessity for such a measure.' Wicklow rightly denounced this as a fabrication:

Every Peer in the House who was connected with Ireland was in favour of the proposition ... he should bear in mind that the Roman Catholics were not the only persons in Ireland, and that their prejudices ought not to be allowed to deprive the

---

[27] *The 'Newsman's' full and revised report of the extraordinary marriage case, Thelwall v. Yelverton, tried before Lord Chief Justice Monahan, the Court of Common Pleas, Dublin ... 1861* (London, 1861), cited p. 67.

[28] *The Times*, 5 March 1861.

[29] The House of Lords heard the case on appeal in 1864 and found in Captain Yelverton's favour. Theresa tried to appeal this decision until 1868. The case prompted the 1870 Marriage Case and Marriage Law Amendment Act which legalised religiously mixed marriages solemnised by a Catholic priest (Helena Kelleher Khan, 'The Yelverton affair: a nineteenth-century sensation', *History Ireland*, vol. 13, no. 1 (January–February 2005), pp. 21–5). See also Horstman, *Victorian divorce*, p. 163; House of Lords debates, 3 July 1873, vol. 216, cols. 1698–1702 and Avril B. Erickson and Fr John R. McCarthy, 'The Yelverton case: civil legislation and marriage,' *Victorian Studies*, vol. 14, no. 3 (March 1971), pp. 275–91.

[30] Sessional papers of the ... Lords, vol. 24 (1861), p. 6. Cork prosecutor J. R. O'Flanagan based the melodrama *Gentle blood, or the social marriage* on the Yelverton case in 1861.

Protestants of Ireland of the benefit of the Act which had been passed in regard to England.[31]

The commission's deliberations were interrupted by the death of its chair, Lord Campbell, in 1861, but evidence had already been gathered from Macqueen. Given his earlier stance, he unsurprisingly stressed that the original intent of both the 1850s commission and the 1857 divorce bill was to include Ireland and the colonies within the jurisdiction of any new court. The resultant lack of uniformity caused legal conflicts which might be deemed 'pernicious when waged in between separate and independent nations', but under the union they were 'mischievous when obstinately kept up within the limits of an amalgamated community'. As evidence, Macqueen cited the Yelverton case as well as the lower-profile Bond case which came before the divorce court in 1860. In the latter, the suit was brought by a wife against her husband who had Irish domicile. The court considered its jurisdiction, with judge Sir Cresswell Cresswell highlighting the couple's English marriage and occasional English residency. Although Bond neither submitted nor contested the jurisdiction of the court, Cresswell, lacking conclusive evidence 'to compel us to deal with him as an Irishman', allowed the case to proceed and declared a divorce for Mrs Bond. This was of dubious legality: the place of marriage and occasional residency should not have substituted for domicile.[32] Robert Phillimore, another lawyer with extensive experience in the divorce court, similarly acknowledged the problem of determining domicile. With no time limit defined for residency, evasion was 'very easy'. It was also in a guilty respondent's interest not to question the court's jurisdiction: '[W]here the wife has no defence, she does not say "I can prove you have an Irish domicil . . . " but she lets him get his remedy.'[33] As Donoughmore earlier confirmed, the precedent of Irish citizens divorcing in court was already established, and Phillimore noted the case of an unnamed Irishman who, much aggrieved and 'extremely ill-used' in being compelled to divorce in Parliament, was willing to give up his Irish home and 'come to England and become an Englishman' to divorce in court.[34]

Yet, when the commission considered extending the 1857 act to Ireland, Queen's Advocate Sir J. D. Harding predicted 'unforeseen difficulties of vast magnitude'. Like Macqueen, he did not support the

---

[31] House of Lords debates, 11 March 1861, vol. 161, cols. 1688–94.
[32] Sessional papers of the House of Lords, vol. 24 (1861), pp. 5–6 and p. 14.
[33] Robert Phillimore was the son of Joseph Phillimore, MP and lawyer who unsuccessfully called for divorce reform in the 1830s.
[34] Sessional papers of the House of Lords, vol. 24 (1861), pp. 28–36. See R. J. Phillimore, *Thoughts on the law of divorce in England* (London, 1844) and *The law of domicil* (London, 1847).

continuance of parliamentary divorce but proposed commencing a dialogue with the Irish Catholic populace.[35] The *Catholic Telegraph* subsequently sought to prove that there was no demand for the reform in Ireland, but inadvertently contradicted the oft-made claims of Harding and the anti-reformers: it was 'a question in which Catholics are but little concerned', whilst few Irish Protestants were 'anxious to avail' of the court.[36] The commission reported in 1865, recommending the introduction of a single statute to unify divorce provision throughout the UK. With two Irish members dissenting, including Irish Lord Chancellor Brady, this transition would have been taxing, but the recommendation was never implemented: Ireland remained legislatively stranded.[37]

A further royal commission, chaired by Lord Chelmsford, considered the laws of marriage from 1865. Ireland was again represented by Brady in his penultimate year in the post, as well as the Irish Chief Secretary Lord Mayo, William Monsell and Justice Thomas O'Hagan of Dublin's Court of Common Pleas. Monsell predicted 'a hard fight with the Protestant Commissioners' but was persuaded by Archbishop of Dublin Paul Cullen to join the commission to defend Catholic interests.[38] A three-year inquiry collated information from the Catholic and Protestant hierarchies and clerics in England, Scotland and Ireland. The Irish submission provides one of the fullest accounts of clerical attitudes to marital dissolution and allows the supposition of popular opposition to divorce reform to be further refuted.

The response of the Irish Catholic hierarchy was less circumspect than in 1857. Privately in the early 1860s Cullen reaffirmed that his church controlled Christian marriage, disdained state regulation and despaired of governmental 'fair play':

Parliament cannot legislate on Catholic doctrine and practices without making great blunders. The Protestant MPs have never given themselves any trouble to learn principles and they cannot legislate on matters of which they know nothing. . . . Everything connected with Catholic marriage was regulated by the Synod of Thurles.[39]

---

[35] Sessional papers of the House of Lords, vol. 24 (1861), pp. 24–5.

[36] *Catholic Telegraph*, 16 March 1861. The paper reiterated its concern for Irish mixed marriages' susceptibility to divorce if reform were introduced.

[37] House of Lords debates, 3 July 1873, vol. 216, col. 1700.

[38] Monsell to Cullen, 27 February 1865, Cullen papers, 41/3/I/16 (DDA). Mayo, preoccupied by his secretaryship, played only a nominal part and was subsequently barred from signing the final report.

[39] Cullen to Monsell, 18 May 1861, Cullen papers, 64/16/50 (DDA). The 1850 synod laid down regulations for the Irish Catholic Church.

His 1862 *Instruction of Marriage* also highlighted the 'anathemas of the new divorce courts'.[40] Following a private meeting, Cullen and Bishops Walshe, Walsh and Furlong responded to the commission, drawing attention to both the 1864 papal reinforcement of the indissolubility of marriage and Ireland's moral currency: '[A] religious respect for marriage still prevails. . . . Ireland can boast that within her boundaries illicit unions are not frequent.' Portraying the marriage of divorcees as 'mere concubinage', the strongest condemnation was reserved for state involvement in marital affairs. This publicised Cullen's earlier private commentary; divorce legislation was 'well calculated to destroy the happiness of families, to spread immorality, and to render the education of children extremely difficult and uncertain'.[41]

Catholic clerics like Bishop Lawrence Gillooly of Sligo made individual submissions to the commission, which was indicative of the independent spirit that prevailed within the Irish hierarchy. Gillooly depicted divorce as 'essentially criminal' and capable of destabilising society. He was also one of several hierarchical respondents calling for the abolition of divorce courts which were 'opposed to Christian faith and morality. . . . We regard the divorce law as a grievance to Catholics, and we should protest against it even though no member of our communion should ever take advantage of it.' The most ominous portent, however, came from Bishop Michael O'Hea of Skibbereen; divorce reform would pitch church against state: '[A]ny enactment of the kind for Ireland would necessarily place us in collision with the authority of the State and its decisions.' Evidence from the Church of Ireland's Bishop of Derry and Raphoe could hardly have been more different. He did not mention divorce but portrayed marriage as a civil contract which could therefore be broken: Beresford's earlier non-combative governmental approach evidently remained steadfast.[42]

The commission's 1868 report recommended that marriage laws, including those on divorce, should be unified throughout the UK. The Irish Catholic members of the commission, Monsell and O'Hagan, not only dissented from the recommendations on divorce as it was contrary to God's law but also reiterated the claim of Irish moral superiority: 'The sexual morality of the Irish people, [was] probably without parallel in Europe or in the world.'[43] Cullen, in private correspondence, accused the

---

[40] Ibid., 27 November 1863, Cullen papers, 64/16/55 (DDA).

[41] Supporting letters were submitted to the commission from Irish Catholic Archbishop Joseph Dixon and Bishops Kelly, Donnolly, Denvir, McGettigan, Dorrian and Kilduff.

[42] *Report of the Royal Commission on the Laws of Marriage* (London, 1868), pp. 9–10, p. 13 and pp. 33–8.

[43] Ibid., p. liii and p. 201. Catholic Bishop Delaney of Cork also made an individual submission to the commission but did not mention divorce.

government of failing to 'recognize the decision of the Catholic Bishops' that separation was the 'only divorce allowed in the Catholic Church', but he worried unduly.[44] Akin to the 1865 report, the 1868 recommendations were never enacted. This was not wholly unremarked upon; questioned on Irish divorce reform in 1869, Lord Chancellor Hatherley refused to prioritise the issue as the laws governing bankruptcy and charitable trusts demanded attention in the remainder of the parliamentary session. More significant was his suggestion that the public needed more time to deliberate on Irish divorce, noting 'considerable doubt whether, in one portion of the country at least' the recommendations would be accepted.[45]

The only change which impacted the dissolution of Irish marriage in the later nineteenth century was the disestablishment of the Church of Ireland in 1869. Fear of this previously encouraged the church's determination not to vex the government, but ultimately proved ineffectual. Posthumously, and overly optimistically, viewed as Ireland's opportunity for equitable divorce provision with England, disestablishment abolished the ecclesiastical courts, transferring their matrimonial jurisdiction to court. This was overdue in Ireland; English ecclesiastical court matrimonial jurisdiction moved to court as part of the 1857 reform. The Matrimonial Causes and Marriage Law (Ireland) Amendment Act of 1870 allowed proceedings for separation and civil nullity to be heard by the judge of the Court of Probate who now sat as a judge in the new Court of Matrimonial Causes and Matters.[46] This 'simplified, cheapened, and improved' the procedures for separation, but the Irish civil courts would not legitimise church annulments and lacked the power to determine custody or education for children, maintenance or property rights, although minors could be made wards of court.[47]

Irish separation was now a civil process, but Irish divorce provision remained within parliamentary realms. Moves to redress this continued but enjoyed no more success than in previous decades. Lawyer and

---

[44] Cullen to J. Blake, 21 February 1865, uncatalogued material, Cullen papers (DDA).

[45] House of Lords debates, 5 April 1869, vol. 195, col. 138 and 3 July 1873, vol. 216, col. 1700.

[46] Arthur S. Quekett, 'Divorce Law Reform in Northern Ireland', *Journal of Comparative Legislation and International Law*, 3rd series, vol. 22, no. 1 (1940), p. 33. Canon law provided the basis for the grounds of nullity in both church and civil hearings (see Report: Nullity of Marriage (Law Reform Commission [hereafter LRC] 9–1984, October 1984), p. 3.

[47] A. W. Samuels, 'The law of divorce in Ireland', *Report of Statistical and Social Inquiry of Ireland*, vol. 4, June 1887, p. 186 and *First Report of the Commissioners* (1853), vol. 1, p. 1. Samuels was a native of Dublin, solicitor general of Ireland from 1917 to 1918 and attorney general of Ireland from 1918 to 1919. A unionist in political persuasion, he was elected for a Dublin University seat in 1917. He was a judge of King's Bench at the High Court of Ireland from 1919 to 1925.

Tipperary County MP Denis Caulfield Heron, for example, moved that Irish private bill business, including divorce, be transferred to a separate Irish tribunal in 1871. Finding that the fees payable on Irish bills would be inadequate to support a new tribunal, and that the balance would be covered by taxation, the motion was dropped.[48] Lord Chancellor Selbourne was not so reticent, noting it 'would be his good fortune' to submit an Irish divorce bill in 1873, but no bill was forthcoming.[49] A decade after the report of the royal commissioners on the laws of marriage, Lord Chelmsford requested the lord chancellor to 'not allow this subject to remain much longer rejected'. The response reaffirmed the conviction that divorce reform would be negatively received in Ireland with Monsell's dissent from the 1865 commission cited as evidence. Whilst this did not justify inertia, 'the Government had to ask themselves what was the proper time to bring it forward with a fair prospect of passing it. ... They all lived in hope', but not to the extent that there was any commitment to reform.[50]

Sporadic calls for divorce reform from the Irish legal profession also failed. Most frequently these were based on the need for equality between Ireland and England and the personal toll of parliamentary divorce. King's Inns' bencher, member of the English and Irish bar and future solicitor general Arthur Samuels took up Brooke's rallying call in 1887. Referring to the 'anomaly' and financial 'hardship' of Irish divorce, Samuels acknowledged that 'most legislators' were not desirous of reform and even he shied away from calling for the English court model to be introduced to Ireland. Samuels's rationale was, like that of many who preceded him, that this would open a 'dangerous question' and a 'storm' of the 'strongest' cross-denominational clerical and lay opposition: '[T]hough we must reluctantly confess that the virtue of Erin's sons and daughters is not in practice as exalted as it is in poetry, yet ... the number of cases requiring the intervention of the Divorce Court, is in proportion to the population, happily very small.' There was no consideration that the limited demand was partly due to the inherent difficulties of the parliamentary divorce process which encouraged the 1857 reform. Samuels's compromise was to propose to increase the jurisdiction of the Irish Court of Probate and Matrimonial Causes to allow maintenance, restitution of conjugal rights, alimony, custody of children and marriage settlements to be considered and to make the adulterer a co-respondent in

[48] Clifford, *History of private bill legislation* (vol. 2), p. 749. Heron was former professor of jurisprudence and political economy at Queen's College, Galway, and was called to the Irish bar in 1848. He was an MP from 1869 to 1874. Samuels was also concerned about the cost of Irish private bill legislation but did not apply this to divorce cases.
[49] House of Lords debates, 3 July 1873, vol. 216, cols. 1701–2. [50] Ibid., cols. 7–9.

adultery suits. This would partly standardise Irish and English court practices as, unlike in England where the court would determine maintenance to be paid by both husband and co-respondent for wifely and child maintenance, in Ireland an adulterer could 'throw aside the wife he has seduced from the shelter of her home, and contribute nothing to her maintenance when worse than widowed. The husband cannot in any way be compelled to support her, for the wife, unwifed, without home, and without hope, and without help, what remains?'

Similarly, with regards to custody, the Irish court, unlike that in England, had no jurisdiction. The best that could be hoped for was an intervention from the lord chancellor to make children wards of the court if paternal unsuitability threatened a child's welfare. As the law stood, a woman, even if innocent of adultery, had little chance of gaining custody: 'In Ireland, the father, no matter how guilty and unfit for it, can claim and retain complete control over the children of the marriage, and the innocent mother cannot secure for herself the solace of their society.'[51]

Samuels's proposed reform would have stemmed the multiplicity of suits required in Irish marital disputes, but as Lord Braye, Catholic spokesman in the House of Lords, astutely observed, attempted divorce reforms frequently coincided with 'times when the question of the future of Ireland' was to the fore.[52] Samuels fell foul of this in 1890 when he drafted an Irish divorce bill to address the procedures for Irish divorce rather than its grounds at the request of the Council of the Irish Bar. Judge Warren, president of the matrimonial division, approved the bill and Samuels later noted that 'it would probably ... [have been] unopposed', as it would have prevented 'the public disadvantage of recounting private scandals in different phases of a litigation which might well be terminated in a single cause'. The bill would thus have maintained the current basis of the law but moved the procedure from Parliament, although whether this would have been to the Irish or English courts was unspecified.[53] This cautious draft bill was, however, torpedoed by Irish Parliamentary Party leader Charles Stewart Parnell's citation as co-respondent in the divorce of one of his party lieutenants, William O'Shea, in the same year.

The O'Shea divorce not only crystallised the nonconformist voice and fractured the unity of Irish nationalism but also negated chances for Irish divorce law reform in the late nineteenth century.[54] Katharine Wood, the

---

[51] Samuels, 'The law of divorce in Ireland', pp. 186–9.
[52] House of Lords debates, 28 April 1921, vol. 45, col. 84. Braye was a Catholic convert.
[53] Samuels to *The Royal Commission on Divorce (1909) ... Minutes of Evidence*, vol. 3, pp. 457–8.
[54] For an example of extreme nonconformist criticism of Parnell, see Rev. Hugh Price Hughes in the *Methodist Times*.

daughter of a baronet and Anglican cleric from Essex, was age twenty-two when she married Irishman and later MP William O'Shea in 1867. She may seem an unlikely culprit to thwart the Irish home rule cause, yet she was accused of this and more. Meeting Parnell in 1880, Katharine was soon romantically involved with him; she bore him the first of three children in 1882.[55] O'Shea's English domicile meant a parliamentary divorce was avoided: in 1889, he successfully filed for divorce in the London court on the ground of Parnell's adultery with his wife from 1886. A defence of connivance, conduct conducive to adultery, wilful separation, unreasonable delay in bringing a suit, cruelty and adultery with Katharine's sister Anna was quickly abandoned.[56] This was not uncommon as it could bar the legal proceedings and amounted to a *de facto* admission that adultery had occurred.

Those who clamoured into court were ultimately disappointed; neither Parnell nor Katharine was present. Katharine further distanced herself from the case by declining to let her counsel cross-examine or call witnesses. Hundreds of letters were, however, presented as evidence, proving O'Shea's knowledge of the affair and Katharine's fortitude: 'I have not the slightest intention of allowing you to make the rest of my life utterly miserable by nagging at me from morning until night.' Servant testimony was also heard, describing Katharine's appearance as 'anything but that of a respectable woman' when Parnell was in attendance.[57] After a two-day hearing, the jury's decision was so rapid that they did not leave the box; 'after consulting for two minutes' they found Katharine guilty of adultery with Parnell and O'Shea free from connivance.[58] Parnell was to pay costs of £778 which he tried to avoid on the basis of his Irish residency and monies owing to him by O'Shea. A case, later brought to the bankruptcy court in London, was dismissed. Costs were also reserved against Katharine until it was known if she had a separate estate. O'Shea got custody of the two children under the age of sixteen, but he returned the children to Katharine in 1892.

---

[55] The first child died in infancy. Katharine tellingly omits mention of the two later children from her memoir. See Katharine O'Shea, *Charles Stewart Parnell. His love story and political life* (London, 1972 reprint of 1914 edition).

[56] This adultery was unproven. The claim was possibly provoked by sibling wrangles over their aunt's inheritance (William T. Stead, *The discrowned king of Ireland ... with some opinion of the press on the O'Shea divorce case* [London, 1891] [British Library, 8145. f.11], p. 18).

[57] 'Full report of the great sensational divorce suit of O'Shea and Parnell' (1890) (London School of Economics, Selected Pamphlets, D(42)/D283), p. 8, p. 9 and p. 15. This sixteen-page pamphlet was priced at one penny.

[58] *The O'Shea-Parnell divorce case. Full and complete proceedings* (Boston, n.d.), p. 29.

The first public critique of Parnell came not from the Catholic Church but from his former political ally Michael Davitt. Their relationship deteriorated over the question of land nationalisation from 1882; writing to the *Labour World* three days after the divorce hearing, Davitt urged a Catholic response. The most prominent member of the Irish hierarchy, William Walsh, archbishop of Dublin and president of Maynooth, would initially not be publicly drawn in although he threw out a bust of Parnell which had previously 'held a prominent place' in his hall.[59] Walsh tactically asked for consultation with his 'episcopal brethren . . . to afford Mr. Parnell an opportunity of solving the difficulty himself'.[60] The *Irish Catholic* was not so judicious; it called for Parnell's resignation.[61] Correspondents of Tobias Kirby, rector of the Irish College in Rome, also branded pro-Parnellites as the 'Anti-Clerical Party'[62] while Primate of all Ireland Michael Logue wrote to Walsh from Rome expressing no compassion for Parnell: 'A man having the destinies of a people in his hands and bartering it away for the company of an old woman is certainly not the person to beget confidence.'[63] Kirby, Bishop Moriarty and Archbishop Croke also reassured the Pope that Parnell would be removed from public life.[64] Many in the hierarchy were adamant that the church needed to raise its head above the Parnell parapet; their duty was 'to speak for our people. . . . God's commandments must be respected. . . . What a grand Old Man Gladstone is! and are we to allow him and a lot of nondescript Ministers to proclaim the laws of Christian morality?'[65] But, clerical intervention was not always welcomed: in Galway it was claimed that

---

[59] Conor Cruise O'Brien, *States of Ireland* (London, 1972), pp. 26–7. Walsh initially thought Parnell should temporarily retire and five county conventions in Ireland, including more than 100 priests, supported Parnell at the time of the divorce suit (St John Ervine, *Parnell* [London, 1928 ed.], p. 275).

[60] Notes on a private conversation between Walsh and Parnell via an intermediary, 16 December 1890, Walsh papers (DDA).

[61] *Irish Times*, 29 November 1890. O'Shea was not impressed by Walsh's intervention and asked him to 'retract . . . the extra-ordinary innuendo respecting my divorce case' (William O'Shea, London to Walsh, 30 November 1890, Walsh papers [DDA]).

[62] Bishop J. Dunne, Edenderry to Walsh, undated, KIR/UN/10, Kirby papers (Irish College, Rome). Kirby held this position from 1850 to 1895.

[63] Bishop Michael Logue, Milan to Walsh, 18 November 1890, Walsh papers (DDA). Logue hoped Parnell would retire.

[64] See letter of 30 November 1890, KIR/NC/1890/40, Kirby papers (Irish College, Rome). Croke also spoke after mass against Parnell and issued a confidential anti-Parnellite circular to his clergy (Croke to Kirby, 6 March 1891, KIR/NC/1/1891/12, Kirby papers [Irish College, Rome]).

[65] Bishop Woodlock to Walsh, 26 November 1890, Walsh papers (DDA). Woodlock also asked for the special committee to convene. Bishop Gillooly made similar comments on 19 November and 28 November 1890 (ibid.).

priests who attempted to express their views on Parnell were told that it was a political issue.[66]

Pressure mounted on the Irish Catholic hierarchy to make a formal pronouncement. Even Parnell was critical of the delay, waiting until Gladstone, journalists like W. T. Stead 'and every miserable old woman in England ... had interfered'.[67] The hierarchy's standing committee, composed of four archbishops and six bishops, met on 3 December 1891. Their subsequent declaration 'to the Catholic people of Ireland' was the clearest indication to date that divorce would not be tolerated. Parnell, 'dishonoured and wholly unworthy of Christian confidence', could not lead without fragmenting the party of his making, jeopardising home rule and further land reform.[68] Hierarchal uniformity was, however, undermined by Bishops Healy of Clonfert, Coffey of Kerry and O'Dwyer of Limerick who deigned to sign the manifesto as they did not see this as a moral question. O'Dwyer further sought to curb clerical political engagement.[69]

Dealing with the O'Shea's divorce became a question of maintaining Catholic hierarchical authority which 'required the total political destruction of the man whom it had denounced'. That authority was thrust against Parnell in a series of by-elections; the South Meath election was declared void due to undue clerical influence.[70] Some also called for the suspension of pro-Parnellite clerics.[71] Yet, privately Walsh sought mediation with Parnell. Notes of a conversation in mid-December record Walsh offering to assist Parnell and garner his response to the allegations made in the divorce suit. This formed part of a twenty-two-point plan which is lost, but a five-page dossier of Parnell's public references to the divorce case survives. Via an intermediary, likely Edward Byrne, the editor of the

---

[66] Bishop F. J. MacConvach, Galway to Walsh, 28 November 1890, Walsh papers (DDA).

[67] Callanan, *Parnell split*, cited p. 261.

[68] The declaration was reprinted in the *Irish Times*, 4 December 1890. A circular from several bishops to their clerics followed, calling for support of the hierarchy's statement (Bishop John Moriarty to Walsh, 4 December 1890, Walsh papers [DDA]).

[69] Bishop E. T. O'Dwyer to Kirby, 6 December 1890, KIR/1890/429, Kirby papers (Irish College, Rome). O'Dwyer was aware of the affair from 1888; one of his missives to O'Shea was presented in the divorce suit. Croke asked Kirby to seek confidential advice from propaganda at the Vatican on O'Dwyer's role in ordering, or at least discouraging, clerical involvement in the Parnell case but was swiftly rebuked: 'a true pastor of souls ... [does] his own duty, and not mind if any other bishop should fail' (Mark Tierney, 'Dr. Croke, the Irish bishops and the Parnell crisis, 18 November 1890–21 April 1891', *Collectanea Hibernica*, vol. 11 [1968], cited p. 142).

[70] O'Brien, *States of Ireland*, pp. 27–8. Archbishop Croke and Bishop Dorrian previously tried to reassure Kirby of Parnell's reliance. See KIR/1879/510 and KIR/1880/36a, Kirby papers (Irish College, Rome).

[71] Logue to Kirby, 18 March and 13 April 1891, KIR/1891/160 and /212, Kirby papers (Irish College, Rome).

Freeman's Journal, Parnell enquired of Walsh what impact his marriage to Katharine O'Shea might have on any 'final settlement'?[72]

That marriage in June 1891 made it impossible to continue to proclaim Parnell's innocence.[73] A printed circular, issued to Catholic bishops on the same day as the marriage, was signed by all the hierarchy with the exception of O'Dwyer. This sealed Parnell's fate: his leadership was repudiated.[74] Bishop Gillooly asked at the time of the divorce hearing: '[S]hould Parnell marry the adulteress ... can we still condone the outrage to Catholic doctrine and morality, by our silence?'[75] The hierarchy could not: Archbishop Walsh decried the marriage as 'a public compact for the continuance of their shameful career' and to Bishop O'Donnell of Raphoe it was the 'climax of brazen horrors'. The anti-Parnellite *National Press*'s denunciation of the marriage as 'pagan' vied with the *Nation* for the most incensed response; it printed the marriage announcement beneath the words of Matthew 14: 'And he that shall marry her that is put away commiteth adultery.'[76] Even pro-Parnellites, like William O'Brien, were shocked by the marriage and the *Freeman's Journal* ended its controversial patronage of Parnell.[77]

Parnell's union with Katharine was brief: he died at age 45 in October 1891. However, the chances for Irish divorce law reform in the nineteenth century died before Parnell. The O'Sheas' divorce and Parnell's subsequent marriage to Katharine drew the association between divorce and immorality ever tighter. The invective directed at Katharine O'Shea was virulent. Labelled 'Kitty' by the press, a name she never used, this misnomer intimated moral laxity and depravity.[78] To Gladstone, she was 'at the very root of all the mischief'[79] and James Joyce later claimed that 'A woman ... brought Parnell low.'[80] Parnell's fictitious exit from Katharine's home via a non-existent fire escape became music hall fodder

---

[72] Notes on a private conversation between Walsh and Parnell via an intermediary, 16 December 1890 (Walsh papers, DDA).

[73] Some clerics earlier backed pro-Parnellite candidates in Carlow in defiance of church-approved candidates. Fr W. Hurley was an example of a Catholic cleric who refused to believe the allegations and claimed to have been 'grossly insulted' for defending Parnell. See his letter to Walsh, 13 December 1890, Walsh papers (DDA).

[74] Printed circular, 25 June 1891, Walsh papers (DDA).

[75] Bishop Gillooly to Walsh, 19 November 1890, Walsh papers (DDA).

[76] Callanan, *Parnell spilt*, p. 126 and p. 127.

[77] Parnell established the *Irish Daily Independent* when the *Freeman's Journal* stopped supporting him. By comparison, most of the English press reacted positively to the marriage.

[78] 'Kitty' was also a slang name for female pudenda. See Mary Rose Callaghan, *'Kitty O'Shea'. The story of Katharine Parnell* (London, 1989), p. 5.

[79] Callanan, *Parnell split*, pp. 187–9. See also H. C. G. Matthew (ed.), *The Gladstone diaries, 1887–91*, vol. 7 (10 vols., Oxford, 1994), cited p. 345. Gladstone thought that home rule would be delayed for five to six years in consequence of the divorce.

[80] James Joyce, *Ulysses* (London, 1922), p. 34.

and a fire escape toy was produced.[81] Sexual innuendo abounded at political meetings and IPP member T. M. Healy was the most immodest, declaring, to Parnell's face, that Katharine was 'the mistress' of the party whose affection was purchased by political favours. After Parnell's death, Healy confounded many by twice calling Katharine a 'proved British prostitute'.[82] She was also dehumanised as an animalistic 'she-wolf' and the demonic 'Banshee of Brighton'.[83] The abuse was not limited to Ireland or solely verbal: Balfour, addressing a Conservative Primrose League meeting at Hatfield Park, faced jeers of 'Kitty O'Shea'.[84] At the Carlow by-election, a placard on a pole depicted a female effigy holding a kettle (when Andrew Kettle, MP for Cork, was addressing the meeting with Parnell), with the words 'Kitty, damnation, but I am scalded'. Denounced as 'degrading politics', the local chapel was also 'desecrated by bawdy inscriptions under the very nose of the parish priest'.[85] A petticoat raised on a pole at another meeting asked, 'Will the petticoat of Kitty O'Shea be the flag of Ireland?'[86]

The censure of Katharine was highly gendered and, at times, racial. This was epitomised by William Stead's portrayal of her as a 'sinister figure' with an incomparable 'standard of morality' to Irish women. Nor would he portray her as a victim of a man's seduction which contradicted the prevailing portrayal of adulterous women:

[N]o one can profess to find in this middle-aged, ambitious and intriguing woman the almost childish victim of the seductive art of an experienced man of the world ... the balance of the fault probably lies at the door of the weaker, who is, in this case, the richer sex ... only when he dallied in the lap of Delilah ... he became another man.[87]

Of Captain O'Shea, although a 'willing and complacent party to the dishonour of his wife', Stead, casting a watchful eye over the possibility of a libel action, had little to say.[88]

---

[81] Jules Abels, *The Parnell tragedy* (London, 1966), p. 321. See also Callaghan, '*Kitty O'Shea*', p. 134. Clark Gable and Myrna Loy starred in the Hollywood film *Parnell* in 1937.

[82] Elizabeth Kehoe, *Ireland's misfortune. The turbulent life of Kitty O'Shea* (London, 2008), p. 423. Healy did not apologise but agreed not to use such language after Labouchere read him a letter from Gladstone.

[83] *Freeman's Journal*, 13 July 1891. W. T. Stead also referred to her as the 'were-wolf of Irish Politics' (Callaghan, '*Kitty O'Shea*', cited p. 155).

[84] *Freeman's Journal*, 20 July 1891. Established in 1883, the Primrose League was a popular Conservative association with male and female branches which were known as habitations. The league peaked in popularity in the early twentieth century and disbanded in 2004.

[85] MP Conway in *Irish Times*, 4 July 1891.   [86] Abels, *Parnell tragedy*, p. 358.

[87] Stead, *Discrowned king of Ireland*, pp. 3–6, p. 8 and pp. 11–12.

[88] Ibid., p. 9 and pp. 15–17. Gladstone read Stead's work in 1890.

The hierarchy joined the defamation of Katharine; Archbishop Croke asked 'What has shorn us of our strength?' to which Dean Kinane replied 'Kitty O'Shea'.[89] This conflicted with the sympathy and sense of passivity usually associated with adulterous women, suggesting that Parnell, rather than being the scorned adulterer, was prey for a predatory woman. Indeed, into the twentieth century, William O'Brien maintained that Parnell was 'the victim [rather] than the destroyer of a happy house'.[90] Nationalists like O'Brien, Redmond and Davitt objected to the vitriol of much of the debate, but Katharine would never evade this social death. Her 1914 memoir, significantly written under her first married name of O'Shea, was published for profit and sold well, reprinted twice in its first year of publication. It was, however, sufficiently belligerent to merit censorship by the Dublin Vigilance Committee whose call for Catholic booksellers not to stock it was partially successful.[91] Its subtitle prioritised Parnell's 'love story' over his 'political life' and Katharine understandably felt 'the hate that followed [Parnell] ... to the grave' turned on her: 'From one end of chivalrous Ireland to the other ... the name of "Kitty" O'Shea was sung and screeched, wrapped about with all the filth that foul minds, vivid imaginations, and black hatred [create].' Parnell, she maintained, found solace in the fact that she was never known by that name. Katharine did not, however, consider the gendered law and social mores which placed her in this position or the impact that her unprecedented denouncement as an adulterous woman might have on those considering divorce or its reform.[92]

Debates on Irish home rule, specifically the power of any semi-autonomous assembly, drew parliamentary attention back to the country's divorce provision. In the committee stages of the second home rule bill in 1893, Gladstone, previously pitted against the 1857 divorce reform, now heralded Ireland's lack of divorce provision as 'a very great distinction ... and ... it is one that Ireland highly prizes, and in that I think Ireland is right'. Gladstone interpreted the lack of any popular call for reform as evidence that the country 'rested contentedly' under the existing law: why should 'we take [it] out of her hands and keep hanging over her this dread of our Divorce Law'?[93] By comparison, a body of both

---

[89] *Irish Times*, 2 May 1891.

[90] Sally Warwick-Haller, 'Parnell and William O'Brien. Partners and friends from consensus to conflict in the Land War' in D. G. Boyce and Alan O'Day (eds.), *Parnell in perspective* (London, 1991), cited p. 72. See also *Freeman's Journal*, 7 October 1891.

[91] Kehoe, *Ireland's misfortune*, p. 437. On Katharine's financial position in widowhood see ibid., pp. 421–8.

[92] O'Shea, *Parnell*, p. viii and p. 299. Katharine claimed that Gladstone knew of her relationship with Parnell for a decade and that her husband sought the advice of Cardinal Manning.

[93] House of Commons debates, 12 May 1893, vol. 13, col. 851 and col. 942.

conservatives and unionists poignantly predicted that placing divorce jurisdiction in the hands of an Irish parliament would facilitate the introduction of retrogressive legislation and further the divergence of divorce law in the UK.[94] Divorce was never a major preoccupation in the second home rule bill debates; however, by the third home rule crisis of 1912–14, as a result of increased Irish political polarisation, there were more explicit references to religious difference and minority rights. Unionist Ronald MacNeill in 1913, for instance, echoed the same disquiet as did those in 1893, regarding the possibility of Catholic moral teaching dominating any Irish parliament whilst highlighting the contrary church and state positions:

[T]here is a clearly defined ecclesiastical view and a clearly defined civil view. It is idle to suppose that in a Parliament predominantly representing people taking the ecclesiastical view of marriage and divorce the expression from those representatives in such a Parliament will not give full effect to the ecclesiastical view and make it the law of the country.[95]

The process and grounds for divorce were also under review. Lord Gorell, president of the Divorce Court, made a proposal to allow country courts to hear divorce cases to increase lower-class access which led to the 1909 Royal Commission on Divorce and Matrimonial Causes. Unlike its 1853 predecessor, this commission considered the Irish position but indifference again characterised the Irish reaction: '[T]he proceedings of the Divorce Commission are exciting no interest whatever in Ireland. ... It is a somewhat significant circumstance that ... no one in Ireland should suggest even that the status quo in Ireland should be disturbed.'[96] The Irish Newspaper Society, the association for newspaper proprietors, however, informed the commission of a petition it received from a number of organisations in Cork, including the Women's Aid Association and the Women's Christian Temperance Association, which opposed the publication of divorce cases 'which are bound to have a disastrous effect on the morals of the community'.[97]

The evidence also revealed dissent amongst the Irish legal profession. Edward Carson's experience in the London divorce court and, he was 'sorry to say', on the Standing Committee for Divorce in Westminster had not liberalised his views on divorce. Supporting the sexual double

---

[94] See the comments of conservatives Sir Edward Clarke, QC and MP for Plymouth, and Sir Randolph Churchill, MP for South Paddington as well as William Macartney, unionist MP for South Antrim (ibid., 12 June 1893, vol. 13, cols. 852–60).

[95] Ibid., 16 January 1913, vol. 46, cols. 2375–6.

[96] Fitzpatrick, 'Divorce and separation', cited p. 186. The commission's 246 witnesses gave evidence in public.

[97] Hon. H. G. Barnes, *Royal Commission on Divorce ... Minutes of Evidence*, vol. 3, p. 179.

standard, the publication of divorce cases, banning divorcees' remarriage and leaving cases of desertion or abuse without remedy, he claimed that 'Ireland is a very moral country, but I do not set it up as absolutely free from immorality.'[98] This provoked an ill-tempered exchange with Lady Frances Balfour who correctly aligned the cost of parliamentary divorce to the alleged low demand: '[W]onderful as Ireland is ... do you think that it is just that the law in Ireland should be such that you cannot get it [a divorce] under £1000? ... They do not require it because they cannot get it.'[99] Arthur Samuels, giving evidence at the request of the Irish bar, and James Roberts of Inner Temple and the English bar who brought an estimated third of all Irish parliamentary divorce bills to Westminster from 1887, concurred that cost as opposed to morals prohibited Irish divorce. Indeed, Samuels cited cases where he had been 'frequently consulted ... where people would have proceeded to the Lords and the Commons and got a divorce if they had the means ... but the number is not large'. What remained unknown was the number dissuaded by cost before seeking legal counsel. Samuels and Roberts both emphasised the human toll of the parliamentary system: the former recounted a case 'of great hardship' where a woman, likely Mrs Lautour who divorced in Parliament in 1905, 'belonging to one of the best families in Ireland' but hit by land agitation 'became very poor'. She then worked as a hospital nurse to fund a divorce which she secured twenty years after her husband's adultery and thirteen years after separating. Roberts similarly related the case of an Irish mechanical engineer, probably Richard Griffin, who divorced in Parliament in 1896 and delayed bringing a bill for a decade after separating whilst 'the guilty parties were living as husband and wife in America', and another who delayed divorce for eight to nine years and by that stage was unable to proceed as it was no longer known whether the respondent was alive.

Defeated in his earlier reforms, Samuels was convinced that the parliamentary system would endure: 'you would have a great difficulty in getting rid of it. I know you would raise a storm in Ireland if you introduced a Bill to dissolve marriage' or moved to a court-based process.[100] His compromise was to propose the abolition or reduction of the 'very

---

[98] Samuels, ibid., p. 456. Unlike Carson, Samuels felt press coverage of divorce cases was morally damaging.

[99] Carson, ibid., pp. 420–6. Carson also opposed making desertion a sole ground for divorce but suggested that damages against a co-respondent should be increased and wives' alimony was often inadequate.

[100] Lord Gorell suggested that Irish protest regarding court-based divorce would be 'an illogical storm'. Samuels wanted two years' desertion to be a ground for Irish divorce as it was in England (*Royal Commission on Divorce (1909) ... Minutes of Evidence*, vol. 3, pp. 456–62).

oppressive burden' of parliamentary fees which amounted to £75 in the House of Lords and £35 in the House of Commons by 90 per cent and combine the criminal conversation and separation suits to further reduce costs: '[M]ost people have very limited means in Ireland ... money is a very hard thing to get.' Roberts, however, distinguished between the alleged 'determined opposition' of Irish Catholics and Protestants to court-based divorce and those with direct experience of the parliamentary system who 'always said what a ridiculous position the whole system is, and what a tax it is on them having to find all this money and go through so many hearings. That is the view not only of the lay clients but the solicitors as well.'[101]

Unlike earlier commissions, evidence was heard from minority religions in Ireland. Rev. Dr Hermann Adler, the chief rabbi in England, for example, denied any sense of grievance amongst the Irish Jewish community that parliamentary divorce was the only available recourse and that standards of morality differed amongst English brethren as they could access the divorce court.[102] Not all, however, were willing to contribute; the Baptist Union of Great Britain and Ireland did not think that it could 'usefully give evidence'; the church reluctance to engage with the divorce question, so evident in 1857, lingered in some quarters.[103] Reporting in 1912, the commission's majority report found that due to Catholicism, Irish 'conditions of life ... differ materially' from those in England. It further dwelt on the undesirable publicity generated by parliamentary divorce. Its conclusion that separation was an 'unnatural and unsatisfactory remedy leading to evil consequences ... [and was] inadequate in cases where married life has become practically impossible' could have been used as a lever to revive the Irish divorce debate, but this was not the commissioners' primary concern. Rather their focus was the 'urgent' need to equalise and widen the grounds for divorce in court to include desertion, cruelty, drunkenness, insanity and life imprisonment. The First World War, accompanied by opposition to divorce reform from both the Anglican and Catholic Churches in England, however, delayed the recommendations from being enacted.[104]

It was often claimed there was no demand for Irish divorce, but ninety-two Irish citizens divorced in Parliament from 1857 to 1922. Thirty-nine Irish bills passed from 1857 to 1900 which were all undefended and the

---

[101] Roberts, *Royal Commission on Divorce (1909) ... Minutes of Evidence*, vol. 3, pp. 462–3.
[102] Rev. Dr Hermann Adler to *Royal Commission on Divorce ... Minutes of Evidence*, vol. 3, p. 411.
[103] *Report of Royal Commission on Divorce* (1912), p. 35.
[104] Ibid., p. vii and p. 11. Imprisonment under a commuted death sentence was also suggested as a ground for divorce.

pace of increase was steady in the early twentieth century: two divorces passed in the 1857 to 1867 period, three from 1867 to 1877, five from 1877 to 1887, ten from 1887 to 1897, fifteen from 1897 to 1907 and an average of one per annum from 1907 to 1910.[105] Bills for Irish parliamentary divorce averaged two per annum from 1910 to 1922, peaking at seven in 1920.[106] With increasing numbers, Irish parliamentary divorces gained a more diverse social complexion from the 1880s when more middle-class petitioners were evident. Indeed, from 1870 to 1900, 36 per cent of Irish parliamentary divorces, for which the profession of the husband can be determined, were in the middle classes: journalists, master mariners, bank officials, doctors, dentists, veterinarians, Royal Irish Constabulary district inspectors, surveyors, engineers, former MPs, solicitors and barristers all featured. In addition, there were horse dealers and mechanics of sufficient means to proceed. An augmentation of military divorces was also apparent which continued an earlier prevalence and stressed the association between absence from home and infidelity.[107]

The aristocratic petitioner was not, however, extinct. From 1900 to 1922, 11 per cent of Irish parliamentary divorces passed to those with titles or honorifics including Sir Robert McConnell in 1905, the Hon. Flora Irvine in 1916, the Hon. Viola Gore in 1916, Viscountess Georgina de Vesci in 1920, Baroness Jose Carbery in 1920 and Marchioness Bessie Conyngham in 1921. Social boundaries also need to be demarcated by more than aristocratic title: Major Bryan Cooper divorced in 1920, but his 500-acre estate, Markree Castle in Co. Sligo, placed him firmly in the upper classes. Alimony and maintenance payments, awarded in separation and divorce, respectively, also convey the more varied social profile which emerged: Hurly paid permanent alimony of £20 per month whilst Viscount de Vesci paid £550 annual maintenance.[108]

Akin to class composition, the religious affiliation of Irish divorcees diversified which suggests a willingness amongst some to defy church rulings. From 1896 to 1922, 75.5 per cent of Irish parliamentary divorces were granted to Anglican petitioners, but Catholic petitioners comprised 6.6 per cent, Presbyterians 4 per cent, Methodists 2 per cent and Jews 2 per cent.[109] Alice Edith Donovan (née Rodgers) of Cork brought the

---

[105] James Roberts, *Royal Commission on Divorce and Matrimonial Causes. Minutes of Evidence*, vol. 3 (London, 1912), p. 465.

[106] Records of the House of Commons, Minutes of Proceedings on Irish Divorce Bills [1907–22] (4 vols., Parliamentary Archives [hereafter PA], HC/CL/CO/BF/1–4).

[107] Captain Beamish divorced in 1876, Captain Cliffe Vigors in 1890 and Major George Cavendish Clark in 1919.

[108] Printed divorce bills, PA, HL/PO/PB/18/5/4a.

[109] Religion is unknown in 8.8 per cent of Irish parliamentary divorces heard from 1896 to 1922, ibid.

first Irish Catholic divorce to Westminster in 1905. In the House of Lords, her father identified the handwriting and a photograph of his son-in-law Daniel Augustine Donovan, chief of police at Cape Coast castle. Alice sought divorce on grounds of 'alleged misconduct and cruelty'. Married in the Roman Catholic Church of the African Mission in Cork in 1895, from 1899 her spouse 'began to use violent language, and frequently was guilty of various acts of cruelty'. She ceased cohabitation and her spouse was adulterous with a nurse in his employ. There was a six-year delay between separation and divorce, but by the time of the latter her husband admitted adultery; 'Yes ... I did this, but I now ask for forgiveness having done so.'[110]

Married in the Roman Catholic Military Church in Rangoon, Bengal, in 1899 Gwenllian (née Pascoe Morgan) Pascoe Killery's divorce was brought on the same grounds as Donovan's. She divorced St John Brown Killery, a captain in the Royal Army Medical Corps, in 1907: '[H]er husband had frequently beaten her with a whip and gave her a black eye [and] threw a knife at her.' At the time of marriage and the divorce, he was domiciled in Ireland, and Westminster therefore raised no question over hearing this bill.[111]

Despite the broadening socio-religious profile of Irish divorcees, as the deliberations of the 1909 commission confirmed, the cost of a parliamentary divorce and gathering evidence continued to deter and delay both male and female petitioners. Mrs Griffin, for example, waited eleven years before embarking on a parliamentary divorce in 1896.[112] Women, in particular, needed financial assistance to bring divorce proceedings. Violet MacBride's 1913 bill was financed by her father after her abusive spouse left her on his doorstep with her luggage and six shillings.[113] Other women waited for a censorious parent's death to fund divorce, using inheritance money to proceed or initiating proceedings with the help of friends.[114] A sense of propriety could also cause delay. As Charlotte Carolin averred in 1913: 'with reference to my children, I thought it would interfere with their interests if I took any steps

---

[110] *Irish Times*, 29 March and 31 May 1905; Roberts, *Divorce bills*, p. 103. See also PA, HL/PO/PB/1/1905/5E75. The third Catholic divorce, that of Lida FitzGerald, who married in a Catholic church in Los Angeles, was heard in 1907. See PA, HL/PO/PB/1/1907/7E75.

[111] *Irish Times*, 27 February 1907. See also PA, HL/PO/PB/1/1907/7E76.

[112] See also the previously discussed case of Jane Lautour who waited thirteen years between separating and divorcing in 1905, and twenty years from the time of her husband's adultery and desertion.

[113] 16 July 1913, PA, HC/CL/CO/BF/2/1.

[114] For example, Josephine Maxwell waited until her father's death to divorce (28 November 1911, ibid., HC/CL/CO/BF/2/1); Charlotte Carolin divorced with the help of friends (13 July 1913, ibid.).

beforehand because their grandparents are educating them' and they would benefit from their inheritance.[115]

Some financial assistance to wives was, however, available. The practice for husbands to provide funds to enable wives to defend a divorce bill remained, with Parliament having to be informed of the nature of the defence. In Dr Atkin's 1887 bill, a clause was inserted to ensure that he paid his wife a previously agreed amount of £700 on the act's passage.[116] Although wifely maintenance was frequently granted, this was not guaranteed. Criminal conversation damages were also often unpaid which could thwart or delay husbands in financing divorce.[117] These damages also lessened in the mid-nineteenth century. The average amount from cases which were succeeded by a parliamentary divorce from 1896 to 1922 was £851. With the highest award of £3,000, there was no equivalent to the large damages of the earlier period which avers to a growing distaste for the suit.[118] By the early twentieth century, in cases where the parties were legally separated, proving loss of consortium beyond nominal damages of a farthing became futile and Parliament accepted this as justification for not bringing a criminal conversation suit.[119] Divorce select committee member the Rt Hon. J. C. Campbell was also candid regarding the Irish anomaly of criminal conversation: 'We have no proceedings in the slightest degree analogous to this in Scotland or in England' with the cost and likelihood of low damages deemed sufficient to 'deter any man from raising an action'.[120] The result was that men like George MacColl, who earned £200 per annum, had to borrow money from his father to divorce in 1911, whilst John Bishop only divorced with the help of friends and borrowed money in the following year.[121]

It was possible to submit a bill in *forma pauperis*, meaning in the manner or character of a pauper, if petitioners lacked means; house fees would be rescinded and counsel would act without charge. To qualify, petitioners had to earn less than 30 shillings per week and have possessions amounting to a value of less than £25. The 1910–12 Royal Commission on Divorce estimated that fifty such cases came to court per annum, but parliamentary bills did not record in *forma pauperis* cases so it is impossible to gauge their popularity. However, the social standing of those

---

[115] Carolin, ibid.

[116] Atkins lived apart from his wife, he claimed, on health grounds and she was subsequently adulterous (Roberts, *Divorce bills*, p. 59).

[117] The sum of £1,500 damages was, for example, unpaid in Fife-Young's case although he proceeded to divorce in Parliament and secured custody in 1920 (PA, HC/PO/CO/PB/18/5/4a).

[118] Averaged from seventeen criminal conversation awards, ibid., HC/PO/CO/PB/18/5/4a.

[119] See, for example, John Bishop's 1912 divorce bill, PA, HC/CL/CO/BF/1/2.

[120] Ibid., 11 July 1912.   [121] Ibid.

divorcing in Parliament remained comparatively high which suggests that few such bills were submitted. Parliamentary agent Deane, presenting a raft of divorce bills in the early twentieth century, also claimed that this process was largely unknown: 'I did not know until quite recently that one could come in forma pauperis'; as the last case was heard in 1849, 'it is very excusable that one would not know it'. George White thus justified the nine-year delay between his separation and divorce in 1920, as a solicitor earlier informed him that a parliamentary act would cost £500–£600 but learning of in *forma pauperis* he proceeded.[122]

A lack of means was not the only bar to divorce; condonation remained prohibitive, but many Irish divorces were consensual. Even when a separation suit was defended, this was often abandoned in a divorce. The response of Captain William Dooner, encouraging his wife to pursue 'whatever action you may take "quickly"', was commonplace: '[O]ur present life must be extremely distasteful to you. . . . I [cannot] . . . live with you any longer. I absolutely decline to turn you into a prostitute, for that is . . . what the intimacies of married life become in the absence of mutual affection.'[123] Many respondents also waived the right to attend the parliamentary hearings of a bill. This was, at times, pragmatic: in the Murphy Grimshaw Validation Bill of 1907, the wife had left the country, but her affidavit confirmed 'she was fully aware of what was going on and had no wish to oppose the Bill in any way'.[124] Gladys Massy was similarly acquiescent: she wished 'the bill should go through as she wished to marry the co-respondent' and admitted adultery in a letter to her spouse. Lady Viola Gore also promised that 'every facility will be given to your lawyers to prove in the divorce proceedings which I hope you will at once begin'.[125] For other respondents, non-attendance was a means to distance themselves from the hearing: Mary MacColl, served with divorce papers in Belfast in 1913, stated 'I shall not attend – it is no good.'[126] Parliamentary agents presenting bills also successfully requested that respondents and witnesses who had already given evidence to the House of Lords did not attend the select committee's hearing to limit costs.[127] This led the select committee to reiterate that at least one witness

---

[122] Ibid., 10 May 1920, HC/CL/CO/BF/2/4. Cases were also heard in *forma pauperis* in the ecclesiastical courts.

[123] Dooner divorce bill, 1915, ibid., HC/CL/CO/BF/2/1.

[124] 19 June 1907, ibid., HC/CL/CO/BF/1/1.

[125] Massy, 6 July 1915, ibid., HC/CL/CO/BF/2/4 and Gore, 31 July 1916, ibid., HC/CL/CO/BF/2–3.

[126] MacColl divorce, 26 June 1913, ibid., HC/CL/CO/BF/2/1.

[127] See, for example, the 1913 cases of Charlotte Carolin and Emily Dooner, ibid., HC/CL/CO/BF/2/1.

was required to prove 'the cardinal facts of Adultery and Cruelty' in 1907, but even this was occasionally waived.[128]

Evidence in divorce bills came from diverse sources: midwives' attending illegitimate births, doctors detailing the effects of marital cruelty, ship stewards confirming shared accommodations and hotel employees identifying respondents and co-respondents from photographs and providing testimony of shared bedrooms where couples were together 'as man and wife'. Hotel registers and receipts were also accepted as evidence of adultery.[129] Servants, however, provided the bulk of evidence in parliamentary divorces and this could have serious consequences. Giving evidence against a master or mistress almost always resulted in a loss of employment in consequence of their loyalty being deemed suspect. Indeed, in the 1915 Beamish case the House of Commons was asked to dispense with one servant as a witness as she had already lost a 'situation through giving evidence . . . and might risk her present one'.[130] For family members, especially progeny, giving evidence was often emotionally distressing. An eldest son, subpoenaed to give evidence against his mother in 1920, was instructed by his father in military service to 'take all the steps' to prevent the adultery but testified 'I could not take any steps because my mother said for the sake of all to let it go.'[131]

Private investigators were also dispatched to witness adulterous liaisons. Evidence presented during George MacColl's bill recalled that men were sent to London 'to report on her [his wife's] movements alone with men. . . . Her hair was in disorder. . . . She had her dress off . . . she had her corsets in her hand, and was holding her petticoats so that they would not slip down. She entered the bedroom.'[132] Husbands were similarly placed under surveillance. Gerald Denny, formerly of Redmondstown House, Clonmel, was 'watched' in London by his father-in-law's solicitor who 'found that he had committed adultery'. This case also highlighted that bills could cost thousands of pounds especially when marriage settlements had to be negotiated: Phyllis Denny's divorce, on the grounds of adultery and cruelty that so 'injured and terrified' her that she was on 'the verge of a breakdown', cost c. £2,000 in 1915 and she 'wanted to be

---

[128] See, for example, the 1911 cases of Alexander Pilkington and Herbert Watson, ibid., HL/CL/CO/BF/1/1 and HL/CL/CO/BF/2/1. Watson's wife married bigamously in America.

[129] Alexander Pilkington divorce, 5 December 1911, ibid., HC/CL/CO/BF/2/1.

[130] The servant's evidence was considered as significant and she was called before the select committee (Beamish divorce bill, 21 March 1915, ibid., HC/CL/CO/BF/1/2 and 15 April 1915, ibid., HC/CL/CO/BF/2/2). The Beamish separation case was the first heard by a jury in Ireland.

[131] Osborne's divorce bill, 28 July 1920, ibid., HC/CL/CO/BF/2/4.

[132] 26 June 1913, ibid., HC/CL/CO/BF/2/1.

released from all connection with the family'. The result, after lengthy deliberation in Parliament where Lord Chancellor Loreburn stressed that the petitioner's interests should override all other concerns, was that 'Each party was to release the other's funds in the supplement, [with] funds to be paid to petitioner in stock.'[133]

By 1909, there was a sufficient annual tally of Irish divorce bills to vex Parliament. Loreburn, although reluctant to reopen the debate, noted: '[W]e constantly have cases of Divorce Acts being proposed from Ireland. . . . Nobody ever says a word against them . . . because by consent of Parliament it has been held that the evil is more than counterbalanced by the advantages.'[134] The frequency of Irish divorce effectively countered boasts of Irish purity, which gained wider resonance from the late Victorian period. As Judge Baron Dowse in Dublin's Exchequer Court remarked in 1880, 'he was happy to say, they had little necessity for any Divorce Act' in Ireland.[135] Nationalist William Redmond reiterated this in the early twentieth century, depicting Ireland as 'the most civilised country in the world [with] . . . no divorce law'.[136] Yet, in the rare instances where more popular views towards divorce can be adjudged, opines varied. The response to the *Daily Telegraph*'s request for female reactions to Mona Caird's article 'Marriage', published in the *Westminster Review* in 1888, was unprecedented: 27,000 replies were received, including some from Ireland, and many were candid about their marital afflictions. One Belfast respondent, Edith Maxwell, embraced Caird's critique of male superiority and marital degradation:

I shake hands with her in spirit, and think that every woman, especially those unhappily married, should bless her and call her a friend. . . . She is not afraid to expose the wretched married tie in all its mockery . . . there is not a woman in England or Ireland . . . who will not secretly own to that fact . . . bondage of the marriage contract is bitter and galling. . . . Religion steps in, and compels an unhappy woman to live with a man who has repulsed and outraged her with his infidelity and cruelty. What is she to do? Get a divorce; and, if a Catholic, how can that help her? It is supreme cruelty for any religion to compel a woman to sacrifice the rest of her life just because the early part was a failure.

Maxwell sought 'a union free from slavery' but believed that women cowered to air their concerns.[137] Other respondents misconstrued Ireland's divorce law: Anna Liffey of Dublin believed that 'divorce is on

[133] *Irish Times*, 10 March 1915 and PA, HC/PO/PB/18/5/4a.
[134] House of Lords debates, 14 July 1909, vol. 2, col. 504.
[135] Anon., *Authentic report of the crim. con. trial of Joynt v. Jackson*, p. 28.
[136] House of Commons debates, 3 May 1905, vol. 156, col. 729.
[137] Ann Heilmann (ed.), *The late Victorian marriage question: a collection of key new woman texts* (Abingdon, 1998), cited p. 22.

no grounds available for a wife', and such restricted provision was a preventative boon: 'the non-existence of an Irish Divorce Court, with its necessarily polluting influence and outflow of poisonous literature, acts as a bulwark against the spread of evil' and reduced marital breakdown. She suggested a widespread interest in Caird's work, but this did not translate into a sustained Irish contribution to the debate: 'I have heard much surprise expressed in general social circles that so little contribution has been made to the discussion ... from this side of the water, though it is in the mouths of all.'[138] Liffey was right in regard to the latter and the lack of debate provided fertile ground for anti-reformers to claim that most Irish citizens neither sought access to the divorce court nor supported the establishment of an indigenous court.

Irish opposition to divorce was also often muted in comparison to other areas of Europe and the British Empire. Victoria's passage of the Australian divorce bill in 1890, for example, saw the Anglican, Methodist and Presbyterian hierarchies oppose the act and the bishops of Melbourne and Ballarat instructed clergy not to officiate at the marriages of divorcees or issue marriage licenses to them. Three years later, an Italian petition against a divorce bill with 60,000 signatories was presented by a committee of Catholic women, claiming that divorce was 'against religion as well as against the conscience and dignity of woman' and, if enacted, would 'contribute to the ruin of many Italian wives and mothers'.[139] Another Italian divorce bill caused the resignation of government ministers and was subsequently defeated in 1902.[140]

There was no analogous Irish protest, although Earl Russell depicted parliamentary divorce in 1907 as 'entirely the privilege of the wealthy' and of 'hoary antiquity', better suited to preservation in 'museums and in books and not applied to unfortunate living people who have to suffer from their existence'. Noting the 'hardship that because a person is one of a small minority in an overwhelmingly Catholic country he should be deprived of a remedy which would be open to him elsewhere', Russell still did not seek to reform Irish divorce provision.[141] The Irish first-wave feminist movement, evolving from the late 1870s, also failed to invoke reform.[142] This was not unusual; although some Western European feminists championed divorce, more commonplace was the American,

---

[138] Ibid., cited p. 120.
[139] Ibid., 25 May 1893. The 1901 Australian Federal Divorce Bill was introduced to harmonise the acts of Victoria and New South Wales with those of other states.
[140] Argentina rejected a divorce bill in the same year.
[141] House of Lords debates, 16 July 1907, vol. 178, col. 491 and col. 494.
[142] There was limited discussion of divorce in the *Irish Citizen* but see September and November 1919.

British, Canadian and Italian experience where feminists played a low-key role in divorce reform campaigns as the polemic which shrouded this issue prompted fears that it could dilute support for the already controversial campaigns for female enfranchisement.[143]

By comparison, members of the Irish legal profession, especially Brooke and Samuels, became more vocal on the need for reform. Samuels was a particularly patient reformer. Still seeking divorce reform in 1917, he reiterated his suggestion to reduce parliamentary fees to aid Irish petitioners. Parliament, preoccupied with the reverberations of the First World War and the 1916 rising in Ireland, would not be drawn and Bonar Law's advice that a resolution from both houses would be required to lower the minimum standing orders' fee of £100 for Irish divorce bills was never realised.[144] Divorce law was not, however, static as the changing definition of marital cruelty and precedent established in court facilitated more Irish parliamentary divorces, especially from female petitioners.

---

[143] Janice Hubbard Harris, *Edwardian stories of divorce* (New Brunswick, NJ, 1996), p. 25.
[144] *Irish Times*, 25 August 1917. Coverage of reported divorces in *Irish Law Times and Solicitors' Journal* also afforded an opportunity to muse on the 'rather curious state of the law . . . [and] the absurdity of having different laws for different portions of the British Isles' (*Irish Law Times and Solicitors' Journal*, vol. 7 [1873], p. 121).

5   The Widening Definition of Marital Cruelty

Gendered grounds for female divorce such as unnatural offences or incest were highly sensitive. The likelihood of losing custody of children further deterred women experiencing marital strife from seeking legal redress. Even cruelty, the most commonly cited ground by women, was hard to legally define. Cruelty is also impossible to measure with any degree of accuracy, and Lord Stowell's 1794 pronouncement of 'what is tolerable by one may not be by another' epitomised the importance of subjectivity in this aspect of matrimonial law.[1] Cruelty was initially determined as action endangering life and limb. Thus, the English case of Mrs Dawson, whose adulterous spouse routinely flogged her 'sometimes with a horse-whip and sometimes with a hair brush', which came before the House of Lords six times from 1848, was not deemed sufficiently cruel to permit divorce.[2] This was indicative of the centuries' long acceptance of hus-bands' physical chastisement of wives: Dr Marmaduke Coghill, judge of the Prerogative Court of Ireland for instance, held a switch aloft in the midst of a seventeenth-century separation hearing, declaring that mod-erate physical correction was 'within a husband's matrimonial privilege'.[3]

Wife-beating has been depicted as 'a constant in Western society' and many women died in consequence.[4] Royal Irish Constabulary figures recorded 100 men guilty of spousal murder from 1838 to 1892, and surveys of the Irish press in the 1870s reveal weekly cases of wife-beating in the magistrates' court.[5] From 1853 to 1920, more than 1,000

---

[1] Stowell in D'Aguilar v. D'Aguilar (1794) where the woman affected was more than age seventy (Biggs, *Concept of matrimonial cruelty*, p. 8). Biggs suggests that the origins of the concept of marital cruelty lie in it being used as a defence to a petition for the restitution of conjugal rights (ibid., p. 10).

[2] Macqueen, *Practical treatise on divorce*, p. 32.

[3] Doggert, *Marriage, wife-beating and the law*, cited p. 9.

[4] Phillips, *Putting asunder*, p. 343.

[5] Pauline M. Prior, *Madness and murder. Gender, crime and mental disorder in nineteenth-century Ireland* (Dublin and Portland, OR, 2008), p. 91. Most commonly in Ireland, in line with Western European patterns, men killed their wives; ten times as many men (126) as women (12) were accused of spousal murder in Ireland from 1866 to 1892 (Carolyn

appeals by Irishmen convicted of domestic violence were lodged, suggesting not only that many men believed there should be redress for their actions but also the commonality and severity of marital cruelty.[6] The latter is reinforced by Edwards's figures which record 501 sentences passed in Ireland for violent acts against women in 1889: 105 for common assault and 396 for aggravated assault, constituting 14 per cent of all such sentences passed in the UK.[7] Abuse was undoubtedly more frequent than these figures suggest, as many women were unwilling to testify against an abusive spouse or proceed with legal cases as they feared reprisals or economic destitution or were ashamed.[8] It was also widely believed to be to a wife's credit to endeavour to make a marriage work and not seek a legal remedy.[9] Such sentiments were neither new nor unique to Ireland. To Belfast feminist L. A. M. Priestly McCracken, this 'natural shrinking from exposure' was an 'age-long tradition': '[I]n matrimonial affairs what transpires in the home must be carefully concealed from the world without. The quarrels and differences ranging from "incompatibility of temper" … to physical violence and giving of "black eyes," must be kept strictly secret.'[10]

Modern legal practitioners' definition of domestic violence considers the act itself as well as the physical and mental attributes of the parties,[11] but much of the earlier discourse focused on gender-based power as the sexual double standard impacted what constituted cruelty towards a wife. This allowed a husband to 'successfully plead that he was exercising his marital power of correcting her [his wife], even though he had nearly

A. Conley, 'No pedestals: women and violence in nineteenth century Ireland', *Journal of Social History*, vol. 28, no. 4 (1995), p. 807. See, for example, the spousal stabbing of Mrs Ffrench in Co. Westmeath (*Freeman's Journal*, 8 April 1901).

[6] Rosemary Cullen Owens, *A social history of women in Ireland, 1870–1970* (Dublin, 2001), p. 176.

[7] Susan Edwards, '"Kicked, beaten, jumped on until they are crushed." All under man's wing and protection: the Victorian dilemma with domestic violence' in Judith Rowbotham and Kim Stevenson (eds.), *Criminal conversations: Victorian crimes, social panic, and moral outrage* (Ohio, 2005), p. 262.

[8] See E. Steiner-Scott, 'To bounce a boot off her now and again: domestic violence in post-famine Ireland' in Maryann G. Valiulis and Mary O'Dowd (eds.), *Women in Irish history*, p. 130 and p. 132 (Dublin and Portland, OR, 1997). See also the reports from the Watch the Courts Committee in the suffrage paper, the *Irish Citizen*.

[9] Byrne, *New law of divorce*, p. 36.

[10] L. A. M. Priestley McCracken, 'Wife-beating' in the *Irish Citizen*, September 1919. She recommended hard labour for those found guilty of this crime and suggested that wife-beating was 'a hateful form of oppression [and] … a common occurrence … suffered for the most part in silence by the victim for the sake of her social or financial position, or for the sake of her children'. McCracken was a regular contributor to *The Irish Citizen* as well as the English suffrage journal *The Vote*. Collections of her writings *First Causes* and *Shall Suffrage Cease* were reprinted as penny pamphlets.

[11] Alan Joseph Shatter, *Family law in the Republic of Ireland* (Dublin, 1977), p. 117.

killed her, or ... witnesses heard her complaining in her bed or saw her with livid eyes and bandaged face'.[12] This was subject to eighteenth-century censure from English reformer Sarah Capone: 'A good Husband would not desire the Power of Horse-whipping, confining, Half-starving his wife, or squandering her Estate; a bad Husband should not be allowed it', but the toleration of wifely physical chastisement continued.[13]

A husband's cruelty could be considered as a discretionary bar to divorce, but Parliament decided in Rev. Vanston's 1897 parliamentary divorce that this was not the case.[14] Within a year of marriage, Vanston, a clerk in holy orders, and his wife were reportedly living 'unhappily' in Rathgar, Dublin. Henrietta Vanston filed a petition against her husband on the ground of cruelty but did not proceed as a private deed of separation was executed in 1884, providing her with a £65 annuity for life as long as she did not remarry and £25 annual maintenance for their child. The Vanstons lived apart for a year until Mrs Vanston went to America in 1896. She divorced in the Dakota Territory and remarried in New York before returning to Dublin. In a subsequent divorce brought by Rev. Vanston, his cruelty was considered as a possible bar; however, emphasising female forbearance, with the exception of Sir John Dineley's 1739 English divorce bill there was little parliamentary or court precedent for this and, as Mrs Vanston's adultery was not denied, the bill passed.[15]

Women of the higher social orders were also believed to be less resilient to violence than their lower-class counterparts. As Sir John Nicholl noted in Lord Westmeath's 1827 case, one in a litany of marital wrangles which spanned decades, 'A blow between the parties in the lower conditions and in the highest stations of life bears a very different aspect.'[16] Byrne's mid-nineteenth-century legal guide gave a similar emphasis; the 'rank and position of the parties' would be considered in the legal application of cruelty: 'A blow of the fist, which in the humbler classes is followed by reprisals and instantly forgotten, will ... in a higher station, prove ever fatal to conjugal repose.'[17] Such reasoning left working-class women

---

[12] Kitchin, *History of divorce*, pp. 78–9.

[13] Sarah Capone, *The hardships of the English laws. In relation to wives with an explanation of the original curse of subjection passed upon the women. In a humble address to the legislature* (London, 1735), p. 50.

[14] Sir John Dineley failed to divorce Mary Lawford on the ground of her adultery in 1739. In this case, claims of wifely cruelty as well as the lack of a separation in the ecclesiastical court deterred the House of Lords from passing the divorce bill. For Dineley's divorce bill, see *House of Lords Journal*, vol. 25 (1739), p. 376, and Stone, *Broken lives*, pp. 82–116.

[15] Roberts, *Divorce bills*, pp. 92–3 and *Irish Times*, 11 June 1897.

[16] Roberts, *Divorce bills*, cited p. 79.

[17] Ibid., p. 27. See also Fenn, *Thirty-five years*, p. 179. Views on working-class propensity to domestic violence were also common in France. See Mary Trouille, *Wife abuse in 18th-century France* (Oxford, 2009), p. 4.

susceptible to abuse which they could supposedly tolerate. Upper- and middle-class women's vulnerability came from another source: their abuse was easier to conceal than that experienced in lower-class neighbourhoods with close community ties and residential proximity. This was highlighted in the 1859 press reaction to a cruelty case where the unnamed son of an Irish peer beat his wife, forced salt down her throat, threatened her with a meat cleaver, cut her hair, pulled her out of bed when ill and locked her in a room for three weeks without a fire or candles. Thus, as the *Examiner* intimated, 'aristocratic connexion covers a multitude of sins'.[18]

Although Westminster never reformed Irish divorce provision, the law was not inert. Rulings in the ecclesiastical courts and later in the divorce and civil courts impacted the legal definition of cruelty. Irish divorce acts similarly established legal precedent. The solely physical definition of legal cruelty was first challenged in the ecclesiastical courts where the level of violence demanded to constitute legal cruelty waned from the mid-eighteenth century. In 1790, Lord Stowell, in the landmark separation case of Evans versus Evans, introduced fear of violence into the definition of cruelty:

The causes must be grave and weighty, and such as shew [sic] an absolute impossibility that the duties of married life can be discharged. In a state of personal danger no duties can be discharged; for the duty of self-preservation must take place before the duties of marriage. . . . What merely wounds the mental feelings is in a few cases to be admitted where they are not accompanied with bodily injury, either actual or menaced.[19]

This influential ruling was widely cited; it was, for example, the authority in the Irish case of McKeever versus McKeever in 1878 and continued to be referenced in Ireland in the twentieth century.[20] This underscored, as Brown and Dolan suggest, that the '*origins* of the law mattered little. English laws, private and public, could become natural to the Irish.'[21]

In the 1801 case of Oliver versus Oliver, Stowell went further: 'Words of menace, importing the actual danger of bodily harm, will justify the interposition of the court, as the law ought not to wait till the mischief is actually done.' By 1810, Stowell moved towards the inclusion of non-physical conduct which violence could follow in the definition of marital cruelty.[22]

---

[18] *The Examiner*, 26 November 1859.
[19] Hammerton, *Cruelty and companionship*, pp. 120–1.
[20] I am grateful to Maebh Harding for drawing the McKeever case to my attention.
[21] Brown and Donlan, *The law and other legalities*, p. 29.
[22] In the separation case of Holden v. Holden (1810), Stowell moved towards the inclusion of non-violent conduct which violence could follow (Biggs, *Concept of matrimonial cruelty*, pp. 26–7).

This more complex definition also emerged in Ireland's ecclesiastical courts. As Dr Radcliffe summarised in the case of Carpenter versus Carpenter heard in Dublin's Consistory Court in 1827, cruelty was 'something which renders the cohabitation unsafe, or is likely to be attended by injury to the person or health of the party'.[23]

During the extensive debates surrounding the 1857 divorce act, some moves were made to amend the law in relation to marital cruelty. Gladstone, disapproving of the 1850s Royal Commission, staunchly opposed the bill. Making more than seventy 'frenzied ... interventions', including twenty-nine in one sitting, he played devil's advocate in proposing to alter the law relating to cruelty as a ground for divorce.[24] Citing examples of female insanity and suicide resulting from the failings of the law to free wives from the violence of drunken spouses and the 'cruelty of insult, which sends the iron into the soul as deeply, and far more sharply, than any material instrument', Gladstone unsuccessfully called for the definition of cruelty to be extended beyond the physical.[25] However, by the 1860s verbal abuse and insults, also referred to as moral cruelty, were widely accepted as cruel and a similar shift occurred in mid-century America; regardless of location, however, this was a gradual and uneven redefinition.[26]

Much of the legal gaze remained fixed on physical violence at least until mid-century, and the 1863 case of Mrs Fitzgerald emphasised the surviving strictures of marital cruelty. A four-day hearing in the divorce court saw her allege cruelty following the death of an infant and a miscarriage, but the actions of her Irish 'rollicking, careless, easy-tongued husband' were not accepted as constituting cruelty. Although a claim of English residency was accepted, she failed to divorce.[27] Henry Fenn, with three decades of experience as a reporter in the divorce court, also indicated the challenges of substantiating verbal abuse: 'There are men who know how to work on a woman's nerves, to trample on her fine feelings, to humiliate and render her miserable, and yet always keep within the exact limit of the law.'[28]

---

[23] William Duncan, 'Desertion and cruelty in Irish matrimonial law', *The Irish Jurist*, vol. 7, new series (1972), cited p. 213.

[24] Roy Jenkins, *Gladstone* (London, 1995), p. 187. Shanley concurs that Gladstone was 'a master at using egalitarian arguments against legal reforms to aid women' and hoped to defeat the 1857 bill by calling for non-gendered grounds of divorce. Gladstone's approach to female enfranchisement was similar (Mary Lyndon Shanley, *Feminism, marriage and the law in Victorian England* [Princeton, 1989], p. 40).

[25] Kitchin, *History of divorce*, cited p. 195. Henry Drummond also called for a change in the legal definition of marital cruelty during the debates.

[26] Robert L. Griswold, 'Sexual cruelty and the case for divorce in Victorian America', *Signs*, vol. 11, no. 3 (1986), pp. 529–41.

[27] *Saturday Review*, vol. 16, no. 426, 26 December 1863.

[28] Fenn, *Thirty-five years*, p. 180 and p. 191.

Yet, as more women divorced in court, case law gradually determined that if the degree and length of verbal abuse were sufficient to break a woman's health, a husband could be found guilty of cruelty. The divorce court therefore continued the process begun in the ecclesiastical courts in unsteadily expanding the notion of marital cruelty beyond the physical.[29] This was especially true if sustained verbal abuse was accompanied by actual or threatened bodily injury. In addition, cruelty subjected to a child in the presence of the mother with the express purpose of upsetting her became legally validated as an act of cruelty.[30] This, as the Irish separation case of Manning versus Manning proved in 1872, did not extend to husbands witnessing their wives inflict harm on children as men 'are supposed to be made of sterner stuff'; the sexual double standard could also be prejudicial to men.[31]

These legal changes were indicative of transformative social mores concerning men's role in marriage and the marital union more generally. Companionate marriage featured in late-eighteenth- and nineteenth-century rulings on spousal cruelty but never eclipsed gender differences. Indeed, women's supposed emotional composition compared to men's physical strength was a prevailing consideration; for some legal commentators, it provided a 'welcome flexibility in applying the law'.[32] Wife-beating was, however, subject to increasing censure from the 1820s[33] and was averred to as 'unmanly brutalities' from the 1850s.[34] The ground-breaking Liverpool case of Kelly versus Rev. Kelly in 1869 helped embed the emergent legal definition. A separation was granted to Mrs Kelly on the ground of non-violent cruelty at the hands of her Irish spouse which included being denied money, accompanied or followed when she went out and removed as mistress of the marital home. The Kelly case, keenly followed by the press for five months, thus departed from the earlier strict requirement for physical violence.[35] By the 1880s, case law

---

[29] Changes in the definition of marital cruelty made in the divorce court also filtered down to magistrates' courts. See Hammerton, *Cruelty and companionship*, p. 4 and p. 55.

[30] Fenn, *Thirty-five years*, p. 179 and p. 180. In the 1859 separation of Suggate v. Suggate, the first president of the divorce court, Sir Cresswell Cresswell, decided violence inflicted on children in the presence of the mother, without causing injury to the mother, constituted legal cruelty but it took time for this to become embedded.

[31] Report: Divorce a Mensa et Thoro and Related Matters (LRC 8–1983, 16 December 1983), cited p. 8.

[32] At this juncture, companionate marriage referred to a marital union based on mutual consent and equality (Biggs, *Concept of matrimonial cruelty*, p. 20).

[33] John Tosh, *A man's place. Masculinity and the middle-class home in Victorian England* (New Haven, CT, and London, 1999), p. 61.

[34] *The Examiner*, 26 November 1859.

[35] Hammerton, *Cruelty and companionship*, p. 94. For a discussion of Kelly v. Kelly, see Biggs, *Concept of marital cruelty*, pp. 36–9 as well as Frances Power Cobbe's leaders in the *London Echo*, 11 February and 10 March 1870 (see Susan Hamilton, 'The practice of

in the divorce court ruled that proof of actual physical violence was no longer required for a woman to plead cruelty coupled with adultery as grounds for divorce.[36] The court's onus thus shifted, as Stowell earlier advised, to the safety of the wife and her fear of injury.

The 1891 Regina versus Jackson case which prevented a husband from kidnapping, physically chastising or confining his spouse was followed four years later by that of the Earl and Countess Russell who, in a series of suits, counter suits and appeals, uneasily raised the notion that cruelty which did not damage health could make marriage untenable.[37] Therefore, when the idea that a husband could beat his wife with a stick 'provided it was no thicker than his thumb but ... not [with] a cudgel or an iron bar'[38] was called into play in an 1891 court of appeal divorce case, Master of the Rolls Lord Esher could only laugh.[39] Moreover, the justice of forcing a wife to remain with her husband by a restitution of conjugal rights order was waning. By 1899, Lord Halsbury referred to this as lacking 'a due sense of ... respect due to a wife whom the husband had sworn to cherish and protect' and as a 'quaint and absurd dicta ... not now capable of being cited ... in a court of justice in ... any civilised country'.[40] The details of such cases were still carefully considered as it was seen as a wife's duty to submit to her husband's will, and if she could 'ensure her own safety by ... proper self-command' she had no right to complain or institute divorce proceedings. However, wifely provocation of violence became much less frequently cited in divorce cases as

everyday feminism: Frances Power Cobbe, divorce, and the *London Echo*, 1868–1875', *Victorian Periodicals Review*, vol. 35, no. 3 [Fall, 2002], pp. 227–42).

[36] Hammerton, *Cruelty and companionship*, p. 121.

[37] Married in 1890, Countess Russell unsuccessfully tried to separate. The grounds, which included much publicised unnatural offences with a third party, were unsubstantiated. She then brought a restitution of conjugal rights suit hoping that her spouse's non-compliance would allow her to claim desertion as a basis for separation. Earl Russell's counter separation suit claimed wifely cruelty, but the majority in the Court of Appeal disagreed, ruling that her conduct was sufficient to present a defence to the restitution of conjugal rights. The case went on appeal to the House of Lords where the majority upheld the decision of the Court of Appeal and thus rejected the idea that the impossibility of continuing married life should be the basis for separation. See Biggs, *Concept of marital cruelty*, pp. 39–43. Russell's matrimonial battles led him to establish the Society for Promoting Reforms in Marriage and Divorce Laws in England in 1902. Never overly popular, it merged with the Divorce Law Association to become the Divorce Law Reform Union in 1906 (Cretney, *Family law*, p. 205).

[38] Edwards, 'Kicked, beaten, jumped on', p. 249. The rule of thumb is alleged to have originated with Sir Francis Buller's 1782 ruling in the Court of King's Bench. Although some dispute its existence, Edwards notes, 'it was certainly the case in practice in England, and cannot be dismissed as a fiction' (ibid.).

[39] Fenn, *Thirty-five years*, cited pp. 183–4. The 1891 case was the Clitheroe abduction case which began as a restitution of conjugal rights suit in 1889.

[40] Ibid., cited pp. 185–6.

domestic violence was increasingly seen as an abuse of power.[41] Sir Edward Carson, Irish unionist leader and barrister, with experience both in the London divorce court and on the standing committee which heard bills for parliamentary divorce at Westminster, also noted the distinction which many men made between infidelity and cruelty: 'I have had over and over again in my practice men come to say: "I am quite willing to . . . admit I have committed adultery: but I will not have it said . . . that I was cruel to a woman."' Carson explained that this was due to domestic abuse becoming seen as 'unmanly' and at variance with the notion of a husband as his wife's protector.[42] As with the widening definition of marital cruelty, these 'new standards of manhood' also emerged in America and Europe.[43]

The cruelty of wives against men was rarely mentioned in either court-based or parliamentary divorce. Although a recognised matrimonial offence, it was superfluous to legal requirements as men only needed to prove a wife's infidelity to divorce. For example, in Dr Lardner's 1839 divorce bill, witnesses testified that his wife was 'of a violent and uncontrollable temper . . . boisterous and unkind', but her adultery provided the ground for divorce.[44] Moreover, although the physical effects of the violence by the wife were often less, 'simply because cats are weaker than dogs', the moral impact was acute.[45] Just as a woman's infidelity was believed to inflict the most injurious insult on her spouse, her violence had 'profoundly great' moral implications. A woman's violence was also deemed likely to provoke retaliation from her spouse which could put her at risk. Courts would therefore intervene if a husband was continuously provoked by a wife: '[I]t asks itself, what security is there in such circumstances for the wife?' Parliament, however, was averse to legislate on marital cruelty,[46] which significantly disadvantaged Irish women seeking to cite cruelty in a divorce bill.[47]

The idea of varying class resilience to domestic violence also endured. This was widely publicised in the late nineteenth century by Dublin-born

---

[41] Ibid., p. 179.
[42] Carson, *The Royal Commission on Divorce and Matrimonial Causes. Minutes of Evidence*, vol. 3 (London, 1912), p. 425. Carson disliked divorce, informing this commission that he would have opposed the 1857 Divorce and Matrimonial Causes Act. Yet, his definition of marital cruelty was liberal, seeing a man's adultery 'flaunted' before his wife as cruel and 'the grossest insult' which would impact her health (ibid., p. 426). See also Hammerton, *Cruelty and companionship*, p. 3.
[43] Griswold, 'Sexual cruelty', p. 533; Trouille, *Wife abuse*, p. 43.
[44] *Freeman's Journal*, 27 April 1839. Dr Lardner's bill is discussed in Chapter 1.
[45] Frances Power Cobbe in Hammerton, *Cruelty and companionship*, cited p. 46.
[46] Rebecca Probert, *Marriage law and practice in the long eighteenth century. A reassessment* (Cambridge, 2009), p. 14.
[47] Fenn, *Thirty-five years*, p. 189.

feminist reformer Frances Power Cobbe. Her last lengthy work on women, 'Wife-Torture in England', published in 1878, influenced the Matrimonial Causes Act of the same year. This act allowed magistrates to grant maintenance and separation payments to women whose husbands were convicted of aggravated assault.[48] In Cobbe's view, domestic violence in the upper and middle classes, although more commonplace than popularly believed, rarely extended beyond what she referred to as 'an occasional blow or two of a not dangerous kind', claiming that men of the higher classes were constrained by the possibility of being 'betrayed by . . . [a] wife's black eye' and the 'disgrace' they would incur if their violence became known.[49] By comparison, the level of domestic violence in the ostensible 'kicking districts' – working-class areas with high Irish migrant densities in cities like Liverpool – was rife. Cobbe thus called for the grounds for divorce to be equalised between the sexes, but curtailing violence in lower-class marriages would require not only legislative reform but also 'the slow elevation and civilization of both sexes'.[50]

Determining whether the limited availability of Irish divorce impacted the level of class-based domestic violence is fraught with difficulties. The actual level of violence in Ireland, as elsewhere, cannot be ascertained with any degree of accuracy and the Irish case study is further complicated by the destruction of many court records in 1922.[51] Irish trials of those convicted of spousal murder certainly focused more on the association between violence and alcohol than on the lack of means to dissolve a marital union, although in the 1887 trial of Cork surgeon Dr P. H. E. Cross, the police recorded that he poisoned his wife to marry another. This motive was shared by Catherine Delany of Co. Tipperary in 1884, one of only two Irishwomen found guilty of spousal murder from 1900 to 1920.[52] In the post-1857 period, it was also uncertain if case law from the divorce court could be applied to parliamentary divorce. Indeed, although Byrne's legal guide to explain the machinations of the 1857 act to

---

[48] See Frances Power Cobbe (1822–1904), 'Wife-torture in England' (*Contemporary Review*, April 1878) reprinted in Sheila Jeffreys (ed.), *The Sexuality Debates* (New York and London, 1987), pp. 219–53. See also J. W. Kaye, 'Outrages on women', *North British Review*, vol. 25, no. 49 (1856), pp. 233–56. It is questionable whether the 1878 Matrimonial Causes Act applied to Ireland (Duncan, 'Desertion and cruelty', p. 216). The Married Women's (Maintenance in Case of Desertion) Act of 1886 did apply to Ireland; in 1909, eighty orders were issued in Dublin and ninety-six in the remainder of Ireland (Fitzpatrick, 'Divorce and separation', p. 176).

[49] Edwards, 'Kicked, beaten, jumped on', cited p. 249.

[50] Hammerton, *Cruelty and companionship*, cited p. 38.

[51] This was a result of the 1922 Custom House fire in Dublin.

[52] Cross received the death penalty in 1888. Delany's death sentence was commuted to life imprisonment; she served thirteen years (Prior, *Madness and murder*, pp. 92–3, p. 97, p. 151 and p. 155).

an Irish audience confidently claimed that its reforms would extend to Westminster, this was not guaranteed.[53] It took a landmark Irish divorce act in 1886 to ascertain the bearing of court precedent on parliamentary divorce.

In the history of both Irish and parliamentary divorce, Louisa Westropp's case was groundbreaking. Westropp was the first Irishwoman to seek a parliamentary divorce and her act of 1886 established legal precedent. Female divorce was not only rare, with only four previous acts passed to Englishwomen (the last in 1850), but Parliament also discouraged female bills 'except in cases of great and extraordinary enormity'.[54] In 1805, Elizabeth Touche experienced this at first hand when her attempt to divorce met the response that female divorce 'uniformly rendered that house very cautious in entertaining bills of the kind'.[55] Westropp, an Irishwoman of landed stock, was the daughter of Captain Richard and Lady Louisa Morgan and a granddaughter of the late Earl of Mount Cashell.[56] In 1878, age nineteen, she married her first cousin, Edward Morgan, age twenty-two, of Co. Limerick in an Anglican ceremony. Within three months of that union, 'great cruelty' was alleged to have commenced. Three daughters were born; but Edward, frequently intoxicated and using 'violent and indecent language', would spit in his wife's face when 'sober by way of amusement'. He forced her into a stable with loose horses, pointed a loaded revolver and threatened to shoot her, but 'she was so miserable that it did not much matter whether he did so or not ... late at night she was obliged to take refuge in a cupboard from his violence. He was going about the house with a thick stick breaking everything and calling for her.' Louisa and the children were also hit 'with a whip until the blood ran' and a three-year-old child was beaten in front of her. She lived 'in bodily fear' of her spouse and her health suffered.[57] This, coupled with Edward's adultery, led to an informal separation in 1883. In 1885, she formally separated in the Irish Matrimonial Court due to spousal cruelty and a decree from the Irish Court of Chancery gave her custody and control of the children.

---

[53] Byrne, *New Law of Divorce*, preface, p. 1, p. 7 and p. 27.
[54] Macqueen, *Practical treatise on divorce*, p. 217.
[55] House of Lords debates, 9 April 1805, vol. 4, col. 326. Touche failed to divorce.
[56] Louisa was brought up by her aunt at Moore Park, near Kilworth, Co. Cork. Lands at Bridestone, Co. Cork were settled on her with life interest after her father's death and remainder to her husband and children. After marrying, they lived at Moore Park with her grandfather and aunt.
[57] *The Times*, 18 May 1886. Edward Westropp was alleged to have 'said that if he shot her nothing would be done to him, as it could be proved there was madness in the family' (*Irish Times*, 3 May 1886).

The parliamentary divorce was undefended and witnesses, including family members, servants, a bank employee and police constable, confirmed both the adultery and catalogue of cruelty. Louisa's lengthy cross-examination in the House of Lords was deemed 'Extraordinary Evidence' by the press but to date such abuse would have been insufficient to procure a parliamentary divorce.[58] However, as this would now justify a *decree absolute* in the divorce court, Parliament decided to follow suit.[59] Lord Chancellor Herschell determined to do otherwise would disadvantage Irish petitioners, and his summation of Edward Westropp's conduct encompassed many of the changes in the definition of marital cruelty:

[T]o inflict bodily injury upon her on one occasion but to put her in reasonable fear on many other occasions. Moreover, his behaviour to her child in her presence, his threats against her, and his general conduct were such as to put her in bodily fear, and fully justified her in refusing to continue cohabitation with him, and, in fact, rendered it impossible for her to do so with any comfort to herself or any reasonable prospect of maintaining her health . . . it was clear that at the present time the conduct that would justify the passing of a decree absolute in that part of the United Kingdom to which that [1857] Act applied would justify their Lordships in reading a Bill of this kind a second time.[60]

Parliament thus ended 'its old and strict rule against allowing divorce to injured wives, unless in the most exceptional cases'.[61] The legal precedent which this case established was significant. The Westropp principle held that any ground for divorce accepted by court could be applied in Parliament. As the divorce court awarded damages rather than demanding a criminal conversation suit, the Westropp precedent also lessened the parliamentary demand for the latter, although an explanation, usually on the ground of either a co-respondent's unknown whereabouts or foreign domicile, was sought. In the Torrens' divorce bill of 1909, for example, it was held that even though no criminal conversation action had been taken as the co-respondent was not within the jurisdiction, the bill could proceed to its second reading.[62]

The Westropp ruling attracted international comment: to Canadian legal commentator John Gemmill it represented 'a healthy change in sentiment'.[63] Eighty years later, the Northern Irish attorney general

---

[58] *The Times*, 3 May 1886.
[59] A *decree nisi* was usually followed by a *decree absolute* in a period of six weeks.
[60] *The Times*, 18 May 1886.
[61] Clifford, *History of private bill legislation* (vol. 2), pp. 771–2.
[62] *Irish Law Times and Solicitors' Journal*, vol. 44 (26 March 1910), pp. 74–5. See also PA, HL/PO/PB/1/1909/9E71.
[63] Gemmill, *Practice of the Parliament of Canada upon bills of divorce*, p. 55.

similarly reflected on its import: the Westropp principle was 'recognised as the leading authority ... [and] laid down definitely ... that the rule upon which the House of Lords would act in considering whether it would pass into law a Bill granting a divorce in Ireland upon any ground which would have been a sufficient ground for the granting of a divorce by the courts of England'.[64] Through tenacity and desperation and backed by lawyers who wanted to test the law, Westropp thus succeeded where successive reformers failed in providing permanent relief for some Irish victims of domestic abuse in the late nineteenth and early twentieth centuries. The impact of the Westropp principle must also be measured against the sterile backdrop of other legal recourses particularly for dealing with marital cruelty in Ireland: 'None of the landmark English Acts of the latter half of the 19th century increasing the matrimonial jurisdiction of the Magistrates' Court was ... extended to Ireland.'[65] Replicating the emergent pattern in the divorce court, the number of Irish women bringing bills to Parliament augmented post-Westropp: five Irish women divorced in Parliament in the remainder of the nineteenth century and a further twenty-four presented bills to Westminster from 1900 to 1922. This represented 45 per cent of the fifty-three Irish divorce bills heard from 1900 to 1922 with female bills in the majority (54 per cent) from 1914.[66]

Adultery and cruelty became the most commonly cited grounds by Irish wives pursuing a divorce. Beatrice Peacocke's bill was typical of many brought by women from the late 1880s. Peacocke, of Victoria Castle in Killiney, Dublin, also illustrated the continuance of upper-class parliamentary divorce petitioners. After six years of marriage, she divorced her husband on the grounds of adultery and cruelty in 1897. Although the lord chancellor mused on whether 'drunkenness or madness' caused the violent actions of her spouse, there was no denying his 'cruelty and brutality'.[67] The only Irish female divorce bill which did not list cruelty as a ground for divorce was brought by Marchioness

---

[64] Black, Northern Ireland [hereafter NI] House of Commons debates, 2 May 1939, vol. 22, col. 1239.

[65] Steiner-Scott, 'To bounce a boot off her', p. 129. The Aggravated Assaults on Women and Children Act of 1853, for example, did not extend to Ireland or Scotland. Duncan also questioned whether the 1895 Summary Jurisdiction (Married Women) Act, which repealed the 1878 and the 1886 acts and allowed magistrates to grant separation, custody and maintenance for abused wives and imprison and fine abusive spouses, applied or was used in Ireland (Duncan, 'Desertion and cruelty', p. 216) and Fitzpatrick concurs (Fitzpatrick, 'Divorce and separation', p. 176).

[66] PA, Records of the House of Commons, Minutes of Proceedings on Irish Divorce Bills [1907–22] (4 vols., HC/CL/CO/BF/1–4).

[67] *The Times*, 21 May 1897. See also the case of Baroness Jose Carbery, *Irish Times*, 8 November and 13 December 1919. She divorced in Parliament in 1920.

Conyngham in 1921; her successful bill was based on the grounds of adultery and desertion.[68] This furthered underlines the significance of the Westropp precedent; desertion was not recognised as a ground for separation in Ireland, but as it was a ground for divorce in court, it would now be considered by Parliament.[69] Jane Lautour of Castle Cooke in Co. Cork shared Peacock's and Conyngham's social profile and also added desertion to her list of grounds for divorce in 1905. She married in 1884, but her husband was adulterous from the following year, broke up their home and left the country. Without maintenance, she secured a separation on the ground of adultery in 1892 but lacked the finances to proceed to Parliament until 1905. She then added twenty years' desertion to her marital woes and, again due to the Westropp ruling, successfully proceeded. Moreover, from 1883, following Lady Georgina Weldon's English case, non-compliance with an order for the restitution of conjugal rights was considered as constituting desertion. In time, Parliament applied this ruling: Viscountess de Vesci, divorcing in Westminster, for example, used non-compliance and adultery as grounds for divorce in 1920.[70]

The 1869 court ruling in Kelly versus Kelly, where a wife being denied the position of mistress in her own home constituted cruelty, was also applied to parliamentary divorce. Alice Maguire's 1922 bill passed on grounds of adultery and cruelty with the latter proven by her spouse bringing another woman to live in the house 'against the wish of the petitioner, and committed adultery with her on divers [sic] occasions'.[71] This was earlier subject to legal censure; Byrne averred that it placed wives in an intolerable position and vindicated their departure from the marital home: 'No woman would be justified in remaining in the same house with her husband's concubine – sharing the turpitude of his crime, and partaking of his polluted bed – degrading herself before her children and domestics in the sanctuary of repose to which purity is indispensable.'[72] However, it was only post-Westropp that Parliament engaged with this change in the law's application.

The impact of the widening definition of marital cruelty and the Westropp principle, however, needs to be measured against contemporaneous reforms

---

[68] Duncan, 'Desertion and cruelty', p. 214. See also PA, HL/PO/PB/6/158–9.

[69] Barrister Arthur Samuels applied to have desertion added to the Irish separation decree but was refused as this was, unlike in England, unrecognised as a ground for separation in the Irish courts (Roberts, *Divorce bills*, pp. 98–9). Lautour's case was delayed as her husband was in New Zealand, but he was telegraphed and on the grounds of his reply the bill was permitted to proceed (PA, HL/PO/PB/1/1905/5E71).

[70] 20 April 1920, PA, HC/CL/CO/BF/2/4.

[71] *Irish Times*, 3 March 1922. See also PA, HL/PO/PB/1/1922/12&13G52.

[72] Byrne, *New Law of Divorce*, p. 37.

in custody rights. An act of 1839 gave mothers custody of children up to the age of seven, but this was subject to the approval of the lord chancellor whose decision depended on a mother being non-adulterous. With adultery the sole ground to divorce a woman, this effectively barred divorced women from securing custody. A further act of 1873 extended the age that children could be cared for by their mother to sixteen and allowed adulterous women to petition chancery for custody, although success was not guaranteed in the latter case. Custody arrangements could also be included in private deeds of separation. In the Vanston divorce, a private deed confirmed both child maintenance and custody in 1884, but its validity was questioned in Parliament in 1897. As the lord chancellor remarked, 'I do not think … that the bargain between the parties, whereby he surrenders his paternal right, is worth the parchment on which it is engrossed. The law would not give effect to it. Nor is the paternal right capable of being bargained away.'[73] Child welfare was, however, moving to the foreground of custody decisions, and the 1886 Custody of Children Act further enhanced a divorced mother's chances of gaining custody. This act removed the need for a divorced mother to petition chancery for custody in England, but this was maintained in Ireland as the civil courts lacked the jurisdiction to determine custody or property rights.

To avoid an additional chancery suit, Irish female petitioners began to include custody clauses in their divorce bills. In Mrs Hart's 1898 divorce and that of Charlotte Jones in the following year, for example, the bills included a clause to give them custody. This could be done by either making the children wards of chancery or making it unlawful for a father to remove the children from their mother's custody. If a child was left with a mother who had been divorced by her spouse, the lord chancellor retained the right to intervene in custody arrangements.[74] Yet, as the 1905 divorce bill of Charles Gamble, a Dublin solicitor in the Irish Supreme Court, illustrated, women's requests for custody were not always successful. His bill was heard when his wife, Ida, was in Canada, but she appointed a Dublin agent as power of attorney. Married in 1889 in an Anglican ceremony, they had three children. She was adulterous and left her husband in 1894 'and he had not seen her since', only learning of her adultery in 1904. In Parliament, Ida asked for her costs to be paid and for custody of their youngest child or at least access to the children. That request was refused, and access arrangements were deemed not to fall within the remit of Parliament; the divorce bill passed with no recourse but the chancery court.[75]

[73] *Irish Times*, 11 June 1897.   [74] Roberts, *Divorce bills*, p. 37.
[75] Ibid., pp. 95–6; *The Times*, 11 May 1905 and PA, HL/PO/PB/1/1905/5E74.

Following custody reform, more Irish women with dependent children, like Emily Dooner (née Senior of Beevor Hall, Barnsley), began to petition Parliament. Brought on the grounds of cruelty and adultery in 1913, Dooner's was one of an increasing number of military divorces. She married Captain William Dooner of the Royal Irish Fusiliers in 1902 and bore two children. From 1909, she was subjected to violence and threatening language and she subsequently left the marital home. The abuse caused mental and physical suffering which required medical intervention for nervous debility and anaemia by 1911. Correspondence, hotel registers and bills were presented as evidence of the adultery and her mother and niece witnessed numerous acts of cruelty: 'In Hong Kong in 1906 and 1907 he struck her, and exhibited a continual spirit of "nagging". When she left Hong Kong she was quite ill as a result of his illtreatment.' After an absence of seven months, she returned, but 'her husband again displayed frequent outbursts of violent temper'. Having previously 'in fits of rage, informed her that he had lost all love for her [and] ... that he would not live with her any longer', he sought a reconciliation in 1910: 'regretting the past, and saying he would try to treat her properly'. Emily subsequently joined him in Ireland but testified:

He used to gnash his teeth, and I was in a state of terror, thinking he was going to strike me. . . . I was very frightened with him . . . he seized me by the shoulders, and with his feet he kicked and kicked and kicked me, saying dreadful things. . . . Subsequently he said, 'You are a vindictive little beast, and you brought all this on us by your damned coldness.'

Suffering a nervous breakdown, she left her spouse for the last time. Her divorce bill passed with costs and she was advised to apply to the lord chancellor for custody, but although described as 'not very well' off she did not seek any financial settlement; for Emily Dooner this was a chance to start anew.[76]

Although custody remained contentious, the sympathy for Irish petitioners evident in the Westropp case was apparent in the wholesale passage of divorce bills heard from 1907 to 1922 and in the actions of the divorce select committee.[77] In Hewat's divorce bill of 1887, respondent Agnes Hewat was in Diep River in Western Cape but consented to the bill. She cohabited with her spouse until September 1885 when she left the marital home. She gave birth in May 1886, but her husband

---

[76] *Irish Times*, 19 April 1913 and 3 July 1913 and PA, HC/CL/CO/BF/2/1.

[77] This was at odds with Nova Scotia, for example, where Snell depicts both a divorce court bench and legal system that was 'generally unsympathetic' to female petitioners bringing divorce on the ground of marital cruelty, prioritising adultery over cruelty and physical over mental abuse (Snell, 'Marital cruelty', p. 6).

denied paternity and secured a separation in Dublin. In the parliamentary proceedings, the only evidence of her adultery was bogusly passing as husband and wife and sharing a cabin on a trip to Cape Colony with a man other than her spouse. The parties could only be identified by photographs shown to the Lords, but the lord chancellor was more concerned about the propriety of discussing a child's legitimacy, particularly including the name of a punitive father, in the divorce bill. This was allowed to stand, but such an intervention intimates concern for these public proceedings.[78] Evidence, particularly of adultery and cruelty, was also often cut short at the request of members of the select committee in the early twentieth century. Petitioner Anna Stoney, for example, was advised in 1919 to 'make your evidence as short as possible, because, of course, we have got the point'. Relating her spouse's cruelty, her counsel was told: 'I do not think you need to talk her through that.'[79] There was also a growing feeling that a detailed repetition of evidence in separation hearings in the House of Lords and the House of Commons was superfluous. By 1915, member of the select committee Earl Loreburn opined: 'This has all been heard in Ireland, and you need not ask the lady unduly.' Later in the same hearing, he asked, 'Is that not enough about the violence and cruelty?'[80]

The increased frequency of female petitioners, sympathy of the select committee, changes to custody rights and the legal definition of marital cruelty should not obscure how difficult such a course of action remained. Many abused women remained reluctant to take legal action. This was in consequence of economic dependency, fear of provoking further violence and, at times, a disinclination to punish husbands. The area which was most hidden was sexual abuse, most commonly brought on the grounds of wilfully passing on a venereal disease which constituted cruelty.[81] Some husbands were remorseful and sought reconciliation. As the Hon. Flora Irvine's spouse wrote, 'I am dreadfully sorry darling but I had not the slightest notion there was anything wrong with me, and you can't tell how much I feel it', but his wife divorced him in 1916.[82] By comparison, Margaret Miles, who contracted syphilis after living with her spouse for just three days, found no repentance: her husband offered her 15 shillings per week if she 'went away quietly and did not make a fuss in Kerry'.

---

[78] Roberts, *Divorce bills*, pp. 89–90.   [79] 25 July 1919, PA, HC/CL/CO/BF/2–3.
[80] The sum of £650 per annum alimony was previously paid to prevent a divorce (Denny divorce bill, 1915, ibid., HC/PO/PB/18/5/4a).
[81] See, for example, the 1913 divorces of Charlotte Carolin and Emily Dooner, ibid., HC/CL/CO/BF/2/1.
[82] Irvine was suffering from gonorrhoea and syphilis and Parliament heard that only the latter could be 'contracted innocently' on 20 June 1916, ibid., HC/CL/CO/BF/2–3.

Undeterred, she divorced in 1918.[83] The rape of a separated wife, as rape within marriage was not illegal until the late twentieth century, especially the violence associated with the act, inflicting an unwanted pregnancy and then forcibly attempting to cause a miscarriage and forced sodomy could also be cited as cruelty.[84] Understandably, few were willing to discuss such issues in Parliament and some Irish petitioners sought an alternative venue in which to pursue divorce: the divorce court.

[83] Ibid., HC/CL/CO/BF/2–3. See also ibid., HL/PO/PB/1/1918/8&9G51.

[84] On forced sexual marital relations, see Gail Savage, '"The instrument of an animal function": marital rape and sexual cruelty in the Divorce Court, 1858–1908' in Lucy Delap, Ben Griffin and Abigail Wills (eds.), *The politics of domestic authority in Britain since 1800* (Basingstoke, 2009), pp. 43–57.

6 Divorce in Court, 1857–1922

Those of Irish domicile or lacking a permanent home in England or Wales were barred from the divorce court from the time of its creation in 1857, but parliamentary divorce's noxious reputation encouraged some Irish petitioners, anxious to free themselves from the matrimonial bond, to develop means to circumvent its expense and publicity. Indeed, Roberts's evidence to the 1909 Royal Commission on Divorce and Matrimonial Causes emphasised the 'great temptation' to avoid parliamentary divorce by renting a house and paying rates in England for six months to establish domicile and access the divorce court. With the cost of a court-based divorce for Irish petitioners estimated at a quarter of the cost of a parliamentary divorce, it is unsurprising that three Irish cases were before the new divorce court as early as 1859.[1]

The Niboyet versus Niboyet case heard in the English Court of Appeal in 1878 ruled that residence without domicile would allow the divorce court to dissolve a marriage if the marital offence was committed in England. Although disputed, this encouraged Justice of the Peace and Deputy Lieutenant of Londonderry Robert McClintock to divorce in court rather than Parliament in 1888. Irish Queen's Counsel (QC) David Colquhon advised McClintock that in consequence of his Irish domicile and matrimonial home, the divorce court could have no jurisdiction over his case. However, Colquhon recommended that if McClintock could get an English address, prove that his wife, Jessie (née Alexander), committed adultery in England and get both she and the co-respondent to submit to the jurisdiction of the court, then a parliamentary divorce might be avoided.

Jessie McClintock's candid admission of adultery left her spouse 'thunderstruck':

> I am writing to tell you that I have gone off with Mr. Thornhill. We are going abroad at once. He has promised to marry me as soon as you have set me free.

---

[1] Roberts, *Royal Commission on Divorce (1909) ... Minutes of Evidence*, vol. 3, pp. 464–5. Roberts wanted the London divorce court to hear Irish cases.

I know I have wronged you but you know I never cared for you and I do for him. I wronged you more than once when Mr. Thornhill was in Derry.[2]

Although McClintock was named as the father of a fourth child in 1889, he denied paternity: '[T]he child is not mine. . . . I did not cohabit with her for six or seven months before the time of her leaving me. . . . There are servants about her lodgings from whom the information could no doubt be obtained.'[3] Using his mother's English address from mid-1888 and 'delicate management' to avoid the court's jurisdiction being queried, McClintock divorced his wife of seven years in court. He did not apply for custody of the fourth child as he had for the three daughters in the divorce proceeding and was reluctant to maintain his former wife. Unable to claim damages from the co-respondent, a militia officer stationed in Londonderry 'without means and dependent on his relatives', McClintock wanted his wife's £200 jointure fortified and was unwilling to continue to pay her £2 alimony per week: '[W]hen a wife leaves her husband, without his knowledge and consent, and then writes him a confirmation of the adultery, the claim would be considered ridiculous.'[4] He agreed to pay her costs of £15.15.0 as he was 'desirous more for his wife's sake than his own . . . that she may be enabled to marry'. She remarried in 1889, but legal disputes followed: a month after the divorce, McClintock sought to remove his former wife's life interest in Irish lands worth £200 a year and was advised that he should apply for custody of the fourth child, whose paternity he denied, to help with a variation of settlement.[5]

Although Roberts charitably declared the 'lay mind somewhat hazy on domicile', the McClintock case underlines the risks that some Irish petitioners were willing to take to divorce in court.[6] A covert court divorce could invalidate second marriages, bastardise issue, contest marriage settlements and lead to a divorce bill being presented in the very venue that petitioners tried to bypass: Parliament. Subsequent legal challenges could also come years after the decree. Edward Carson recalled an Irish case where, eighteen years after a court-based divorce and the establishment of a large grown-up family from a second marriage, the validity of the decree was questioned. This was one of 'many cases [where] . . . persons who were at the time domiciled in Ireland have resorted to the English Court' with 'very disastrous results'.[7] The court-based divorces

[2] Her letter of 17 April 1888 is included in case for counsel, 1888 (PRONI, D2753/1).
[3] McClintock to 'Gentlemen', 16 July 1888 (ibid.).   [4] Ibid., 26 June 1888.
[5] Ibid., Case for counsel, 1888.
[6] Roberts, *Royal Commission on Divorce (1909) . . . Minutes of Evidence*, vol. 3, pp. 464–5.
[7] Roberts, *Divorce bills*, p. 12.

of domiciled Irishmen Colonel Sinclair and Colonel Malone were the most widely publicised of these cases. The legitimacy of their divorces was questioned, and problems arose regarding marriage settlements. Lieutenant Colonel Alfred Sinclair, formerly of the Indian Staff Corps, from Strabane in Co. Tyrone, was a domiciled Irishman. He married Isabella in Bombay in 1878 and they had one child before she left him for another man. Sinclair did not conceal his Irish domicile from the divorce court in 1885; due to the non-attendance of his wife and the co-respondent at the trial, this was not raised.[8] An English court order of the next year altered the marriage settlement but trustees refused to acknowledge its validity. Sinclair then proceeded to the Irish courts to pursue a separation which marked the start of his quest for a parliamentary divorce. The president of the Irish Probate Division sidestepped the issue of the validity of the English decree in 1896 but, recalling the Niboyet ruling of 1878, highlighted the location of the adultery and the law of nations which limited the validity of a divorce to the country where the decree was granted 'unless it was their country of domicile ... for this purpose, as regards English decrees, Ireland is a foreign country'. He advised that the case be sent to the House of Lords, which passed Sinclair's divorce bill in 1897.[9]

Domiciled Irishman Colonel John Malone of Co. Westmeath, formerly of the Westmeath militia, married the Hon. Mildred Yarde Buller in London in 1872. Her adultery was uncovered in 1890 and he divorced in court in 1892, seeking custody of their three children; his wife remarried abroad the next day. Malone remarried in the following year and had three children by his second wife. Attempts to consolidate his estates led to the validity of the court divorce being challenged as the English court had no jurisdiction over Irish trustees of Irish land settlements or Irish land. Malone then brought a divorce bill to Parliament which included a clause to make the parliamentary divorce operative from the date of the court divorce. The Lords, in a move which was reminiscent of the tradition of divorce acts passed in the Irish parliament being approved by Westminster before 1782, agreed to hear Malone's case in 1905. This case changed court process; it subsequently refused to grant a divorce if a husband was not domiciled in England.[10] Malone's case also

---

[8] *The Times*, 4 March 1897. Isabella Sinclair remarried.

[9] Roberts, *Divorce bills*, cited p. 12. See also p. 15 and PA, HL/PO/PB/1/1905/5E73. The divorce court also failed to recognise the validity of the Tollemache Scottish divorce in 1857.

[10] Roberts, *Divorce bills*, pp. 14–15. See also, for example, the case of Irishman Colonel Skinner who divorced in court without English domicile in 1897. The property settlement was later questioned and a divorce bill subsequently passed in Parliament.

established that if the validity of a court divorce granted to a domiciled Irishman was in question, 'the proper course' was to apply for a parliamentary divorce. This procedure was subsequently adopted in the Murphy Grimshaw Divorce [Validation] Bill of 1907.[11] The commentary of Lord Watson in the 1895 case of Le Mesurier versus Le Mesurier was similarly influential: '[T]he domicile for the time being of the married pair affords the only true test of jurisdiction to dissolve their marriage.' The jurisdiction of the English court in this French case was challenged and a parliamentary divorce bill was subsequently, although unsuccessfully, brought in 1897.[12]

Despite this formalisation of process, some Irish citizens still conspired to access court. In the Bray divorce of 1899, notwithstanding claims of nineteen years of English residency, domicile was challenged. Noting Bray's Dublin birth, neither divorce nor separation was granted. The Sproule versus Hopkins case of the following year saw the respondent plead English domicile at both the times of marriage and divorce, but court evidence showed that his domicile was Irish.[13] Detecting Irish petitioners in the divorce court was, however, testing. As barrister C. J. Willock averred, solicitors always considered their clients' domicile: '[I]t is a very rash practitioner who would let the case come into court until he had looked into the facts.' An Irish accent on the part of a petitioner in court could call their domicile into question. As Lord Gorell confirmed, when he 'heard the sound of the Scotch or Irish tone' in court, he inquired as to domicile 'at once'. Yet, as the archbishop of York suggested in 1910, this was an ill guide: '[T]hose who are likely in the upper classes to get into matrimonial difficulties will not have that delightful sound.'[14] The court was therefore increasingly rigorous about testing domicile as Gorell introduced a rule that all divorce court petitioners would have to swear English domicile and falsification would bar the proceedings.[15]

This caused serious problems for several Irish petitioners and allowed some respondents to thwart divorce proceedings. Maurice Desmond, proprietor of a well-known shirt factory in Londonderry, brought his

[11] *Irish Law Times and Solicitors' Journal*, vol. 44 (26 March 1910), pp. 74–5. William Murphy Grimshaw married Mary (née Woodward) in 1888 and the 1907 parliamentary divorce validated that granted in the divorce court. See House of Commons debates, 4 June 1907, vol. 175, cols. 463–4 and PA, HL/PO/PB/1/1907/7E74.

[12] Memorandum on the position of foreign decrees of divorce in Ireland, 27 October 1940 (National Archives, Ireland [hereafter NAI], S12506).

[13] *New Irish Jurist and Local Government Review*, vol. 2 (13 June 1902), p. 225.

[14] *Royal Commission on Divorce (1909) ... Minutes of Evidence*, vol. 1, p. 198 and p. 266.

[15] Gorell noted a judge, 'not of the Divorce Division', who accepted cases of Irish petitioners claiming English domicile 'for a certain time' (ibid., vol. 3, p. 426).

case to court in 1922. He claimed to live in Surrey, but his wife's affidavit maintained Irish residency and averred that he made no attempt to establish a home for her in England after they married in 1918. This was accepted; the divorce petition was dismissed with costs.[16] Violet McBride (née Haines) married in London in 1905, but from 'almost the first day of the marriage' her husband was alleged to be 'indifferent to his wife's society; he often left her for days, and sometimes for weeks'. They cohabited in London until 1908 'when he told her he would not continue to live with her [and] . . . took her in a cab to her mother's house and left her on the doorstep. He did not give her any money since, and she had not seen him from that time.' In 1910, she petitioned the divorce court on the grounds of 'misconduct and desertion'. However, her husband raised the question of his Irish domicile which she shared as a married woman. This was fatal; the petition was dismissed from court, but she successfully divorced in Parliament in 1913.[17]

Aristocratic titles were also deceptive. Lady Kathleen Drogheda, for example, divorced Lord Drogheda, the Right Hon. C. Ponsonby of Co. Kildare, in court on the grounds of desertion, adultery and non-compliance with an order for restitution of conjugal rights in 1922:

The Court might think a question of domicile might arise, it being an Irish title, but in fact the permanent home had been in London. The connection with Ireland was at Moore Park, which the parties had vested, but that was the only connection. The Earl had been unable to get rid of it because it was entailed.

Married in 1909, then after two children were born, Lady Drogheda was deserted in 1920. Referring to the restitution order, her spouse wrote, 'Nothing will induce me to comply with the order, and if at any time you desire to divorce me I think you will . . . [find] all the evidence you require at the Great Central Hotel.' This letter was presented as evidence in court and Lady Drogheda was granted the decree with costs and given custody.[18] Some non-titled Irish petitioners were also legitimately heard in court. Eileen Margaret Barbour of Londonderry, for instance, divorced her husband in court in 1920. They married in 1908; her husband was in the army Medical Service and served in India where they were 'not very happy . . . he neglected her . . . [and] drank heavily every day'. She was adulterous in 1911, but they reconciled until he committed adultery. His refusal to comply with a restitution of conjugal rights order led his wife to divorce. With adultery on both sides, the judge deemed it 'a very bad case' as Eileen Barbour 'violated her marriage vows. It was not like a poor

[16] *Irish Times*, 14 June 1922.   [17] PA, HL/PO/PB/1/1913/3&4G54.
[18] *Irish Times*, 23 November 1921.

woman who went wrong for the sake of food and shelter. . . . A woman who did this sort of thing did not deserve much sympathy', but, as English residency was proven, a *decree nisi* was granted.[19] Frederick Clarke, a staff sergeant in the Field Artillery stationed in Kilkenny, also divorced his wife, Mary, in court in the midst of the Irish War of Independence in 1921. Married 1912, they lived in Londonderry and two children were born, but Clarke, like many military petitioners, brought the case on the basis of wifely misconduct whilst he served abroad. Clarke defended his use of the court: '[H]e had been unable to go the Registry at Londonderry because of the military fearing that he would be shot, as William Street was the heart of Sinn Fein in Derry. They would not "guarantee" him beyond Belfast.' A *decree nisi* was granted which further indicated a degree of compassion for Irish petitioners.[20]

As Joyce reflected with Leopold Bloom's consideration of a court-based divorce in *Ulysses*, although domicile was more stringently tested, Irish cases were presented to the divorce court with increased regularity in the early twentieth century.[21] This mirrored an overall rise in court-based divorces. With an estimated 1,500–2,000 cases presented in one court sitting in 1919, the *Irish Times*'s headline of 'A Divorce Mill' was not unwarranted. This also revealed the paper's partiality; although 'a sad comment on the morality of the times . . . at least the Court will perform its work efficiently and carefully, and that in the vast majority of cases justice will be done'.[22] Yet, Irish use of the divorce court never guaranteed success. The Beauclerks' 'remarkable Irish Divorce Suit', referred to by Sir Charles Russell, QC, as 'one of the saddest and most cruel cases', was heard in court in 1890. Evelyn Beauclerk of Ardglass Castle, Co. Down and London attempted to divorce her husband, Aubrey, on the grounds of cruelty and adultery. Married at age seventeen in 1858, Evelyn soon remonstrated with her spouse 'in consequence of his familiarity with women'. She was 'very much shocked' by his 'flaunting before her his amours, and . . . giving another person the name of his wife . . . her health gave way'. An 1870 separation deed, much encouraged by her father, gave her custody of their son and £1,000 per annum. She subsequently lived apart from her spouse. Delaying divorce proceedings until her son

[19] Ibid., 30 November 1920.

[20] Ibid., 24 February 1921. See also the case of Kathleen Farley who divorced James Farley for desertion and adultery in court in 1921. Married in 1908 and with two children, they lived in Clonmel, but she was deserted in 1916 and evidence of his adultery was presented. No defence was proffered and a *decree nisi* was granted with costs (ibid., 8 March 1921).

[21] Bloom, concerned by condonation and publicity, decided against this course of action. See Peter Kuch, *Irish divorce/Joyce's* Ulysses (Basingstoke, 2017).

[22] *Irish Times*, 7 October 1919 and 4 April 1921.

came of age as well as not 'the slightest molestation by the husband' whist they lived separately for two decades prejudiced Evelyn Beauclerk's case. Although undefended, an additional court hearing was needed to determine whether cruelty could be proven. Cases such as Kelly versus Rev. Kelly where a separation was granted on the ground of non-violent cruelty in 1869 were cited and the court heard that 'her husband's conduct had nearly killed her' and was premeditated to exacerbate her health problems, but this was insufficient to meet the still partial definition of cruelty within marriage; only a separation was granted.[23]

Boasts like that made by Lord Braye in the House of Lords that 'even the enemies of Ireland are bound to confess that the purity of the Irish race is one of the lights of the world' are abrogated by the increasing number of Irish petitioners divorcing in both Parliament and court by the early twentieth century.[24] However, divorce only provided a means of escape from an unhappy or abusive union for a minority. Countless numbers of people could ill afford, either financially or morally, to pursue a divorce. Many more lacked the legal grounds to divorce. Although remarriage provided the best chance of social rehabilitation, second unions of the aristocratic and wealthy were often less prestigious than their first marriage. Moreover, those who divorced, especially women, could still be stigmatised. Irish nationalist Maud Gonne divorcing John McBride, after three years of marriage in 1906, certainly worried about its political fallout. A resolution calling for her resignation from the presidency of the female nationalist association Daughters of Ireland (*Inghinidhe na hÉireann*) was defeated, but the attempt illustrated the engrained moral conservatism which endured. As a 1920 resolution from the Mothers' Union of Down, Connor and Dromore averred, the publicity of divorce trials was 'degrading ... especially on the young' as it familiarised them with divorce.[25] Catholic and Protestant clerics also remained critical of divorce: the 'Problems of Divorce' provided the topic for Rev. R. H. Murray's address to the Anglican Magdalen Church in Dublin in the same year,[26] whilst Rev. M. A. Garrahy's 1922 Lenten lecture in St Frances Xavier Church, Dublin, on 'Idolatry in the Mire' noted a now familiar association: 'The increase in the facilities for divorce was an

[23] Ibid., 1 and 19 November 1890. Evelyn Beauclerk (née Fitzroy) was from Northamptonshire gentry stock and a sister of the Duchess of Rosslyn. The Kelly versus Rev. Kelly case is discussed in Chapter 5.
[24] House of Lords debates, 28 April 1921, vol. 45, col. 84. Braye refuted the idea that an Irish divorce court could ever be established in Ireland.
[25] *Irish Times*, 24 April 1920. This was in reaction to Lord Buckmaster's Matrimonial Causes Bill then before Parliament. The Mothers' Union was established in England in 1885. Initially an Anglican body, it later extended membership to baptised women.
[26] Ibid., 19 September 1920.

outstanding contribution to the evidence which indicated a moral degeneration.'[27] However, few envisaged that Irish divorce law provision could further diversify. With the partition of Ireland in 1920 and the creation of Northern Ireland and the Irish Free State in 1921 and 1922, respectively, the practice of parliamentary divorce ceased at Westminster. Its jurisdiction was transferred to the new parliament of Northern Ireland, but this was not reciprocated in the Irish Free State where the non-availability of divorce came to symbolise the alleged purity of the newly independent state.

[27] Ibid., 4 April 1922.

7 'An Exotic in Very Ungenial Soil': Divorce in the Northern Ireland Parliament, 1921–1939

The history of Irish divorce highlights that the Act of Union did not guarantee legislative uniformity. The partition of Ireland further diversified divorce provision and saw debates on its existence become highly politicised. Its non-availability in the Irish Free State was often cited as evidence of a disregard of minority rights and a barrier to the reunification of Ireland. In Northern Ireland, the parliamentary system of divorce, replete with the shortcomings of Westminster's practice, was introduced as a stopgap measure in 1925. Inherent conservatism and the long-lived reluctance to debate an issue with the potential to deepen the religious divide meant that this system survived in Northern Ireland until 1939. However, divorce remained controversial in the rest of the United Kingdom at least until the 1930s; in consequence, there was often much commonalty in the debates that accompanied divorce reform, particularly with regards to familial stability and financial and property rights.[1]

The 1918 Matrimonial Causes Bill proposed that divorce be made available after three years of marriage in England. Ireland was again excluded, but the bill still met a spikey cross-denominational reception: '[A]lthough it does not apply to Ireland, it obviously affects this country in various ways. Nations like individuals cannot live to themselves.'[2] The Belfast-based Methodist *Christian Advocate*'s response embodied the various tropes which characterised much of the opposition to divorce reform in Ireland throughout the twentieth century: this was proclaimed 'easy divorce' which might increase 'immorality and crime' and 'a dangerous and unscriptural measure', endangering the family and heightening the likelihood of state dependency for the progeny of divorcees. Charles D'Arcy, Anglican bishop of Down, Connor and Dromore expressed his 'fear' of the resultant moral contagion in the *Eugenic Review*. The choice of periodical was explained by D'Arcy's association of divorce with

---

Quote in chapter title comes from Campbell, NI Commons debates, 2 May 1939, vol. 22, cols. 1250–5.

[1] Cretney, *Family law*, pp. lix–lxi.
[2] *Christian Advocate*, 22 March 1918. This journal was published in Belfast from 1883.

societal rates of childbearing; allowing divorce within three years of marriage might increase the number of children born in second unions of 'lower types'. This was juxtaposed to the higher classes who were supposedly aware that marriage could be a 'trial trip ... [and] will most certainly try to avoid the responsibilities and complications of parenthood'.[3] Further debate was, however, stymied as both Northern Ireland and the Irish Free State inherited the embittered politics of the pre-partition era. Security and the establishment of state apparatus, often to the detriment of their respective religious minorities, were the over-riding concerns. Divorce's divisive reputation also meant that neither jurisdiction would engage with the topic until forced to do so. In Northern Ireland, this came in 1925 with the first divorce bill presented to Westminster since partition. The law lords' decision that it should be heard in the Northern Irish parliament ignited the divorce debate.[4]

Standing Orders of the Northern Ireland House of Commons and Senate were included in the 1921 regulations for local bills: divorce petitions were limited to those of Northern Irish domicile and the process was closely modelled on Westminster's. A divorce bill would be read twice in the House of Commons and then proceed to the Northern Ireland Senate for a first and second reading before being heard by the Joint Committee on Divorce Bills. With no Northern Irish equivalent to Westminster's law lords, this committee was appointed at the start of each parliamentary session. Chaired by the Senate's speaker, it was composed of four members of the House of Commons and three members of the Senate who were appointed by their respective houses. The joint committee's consideration was the hearing of the case. It heard evidence and the petitioner could be cross-examined primarily to determine collusion or any other legal action such as a criminal conversation suit. The committee then reported to both houses, stating whether the bill should pass and if amendment was required before its third reading. An amended bill would lie on the table of the House of Commons or Senate for three days.[5] If unamended, it would be read for a third time in the House of Commons and then passed to the Senate. Again, if a bill was amended by either the committee or the Commons at this stage, it would lie on the table of the Senate for three days before being read for a third time in that house.

The fees charged by the Northern Irish parliament averaged £45 in the 1920s, which amounted to considerably less financial outlay than

[3] Charles D'Arcy, *The Eugenic Review*, vol. 10, no. 1 (April 1918), p. 44.
[4] NI Commons debates, 16 May 1925, vol. 6, cols. 495–7.
[5] *Standing Orders of the Parliament of Northern Ireland Senate and the House of Commons relative to the bringing in and proceedings on local bills* ... (Belfast, 1926) (NI Assembly Library, Belfast [hereafter NIAL]), pp. 51–3.

Westminster's house fees which were in excess of £100.[6] Travelling to the parliament in Belfast was also less costly than bringing witnesses and counsel to Westminster, but there was no discussion of the impact this might have on the number of petitioners. The unease which divorce earlier aroused, however, was evident in leader of the Senate Lord Londonderry's introduction of these standing orders in 1925. Stressing that the responsibility of the devolved parliament was not to reform divorce law but to provide continuity in provision, his dislike of the parliamentary process was manifest: 'It is not for me … now to pass judgement upon a system which kept the method of dealing with matrimonial causes in Ireland in a fashion so antiquated and comparatively so costly, a fashion which had long been abandoned elsewhere throughout the British Empire.'[7]

Londonderry also offered reassurance on the differences between the composition of the Northern Irish Standing Committee and Westminster's law lords: as a divorce bill would be preceded by a court separation, 'matters of the law will already have been threshed out between the parties and the decision for or against the Bill will probably rest upon the proof of facts alone'.[8] This prompted three senators, all members of the legal profession, to appeal for divorce to be a court-based process in the new state. James Leslie, for example, emphasised that the parliamentary process should only be a temporary expedient: '[B]ecause I am sure that we should all prefer that these unfortunate matters should be dealt with by our Courts of Justice.' Although the standing committee would be assisted by the Examiner of Affidavits or counsel, Thomas Greer was similarly convinced that court was a more appropriate venue: 'There is no reason why parties should have to come here with a Bill to get a complete divorce, and I do not think a Committee of the kind suggested is a very good body for considering the matter.'[9]

Despite reservations, the transfer of divorce to the Northern Ireland parliament sparked no sustained debate. Londonderry's Senate manoeuvrings deftly avoided the question of morality, and solace was sought in the belief that demand for divorce would be limited: 'Of course, in this country, for reasons that we cannot explain, we have not as much business of this kind as they have in England and therefore the matter is not of such great importance.'[10] Thus, the notion that parliamentary divorce in

---

[6] Ibid., p. 56.   [7] NI Senate debates, 14 May 1925, cols. 115–18.

[8] Ibid., cols. 118–20.

[9] Greer moved a successful amendment to allow respondents living outside Northern Ireland sufficient time to respond to a divorce bill (NI Senate debates, 14 May 1925, cols. 121–2). Senator Henry Armstrong also supported court-based divorce.

[10] Ibid.

Northern Ireland, as in Westminster, would remain the preserve of those of 'sufficient finances and influences' prevailed and was intimated by the Northern Ireland Office of Law Reform as late as the 1990s.[11] However, a case analysis of divorce bills heard by the Northern Ireland parliament challenges such an assertion.

The first divorce bill was introduced to the Northern Ireland parliament in 1925. Isabella Wright (née Weir), a farmer's daughter from Armagh and of 'rather humble circumstances', married John Wright at Riverstown Catholic Church, Co. Sligo, in 1913 before moving to Portadown, Co. Armagh.[12] They had one daughter in 1915, but Isabella claimed 'great unkindness and cruelty' on her husband's part: 'he frequently in gross and filthy language abused [her], . . . swore at and beat her and struck her and wounded her; and in divers [sic] other ways has been guilty of cruelty – in the legal sense of the term'. Her mental and physical health was seriously affected. In 1914, she 'was forced' to leave her spouse, spending a short time in Canada before returning to him in November where she remained until 1919. She then left permanently and had no communication with her husband from 1921. In 1924, she separated in the King's Bench Division of the Northern Ireland High Court on the grounds of adultery and cruelty.[13] The divorce bill extended these grounds to include desertion in a successful attempt to counter any charge of condonation caused by the earlier reconciliation. John Wright's triumvirate of misdemeanours thus 'dissolved the bonds of matrimony on his part' and his wife would be 'deprived of the comforts of [future] matrimony unless the said marriage be declared void and annulled by Act of Parliament'. John Wright was to pay his ex-wife £3 weekly as well as the costs of the bill – £170, including £49 in house fees, equivalent to £9,829 today, the highest in the history of divorce in the Northern Ireland parliament. The bill passed without amendment and received royal assent in November.[14]

The Westminster inheritance was ever apparent in this and other Northern Irish divorce bills. Clauses to prevent the marriage of the adulterous parties were routinely struck out by Westminster from 1809 unless such a union would be within the banned degrees of affinity.[15] That the Northern Ireland parliament willingly maintained a defunct practice aimed at punishing an adulterous spouse underscores its timidity

---

[11] *Divorce in Northern Ireland. A better way forward. A consultation paper from the [NI] Office of Law Reform* (1 December 1999), p. 15.
[12] Fees on private bills, 1925–50 (PRONI, FIN/18/6/53).
[13] Jurisdiction of the Court for Matrimonial Causes was transferred to the High Court by the Courts of Justice Act, 1924.
[14] Wright's Divorce Act (1925) (NIAL).   [15] Roberts, *Divorce Bills*, p. 35.

to waver from Westminster's practices. In Wright's bill, the matrimony of her husband and the 'female unknown' with whom he committed adultery was therefore 'declared to be illegal and void'. Moreover, any children resulting from such a union 'shall be illegitimate and subject to all disabilities[,] privations and restrictions to which any child or children born out of lawful wedlock is or may be subject by the laws and customs of the United Kingdom'.[16] This interdiction of remarriage was more a female than a male preserve in the Northern Ireland parliament. An additional four female petitioners included similar bans and sometimes named the 'other' woman, but these clauses were routinely removed from the final bills. Only one man tried to prevent such a union taking place: Hubert Hunter's 1933 bill included an identical proviso which met the same fate as that of female petitioners; it was amended by the joint committee.[17]

From Wright's act in 1925 until 1939, the Northern Ireland parliament heard sixty-three divorce acts. The wholesale passage of these acts confirmed what Londonderry earlier inferred: as parliamentary divorce customarily followed a court-based separation, there should be few legal impediments to divorce. The suggestion that divorce would be uncommon is, however, harder to sustain. A clear increase in demand was discernible in the 1930s; fifty acts were passed in this decade, comprising 85 per cent of all divorce acts in the Northern Ireland parliament The annual figures peaked in 1933 when nine divorces received royal assent, surpassing the highest annual number of Irish divorce bills passed by Westminster in 1920. A case analysis also allows a geographical and gender profile of those divorcing in the early years of the Northern Ireland state to be drawn. The majority of petitioners were Belfast-based, comprising 57 per cent of the total; 11 per cent were from Co. Down; 10 per cent from Co. Antrim; 5 per cent from Co. Fermanagh; 5 per cent from Co. Londonderry; 2 per cent from Co. Armagh. Eight per cent listed English addresses, an additional 2 per cent cited Scotland and one petitioner was resident in Ceylon. The gender profile is similarly distinct: women brought 54 per cent of bills. In the 1920s, women brought half of the ten bills introduced, but in the 1930s, women brought thirty bills, representing 57 per cent of all divorce bills introduced in this decade; 46 per cent of all divorce bills brought by women to the Northern Irish parliament were on the grounds of adultery and cruelty which continued the emergent pattern in Westminster after Westropp's 1886

[16] Wright's Divorce Act (1925) (NIAL).
[17] Elizabeth Lemon's Divorce Bill (1927); Christabel Macartney's Divorce Bill (1931); Josephine McCleane's Divorce Bill (1931); Margaret Robinson's Divorce Bill (1931) and Hunter's Divorce Bill (1933) (NIAL).

act. Twenty-six per cent of women brought bills for adultery and desertion and 9 per cent mirrored that of Isabella Wright, being brought on the
triplicate grounds of adultery, cruelty and desertion.

The grounds for divorce in Northern Ireland were subject to change.
Like much of the state's early legal apparatus and impetus for reform, this
was routinely inspired by Westminster. The 1923 Matrimonial Causes
Act equalised the grounds for divorce in court and application of the
Westropp principle extended this reform to the Northern Ireland
parliament.[18] It took some time for this to be realised, but from
Margaret Robinson's 1931 bill, women began to divorce their spouses
solely on the previously male preserve of spousal adultery: 20 per cent of
all female petitioners subsequently brought bills to the Northern Ireland
parliament on this ground. Marrying in Belfast in 1907, Margaret
Robinson's husband was adulterous in 1930; she separated in
January 1931 and divorced in December of the same year.[19] May
Barbour of Belfast also divorced on this sole ground after seven years of
marriage in 1936. The couple separated in 1935 and the divorce bill
stated that 'the bond of matrimony ... [was] violated and broken by ...
manifest and open adultery'. Married in 1914, Dulcie McClure similarly
divorced due to her husband's adultery in 1938 even though she separated because of adultery and cruelty which she endured for more than
a decade when her husband 'declined to speak to her and ... recognise her
as the mistress of his household, and has otherwise neglected and ill-
treated' her. This evidences the continued female disinclination to publicly discuss cruelty.[20]

Other women, such as Elizabeth Lemon from Middlesex who divorced
her spouse and first cousin in 1927, continued to bring bills on the
grounds of aggravated adultery, most commonly cruelty or desertion.
Dependent domicile also meant that Lemon had to divorce in the
Northern Ireland parliament rather than court. Adultery and cruelty,
causing 'danger and injury' to her health by 'systematic insults before
servants and guests, which ... amounted to a course of terrorism' as well
as a lack of financial provision since their marriage in 1902, provided the

---

[18] A confidential draft of the 1939 NI Matrimonial Causes Bill recorded that the 'habit' and
'practice of the Northern Ireland Parliament has been to pass Divorce Bills on the same
grounds for divorce as those which were statutory in England under 1857 and the
amending Act of 1923' (Confidential notes on clauses of the draft of the Matrimonial
Causes Bill [NI], October 1938 [PRONI, CAB4/403/24], pp. 3–4). For a confidential
draft of the bill, see PRONI, CAB4/403/25.

[19] Robinson's Divorce Act (1931) (NIAL).

[20] Barbour's Divorce Act (1936); McClure's Divorce Act (1938). See also the divorces of
Mabel McMullan (1938) and Margaret McGugan, Mary Plumb and Isabel Stuart
(1939) (NIAL). Stuart brought the last divorce bill to the Northern Ireland parliament

basis of her bill.[21] She was only supported by a small parental allowance with the exception of seven weeks in 1916 when she received a separation allowance of 24 shillings per week when her husband was a private in the Royal Army Service Corps. Lemon had not seen her husband since 1918 and was consequently unable to separate, but her divorce bill passed.[22]

Lemon's endurance of abuse was commonplace. Josephine McCleane of Belfast, divorcing in 1931, was 'treated with great unkindness and cruelty … he frequently in gross and filthy language abused [her] … and beat and struck her and wounded her; and in divers [sic] other ways he had been guilty of cruelty'.[23] Measuring the impact of such cruelty on a woman's mental and physical well-being remained paramount to the select committee. May McMeekin, for example, experienced domestic violence soon after her marriage in 1923. Her spouse 'frequently gave way to outbursts of bad temper under the influence of drink and insulted and frightened' her. In 1929, after objecting to the way he spoke to her, she was

struck … with his clenched fist a violent blow on the jaw, knocking her down … he rushed at her and caught her by the throat and threatened to break her 'bloody neck,' and pushed her out of the house … being in fear of her life [she] was compelled to remain outdoors for some time but succeeded in getting back into the house through the window of the morning room.

Further abuse led a maid to intervene by 'pulling him away' from his wife's neck. The bill also noted a possible case of syphilis which Ivan McMeekin 'blamed … on a girl with whom he had been going about'. May McMeekin left her husband in 1930 and separated in the same year but delayed divorcing for seven years although whether this was caused by moral or financial considerations, or a combination of both, remains unknown.[24]

Ethel Anderson was similarly subjected to abuse from three months after her marriage in 1915, but she did not divorce until 1931: 'kicked … violently out of bed and then struck and brutally assaulted' with three attempted strangulations, including one when she was pregnant, she was also threatened 'with a stick … locked … in a bedroom' and 'throttled'. Her husband later 'assaulted and threatened' her in front of their son, 'brandishing a large stick over him in such a threatening manner that

---

[21] *Irish Times*, 15 January 1927.   [22] Lemon's Divorce Act (1927) (NIAL).
[23] McCleane's Divorce Act (1931) (NIAL).
[24] McMeekin's Divorce Act (1937) (NIAL). The breakdown of Elizabeth Huddleston's marriage was also caused by her husband's adultery and cruelty which included being 'forced … to work for his support and her own when she was unfit to do so and whilst he remained idle'. This affected her health and caused 'pain both mentally and physically' (Huddleston's Divorce Act [1937] [NIAL]).

[she] ... feared that her said husband would take the life of the said child'. This was pronounced as 'the upmost violence, brutality and cruelty' causing her to live 'repeatedly in terror and in actual danger of her life in consequence suffered severely in her health'.[25] Christabel Macartney's 1931 bill, brought on the same grounds, also detailed serious abuse. Frequently subjected to 'great unkindness ... gross and filthy language ... beat and struck ... and wounded ... violently assaulted'. When threatened with a gun she 'went in fear of her life and her health became greatly impaired both in mind and body'. In 1924, her husband was 'so violent and abusive ... threatening to kill her that she was compelled to leave the house in charge of her Doctor'; she subsequently resided with her mother. Her husband also contracted an unspecified but 'loathsome venereal disease' in their first year of marriage in 1922 which he 'wilfully and recklessly' transmitted to his wife. She required medical treatment but was not informed by the doctors of the nature of the condition until separating in 1930.[26]

By comparison, men only needed to prove a wife's adultery to end a marital union. William McCaldin of Banbridge, Co. Down thus claimed to have been 'deprived of the comforts of matrimony' and was 'liable to have spurious issue imposed upon him' unless a divorce was granted from his adulterous spouse in 1926.[27] However, some male petitioners began to enter additional grounds like desertion to more accurately record the level and cause of marital discord after the English grounds for divorce were equalised in 1923. The only overseas petitioner to the Northern Ireland parliament, Alexander Egan of Colombo in Ceylon, for instance, divorced his wife on the grounds of adultery and desertion in 1928. Egan could petition parliament as prior and subsequent to his marriage in 1918 and at the time of the divorce petition he was domiciled in Ireland.[28] Determining domicile in other cases was more complex: Edith Rankin of Belfast petitioned for divorce in 1929 on the basis of her husband's adultery and cruelty. At the time of her marriage to Leslie Rankin in 1912, her spouse was domiciled in Northern Ireland, but he subsequently lived in Montreal, Toronto, the United States, Liverpool and London. Edith Rankin attempted to separate in the Northern Ireland High Court in 1928 and 1929. Whilst the grounds

---

[25] Ethel Anderson also brought the bill on grounds of adultery and desertion from 1917 (Anderson's Divorce Act [1931] [NIAL]).

[26] Macartney's Divorce Act (1931) (NIAL).

[27] McCaldin's Divorce Act (1926) (NIAL).

[28] Egan's Divorce Act (1928) (NIAL). See also Timbey's Divorce Act (1929); McNulty's Divorce Act (1930); Clarke's Divorce Act (1932) and McAllen's Divorce Act (1937) (NIAL) where husbands brought bills on the grounds of adultery and desertion.

for adultery and cruelty were undisputed, her domicile was questioned. Born in Belfast and residing there until the age of thirty, Leslie Rankin left in 1910 prior to the Government of Ireland Act of 1920 and, as the Lord Chief Justice found in 1929, there 'was no evidence that he had ever acquired a domicile of choice'. The separation was adjourned and Edith Rankin was advised to apply to parliament: a divorce bill, presented in 1929, subsequently passed.[29] Others were unsuccessful: the Northern Ireland Court of Appeal in 1937, for example, refused to recognise Lyons' US divorce as the parties were not domiciled in Northern Ireland.

Condonation remained another key consideration. Proving this as a bar to divorce was previously taxing in Westminster, particularly for female petitioners who were popularly encouraged to forgive errant spouses. In the Northern Ireland parliament there were, however, several examples of leniency which replicated Westminster and the divorce court's sympathy for Irish petitioners. Mary Patterson's bill saw her condone several acts of adultery on the part of her spouse committed three years after their marriage in 1917. Further adultery in 1928, coupled with long-standing cruelty from 1920 to 1928, culminating when she was beaten 'on the head and turned ... out of the house', saw her permanently flee the marital home in 1928 and she secured a parliamentary divorce in the following year.[30] Other women also divorced after forgiving an errant or abusive spouse several times. Housekeeper Phoebe Gibson married in 1899 but was deserted by her husband in 1921 when he left for the United States with another woman. He returned to Northern Ireland in 1922 and lived variously with this woman and his wife as the latter was report-edly 'very fond of her husband'. In 1922, against his wife's wishes, he left for a final time: she separated in 1930 and divorced in the following year.[31] Condonation thus waned as a bar to divorce and the Northern Ireland parliament remained confident that if a separation was granted, or an explanation proffered for its absence, divorce should be automatic.

Demands for a criminal conversation suit also lessened, although it only became defunct in the late 1930s. As in Westminster, application of the Westropp precedent explains this shift. Criminal conversation suits were therefore brought in some but not all Northern Irish parliamentary divorces. Richard Dobbs brought a criminal conversation action in the

---

[29] Rankin's Divorce Act (1929) (NIAL).
[30] Patterson's Divorce Act (1929) and see also Rankin's Divorce Act (1929) (NIAL).
[31] Phoebe Gibson worked as a cook 'to support herself'. Her husband initially sent her £1 per week which he later reduced to 10 shillings (Gibson's Divorce Act [1931] [NIAL]).

Northern Ireland High Court in 1930, for example, and secured £350 damages; he divorced in 1931.[32] Francis Clarke took the same action in 1931, receiving £250 damages before divorcing in the following year and Robert Hall received £500 in damages in 1932 and divorced in the same year.[33] Replicating the trend evident in Westminster, the scale of damages diminished. There are no Northern Irish examples of the very sizeable damages of the preceding century which infers a growing abhorrence to the criminal conversation suit; Thomas Trew was only awarded £50 in his 1934 action.[34] Others who, by virtue of social rank, might have been expected to levy substantial claims, did not pursue damages. The Rt Hon. John Cole, Earl of Enniskillen, divorced his wife, Irene, in 1932 on the ground of adultery. Married in 1907, she was adulterous in 1931, but the lack of a criminal conversation suit in this case was not morally grounded or an expression of kindness towards an errant wife; the whereabouts of the paramour were unknown.

Financial considerations regarding the means of a wife's lover to pay damages were an additional deterrent. Joseph Anderson, divorcing in 1934, was unable to bring a criminal conversation case as his wife's paramour was in the Irish Free State Army and 'without means to pay damages or costs in the event of a verdict being obtained against him'. Anderson separated in 1933, a decade after he uncovered his wife's infidelity, with the delay explained by his 'ill-health, unemployment and poverty'.[35] Similar concerns prevented both John Agnew and Hugh Armstrong from bringing criminal conversation suits. Armstrong divorced in 1936 and Agnew followed in the next year, declining to bring a suit against his wife's lover, a 'Labourer without means to pay damages or costs'.[36] This was the last mention of a criminal conversation suit in the Northern Ireland parliament and provides more evidence of an application of the 'wide policy' favoured in the English court system. To do otherwise would impose 'a hardship and a limitation' on Northern Irish divorce petitioners which they 'would not be liable to if the Government of Ireland Act, 1920, had not passed' and would refute one of its key principles which stated that 'no person should suffer by reason of the Act'. It was therefore deemed just that the rights of divorce available in the English court should be available in the northern parliament.[37]

---

[32] Dobb's Divorce Act (1931) (NIAL).
[33] Clarke's Divorce Act (1932) and Hall's Divorce Act (1932) (NIAL).
[34] Trew's Divorce Act (1936) (NIAL).   [35] Anderson's Divorce Act (1934) (NIAL).
[36] Agnew's Divorce Act (1936) and Armstrong's Divorce Act (1932) (NIAL).
[37] Memorandum of the Minister of Home Affairs on Divorce Programme in NI, 15 May 1931 (PRONI, CAB 4/284/19).

The earlier reliance on criminal conversation damages to finance divorce and the delay in bringing divorce bills to parliament due to financial constraints intimates a varied social profile. Divorcees' occupations also counter the oft-proclaimed notion that parliamentary divorce remained a wealthy preserve.[38] Male occupations ranged from horse dealer David McCaldin (1925) to Constantinople commission agent Thomas Gray (1937) and labourer David Marks (1938). Military occupations were listed for three men with rank varying from lieutenant colonel Richard Dobbs (1931); private John Lemon, who was also a linen merchant (1926); to naval staff instructor James Boyle (1929). Skilled tradesmen such as crane man James Harper (divorcing in 1931), plumber Samuel Morrison and fitter Hugh Armstrong (both divorcing in 1937) brought bills alongside professionals like insurance broker John Sumner (1933), journalist Joseph Anderson (1934) and engineer Hector McAllen (1938). By comparison, the occupation of Northern Irish female petitioners was rarely recorded, but where known it reveals a comparable middle- and working-class complexion: Phoebe Gibson, divorcing in 1931, worked as a cook and housekeeper following her engineer spouse's desertion; Annie Adair, divorcing in 1937, was a hotel owner in Bangor, Co. Down and Elizabeth Huddleston was a laundress in Vancouver at the time of her 1937 divorce.

This discrepancy from the higher social profile of many Westminster divorces was due to cost. Although the parliamentary procedure for divorce in Northern Ireland was modelled closely on Westminster, bills were subject to less delay in a smaller, devolved assembly and could often be dealt with in three to four days, whereas in Westminster the process could take weeks and sometimes months. As fees for private bills were charged at a daily rate, the cost of securing a parliamentary divorce in Northern Ireland was lower than in Westminster. The possibility of further reducing the northern parliament's fees from an average of c. £45 to c. £13 evoked some support in 1929 and further countered the association between the higher classes and divorce. Labour MP Samuel Beattie, for instance, supported the reduction as those seeking divorce were 'the poorer class people'[39] but nationalist MP Cahir Healy averred, 'Surely no Christian, no matter on what side of the House he may sit, wants to make divorce so cheap that it will put temptation in the way of people . . . that is what you are going to do.'[40] Despite Healy's protests, the

---

[38] This is derived from divorce bills and the press as the Northern Ireland census of 1926 was destroyed in the Second World War. Northern Ireland was excluded from the 1931 census as less than a decade had passed since the previous census.

[39] Beattie, NI House of Commons debates, 11 December 1929, vol. 11, col. 1853.

[40] Healy, ibid., col. 1962.

lower fee was agreed: the daily rate for the Examiner of Petitions of Local Bills to inquire into a divorce bill's compliance was reduced from £5 to £2.10.0 and counsel fees to appear before the joint committee halved to £5 which explains the rise in the number of divorces in Northern Ireland in the 1930s.[41]

As in Westminster, the husband normally paid the cost of the parliamentary proceeding regardless of whether or not he was the petitioner, but there were exceptions as a more equitable and less gendered approach emerged. In 1938, Hector McAllen divorced his wife on the grounds of adultery and desertion when, after three years of marriage, she migrated to Australia in 1926; she was ordered to pay the costs of the bill. David Marks's spouse met a similar fate in the same year, ordered to pay costs after being divorced on identical grounds.[42] Other women divorcing on these grounds were not charged with costs; in Hubert Hunter's 1933 bill, an attempt to make his wife, Isabella, liable for costs was struck out by the joint committee. Such a move was not restricted to women; Samuel Morrison and James Harper, divorcing their spouses in 1931 and 1933, respectively, were both noted in the bill as responsible for costs, but this was not included in the final divorce acts.[43]

Like occupation, the religion of petitioners was mostly unrecorded in divorce bills. However, the church where the couple married gives an indication of the religious denomination of at least one of the parties. Of the sixty-three Northern Irish divorce petitioners, 10 per cent married by special licence, in a private residence or hotel and in one instance in an unspecified Christian ceremony in India. An additional 10 per cent married in a registry office whilst another married in a Russian Orthodox Church in Constantinople in 1920.[44] Only one Jew divorced in the Northern Ireland parliament: Henry Solomon married in the Jewish Synagogue in Blackpool in 1924 and divorced in 1931.[45] One Congregationalist also divorced: Thomas Trew married in Belfast in 1919 and divorced in 1936.[46] Two petitioners, representing 3 per cent of the total, married in a Methodist Church: Annie Adair married in Bangor in 1913 and divorced on the ground of cruelty in 1937,[47] whilst Alexander Egan married in the Wesleyan Church at Galle, Ceylon, in

---

[41] Fees on private bills, 1925–50 (PRONI, FIN/18/6/53).

[42] McAllen's Divorce Act (1938) and Marks's Divorce Act (1938) (NIAL).

[43] Morrison's Divorce Bill and Act (1931) and Hunter's Divorce Bill and Act (1933) (NIAL).

[44] Ellen Gray's Divorce Act (1937) (NIAL).

[45] Solomon's Divorce Act (1931) (NIAL).

[46] Trew's Divorce Act (1936) (NIAL). The Congregationalist Church is in the reformed tradition of Protestantism.

[47] Adair's Divorce Act (1937) (NIAL).

1918 and divorced in 1928.[48] Three per cent of petitioners married in a Catholic ceremony including the first petitioner to the Northern Irish parliament in 1925, Isabella Wright. John McNulty of Belfast married in a Catholic Church in Middlesex in 1920 but only resided with his wife for two weeks and the marriage remained unconsummated. He could therefore have sought an annulment but divorced on the grounds of adultery and desertion in 1930.[49] Twenty-one per cent of petitioners were married in Presbyterian ceremonies[50] but the largest proportion of petitioners (48 per cent) were Anglican. The latter was the only denomination whose divorce rate exceeded its demographic representation and continued a trend evident from the eighteenth century.[51] Although this profile was underpinned by the higher social status of many Anglicans, the 1908 ruling of the Lambeth conference that innocent divorced parties could receive communion after a civil marriage began to lessen the stigmatisation of divorcees in at least one denomination.[52]

The longevity of marital unions prior to divorce was variable for Northern Irish petitioners. A disagreement 'about a week or nine days' after marrying in 1929 led Ellen McGeagh to return to live with her mother. That marriage produced a child, born in 1930, but McGeagh separated from his wife in 1936 on the grounds of adultery and divorced in the following year.[53] However, the shortest time between a marriage and divorce in the Northern Irish parliament was four years; Annette Gilfillan divorced on the grounds of adultery and desertion in 1937. More commonplace was the longevity of many unions. Many couples were married for decades before instituting divorce proceedings: the average length of a marriage before divorce in the Northern Irish parliament was fourteen and a half years. Phoebe Gibson's thirty-two-year marriage was the longest union of the Northern Irish parliamentary divorce petitioners. The marital dislocation, rushed unions and six-fold increase in English

---

[48] Egan's Divorce Act (1928) (NIAL); 3.9 per cent of Northern Ireland's population was Methodist in 1926 (*Irish Times*, 14 June 1929).

[49] McNulty's Divorce Act (1930) (NIAL); 33.5 per cent of Northern Ireland's population was Catholic in 1926 (*Irish Times*, 14 June 1929).

[50] See, for example, Taylor's Divorce Act (1933); Morrison's Divorce Act (1933); Hunter's Divorce Act (1933); Annette Gilfillan's Divorce Act (1937); Marks's Divorce Act (1938) and Mabel McMullan's Divorce Act (1938) (NIAL); 31 per cent of Northern Ireland's population was Presbyterian in 1926 (*Irish Times*, 14 June 1929).

[51] See, for example, Anderson's Divorce Act (1931); Gibson's Divorce Act (1931); Perry's Divorce Act (1933); Irene Richard's Divorce Act (1933); Gilbert's Divorce Act (1934) and Fanny McWilliams's Divorce Act (1935) (NIAL); 27 per cent of Northern Ireland's population was Anglican in 1926 (*Irish Times*, 14 June 1929).

[52] This decennial assembly of bishops from the worldwide Anglican Communion first met in 1867. Anglicans accepted adultery as a ground for divorce but did not accept remarriage in church at the juncture.

[53] McGeagh's Divorce Act (1937) (NIAL).

divorce rates seen during the First World War and its aftermath was not reflected in the Northern Irish divorce figures. Wartime marriages, such as that of Ethel Anderson who married in 1915, and John Agnew, who married in 1917, lasted sixteen and nineteen years, respectively. Divorce was not entertained lightly even under the strains of war; however, given the severity of cases involving long-term infidelity, desertion and cruelty, many either separated informally or endured years of mental, physical and financial hardship before seeking permanent legal redress. Once that decision was taken, however, most divorced within a year of separating.[54]

Concerns regarding custody also lengthened the duration of many unhappy unions. In Richard Dobb's 1931 divorce, he retained custody of three children. The Earl of Enniskillen did likewise for his four children after divorcing in the following year.[55] Yet, as emerged in Westminster, the welfare of children came to the fore of custody decisions and paternal custody was no longer an inalienable right. For instance, the first divorce bill presented to the parliament of Northern Ireland in 1925 saw petitioner Isabella Wright retain custody of her daughter.[56] For Robert Hall, divorcing in 1932, custody was decided during the earlier separation. His wife's adultery was deemed, under Section 7 of the 1886 Guardianship of Infants Act, to make her 'unfit to have custody' of their two daughters and this was confirmed in the subsequent divorce bill.[57] That bill also tried to secure 'the virtuous education' of the children, away from their mother's allegedly corrupting influence, but the joint committee ruled out such moral castigation. Only the following wording remained in the final act: '[I]t shall not be lawful for the said Geraldine Elsie Hall to remove her ... daughters ... from the care and custody of their father ... during their respective minorities.'[58]

Despite an evolution in attitudes regarding the moral issues encircling divorce and a reduction in cost, not all who wanted to divorce could proceed. Belfast Council for Social Welfare's self-titled Poor Man's Lawyer Department was operative from the 1930s, providing a fortnightly free legal-aid service to those with an income of under

---

[54] Mary McMeekin separated in 1930 and divorced in 1937; William Perry separated in 1922 and divorced in 1933; Clara Henderson separated in 1931 and divorced in 1938 (NIAL).

[55] Dobb's Divorce Act (1931) and Enniskillen's Divorce Act (1932) (NIAL).

[56] The following female divorcees also maintained custody: Mary Burns, divorcing in 1929; Mary Patterson (1929); Edith Priestly (1930); Josephine McCleane (1931); Ethel Anderson (1931); Alicia Sumner (1933). The Sumner case was unsuccessfully brought to appeal in Belfast's Chancery Court in 1935 as John Sumner tried to set aside his ex-wife's deed of settlement.

[57] Section 7 of the act would previously have not applied to Ireland as its courts could not determine custody, but the rest of bill applied from 1886.

[58] Hall's Divorce Bill and Act (1932) (NIAL).

£2 per week or less than £4 joint income. It advised on custody, the grounds and cost of divorce, women's dependent domicile, defending a suit as well as signing divorce papers.[59] The case of C. T. of Belfast was characteristic of many. Married in 1927, she sought advice in 1938 as her spouse was in Canada, but she lacked an address and efforts to find him through the Salvation Army's publication *War Cry* failed. English by birth, C. T. hoped that when the new English divorce bill passed, she could divorce on the grounds of desertion in the English courts but was advised that it was 'Practically impossible to get a divorce anywhere' as she had no domicile independent from that of her spouse.[60] M. M. of Londonderry, who described herself as 'only a poor working woman with one child. It takes me all my time to keep us from poverty', sought advice in 1941. Married in 1929, she only resided with her spouse for a year in consequence of domestic violence: 'beating me or baby . . . the last time he struck me I decided I could not endure him any longer. . . . He lifted the poker and said he was going to finish me.' She had not seen her spouse in a decade but believed he was in England. She was therefore advised to try to locate him and divorce in England.[61] The inability to divorce within three years of marriage was also problematic; many experienced infidelity, desertion and abuse within the first year of marriage, but all the Poor's Man's Lawyer could advise in such cases was patience. It is therefore unsurprising that, in rare instances, people entered bigamous unions. William Perry, divorcing in 1933 after nineteen years of marriage, recorded that his wife was adulterous from 1921. They separated in 1922 but Frances Perry was convicted of bigamy in Belfast in 1932. Pleading guilty, she was imprisoned for nine months.[62]

Although the number of parliamentary divorces increased in Northern Ireland in the 1930s, the cost of divorce remained prohibitive to many. This was compounded as, unlike in the rest of the UK, a poor person's procedure, as the process of in *forma pauperis* enabling those of low income to pursue legal proceedings became known in the twentieth century, was unavailable in Northern Ireland. The poor person's procedure reduced the cost of a divorce to £5 and prohibited solicitors from charging fees or making a profit. Its non-availability in Northern Ireland indicates that Healy's concerns for a more affordable divorce process were more widely held. Elsewhere, the poor person's procedure was

---

[59] It advised on an array of legal issues including property and tenancy, wills, pensions and compensation.
[60] Belfast Council for Social Welfare [hereafter BCSW] file 112B, 29 September 1938 (PRONI, D2806/DE/1). All named have been anonymised to protect identities.
[61] BCSW file 795B, 18 November 1941 (PRONI, D2806/DE/2).
[62] Perry's Divorce Act (1933) (NIAL).

similarly contentious, but not all misgivings were morally based; most Welsh solicitors refused to take poor persons' cases in the 1940s due to the financial implications.[63] Poignantly using under her maiden name, Ethel Keys, writing from Glasgow, contacted Northern Irish premier James Craig in 1937 regarding Northern Ireland's exclusion.[64] This was one of several pleading letters he received from the 1920s, calling for a poor person's procedure and augmented grounds for divorce. Much of the correspondence was highly gendered: women stressed their respectability whilst men invoked the language of civil rights. Keys wanted to remarry 'like a lady. ... I have worked to keep myself. ... I am a good woman and wish to remain as such. ... Surely there is some way out without having to sin from soul to get freedom.'[65] By comparison, William Locke claimed, 'Legislators for the six counties promised to make the laws of Ulster the same as Great Britain ... the Government should start immediately to atone for past neglect.'[66]

Case files of Belfast's Poor Man's Lawyer Department reveal that without a poor person's procedure, many with legitimate grounds for divorce could not proceed. Despite the reduction in house fees, in the mid-1930s Belfast Council for Social Welfare was citing collective costs of £100 for a parliamentary divorce which was beyond the reach of many. This included M. C. of Co. Armagh. Seeking advice in 1939 after thirteen years of marriage, she only lived with her spouse for months: '[H]e never got me a home or supported me or his child[,] he left me to die with hunger.' Like many others, she was advised to wait for the introduction of a cheaper court-based system of divorce.[67] That system was called for from the beginning of the Northern Irish state, but the government of Northern Ireland continued 'to walk very warily where divorce is concerned' due to fears of religious strife with the Catholic, Methodist and Presbyterian Churches and some undoubtedly suffered in consequence.[68]

---

[63] BCSW file 772B, 31 October 1941 (PRONI, D2806/DE/2).

[64] 4 July 1937 (PRONI, PM/2/11/84). Keys left her Belfast spouse after eighteen months of marriage in 1920.

[65] Ibid.   [66] 26 January 1925 (PRONI, HA/8/160).

[67] BCSW file 202, 20 July 1939 (PRONI, D2806/DE/1).

[68] J. Chuter to Rt Hon. Viscount Jowitt, Lord Chancellor, 10 April 1951 (PRONI, HA/8/160).

8   With as 'Little Provocation as Possible': The Northern Ireland Move to Court

The Northern Ireland government liaised with Westminster regarding the removal of divorce from parliament's jurisdiction from 1931, but not all concurred that this was a priority for the state. Richard Dawson Bates, the Northern Ireland minster of home affairs, failed to 'see any serious objections to a continuance of the existing arrangements', suggesting only a 'far distant . . . day' when divorce reform might be required. Bates thus advised that they should proceed along the lines suggested by the attorney general, Anthony Babington, and parliamentary draftsman, Sir Arthur Queckett – amending section 47 of the 1920 Government of Ireland Act to empower the Northern Irish parliament to legislate in all matters within its jurisdiction. Proceeding in this way, as opposed to introducing a divorce bill, was a compromise to minimise 'the criticism and opposition which undoubtedly would be centred upon it in the Imperial Parliament if it referred to the Divorce Laws'. Rankling Westminster and causing tension with the Standing Committee on Divorce, which was calling for the relocation of divorce to court, certainly fostered governmental reticence. Indeed, Bates averred that the Standing Committee 'may resent advice or direction from the Government',[1] but there was also the perennial concern, present before the establishment of the state, that divorce 'will probably stir up a sectarian controversy'.[2]

Northern Irish premier James Craig consequently pressed for the introduction of a miscellaneous provisions bill, but there were fears that this could constitute an *ultra vires* act which was beyond the state's legal authority: 'While our Parliament might be able to give jurisdiction to the Supreme Court as a whole it could not designate the particular Court, Division or Judge by whom the jurisdiction may be exercised.'[3] Therefore, although

---

The quote in the chapter title is from NI Cabinet papers, 15 May 1931 (PRONI, CAB 4/284).

[1] Memorandum of the Minister of Home Affairs on Divorce Programme in NI, 15 May 1931 (PRONI, CAB 4/284/19).

[2] John Moorhead, Chief Crown Solicitor to A. P. Magill, 15 February 1924 (PRONI, HA/8/150).

[3] NI Cabinet papers, 15 May 1931 (PRONI, CAB4/284).

some of the restrictions on the Northern Irish parliament's power over the Supreme Court were removed by the Northern Ireland (Miscellaneous Provisions) Act of 1932, which allowed the Northern Ireland parliament to move its matrimonial jurisdiction to the High Court, a question remained over appeals and informal discussions with the Home Office ensued.[4]

Plans for new law courts in Belfast furthered calls for divorce's relocation in the early 1930s: '[I]t is perfectly ridiculous that unfortunate people [seeking to divorce] have to get a Bill when they ought to have a court of their own to carry through their business.'[5] By 1936, the Bar Council of Northern Ireland, following Brooke and Samuels, criticised the complexity and cost of the parliamentary process which 'in numbers of really shocking cases ... is a complete denial of justice'.[6] A highly selective response from Craig conveniently interpreted their censure as relating to the cost of the proceeding rather than to the system per se and further consideration was postponed.[7] It was only Westminster's revival of divorce law reform that prompted change in Northern Ireland. A. P. Herbert's private bill, passed by Westminster in 1937, added desertion of three years' duration; presumption of a spouse's death; cruelty, although still legislatively undefined; and incurable insanity as sole grounds for divorce. A case would not, however, be heard within three years of marriage unless there was exceptional hardship or depravity. The act thus embraced many of the recommendations of the majority report of the 1912 Royal Commission, but it was still controversial and, like the 1857 act, only passed after considerable pressure was exerted. Its impact was immediately apparent: the English and Welsh rate of divorce nearly doubled in 1938.

Herbert's act initially only encouraged a consideration of the grounds of divorce rather than the site of hearings in Northern Ireland.[8] MP Sir Robert Johnstone broached this with Craig, noting the 'unsatisfactory state of the law' and the 'hardships imposed upon applicants for divorce by the ordeal of several trials, and the expense of the present procedure'

---

[4] 'Divorce Law in Northern Ireland', confidential memorandum by parliamentary draftsman Arthur Queckett, 19 May 1938 (PRONI, CAB4/403/26), p. 6 and pp. 15–16.
[5] Blakiston-Houston, NI Commons debates, 26 April 1932, vol. 11, col. 830.
[6] A. B. Babington, Royal Court of Justice to Craig, 26 November 1936 (PRONI, HA/8/160).
[7] NI Cabinet papers, 15 December 1936 (PRONI, CAB4/369/13).
[8] A wife could still petition on the grounds of rape if she was separated or the rape of another as well as sodomy or bestiality on her person. Reasonable ground for a presumption of death was a period of at least seven years. Herbert's act also extended the grounds for nullity. Explanatory document on the draft Matrimonial Causes (NI) Order, 1978 (PRONI, D4179/1/5/3) and Matrimonial Causes Bill (NI), 1939 (PRONI, CAB4/411/16).

and, like many before him, called for uniformity of provision with the UK.[9] Yet, when the possible move of divorce to court in Northern Ireland was noted in a 1937 High Court case, the suggestion, even after eighty years of English court-based divorce and numerous international reforms, was still deemed 'remarkable' by the *Irish Jurist*.[10] There were, however, some signs of more popularly held discontent particularly concerning the lack of a poor person's procedure. *Daily Mail* journalist Paul Brewster travelled to various parts of the UK, including Belfast, to ascertain women's views on divorce in 1938. His investigation was sufficiently worrying to merit retention in the Northern Ireland Department of Home Affairs' files with an accompanying handwritten note from G. C. Duggan highlighting that 'The question of divorce is getting publicity'. Bates's response suggested that 'It looks as though the divorce bill would have a good pass.'[11] Most of Brewster's Belfast interviewees abhorred the class bias of parliamentary divorce. Alderman Lily Coleman, the sole female member of Belfast Corporation, favoured a court-based system, claiming that the exalted moral standards in the province would prevent any abuse of a more affordable process: '[T]he people of Northern Ireland are more rigidly moral than in many other parts of the British Isles. One reason is they don't travel so much – and they take their home life more seriously. They are a dour people – more level-headed and dogmatic than in many other places.'[12] Mrs W. J. Holmes, the wife of a Belfast solicitor, however, refused to align the low rate of divorce to exalted morality; she effectively gendered the issue: 'The women's vote will certainly be behind the Government ... because women have suffered more than men from the difficult divorce laws.'[13]

A draft bill, presented to the Northern Irish cabinet for final approval in 1938, proposed to transfer divorce jurisdiction to the Northern Ireland High Court and reform the grounds for divorce along English lines. Queckett, convinced that reform was needed, informed the cabinet that the present system was 'unsatisfactory ... slow, cumbrous and expensive, and ... enables the well-to-do to obtain relief from a marriage which has irretrievably failed, but leaves the poorer sufferer to bear his misfortune'. His attempt to reassure the cabinet with a dubious claim that Herbert's bill met 'little opposition' was tempered by an admission that some of the

---

[9] Queen's University representative Johnstone, NI Commons debates, 10 May 1938, vol. 21, col. 968.
[10] 'Divorce Law', *Irish Jurist*, vol. 3, no. 2 (Easter 1937), p. 18.
[11] Duggan was assistant secretary in the NI Ministry of Finance. See PRONI, HA/8/160.
[12] 'The voice of women', *Daily Mail*, 29 November 1938. The Belfast City Council replaced the Belfast Corporation 1973.
[13] Ibid.

new grounds were potentially contentious.[14] Queckett also determined that the existing process 'was open to serious criticism on the ground of uncertainty, because upon each case Parliament is a law unto itself'. With new grounds introduced by Herbert's act, that would only augment: 'An application here on one of those grounds might possibly be "tried out" in another application of the Westropp principle.'[15] The bill would, as in the English reform of 1857, also end the faltering criminal conversation action, replacing it with a statutory action for damages. As the High Court already had matrimonial jurisdiction in Northern Ireland, the reform essentially presented an extension of their power with the chief crown solicitor and the attorney general proposed as having similar roles to the King's Proctor in England.

Closely modelled on the recent Westminster reform, the Matrimonial Causes Bill (Northern Ireland) sought to remove the parliamentary basis of divorce. Unlike Herbert's act, this was a government-sponsored measure and, introducing its second reading to the Northern Ireland House of Commons in 1939, the newly appointed attorney general Arthur Black was more openly critical of the existing procedure than any of his predecessors. Citing the 1850s commission's reproach of parliamentary divorce, he described it as 'ill-suited … as well as being cumbersome [it] bore on its face marks of great injustice'. Thus, whilst the 1857 act stood as 'a great landmark in the history of divorce … the unfortunate part, so far as Ireland is concerned, is that there was no reform here'. Even at the time of that bill's passage, it was 'recognised … that it was somewhat of an absurdity that the position should be left in this way … [with] a grotesque procedure':

It is not a credit … to think in a matter such as divorce that it is open readily to the man or woman who has considerable means … while … it is closed entirely to the humbler man … with slender resources. … Would anyone in England in this year 1939 propose to scrap the judicial system which was initiated 82 years ago and go back to the old system of obtaining a complete divorce only by promoting a Bill in Parliament. I think that question answers itself.

The criminal conversation action was similarly 'hard to defend in any logical way'.[16]

---

[14] Richard Dawson Bates, NI Minister of Home Affairs, citing Queckett, memorandum for the Cabinet, 31 October 1938 (PRONI, CAB4/403/26). For the bill, see PRONI, CAB4/411/16. On the difficulties Independent MP Allen Herbert faced, see Sharon Redmayne, 'The Matrimonial Causes Act 1937. A lesson in the art of compromise' in *Oxford Journal of Legal Studies*, vol. 13, no. 2 (Summer 1993), pp. 183–200.
[15] 'Divorce Law in Northern Ireland', confidential memorandum by parliamentary draftsman Arthur Queckett, 19 May 1938 (PRONI, CAB4/403/26), p. 6 and pp. 15–16.
[16] Black, NI Commons debates, 2 May 1939, vol. 22, col. 1239.

The proposed new grounds for divorce aroused more debate than the cessation of both parliamentary divorce and criminal conversation. Defining incurable insanity as five-year's treatment prior to a divorce being instituted was particularly divisive and prompted cross-party censure. Deemed 'a terrible flaw' by John Nixon, unionist MP for Woodvale in Belfast, he made the critique personal by denigrating the bachelor attorney general: he 'does not know anything ... except what he sees and reads'.[17] Others sought to test public opinion,[18] but Richard Byrne, nationalist MP for Falls, Belfast, overlooked Catholic parliamentary divorce petitioners, claiming that it was unjust to 'force' the bill on Catholics who allegedly did not believe in divorce.[19] Thomas Campbell, barrister and nationalist MP for Belfast's Central Ward, similarly opposed what he saw as a 'very disagreeable' bill but on the ground of widening accessibility even though a poor person's procedure was not enshrined: this was 'certainly not an Irish Bill ... [it would] open the door of divorce to the very poorest of the poor. ... A great principle is at stake.' Like Nixon, he disliked the insanity clause and, even though the number of parliamentary divorces was augmenting, the reform was claimed to foster 'heathenism' and 'for the first time in Irish territory [see] the scandals with which the London divorce courts reek week by week ... [and] the lewd people who want a divorce':

This Bill will disgrace the law in the Six Counties ... no Government of that Parliament ever asked that the measure of 1857 should be extended to Irish territory. ... To vast numbers this Measure will be abhorrent. In the rest of Ireland there is no divorce law[;] there is no divorce court. I think that is one of the peculiar glories of the Eire part of Ireland ... it is a bitter and evil fruit of partition that this Bill should be brought in here.

Campbell's moral castigation, recalling the opponents of the 1850s reform, concluded with the claim that 'No type of legislation is more calculated to interfere with domestic happiness or more fraught with danger to the present interests of society.'[20]

Members of the Standing Committee on Divorce like William Grant, the unionist MP for Duncairn in north Belfast, drew a different conclusion. Commenting on cases which were 'too horrible to note in any

---

[17] Nixon was also critical of following Westminster initiatives (Nixon, ibid., col. 1247).
[18] See James Brown, MP for South Down, ibid., col. 1257.   [19] Ibid.
[20] NI Commons debates, 2 May 1939, vol. 22, cols. 1250–5. Campbell's views were static; his reminiscences referred to this act as 'uncalled for, unwelcome and thoroughly pernicious. ... Against it I made my strongest protest. ... The British Parliament never ventured to foist such an Act on Ireland. Eire is in the happy position of having no Divorce Court. There the sanctity and indissolubility of the marriage tie are scrupulously safeguarded' (T. J. Campbell, *Fifty years of Ulster, 1890–1940* [Belfast, 1941], p. 132).

company, respectable or otherwise', the reform afforded important protection to women and children which was a common line of argument in twentieth-century international divorce reform: 'This will give these people a new outlook on life – freedom from individuals unworthy of the name of man.'[21] The bill garnered further support as divorce was already an actuality; costs would be reduced in court and provision would be broadly equitable with that of England. The attorney general also defended the bill by a prudent, if brief, negotiation of religious opposition: Catholics would not be compromised as those with moral objections would not institute divorce proceedings.[22] The Northern Irish divorce debate was ultimately much less ideologically charged and sustained than that in the Irish Free State. The removal of divorce from parliament to the judiciary in 1939 thus ended what Queckett rightly depicted as 'an antiquated system . . . an unconscionable time a-dying'.[23]

The act contained progressive elements including the treatment of an unsound mind for five years continuously in England, Scotland or Northern Ireland as a ground for divorce. By comparison, English law only considered treatment within its jurisdiction and Scottish law included that administered in England and Scotland. The end of parliamentary divorce, however, met with little applause. Those who divorced in the Northern Ireland parliament remained a minority of the population but showed determination and, at times, desperation to legally end a union that was already obsolete. Women exercised considerable agency by utilising legal redress more readily than men. This was often fuelled by a desire to remarry or the need for permanent release from an abusive spouse to protect both themselves and their children. Collectively, the divorce bills brought to the Northern Ireland parliament, in consequence of the Westropp principle, lessened the gendered bias of the law and the demand for criminal conversation suits without legislative reform. The reduction of fees in 1929 also highlights a degree of sympathy for petitioners similar to that which emerged in Westminster in the late nineteenth century.

Court-based divorce, however, could never be a cure-all. Lily Chambers of Tullyraine in Co. Down sought to divorce her husband, weaver Holt Waring Chambers of Lurgan, Co. Armagh in court in 1940. Her case, like many previously heard, detailed a litany of abuse. Married

[21] NI Commons debates, 2 May 1939, vol. 22, col. 1256. The protectionist line of argument was, for example, evident in early twentieth-century divorce reform (see Phillips, *Putting asunder*).

[22] Black, NI Commons debates, 2 May 1939, vol. 22, col. 1266.

[23] Arthur S. Queckett, 'Divorce law reform' in *Journal of Comparative Legislation and International Law*, 3rd series, vol. 22, no. 1 (1940), p. 32 and pp. 34–5.

in 1931, she lived with her parents as her husband 'never asked her to go home. Three weeks after [they] married [she] asked him what his intentions were and mentioned two houses that were vacant and he said what would you have done if I had not married.' A son was born in 1932, but she was deserted two years later. The clerk of Armagh Petty sessions wrote to her spouse 'requesting him to provide a home for herself and her infant son, and to maintain them. . . . No reply has been received' and a summons for desertion was issued.[24] Her testimony, seeking maintenance under the Married Women's (Maintenance in Case of Desertion) Act of 1886, in Gilford Petty Sessions in 1934, recorded the following:

I never new [sic] what his wages was for he never told me anything about his work. . . . I asked him . . . was he not going to make me a home as there was not much roam [sic] for me in my mother's house and he just told [me] if he hadent [sic] took me what would I have done . . . he told me he had his mother to keep no matter a dam [sic] about me. . . . I told him if I could not make him do what was write [sic], that the law would make him do what was write [sic].

After several adjournments, they reconciled and he promised 'to get a house and support his Wife and they left the Court together'. Until 1936 he came to see her 'occasionally . . . and . . . made two payments of 10/- each. She has not seen him to speak to since that date and he is still living with his parents'. A case for divorce was brought to the High Court in 1940 when Waring had yet to provide a marital home. Chambers sought alimony and costs, but the financial burden of divorce even in court was too great:

Sorry to say I can['] t go on with my case. . . . I cannot face the money myself hoping you will let it drop for a few months till I see what I can do[.] I am very sorry that I started it when I see the way it has turned out hoping you will not be angry after giving you the trouble writing for me.[25]

Fees of three guineas were outstanding but counsel was confident that she would be granted a divorce on the grounds of desertion with 'a good chance' of costs and maintenance 'even if not for herself at least for the boy'. Overseeing the case, Isaac Copeland noted this was not an isolated instance:

I hear a lot of talk about costs being £40 to £50. . . . I have been doing a big trade in this stuff recently. My notion is that the outlay apart from Counsel (always the bogeyman) is small . . . in this type of case from A to Z inclusive I usually get 15 gu[inea]s: – Pet[itio]n 3 g[uinea]s[.] Brief 5. Consultation 2[.] Proofs 3 gu[inea]s

---

[24] Case for counsel, 1934 (PRONI, D1046/541/1–3).
[25] Case for counsel (PRONI, D1046/541/6, D1046/541/14 and D1046/541/17).

and 2 gu[inea]s for making order absolute. Of course in larger cases we make the aid of the higher scale.[26]

The Poor Man's Lawyer Department of Belfast Council for Social Welfare also fielded more than twice the number of divorce inquiries post-1939 and frequently cited a similar financial outlay to Copeland. The cost of a parliamentary divorce earlier deterred canvasser A. W. of Portadown from proceeding against his adulterous spouse who was living with another man in England in 1936, but his expectant return for advice after divorce moved to court in 1939 proved futile; without a poor person's procedure in the Northern Ireland High Court, he was unable to proceed.[27] With the outbreak of war in 1939, the council advised that 'prophesy is unsafe' regarding the likelihood of this being introduced; however, by 1944 they anticipated its introduction, advising clients that it would be 'imprudent' to divorce at this juncture of the war.[28] This left many facing desertion and abuse. J. G.'s husband made several attempts on her life and had 'often beaten and abused' her: 'I cannot live with him he is so cruel. ... I would rather die.' Described as of the poor class, although 'young[,] ... strong' and able to earn her own living, the cost of divorce was prohibitive.[29] There were also rare instances of wifely abuse on husbands. G. R.'s wife was certified insane and 'so violent that it was impossible ... to manage her' with the result that his 'life ... has been anything but happy', but without financial assistance he was unable to divorce.[30] Unpaid costs could also delay a *decree nisi*, and there were further examples of women being pursued for the unpaid divorce costs of their spouses.[31] With these difficulties, more informal methods to end a union remained: private separation deeds were still being drawn up in Northern Ireland in the late 1930s[32] and tearing up a marriage certificate or seven years' desertion was wrongly believed to end a union as late as the 1940s.[33]

The reluctance to legislate without Westminster's precedent also continued in Northern Ireland. Anticipating a rise in divorce, the Church of

---

[26] Isaac Copeland to Robert S. Heron, 13 and 18 March 1940 (PRONI, D1046/541/12).

[27] The poor person's procedure only operated in petty sessions and county courts in Northern Ireland (BCSW file 3D, 28 December 1936 and 2 December 1939 [PRONI, D2806/DE/1]).

[28] BCSW file 562B, 10 April 1941 (PRONI, D2806/DE/2) and file 3108B, 30 November 1944 (PRONI, D2806/DE/10).

[29] BCSW file, 340B, 9 April 1940 (PRONI, D2806/DE/1).

[30] BCSW file 259B, 1940 (PRONI, D2806/DE/1).

[31] See, for example, BCSW file 797B, 20 November 1941 (PRONI, D2806/DE/2).

[32] BCSW file 3048B, 9 October 1941 and file 488, 21 September 1944 (PRONI, D2806/DE/10).

[33] See, for example, BCSW file 727B, 9 October 1941 and file 488, 2 January 1941 (PRONI, D2806/DE/2).

Ireland sought clarification on its ministers' right to refuse to remarry divorcees which formed part of the 1857 divorce act and asked for legislation enshrining this to be extended to all Protestant churches in 1943.[34] A call for parental consent for marriage of the under-sixteens to limit the number of divorces resulting from hasty unions was also made in the Northern Ireland parliament in 1946 but neither appeal provoked reform.[35] The aftermath of the Second World War, however, led the Northern Irish parliament to consider legislation, similar to that of Britain, to allow women to take out divorce proceedings against 'strangers' – American, Belgian or other allied soldiers who deserted them after wartime marriages.[36] The Belfast Council for Social Welfare was inundated with requests for advice on divorce in the later stages of the war: this amounted to close to a quarter of all cases in 1944–45. Under the 1942 Army Council Instruction 1398, an agreement was reached with the Incorporated Law Society of Northern Ireland to allow military personnel who were not on overseas service free legal aid if they paid a £10 deposit from their army allowance to fund High Court cases costing less than £50 or £100 in special circumstances. Charitable organisations like the Incorporated Soldiers', Sailors' and Airmen's Help Society also assisted with this payment.[37] In addition, Section 16 of the Army Welfare Regulations allowed military personnel to incrementally pay off the cost of a divorce from their army wage. It was therefore unsurprising that requests for advice from the Poor Man's Lawyer from servicemen and their wives became commonplace.

Wartime unions also foregrounded the issue of a wife's dependent domicile. Some statutory exceptions existed in both Section 26 of the Matrimonial Causes Act (NI), 1939, and Section 3 of the Matrimonial Causes Act (NI), 1946. Under the 1939 legislation, a wife could petition for divorce if a husband's Northern Irish domicile was changed by his desertion or deportation. The 1949 section included a temporary provision whereby, until the end of 1950, a husband or wife could take court proceedings if the marriage occurred during the Second World War, if a husband at the time of marriage was domiciled outside the UK and the wife was domiciled in Northern Ireland for three years before the divorce

---

[34] Deputation of Lord Primate, Lord Bishop of Clogher and H. M. Thompson, KC, NI Cabinet meeting, 10 June 1943 (PRONI, CAB4/546). The remarriage of divorcees in the Church of Ireland was permitted from 1996 although clergy can still conscientiously object to perform the ceremony.

[35] Resolution from Stewart Blacker Quin, NI Cabinet meeting, 24 June 1946 (PRONI, CAB4/676).

[36] Thompson, NI House of Commons debates, 15 January 1946, vol. 29, col. 1841.

[37] See BCSW file 3080B, 30 January 1944 (PRONI, D2806/DE/10).

petition was presented. This was another example of Northern Ireland's reliance on external factors to inspire reform:

> It has long been recognised that the old law inflicted a tremendous hardship on deserted women, but it took the influence of strangers in the war years and the spate of desertions which followed, to bring this desirable amendment to fruition in the United Kingdom. There is a substantial number of cases in Northern Ireland where the new proposal will afford relief.[38]

Post war, the number of divorces increased, but this was more than a temporary aberration caused by hurried wartime unions. By comparison, few sought to separate or annul marriages; there were only two petitions for separation and twenty-one petitions for civil nullity in Northern Ireland from 1953 to 1955. Over the same period, 421 divorce petitions were submitted which averaged 0.10 divorces per 1,000 of the population.[39] These numbers pale in comparison to England and Wales where the 1939 figure of 8,517 divorces, representing 0.22 per 1,000 of the population, rose to a new high of 24,857, representing 0.64 per 1,000 of the population, by 1945.[40] The belated post-war introduction of a poor person's procedure in Northern Ireland in 1947 allowed some who previously sought divorce to proceed, but a husband's means were taken into account in a wife's application, making eligibility for the income restriction of £2 (or £4 in special circumstances) per week difficult at times.[41] As transpired during the war, some also needed charitable aid to raise the £10 deposit required.[42] However, an increasing number of women sought advice on divorce from the Belfast Council for Social Welfare; 69 per cent of divorce advice cases were brought by women from 1948 to 1951 and 85 per cent from 1955 to 1958.[43] However, 'moral misgivings' continued to keep Northern Ireland divorce rates comparatively low and deterred some from continuing with a divorce even after proceedings were instituted; others were dissuaded from proffering a defence from a fear of having to attend court.[44]

The government provided a modest £150 grant to the Northern Ireland Marriage Guidance Council which saw more than sixty couples per month by 1951. This, as well as the division of divorcees and widowers into two categories in the 1951 Northern Ireland census, was

---

[38] NI Cabinet meeting, 17 October 1951 (PRONI, CAB4/855/3).
[39] *Ulster Year Book* (Belfast, 1956), p. 254.
[40] Separations also declined in popularity in England and Wales following the move to court-based divorce in 1857. In 1900, the London court received 89 separation petitions; by 1939, there were fewer than thirty separations per annum (Cretney, *Family law*, p. 153 and p. 281).
[41] Rules included in BCSW file 547B (PRONI, D2806/DE/2).
[42] BCSW file 2990B, 27 May 1948 (PRONI, D2806/DE/10).
[43] BCSW advice files, 1948 and 1955 (PRONI, D2806/DE/11 and /16).
[44] BCSW file 6555B and 6557B, 2 August 1962 (PRONI, D2806/DE/18).

indicative of a growing acceptance of marital breakdown.[45] Yet, the census figures for male and female divorcees rarely tallied: the number of divorced men was sometimes half that of divorced women due to higher rates of male remarriage and post-divorce migration which was often impossible for women with dependent children.[46] The 1961 census, for example, recorded 538 men and 1,165 women in this category, age 20 to 85–89, but with a predominance in the 40–44 age groupings for both sexes. By 1966, the number of divorcees increased slightly but the variance in figures between the sexes remained: 614 men and 1,291 women were recorded as divorced with the majority in the 40s age range.[47] By 1971, the number of divorcees recorded in the census doubled from that of the mid-1960s period; more than 1,000 male and close to 2,000 female divorcees were recorded. In the next decade, the rate of male remarriage was estimated as four times higher than that of women in Northern Ireland, provoking some feminist misgivings about divorce particularly on the 'double standard of aging'.[48]

Although divorce rates increased in Northern Ireland, the fears of the anti-reformers were never realised. In 1967, divorce rates were lower per 1,000 of the population than in England and Scotland: Northern Ireland's rate was 0.08 compared to English and Scottish figures of 0.72 and 0.46, respectively. In actual terms, this amounted 211 *decrees nisi* and 174 *decrees absolute* in Northern Ireland. These figures rose to 299 *decrees nisi* and 266 *decrees absolute* in the following year. The partial remedy that separation afforded meant that numbers remained low: eight were granted in 1967 and nine in 1968.[49] By 1970, the Northern Ireland divorce rate was 300 per annum. There was also an increase in the number of divorcees in their thirties (1971 saw a 45 per cent and 54 per cent increase for male and female divorcees in this age range, respectively) but rising numbers also emerged in the fifties age bracket.[50] A correlation was also clear between the instance of divorce and the regional religious composition. The border counties of Fermanagh, Armagh, Tyrone, Londonderry County and County Borough had the lowest instances of divorce recorded at 24, 178, 107, 133 and 87, respectively, in 1971. By comparison, Antrim, Down and Belfast recorded 616, 601 and 1,258 divorcees, respectively. These areas

---

[45] NI Cabinet meeting, 17 October 1951 (PRONI, CAB4/855/3).
[46] In the NI census for 1961, for example, 100 men are listed in the 40–44 age group compared to 238 women. See W. E. Vaughan and A. J. Fitzpatrick (eds.), *Irish historical statistics. Population, 1821–1971* (Dublin, 1978), p. 101.
[47] Ibid., p. 102.   [48] Mark Hamilton, *The case against divorce* (Dublin, 1995), p. 31.
[49] NI House of Commons debates, 29 November 1967, vol. 67, col. 2262.
[50] A total of 1,056 men and 1,950 women were recorded as divorcees in the 1971 NI census (Vaughan and Fitzpatrick, *Irish historical statistics*, p. 103).

were not only more densely populated but also had lower concentrations of Catholic communities, especially in north Down and Antrim.[51]

In addition to a prevailing moral conservatism, financing divorce remained testing for many. Resistance to the introduction of legal aid in Northern Ireland, available to those with a net income of £700 per annum with reduced assistance available to those with higher incomes, was a reprise of the late application of the poor person's procedure. The Council for Social Welfare continually had to advise clients experiencing marital problems to await this reform throughout the 1950s and early 1960s. C. G. in Belfast believed she could 'not await the NI Legal Aid Act' as 'sickened ... by her husband's advances [for] ... too much sexual intercourse', she was also subjected to violence and not allowed to leave the house, although which recourse she turned to was unrecorded.[52] Legal aid was introduced in Northern Ireland, with Labour Party backing in 1964, but by 1966, with a growing backlog of applications, it had not been implemented. Norman Murray, secretary of the Law Society, estimated that 190 divorce cases could be heard in the first year, compared to the pre–legal aid average of 120 cases with deserted wives who formerly lacked the means to pursue spouses through the courts anticipated to benefit most.[53] Married women's dependent domicile, however, remained a bar; if a husband had foreign domicile, his wife could not claim free legal aid in Northern Ireland. Legal aid for divorce was also not universally welcomed, arousing dissent that it might remove the final barrier to lower-class divorce as well as protest from the senior bar which considered it an unnecessary intervention.[54] The gross cost of legal aid for divorce and separation cases in Northern Ireland in its first year of operation, 1966–67, was £259 but, as Murray anticipated, this rose to £16,790 by 1968–69. Of these costs, more than half (£194 and £9,188, respectively) were paid from public monies for damages levied in divorce cases.[55]

Motivated by the Law Reform (Husband and Wife) Act passed by Westminster in 1962, the Northern Ireland government also sought to standardise procedures in relation to maintenance. A family allowances

---

[51] Ibid., pp. 233–40. In 1971, 34 per cent of Northern Ireland was recorded as Catholic.
[52] As C. G had not seen a doctor, she was deemed to lack evidence for cruel conduct (BCSW file 6991, 14 January 1965 [PRONI, D2806/DE/18]).
[53] *Belfast Telegraph*, 10 July 1965.
[54] Desmond G. Neill, 'Some consequences of Government by devolution' in F. H. Newark et al. (eds.), *Devolution of government. The experiment in Northern Ireland* (London, 1953), p. 86 and p. 99. The senior bar is composed of senior barristers.
[55] NI House of Commons debates, 24 June 1969, vol. 73, col. 1770. An estimated £2.5m. per annum was spent on legal proceedings relating to marriage breakdown in Northern Ireland in the late 1990s (*Divorce in Northern Ireland*, pp. 15–18).

bill to consolidate Northern Irish legislation passed between 1945 and 1964 was routine in content, but the lingering sensitivity towards divorce was epitomised by a secret memorandum on the subject prepared for the cabinet by Minister of Home Affairs Brian McConnell in 1965.[56] The Northern Irish response to a 1963 United Nations questionnaire on the legal conditions and effects of the dissolution of marriage, annulment and separation similarly saw the English and Scottish submissions being requested before Northern Ireland made its response even though it was acknowledged that there was 'very little difference between the law here [in Northern Ireland] and that in England and Wales.'[57] However, the High Court in Northern Ireland continued to hear divorce cases, as opposed to the county courts in England; therefore, even with legal aid, divorce remained more costly in the former jurisdiction. Dependent domicile was also only permanently abolished by the 1973 Northern Ireland Domicile and Matrimonial Proceedings Act which replicated Westminster's Domicile and Matrimonial Proceedings Act of the same year. Under its terms, a wife could petition for divorce if she was domiciled in Northern Ireland and her spouse was domiciled elsewhere with the basis of domicile reduced to one year's Northern Irish residency. This was an overdue recognition of married women's legal status which had been subject to piecemeal reform since the mid-nineteenth century.

A desire for parity again prompted Northern Irish divorce reform following the English Divorce Reform Act of 1969, operative from 1971, which introduced irretrievable marital breakdown, proven by separation, mutual consent or the fault of a spouse, as the sole ground for divorce. However, the reintroduction of direct rule to Northern Ireland in 1972 relegated family law to the political backwaters.[58] As Northern Ireland drifted into civil disorder, many were understandably wary of igniting more sectarian discord with 'a subject which would create much discussion and debate … we in the Government must be very careful in considering this whole subject'.[59] The reform was therefore only considered in Northern Ireland from 1974 when Alliance Party

---

[56] Secret NI Cabinet memo, 14 April 1965 (PRONI, CAB1300/5). Northern Ireland earlier followed the English 1925 Guardianship of Infants Act which only permitted maintenance to be given to children, although this was amended in 1951. A wife found guilty of a matrimonial offence was excluded from maintenance in 1945. The 1965 (Husband and Wife) Act (NI) dealt with actions in tort between husband and wife, extending Section 17 of the 1882 Married Women's Property Act, as introduced in Britain in 1962 (PRONI, CAB9/B/241/1 23).

[57] A. J. Kelly to R. Lloyd Thomas, Home Office, 11 January 1963 (PRONI, CAB9R/15A/43).

[58] Dunleath, House of Lords debates, 8 February 1977, vol. 379, no. 25, cols. 1084–8.

[59] Taylor, NI House of Commons debates, 8 February 1972, vol. 84, col. 167.

leader and first and only legal minister in the Northern Ireland power-sharing executive Oliver Napier suggested that it was already 'overdue'.[60] Napier anticipated resistance; his draft green paper urged a free vote to accommodate conscientious objectors.[61] Encouraging debate as 'politically healthy', he wanted to dispel 'suspicions about the influence of the Catholic hierarchy on our thinking' and deemed the fault basis of the existing process: 'not far from the worst that can be devised, running counter not only to commonsense but to basic Christian ethics'. The result was stage-managed legal proceedings 'either ... planned adultery or ... perjury so obvious that it brings the law into contempt and ... taints the whole institution of marriage with an odour of hypocrisy'.[62] Fault-based divorce also made deserted wives particularly vulnerable: 'deserted by their partners in marriage, but who cannot obtain a divorce because their matrimonial offence cannot be proved. Such a situation causes great misery and has a highly detrimental effect on any children which may have been conceived while the husband and wife were living together.'[63]

Alliance Party peer Lord Dunleath championed the Divorce Reform Northern Ireland Bill in the UK House of Lords in 1977, which embraced not only the English 1969 act but also the liberal Divorce (Scotland) Act of 1976 which allowed adultery as a sole cause for divorce and permitted a wife rather than a court to decide if a husband's infidelity made it impossible to continue cohabitation and reconcile. The English act's onus on solicitors certifying that reconciliation was discussed but was 'thought not to have proved of much practical value' and, as this was not required in Scotland, Dunleath followed the latter's lead. The bill also abolished 'outdated remedies' such as the right to claim damages for adultery, the restitution of conjugal rights suits[64] as well as a wife's common law agency of necessity which had ceased in England.[65] To Dunleath, the eight years since the passage of the 1969 English act proved

---

[60] The post of legal minister in the Northern Ireland Executive was not revived after the collapse of power sharing in Northern Ireland in 1974.

[61] A green paper is a consultation document issued by the government to facilitate parliamentary and public feedback.

[62] Napier also suggested that a free vote would allow the Northern Ireland Assembly to survive the defeat of a subsequent divorce bill (Oliver Napier's memorandum [PRONI, EXMEMO 27/74], 22 February 1974 and meeting of the NI Executive, 5 March 1974 [PRONI, OE/2/10]).

[63] Alliance Party press release, 19 January 1977 (PRONI, D4179/1/5/8).

[64] Restitution of conjugal rights was already practically defunct. Belfast Council for Social Welfare advised R. H. of Belfast, for example, that there was 'no legal means by which you can compel your wife to return to you' in 1940 (BCSW file 416B, 26 September 1940 [PRONI, D2806/DE/2]).

[65] Explanatory document on draft Matrimonial Causes (NI) Order, 1978 (PRONI, CAB4179/1/5/3).

that its application was 'reasonably satisfactory' and justified Northern Irish reform:

In the ideal circumstances, divorce ought not to be necessary; but . . . it is a fact of life that human relationships do break down. What I am aiming at is that divorce in itself should no longer be considered to be an offence or a sin. . . . It is regrettable; it is perhaps even deplorable; but, rather like someone who has a serious illness, it is something that you pity them for rather than censure them for it.[66]

As in the 1969 act, Dunleath wanted to improve financial provision for wives, rid divorce of acrimony and 'try to reduce the risk of physical violence which can take place when a marriage has broken but cannot be dissolved'. In a statement that was reminiscent of Power Cobbe, this was presented as more likely 'among the lower income brackets where they live in a small house. They cannot get away from each other.' Some support for this reform, including from the Methodist Church Council on Social Welfare and the Christian Marriage Committee of the Presbyterian Church in Ireland, was forthcoming as the number of divorce petitioners in Northern Ireland markedly augmented (650 in 1976 representing a 40 per cent increase from 1966). A growing acceptance of divorce might therefore be expected, but the perennial resistance re-emerged.[67] As in previous reforms, this was not limited to the Catholic Church. Indeed, in 1977, unionists and elements of the Protestant churches were more strident, objecting in particular to the proposed no-fault proceeding. Moral sensitivities were, however, significantly heightened by a bill to decriminalise homosexuality in Northern Ireland which was also under consideration. For many this was a liberal step too far and the reforms became conjoined: Merlyn Rees, Northern Ireland secretary of state, referred to these as 'one area' in the House of Commons in 1976. The contemporaneous Standing Advisory Commission on Human Rights' *Report on the Law of Northern Ireland in Relation to Homosexuality and Divorce* similarly interwove the reforms. It scrutinised the archbishop of Canterbury's 1966 divorce report *Putting Asunder* along with the findings of the Law Commission on divorce to assess whether Northern Irish law should conform to that of the rest of the UK. Written and oral testimony was collected from individuals and a range of church-based, voluntary, government, legal, welfare and political bodies including all the larger Protestant denominations; the Catholic Church; the Northern Ireland Women's Rights Movement; the Royal Ulster Constabulary; and

---

[66] *Irish Press*, 22 March 1977; Dunleath, House of Lords debates, 8 February 1977, vol. 379, no. 25, cols. 1082–3.
[67] *Irish Times*, 25 November 1977.

the Incorporated Law Society of Northern Ireland.[68] One member of the commission recalled that 'the prevailing culture in NI at that time, and the strength not only of Irish Catholicism, but of Anglicanism and Presbyterianism' culminated to make homosexuality and divorce 'very difficult to discuss in any open or meaningful way. Presbyterianism and Roman Catholicism seemed to me to be the two sides of the same coin. Of course, there were very brave exceptions on all sides, but conservatism merging into bigotry ruled the day.'[69] By comparison to homosexuality, divorce was seen as a 'simple and safe' reform which 'reflected human frailty, rather than right or wrong, although there would always be innocent or guilty parties'.[70] Ultimately the commission, like Dunleath, viewed divorce as 'necessary however sad'[71] and 'went as far as we could but essentially played it safe so that when we did stand above the parapet we would be heard at least by other parts of the world'.[72]

Although there was no divorce equivalent to the Rev. Ian Paisley's 'Save Ulster from Sodomy' campaign, Official Unionist Party (OUP) MP and head of the Orange Order Rev. Martin Smith declared that 'divorce would lower marriage standards', prompting 'immorality' and undermining society.[73] These were well-plied anti-divorce arguments, but OUP leader Jim Molyneaux's letter to Secretary of State Roy Mason claimed, with some justification, that the morally conservative nature of Northern Irish society meant 'these things are even more delicate and controversial . . . than in Great Britain'.[74] Such views aligned to those held by many Catholics leading the *Catholic Herald* to remark: 'The Bishops find their usual enemies acting as allies on this issue.'[75] Indeed, the Northern Irish Catholic Bishops' 1978 statement replicated unionist concerns for the stability of the family and the social implications of 'radical' divorce law reform; they called for further debate and a vote in the Northern Ireland parliament which, due to direct rule, was impossible.[76] Not all viewed a potentially right-wing concord positively: to the feminist Belfast Women's Collective this united 'reactionaries from both sides of the religious divide', but that schism was too entrenched for any collective resistance.[77]

---

[68] *Standing Advisory Commission of Human Rights' Report on the Law of Northern Ireland in Relation to Homosexuality and Divorce* (HMSO, London, 1977), p. 5.
[69] Email to author, 25 August 2013.   [70] Ibid., 26 August 2013.
[71] Ibid., 28 August 2013.   [72] Ibid., 25 August 2013.
[73] *Fortnight*, 26 June 1986, p. 6. The Orange Order is a Protestant fraternal society established in 1795.
[74] Ibid.   [75] *Catholic Herald*, 31 March 1978   [76] Ibid.
[77] *Women's Action*, vol. 2, no. 3 (August–September 1978). This socialist collective sought access to contraception and abortion, equality, free childcare, an end to sexism and the right to divorce.

Those in opposition found an ally in former Northern Ireland Lord Chief Justice MacDermott. His letter to the press on divorce's destabilising familial influence generated a considerable response as well as support from Cardinal Conway, Catholic Primate of All Ireland. Prior to this, the commission had only received two objections to the proposed reform, but MacDermott denied popular support, suggesting, like Molyneaux, regionally exceptional attitudes towards marriage and divorce. The possibility for a spouse who was 'guilty' of a matrimonial offence to divorce particularly riled MacDermott: '[D]ivorce brings, even in quite young children, a sense of shame and insecurity and resentment which works greatly to their disadvantage. I cannot measure the likely extent of this evil; but I am sure it exists and is substantial.'[78]

The Northern Ireland Women's Rights Movement, seeking divorce reform for the past three years, contextualised rather than disputed MacDermott's claims: one in four marriages ended in divorce with high levels of remarriage; nine out of ten remarried within five years of the end of their first union. Divorce thus extended rather than severed familial bonds. They also refuted the suggestion that children of divorced parents were damaged: 'What would cause a child greater unhappiness to live in an unhappy home, often witnessing rows or violent scenes, or to live in a home free of marital tension?'[79] A subsequent radio interview by Dunleath further bolstered the public response: 312 letters and 28 telephone calls were received of which 88 per cent and 75 per cent, respectively, favoured reform. The commission thus concluded that there was 'a widespread desire' for a standardisation of the law with that of England and Scotland.[80] The resulting bill was an anomaly: Westminster considered legislation originating in Northern Ireland and sponsored by the Alliance Party which lacked members in the English House of Commons. The English divorce model was also not without critics.[81] English judge Lord Simon of Glaisdale, president of the Probate, Divorce and Admiralty Division of the High Court, saw it, and the Scottish reform of 1976, as the embodiment of 'humbug and injustice', recapitulating

---

[78] Lord MacDermott cited the increase in divorce following the 1969 English reform as evidence. The number of English divorces rose from 60,134 in 1969 to 190,822 in 1972 but fell to 140,064 in 1975.

[79] The Northern Ireland Women's Rights Movement (NIWRM) further highlighted that a third of divorces were granted to childless couples and another third to families with one child (*Irish Press*, 22 March 1977).

[80] *Standing Advisory Commission of Human Rights' Report on the Law of Northern Ireland in Relation to Homosexuality and Divorce*, p. 7. The commission also recommended that homosexuality laws be reformed to comply with the English 1967 act, but further amendments to homosexuality law should not 'automatically apply' to Northern Ireland, ibid., p. 11.

[81] Lord O'Neill, House of Lords debates, 8 February 1977, vol. 379, no. 25, col. 1095.

some of the former grounds for divorce and adding the right of a husband to 'repudiate his wife, because she has ceased to find favour in his eyes, after he has deserted her for five years'. Safeguarding a wife from financial hardship after five-years' separation, enshrined in Clause 4 of the bill, had also never 'been successfully invoked'. For Simon, the bill thus allowed men to rid themselves of wives too easily and encouraged one-parent families, but he did not ask the Lords to oppose the bill in the interests of legislative uniformity: 'You get false claims of domicile . . . things have got to get worse before they get better. . . . There has to be wider recognition of the misery that has been caused by throwing over established institutions and traditional ideas.'[82]

The pro-reform campaign was based on the more equitable division of property and opposition was muted, especially from the Catholic Church which distanced itself from the reform, declaring 'that civil divorce in the North is not one of its primary concerns'.[83] The Church of Ireland was conciliatory whilst considering a broader liberal agenda: its Role of the Church Committee urged all churches to assess their relations with one another and the 'harsh essential' of reconciling freedom of conscience to contraception, Sunday observance, marriage breakdown and divorce.[84] As the Human Rights' Commission found, the Presbyterian Church was more tentative; it would not oppose the reform as long as reconciliation was encouraged and divorce was not made easy. The Democratic Unionist Party (DUP) and the Free Presbyterian Church, both of Paisley's creation, protested most vociferously on the ground that marriage and morality would be undermined.[85] Yet, even Paisley's opposition was not absolute; he favoured a move to the county courts as a means to reduce delays as well as the legal aid bill: '[I]n some instances there is grave hardship to wives who have been divorced or have had to divorce their husbands . . . a terrible backlog of debt is accruing and . . . this should be taken from the wages of the people who rightly should pay it to the parties who have been aggrieved in these law suits.'[86]

A decade after Westminster's reform, the law allowing divorce on the ground of irretrievable marital breakdown was introduced to Northern

---

[82] Simon, House of Lords debates, 8 February 1977, vol. 379, no. 25, cols. 1089–94.

[83] *Irish Times*, 25 November 1977.   [84] *The Furrow*, vol. 28, no. 4 (April 1977), p. 256.

[85] *Irish Times*, 25 November 1977. The Free Presbyterian Church, like the Presbyterian Church, has foundations in Calvinism. Free Presbyterians' central tenet focuses on the individual as a sinner and the need to discipline and judge its congregation and wider society. The church opposes ecumenicalism, abortion and homosexuality (Rob Kitchen and Karen Lysaght, 'Sexual citizenship in Belfast, Northern Ireland', *Gender, Place and Culture*, vol. 11, no. 1 [2004], p. 88).

[86] NI House of Commons debates, 8 February 1972, vol. 84, col. 166.

Ireland in 1978. Unionists introduced twenty amendments, making divorce more complex and expensive than its English counterpart. Divorce was allowed on the grounds of adultery, unreasonable behaviour, desertion of at least two years' duration or the parties lived apart for at least two years if the respondent did not object to a divorce or five years if the divorce was non-consensual and would not cause 'grave financial or other hardship to the respondent' to the extent that 'it would be wrong to dissolve the marriage'. Couples without children who had been separated for two years now had the option to have their case heard in a county court.[87] Connivance and condonation, such as living together for a period of at least six months after the fault occurred or for a period totalling six months, remained bars to divorce. One of the few advantages of Northern Ireland's delayed divorce reform was that it could adjudge English and Scottish law. The 1978 Northern Irish act therefore differed from the English legislative provision in several regards: the discussion of reconciliation was not conditional and a petitioner would be heard orally.[88] The reform thus standardised and diversified divorce law provision in equal measure.

Feminists' reaction, like that of the Belfast Women's Collective, was subdued, questioning the length of separation required and the expense and the requirement to appear before the High Court for defended cases and those with property and maintenance settlements.[89] The impact of the reform was, however, striking. The increase in divorce rates in Northern Ireland mirrored the English post-1969 situation. The pre-reform annual Northern Irish divorce rate rose by 45 per cent from 1971 to 1979 (from 337 petitions to 757); in 1981, the year that the new law came into effect, figures rose by another 45 per cent to 1,673 petitions and 1,498 *decree nisi*. Numbers continued to rise: 1,740 petitions and 1,467 *decree nisi* were granted in 1982 with 1,609 petitions and 1,513 *decree nisi* in the following year.[90] This was partially a consequence of those who previously lacked the fault basis to institute proceedings: from 1978, 70 per cent of all Northern Irish divorces were brought on the basis of irretrievable breakdown and women were twice as likely as men to file for divorce. The stresses of married life and the impact of the Northern Ireland troubles, causing economic deprivation, unemployment and separation from partners imprisoned for paramilitary-related activities,

---

[87] Explanatory memorandum on the Divorce Reform (NI) Bill, House of Lords, 1977 (PRONI, D4179/1/5/4). For the bill see PRONI, D4179/1/5/4.

[88] Clare Archbold, 'Divorce. A view from the north' in Geoffrey Shannon (ed.), *The divorce act in practice* (Dublin, 1999), pp. 47–8.

[89] *Women's Action*, vol. 2, no. 3 (August–September 1978).

[90] *Fortnight*, 23 June 1986, p. 6.

were additional causal factors in the rising divorce rate.[91] Yet, as John Chambers of the Northern Ireland Marriage Guidance Council emphasised, 'It's a myth to think that people are rushing to get a divorce. ... Many Protestants are just as reluctant to go for divorce as Catholics.'[92]

Moral conservatism in Northern Ireland thus crossed religious and political bounds. A proposal in 1985 that 'postal divorces' could be introduced in Northern Ireland for uncontested divorces without children was, for example, blocked by the unionist-dominated Grand Committee in the Northern Irish Assembly on the grounds of regional exceptionalism: '[S]uch a move would not be in line with the "cultural traditions" of the state.'[93] The cost of divorce also remained higher in Northern Ireland than in England, estimated at £3,000 and £400, respectively, and moves to amend the Northern Irish provision were again under review in the mid-1980s whilst the first referendum to introduce divorce to the Republic of Ireland was under consideration.[94] The latter saw anti-divorce campaigners cite the rising instance of divorce in Northern Ireland to illustrate the correlation between reform and an increased rate of divorce. Those in support of the reform also called Northern Ireland into play: the Progressive Democrats' 'Stand by the Republic Vote Yes' pamphlet asked: 'What could we ask for the Catholics in Northern Ireland if we legislate only for the majority in our own society?' The referendum also underscored that the common ground which emerged among the churches in Northern Ireland in opposition to the 1978 reform was not indicative of any wider reconciliation. Rather, the sense of moral ownership that the Catholic Church purported to have over divorce was criticised by Dr Robin Eames at the 1986 Church of Ireland Synod and similar sentiments emerged at the Presbyterian General Assembly of the same year.

There was some cross-border support for the proposed constitutional amendment: the Social and Democratic Labour Party (SDLP), Sinn Féin and the Alliance Party concurred with the Progressive Democrats that a 'no' vote in the referendum would 're-inforce [sic] the prejudices against what Unionists see as a priest-run state', thus reviving the 'Rome rule' claims of the home rule era. The DUP and the OUP, however, hoped for the referendum's defeat to stall the emerging involvement of the Republic in Northern Ireland affairs epitomised by the 1985 Anglo-Irish Agreement and nothing could reconcile them to the notion of a thirty-two-county

---

[91] Dr Edward Daly, Catholic bishop of Londonderry, *Fortnight*, 23 June 1986, cited p. 6.
[92] Ibid.   [93] Ibid.
[94] Irish Bishops' Pastoral (Tomás Ó Fiaich, Kevin McNamara, Joseph Cunnarie and Thomas Morris), *Love is for life. A pastoral letter issued on behalf of the Irish hierarchy* (Dublin, 1985), p. 62.

state.[95] As Frank Millar, the OUP's general secretary, informed the Northern Ireland Assembly, 'they would be wrong to think changes would make unification more likely'. Thus, although moral conservatism provided common ground across party and religious divides, this was never to the extent that they would co-operate in any anti-divorce campaign. The northern Catholic Church was also unwilling to become actively involved. In the words of one cleric, 'we've enough problems of our own without getting involved in that'.[96]

Although the 'no' campaigners placed considerable emphasis on the post-1981 Northern Irish divorce figures, their protestations were increasingly ill founded. Northern Ireland's divorce rate remained lower than England's and levelled as the pent-up demand from those living apart but previously lacking the evidence to bring a petition forward under the former fault-based system ended: in 1984 there were 1,776 petitions and 1,611 *decree nisi* which increased to 2,007 petitions and 1,656 *decree nisi* in 1985. Seventy per cent of divorces continued to come before the High Court as opposed to a county court as they were defended or entailed property and maintenance settlements. Women remained twice as likely as men to file for divorce, a situation which had been constant for the past seven years and was apparent in the earlier parliamentary divorce proceedings. Indeed, female petitioners, at times, outnumbered men by three to one; in 1983, for example, 1,855 divorce petitions were filed by women and 585 by men. Such figures countered the anti-divorce lobby's claim that women were the moral and economic victims of divorce.[97]

Progressive views like that of Jim Meehan of the Catholic Marriage Advisory in Belfast, which saw 2,000 couples a year by the mid-1980s, also challenged the long-standing notion that divorce reform augmented demand:

Divorce doesn't make a button of difference to the stability of marriage. ... I would take issue with the Catholic bishops who think Catholic marriage is undermined by divorce. ... There are no figures to show that more Catholic marriages in the North break down than in the Republic. What the bishops are alluding to is an ideal, but it's an ideal they are pushing to breaking point.

John Chambers of the government-backed Northern Ireland Marriage Guidance Council concurred: 'It's a myth to think people are rushing to

---

[95] The Anglo-Irish Agreement between Britain and the Republic of Ireland gave the latter a consultative role in Northern Ireland without changing its constitutional position.

[96] *Fortnight*, 23 June 1986, pp. 5–6.

[97] Figures from the Northern Ireland Court Service, *Irish Times*, 26 May 1986. Women also more commonly cited unacceptable behaviour as a ground for divorce, but most did not cite specific grounds.

get divorced. When you work with people going through marriage break-down you see the absolute heartache, frustration and disappointment. ... Even people in very bad marriages are often slow to get a divorce. It's a very sad and miserable decision for most people to make.'[98] Northern Irish divorce rates consequently only increased slowly: the 1990s saw an annual Northern Irish rate of more than 2,000 divorces per annum; in 1991, for example, there were 2,310 divorces, with half brought on the basis of two years or more separation.[99]

Further English reform, the 1996 Family Law Act, prompted another Northern Irish reassessment of divorce. The Republic of Ireland's successful second divorce referendum of 1995 and the subsequent Family Law (Divorce) Act of the following year which enshrined no-fault provision also contrasted unfavourably to Northern Irish inertia. A review by the Northern Ireland Office of Law Reform depicted a still traditional society, bound by religious conviction but where 25,000 couples were divorced: 2,538 divorces, involving 2,440 children, representing 3.4 per 1,000 of the population, were granted in Northern Ireland in 1996. This rate remained lower than the rest of the UK, with England's divorce rate at 13.5 per 1,000 population and Scotland at 10.9, but Greece, Spain and Italy recorded lower levels than Northern Ireland: the claim of regional moral exceptionalism was losing veracity.

Variations, however, remained between the Northern Irish and English provision. In Northern Ireland, for example, adultery simpliciter, an act of adultery not needing proof, was required to divorce whereas in England proof of adultery and the inability of the petitioner to live with their spouse were required from 1973. The oral hearing also survived in Northern Ireland, whereas in England special procedures and undefended cases could be submitted in writing, popularly referred to as 'divorce by post', rather than attend court, from 1977.[100] Although previously defeated, this provision was on the Northern Ireland statute book from 1993 but had not been implemented, a latitude the Office of Law Reform was right to suggest was due to 'attitudinal differences'. Northern Irish petitioners also did not have to prove that they had discussed reconciliation even though a 1978 order replicated provisions for this from the 1973 English act.[101] Until 1995, a social worker's welfare report was, however, required in all cases of divorce involving children younger than age eighteen in Northern Ireland. This often caused delay so its removal was

---

[98] *Fortnight*, 23 June 1986, p. 6.   [99] Hamilton, *The case against divorce*, p. 14.
[100] 'Special procedure' refers to the process for undefended petitions for divorce where a *decree nisi* can be issued without either spouse appearing in court.
[101] There was only one mediation body, the Northern Ireland Family Mediation Service, which received individual referrals as well as those from its parent body, Relate.

widely welcomed. There was also considerable use of magistrates' courts in Northern Ireland to secure maintenance orders and, prior to the establishment of the Child Support Agency in 1993, to determine child-care issues.

Of those divorcing in Northern Ireland, 70 per cent did not proceed on the basis of fault but cited separation as the cause of their marriage breakdown. This was higher than the Scottish rate of c. 60 per cent but lower than that of England and Wales where 75 per cent cited fault. This variant was a result of a desire to make it easier to proceed than indicative of the cause of marriage breakdown. Fifty-nine per cent of Northern Irish petitioners interviewed by the Law Reform Office affirmed this, citing following solicitors' advice or fear of a partner after domestic violence, which a quarter of women interviewed had experienced, using it as a bargaining tool and a means to facilitate more amicable divorce proceedings. The long-standing reluctance to publicly discuss marital problems also encouraged citing separation as a ground for divorce. Indeed, for wives' separation of two years coupled with unreasonable behaviour (most commonly domestic violence) was an increasingly popular ground of divorce: adultery and desertion accounted for only 7.5 per cent and 0.4 per cent, respectively, of Northern Irish cases in 1996.[102] This was a significant shift from the earlier parliamentary basis of divorce when adultery underpinned every bill. Divorce remained slower in Northern Ireland than in England, requiring two as opposed to one year's separation and consent from the parties or five years' separation without consent. Religious and moral objections were used to extend the period of separation beyond five years but were rarely proven in court. A proposed reduction to three years' separation where the divorce was non-consensual was considered in 2002 but was not implemented which highlights the surviving moral conservatism and continued aversion to 'easy' divorce.[103]

In consequence, although the number of divorces increased in Northern Ireland, this was gradual and not always incremental: 2,572

---

[102] *Divorce in Northern Ireland*, p. 22.

[103] *Divorce – the new law in Northern Ireland. An equality impact assessment of the Matrimonial Proceedings and Family Law Bill 2002* (Office of Law Reform, Department of Finance and Personnel, Belfast, 2002), p. 5. The mixed-fault and no-fault divorce system operative in Northern Ireland was also in existence in countries such as the Netherlands, Germany, England and Wales and France. No-fault systems were operative in, for example, Australia, New Zealand, Sweden and some US states. Mutual consent as the basis for divorce was available in Belgium, France and Sweden whereas unilateral demand was only available in the latter. The length of separation required before divorce also varied from a year in Canada and Australia to ten years in Belgium. When divorce was legalised in the Republic of Ireland in 1996, separation for four of the past five years was required (ibid., pp. 33–4 and pp. 81–1).

divorces were granted in Northern Ireland in 2016 which was below the high point of 2,913 recorded in the immediate pre-recession year of 2007.[104] Nor was divorce hastily considered: in 2016, most petitioners sought an end to marriage in their mid- to late forties and after ten to twenty-four years of marriage. Although statistics are not available for the religious beliefs of those divorcing in court in Northern Ireland, using the method of celebration of marriage, 27.5 per cent of divorces were by Catholics compared to 13.9 per cent Presbyterian, 10.4 per cent Church of Ireland, 3 per cent Methodist and 0.66 per cent Free Presbyterian in Northern Ireland in 2016. With a Catholic rate of divorce now marginally above those who married in a registrar's office (25.9 per cent) and nearly identical to the amalgamated total of Protestant divorcees (27.96 per cent), a remarkable shift occurred in both number and religious profile of divorcees in Northern Ireland over the course of four decades.[105] This was indicative not only of the widening grounds of divorce and the availability of legal aid but also the assertion of individual will in a still conservative society. Such changes provided headline fodder for the opponents of divorce whose arguments reached new heights in independent Ireland.

[104] Registrar General 2016 Annual Report Divorce (www.nisra.gov.uk/publications/regis trar-general-annual-report-2016-divorces).

[105] Ibid. A correlation between recording no religion in the census and divorce suggests that church non-accommodation of divorcees could impact faith. This was particularly marked in the Catholic Church; of divorcees professing a religion in the 1991 Northern Ireland census, the majority were Protestant (Archbold, 'Divorce', p. 50).

9   An 'Unhappy Affair': Divorce in Independent Ireland, 1922–1950

Marriage was often afforded high status as a societal stabiliser in newly established states and the Irish Free State, operative from 1922, was no exception.[1] Therefore, when three private divorce bills, the first in November 1922, were brought to the Private Bill Office of the Oireachtas (Irish parliament) Independent Senator James Douglas, chair of the Joint Committee on Standing Orders relating to Private Business, advised that they should not be formally examined in recognition of 'the feeling in the country' and in the Irish parliament. Douglas's rationale was that this would act as a first parliamentary reading and the bills would then be considered in the upper house (Seanad). The bills were withdrawn, but only in 1925 after repeated requests from the petitioners 'that the matter be settled one way or the other'.[2] These were the last private divorce bills submitted to the Irish parliament.

Canada provided a model for the dominion status of the new state, but this did not extend to divorce provision.[3] As early as 1924, Catholic Bishop William McNeely predicted to John Hagan, rector of the Irish College in Rome, that 'strong talking' would ensue on divorce in the new state. Others anticipated that the issue would signal 'deep and dark' trouble with the potential for the Catholic hierarchy to 'assist in the unseating of their canonized government'.[4] With no procedural precedent, first president of the Executive Council W. T. Cosgrave admitted his trepidation to James Downey, bishop of Adara and coadjutor bishop of Ossary: 'I must confess that in the beginning I was a child so far as my information and knowledge of the subject [of divorce] was

---

[1] Nancy Cott, *Public vows: a history of marriage and the nation* (Cambridge, MA, 2000), pp. 1–6.

[2] Douglas to Cosgrave, undated (NLI, MS 49,581/34, folio C72).

[3] In Canada, divorce bills were introduced to the Senate. When the 1996 Irish divorce act was being drafted, Minister for Equality and Law Reform Mervyn Taylor consulted the Canadian divorce act to determine the definition of living apart.

[4] MacNeely, Letterkenny, Co. Donegal to Hagan, 20 October 1924 and M. J. Browne, Westport, Co. Mayo to Hagan, 25 August 1925 (Hagan papers, HAG/1/1924/495 and HAG1/1924/399, Irish College, Rome, accessed at www.irishcollege.org). Hagan was rector from 1904 to 1930.

concerned.'[5] Whilst Cosgrave opposed divorce, he was not willing to devise state policy from personal principle. For direction, he turned not to the legal profession but to the Irish Catholic hierarchy: this was a fatal step for the future of divorce in the new state. Cosgrave also 'kept in very close touch ... and had direct and indirect communication' with Edward Byrne, the archbishop of Dublin on the subject and from whom he learnt that the Catholic Church claimed jurisdiction over all baptised persons.[6]

The expectation was that divorce would be banned in the first constitution of the new state. The draft constitution of 1922 included Article 53 by Alfred O'Rahilly, which noted the 'inviolable sanctity of the marital bond', but this was ruled out by the drafting committee which feared it would be rejected by the British cabinet 'on the ground that it would destroy a right that the Protestant community had enjoyed in Ireland'.[7] This was an ill-based assertion as a number of Irish Catholics had divorced in Westminster but is an early example of the state seeking clerical endorsement; the draft was submitted to the Catholic hierarchy. Cardinal Logue's response was unambiguous: '[S]ee that it is in accordance with the principles of Christianity and with Catholic principles.'[8] The unwillingness to debate this issue, so evident under the union, continued in independent Ireland: the first government, preoccupied with state building and countering internal strife, was ultimately 'unwilling to raise a controversy which called for no immediate solution'.[9] The first constitution therefore made no reference to divorce.

More liberal elements of the Irish press, however, quickly declared divorce a right of citizenship. Freedom of conscience was also guaranteed under Article 8 of the 1922 constitution. Considerable 'embarrassment' was therefore predicted if the new state denied divorce:

[S]trong conflicts of opinion will arise; and the statesmanship of Government and Parliament may be submitted to a severer test than any which it encountered during the framing of the Constitution. ... If the promises of the authors of the [Anglo-Irish] Treaty are to be fulfilled, both in letter and in spirit, it must be made

[5] Cosgrave to Downey, 21 September 1925 (NAI, MS TAOIS/3/S4127). The president of the Executive Council was later known as Taoiseach.
[6] Ibid.
[7] Michael Nolan, 'The influence of Catholic nationalism on the legislature of the Irish Free State', *The Irish Jurist*, vol. 10, new series (1975), p. 133.
[8] Logue writing to Bishop Patrick McKenna in March 1922 (Patrick Murray, *Oracles of God. The Roman Catholic Church and Irish politics, 1922–37* (Dublin, 2000), cited p. 420). Members of the northern Catholic hierarchy, like Bishop O'Donnell, did not want the constitution to contain such a prescriptive marital element as O'Rahilly suggested (ibid.).
[9] Peter Finlay, SJ, 'Divorce in the Irish Free State', *Studies*, vol. 13, no. 51 (September 1924), p. 353.

possible for afflicted husbands or wives to obtain in Ireland the relief they can obtain in Great Britain and throughout the Empire.[10]

As a minimum provision, the continuance of parliamentary divorce was proposed, with the Seanad suggested as the most appropriate venue for hearing divorce bills. Initially this prompted questions of process rather than principle although correspondence between Michael Hayes, the Ceann Comhairle (Dáil [lower house] chairman) and the private secretary of Ard-Chomhairle (the Irish executive council) advised that all references to divorce proceedings should be omitted from the Private Bill Standing Orders under preparation in 1923.[11] Cosgrave was informed early in the same year as follows:

[T]he Church will strenuously resist any legislation providing for divorce even for non-Catholics ... the result of the absence of facilities for divorce in this country would be that persons desiring such facilities would leave Ireland and become domiciled in some other country in which they are available.
The Archbishop's view is that Ireland would not lose anything by this.[12]

In some clerical quarters, the sense of moral contagion and the desire to export those deemed morally suspect clearly endured.

A memorandum, 'Suggested Proceedings of the Select Committee on Divorce Bills', issued to each member of the executive council, illuminates how close the new state came to permitting divorce on similar grounds to those in Westminster. The establishment of a nine-member Select Committee on Divorce Bills to hear counsel and examine evidence and witnesses in the Seanad was entertained.[13] Approaches by the Incorporated Law Society and solicitors seeking clarification of the state's intent regarding divorce, coupled with the divorce bills already presented, now made this a matter of urgency.[14] Attorney General Hugh Kennedy was 'strongly of the opinion' that divorce should be available 'for those who approve of that sort of thing ... there are a batch of cases ripe for disposal if we had the machinery'. Although acknowledging that this was a subject that Cosgrave 'does not like', Kennedy, again aligning divorce

---

[10] *Irish Times*, 11 November 1922.
[11] Ceann Comhairle to the Private Secretary to the Ard-Chomhairle, 9 March 1923 (NAI, S3301).
[12] Parliamentary Secretary to the Executive Council, Eamonn Duggan to Cosgrave, 20 March 1923 (NAI, MS TAOIS/3/S4127).
[13] Memorandum, c. 1923 (NAI, S3301). The proposed Select Committee on Divorce would have been appointed at the start of each Dáil session.
[14] Colm O'Murchadha to the secretary of the Executive Council, 14 September and 16 October 1923 (NAI, S3301) and Letter to Hugh Kennedy from Casey, Clay and Collins, 24 January 1924 (NAI, MS TAOIS/3/S4127).

solely to Protestantism, failed to 'see how we can prejudice the position of the minority in this country by depriving them of this little luxury'.[15]

There was no popular call for divorce, but as Kennedy highlighted, removing the already restrictive parliamentary route from Irish petitioners raised concerns about minority rights in the new state. Some English newspapers inferred that changing domicile would be the only way to attain divorce in the new state, but this would be only available to men due to married women's dependent domicile: 'As matters now stand, a husband who has been wronged can only obtain relief by abandoning his Free State citizenship and crossing the Ulster border or travelling to some other part of the Empire. A wronged wife is in an even worse position, for she will be unable to change her domicile.'[16] Moreover, even if parliamentary divorce were available, the fate of petitioners, as the home rule debates earlier suggested, in assemblies with Catholic majorities was questioned. These concerns initially overrode qualms about the Catholic Church's reaction as evidenced by the moves to introduce standing orders and adhere to the Westminster practice, but this process stalled in 1923.

Any expectation that the Irish Catholic hierarchy might leave divorce for governmental deliberation was terminated by the bishop of Cork's exaggerated claim to Cosgrave that 'Protestants were clamouring for divorce procedures.'[17] Cosgrave subsequently sought Archbishop Byrne's advice. Forwarding a copy of the 1924 *Catholic Teaching on Marriage*, Byrne, like Cosgrave, refused to express any personal opine and brought the question before the Irish hierarchy. Freed from Cullen's conservatism and buoyed by Irish independence, the hierarchy's response was more unequivocal than any issued in the preceding divorce debates:

[U]nder no circumstances could the Church give any sanction to divorce ... the Church regards Matrimony as a Sacrament only, and claims the sole jurisdiction in regard to it ... they could not even sanction divorce for non[-]catholics for the reason that all persons who had been baptised are members of the Church under its jurisdiction.[18]

The church's purported reach thus extended to all Christian marriages: '[I]t would be contrary to Natural Law to permit dissolution of their marriages. And only the church could decide what constituted natural law.'[19] Divorce was therefore deemed a church concern: both the religion

---

[15] Kennedy to Eamonn Duggan, 12 March 1923 (NAI, MS TAOIS/3/S4127).
[16] *Daily Express*, 13 February 1924.
[17] Diarmaid Ferriter, *The transformation of Ireland, 1900–2000* (London, 2004), p. 339.
[18] Dermot Keogh, *The Vatican, the bishops and Irish politics, 1919–30* (Cambridge, 1986), cited p. 128. See the 1924 'Catholic Teaching of Marriage', Byrne papers (DDA).
[19] J. J. Lee, *Ireland, 1912–85. Politics and society* (Cambridge, 1989), p. 157.

of the solicitors handling a divorce bill submitted to the Dáil and that of the petitioner was noted in the hierarchy's resolution. Any earlier Irish association with divorce was also strenuously denied:

Hitherto in obedience to the divine law, no divorce with right to remarry has ever been granted in this country. The Bishops of Ireland have to say that it would be altogether unworthy of an Irish Legislative body to sanction the concession of such divorce, no matter who the petitioners may be.[20]

This highly selective interpretation overlooked the passage of divorce bills by the Irish parliament but does not provide evidence of a theocracy.[21] Rather this was an insecure government in a beleaguered new state which prioritised church support over individual rights. The Catholic Church was always a willing governmental guide, but the advice it proffered on divorce, especially in the early years of the new state, was neither impartial nor always accurate. Decisions based on such partiality had an impact for generations.

Lay bodies like the Catholic Truth Conference were often more fundamentalist than the hierarchy. Their Mansion House conference in Dublin in 1924, despite a varied programme which included housing and home education, was advertised under the by-line of 'The Dail and Divorce': 'The Dail is YOUR SERVANT. It will shortly be called upon to decide for or against Divorce. Do you want Divorce? If not, make your wishes known by attending.'[22] At the conference, in one of the first public expressions of an emergent anti-divorce movement, the Most Rev. Dr Patrick McKenna, Catholic bishop of Clogher, addressing a mass meeting of women, decried divorce as 'dreadful' with the 'catch-cries of "No religion in politics"' maligned as 'absurd'.[23] The Very Rev. Dr J. Byrne further depicted a global church crusade against moral decay with divorce at its core:

[C]onscription and death in service of a foreign country would be much less immoral than a divorce law. .... Divorce laws are tearing homes to pieces, and only for the shreds of decency that remain and a public opinion that is daily weakening, unfortunately society would return to the field of paganism. The world is in a bad way.[24]

---

[20] The resolution was signed by Cardinal Logue, 9 October 1923. Copy letter to Rev. Dr Byrne, archbishop of Dublin to Eamonn Duggan, 10 October 1923 (NAI, MS TAOIS/3/S4127).
[21] Diarmaid Ferriter, *Occasions of sin: sex in twentieth-century Ireland* (London, 2009), p. 7.
[22] *Irish Examiner*, 10 October 1924.
[23] *Irish Independent*, 20 October 1924. Contraception was also condemned as 'Herod's crime of murder' (*Freeman's Journal*, 20 October 1924).
[24] *Irish Independent*, 20 and 21 October 1924 and *Irish Examiner*, 21 October 1924.

Parliament's subsequent consideration of divorce was often religiously charged but, as in both Westminster and Northern Ireland, lacked a regimented religious or party divide. The divorce debate, which had been assiduously avoided from 1857, began in late 1923 when Standing Orders for Private Bills, based on House of Commons' practice, were adopted by the Dáil and the Seanad with an onus on joint house procedures to limit the expense to petitioners. No special provision was made for divorce bills. To Donal O'Sullivan, clerk of the Seanad, 'The reason for the omission is obvious. ... It is hardly too much to say that every Irish Catholic regards the subject of divorce with abhorrence.'[25] Catholic members of the Oireachtas were also instructed to take no part in ending the divine institution of marriage. As Peter Finlay of the Society of Jesus (SJ), cautioned: 'Catholics could not aid anyone to dissolve a marriage or further divorce legislation ... he may not recommend or introduce it to either assembly; he may not approve of standing orders which will facilitate its introduction. He may take no positive part in abrogating a divine command.' As the government's duty was to protect its citizens, Finlay resolved that 'they may not advocate what will prove injurious. ... They may not assent, in public life nor legislation, to what Christ ... condemns and forbids ... they must use their influence and authority on the side of right.' This was an order of faith: '[T]he Irish Executive will be bound to oppose all divorce legislation, and Catholic Deputies and Senators will be bound to attend and vote against it. Catholic electors will be bound to take cognisance of the action or inaction of their representative and to deal with them accordingly.' Finlay was, however, one of the few in the new state to acknowledge the existence of parliamentary divorce, deeming it 'costly' and therefore 'very rare'. He used this to justify divorce's non-availability as only an 'utterly insignificant' Protestant minority would purportedly seek it.[26] Although Catholic censure predominated, this was not an exclusively Catholic preserve. The Church of Ireland's Bishop of Meath Benjamin Plunket, for instance, revived the 1850s call for the criminalisation of adultery, calling for every errant spouse to 'be treated as a robber, a forger, or a murderer'.[27] This was not collectively embraced by his church *Gazette* which, although emphasising shared sensibilities with Catholicism, framed the argument in terms of minority rights:

[25] O'Sullivan, *The Irish Free State*, pp. 163–4.

[26] Finlay, 'Divorce in the Irish Free State', pp. 360–1. The Society of Jesus is the formal name for the Catholic Jesuit Order.

[27] Yeats, Seanad Éireann debates, 11 June 1925, vol. 5, cols. 435–40.

The Church of Ireland like the Church of Rome dislikes divorce intensely ... this is not a religious question at all; it is a matter of civil rights. The minority of Ireland hitherto has enjoyed the right under British law of being able to secure a divorce, and under the Free State constitution that minority is given complete civil and religious liberty.'[28]

The Joint Committee on Standing Orders relative to Private Business, chaired by Douglas, was composed of senators William Barrington (Independent), barrister Samuel Brown (Independent) and Thomas Farren (Labour) and deputies Bryan Cooper (Independent), barrister Professor William Magennis (Cumann na nGaedheal (Society of the Gaels)) and Pádraic Ó Máille (Cumann na nGaedheal). Cooper's inclusion on the committee was especially pertinent: he divorced in Westminster in 1920. The *Catholic Bulletin* was certainly unnerved by the committee: '[W]e fear this is a matter where the majority rule will not apply. There is a big gulf between the treatment of popular, and unpopular minorities.'[29] Yet, the committee's report of July 1924 declared only a stalemate: '[T]he present position is unsatisfactory from every point of view.' Its misconception that Standing Order no. 1, which related to private bills, would give 'unrestricted power to introduce Divorce Bills ... even in cases where a judgment of a court of law has not been previously obtained' could have been avoided by an adoption of Westminster's standing orders which prevented such bills being introduced. The gendered grounds of domicile, which previously tried the more liberal sections of the press, were also disconcerting to the committee: men could pursue a divorce in another jurisdiction, but women could not. With three divorce bills now presented, the spectre of more following in their wake 'practically without any restrictions' overlooked the financial and legal strictures of the parliamentary proceeding and the rules regarding domicile. Indeed, in comparison to Finlay, the committee highlighted the 'many cases' of parliamentary divorce heard from 1701 to 1857 and acknowledged that Irish divorces were passed by both Westminster and the Irish parliament. The committee also reiterated attorney general Kennedy's call for 'definite judgment' from parliament:

[C]onsiderable differences of opinion exist ... there are citizens of the Saorstát [state] who have no conscientious objections to the granting, under certain circumstances, of divorce ... and who believe that the same facilities in this respect should be available that were in existence before the [Anglo-Irish] Treaty, nevertheless the majority feel that such proceedings are contrary to their

---

[28] *Church of Ireland Gazette*, 8 August 1924, editorial.
[29] *Catholic Bulletin*, vol. 14, no. 9 (September 1925), pp. 774–5.

religious convictions and that divorce with a legal right to remarry should not be permitted.[30]

It remains unclear how the views of that majority were determined.

There was no progress until February 1925 when Cosgrave brought a Dáil motion, asking the Joint Committee to submit additional standing orders regarding matrimonial matters other than divorce and alter the orders to prevent the introduction of divorce bills. In a move which was both 'surreptitious' and 'of dubious legality', Cosgrave requested that the Seanad accept his resolution.[31] Cosgrave now claimed that his view of marriage as a sacrament concurred with that of the majority: '[T]he whole fabric of our social organisation is based upon the sanctity of the marriage bond and that anything that tends to weaken the binding efficacy of that bond to that extent strikes at the root of our social life.'[32] Therefore, masked as a debate on parliamentary process, this was essentially a moralistic tirade on the rights and wrongs of marital dissolution. Representing a group of independent members, Professor William Thrift, with 'very great reluctance', responded to Cosgrave, emphasising an attachment to both the sanctity of marriage and the rights of the individual: '[T]here are very hard cases, and I do not feel ... it would be permissible for me personally to say what view other persons ought to take on that question of divorce.' This was a test of inclusivity for the new state: 'You want every Irishman in this Irish nation ... and the way we are going to get them is to ensure for them absolute justice and fair play.' Thrift thus predicted a divorce interdict which could impose a barrier to Ireland's reunification.[33] Yet, if divorce was the price of 'friendship and co-operation of the Six Counties', some refused to 'purchase that ... of national dishonour'.[34] Others declared their religious credentials to the house: George Wolfe did not 'worship at the same alter as the majority' but favoured an outright ban on divorce and revived the connexion between increased facilities for divorce and augmented demand.[35]

[30] Report of the Joint Committee on Standing Orders (Private Business on the position of Saorstat Eireann of bills relating to matrimonial business, 11 July 1924 [NAI MS TAOIS/ 3/S4127]), pp. 1–3. The report was signed by James Douglas.

[31] Christine P. James, 'Céad Míle Fáilte? Ireland welcomes divorce: the 1995 Irish divorce referendum and the Family (Divorce) Act of 1996' in *Duke Journal of Comparative and International Law*, vol. 8 (1997–8), p. 182.

[32] Cosgrave, Dáil Éireann debates, 11 February 1925, vol. 10, cols. 156–8. Vice-president Kevin O'Higgins seconded the motion.

[33] Thrift also cited Article 8 of the 1922 constitution (ibid., cols. 159–63). Blythe did not agree that partition would be embedded by banning divorce. See ibid., col. 173.

[34] Davin, ibid., col. 176.

[35] Wolfe, ibid., cols. 164–5. Deputy Ernest Alton, who like Thrift was a future provost of Trinity College, Dublin, concurred. See ibid., col. 179.

There was also considerable moralising about those who might seek divorce; only those lacking conscience would allegedly divorce and the 'moral welfare' of the country would be damaged by polygamous second unions if divorce was permitted.[36]

Cosgrave's motion was carried, coming before the Seanad in March when its constitutionality was more fully deliberated. Former unionist landowner, Seanad chair and barrister Lord Glenavy ruled the motion out of order on the ground that it opposed the constitution as the right to petition parliament by private bill existed under common law. It was therefore protected by Article 73 of the 1922 constitution which ensured that statutes in place at the time of its passage remained in force until repealed or amended by the new state's parliament. Cosgrave's motion would therefore deny parliament the constitutional right to legislate on divorce.[37] This was astute but was popularly cast as a critique on both government and parliament: 'If the motion was out of order in the Senate, it was equally so in the Dáil, and so there was an implied (but unavoidable) censure on the Government for proposing it and on the Chairman of the Dáil for permitting it to be moved.'[38] The level of Protestant representation in the Seanad, including its chair, provided an easy scapegoat for those seeking to discredit Glenavy: the proposed motion was withdrawn.

Thrift was, however, more highly criticised than Glenavy. The *Catholic Bulletin* lambasted his 'Divorce Stunt' as well as his Trinity and freemasonry connections.[39] The earlier existence of divorce under the jurisdiction of the Irish parliament could also only be accommodated by an association with the alleged immoralities of ascendancy rule.[40] Although chairman of the Joint Committee on Private Business, Douglas privately advised against public controversy on divorce, the *Irish Statesman*'s publication of W. B. Yeats's undelivered Seanad speech notes on divorce intensified the sectarianism of the debate.[41] Yeats portrayed efforts to make divorce unattainable as 'an act of aggression' that merited

---

[36] Davin, ibid., col. 176 and O'Sullivan, ibid., cols. 177–8.
[37] See Glenavy to James Douglas, undated [1925] (NLI, MS 49,581/53, B38 2/27). Glenavy practiced in the Divorce Division in England and was appointed English attorney general in 1905. In 1916, he became Irish attorney general and lord chief justice and served as Irish lord chancellor from 1918 to 1921.
[38] O'Sullivan, *Irish Free State*, pp. 165–6.
[39] *Catholic Bulletin*, vol. 15, no. 3 (March 1925), p. 200. See also James Doyle, Vicar-General of Ossary's similar comments in the *Kilkenny People*, 8 September 1925.
[40] *Catholic Bulletin*, vol. 15, no. 3 (March 1925), p. 201 and p. 203.
[41] See Senator James Douglas letter to 'AE' (George Russell) the editor of the *Irish Statesman*, 27 March 1925 (NLI, MS, 581/32, folio C1). Douglas advised that it would be advisable to publish such material as articles rather than speeches although he encouraged debate on such issues (ibid.).

a Protestant counteroffensive: 'I want those minorities to resist, and their
resistance may do an overwhelming service to this country. ... We must
become a modern, tolerant, liberal nation.' His inference that Cosgrave's
motion breached 'the religious truce in Ireland' riled the *Bulletin* to new
heights: Yeats was now the 'show performer ... imitating the Cicero of
Ancient Rome', and if the Irish parliament had been guilty of ascendency
rule, Yeats's 'sarcastic note of the New Ascendency' with their 'plastic
consciences' was equally abhorrent.[42]

Douglas tabled a revised divorce motion in the Seanad in mid-1925.
Seeking the support of both houses, he proposed that the Joint
Committee's consideration of divorce bills be removed from Standing
Order 55 and that such bills be read a first time in each house before
being further considered by the Seanad. Douglas's explanation was
deliberately less technical than that of Glenavy who encouraged its
introduction, believing it was 'the best way out of an awkward position'
and, with government backing, 'they could easily get the Dail [sic] to
accept it as the Deputies will realise that they cannot coerce the Senate
to pass the resolution. In this way we could get rid of this divorce
business by constitutional methods so that no grievance would be felt
in any quarter.'[43] Many in the government, including Cosgrave, sought
to reassure Protestants in the new state and were unwilling to introduce
specific legislation to prohibit divorce. Indeed, Cosgrave acknowledged
that to have no provision for divorce would be 'more severe' than
Catholic Church strictures.[44] There was, however, an awareness, as
was earlier inferred, that a private divorce bill requiring the approval of
both houses with Catholic majorities 'was a plain impossibility ... no
individual would be likely to waste time and money in promoting such
a Bill'.[45]

Debates on the Douglas motion gave Yeats a platform to address the
country. Although he was not the first to align disrespect for minority
rights with partition, the assertion that this would cause harm of historic
proportions was new:

---

[42] The speech was undelivered as the Dáil ruled the debate out of order (*Catholic Bulletin*,
vol. 15, no. 4 [April 1925], pp. 292–4). For various versions of the speech, see NLI, MS
30,080. Roman statesman and acclaimed orator Cicero was declared an enemy of the
state before his execution in 43BC.

[43] Glenavy to Douglas, undated [1925] (NLI, MS 49,581/53, B38 2/27).

[44] Cosgrave to Dr James Downey, bishop of Adara and coadjutor bishop of Ossary noting
'some Court (whether Dail, Senate or Joint Committee) should be provided which would
consider cases of hardship. ... To have a case considered and relief refused ... was one
thing, but to have no Court was entirely different', 21 September 1925 (NAI, MS
TAOIS/3/S4127).

[45] O'Sullivan, *Irish Free State*, p. 167.

If you show that this country, Southern Ireland, is going to be governed by Catholic ideals and by Catholic ideals alone, you will never get the North … you will pass more and more Catholic laws, while the North will, gradually, assimilate its divorce and other laws to those of England. You will put a wedge into the midst of this nation. I do not think this House has ever made a more serious decision … the minority will make it perfectly plain that it does consider it exceedingly oppressive legislation to deprive it of rights which it has held since the 17th century.

Yeats's claim that denying 'a practice which has been adopted by the most civilised nations of the modern world' would amount to a discourtesy of 'monstrous' proportions might have been palatable in some quarters, but his now infamous questioning of the morality of dead generations of Irish heroes neared blasphemy. This ranged from Daniel O'Connell, who 'in his own day … you could not throw a stick over a workhouse wall without hitting one of his children', to Charles Stewart Parnell, who although experiencing a 'good deal of trouble … in the opinion of every Protestant gentleman in this country' made an honourable marriage. Yeats's attempted explanation that 'the memories of these great men of genius' were not 'swept away by their sexual immoralities' was largely ineffective.[46]

Yeats did not deny the existence of a conservative Protestantism, but he depicted the fight for divorce as a religious mêlée:

We … are no petty people. We are the people of Burke; we are the people of Grattan; we are the people of Swift, the people of Emmet, the people of Parnell. … If we have not lost our stamina then your victory will be brief, and your defeat final, and when it comes this nation may be transformed.[47]

Dismissed by some as a 'sectarian' and indulgent 'diatribe', 'maligning the dead' and 'blackening the character of the people of this country', others cast doubt on Yeats as a moralist and statesman.[48] However, some Protestant senators, lacking Yeats's invective, concurred that parliamentary divorce should be maintained:[49] to Senator John Bagwell any other

---

[46] Yeats, Seanad Éireann debates, 11 June 1925, vol. 5, cols. 435–43.

[47] Ibid., col. 443.

[48] Maurice Moore, ibid., 11 June 1925, col. 445 and col. 448; Thomas Farren, ibid., col. 475 and J. T. O'Farrell, ibid., col. 470.

[49] Yeats, ibid., cols. 479–80. To the *Catholic Bulletin*, Yeats thus graduated from 'impudence' to 'satanic arrogance', a man who 'excelled in evil' with the result that 'Catholic people of Ireland … are to be abused and jeered at' (*Catholic Bulletin*, vol. 15, no. 7 [July 1925], pp. 642–3). *The Tablet* was more measured, suggesting that the Douglas motion limited the facilities for divorce as both houses' approval was required (*The Tablet*, 20 June 1925). Yeats was personally affected by the experience: 'weary in body and weary of a Seanad which no longer counted for anything in the government of a nation', he did not stand for re-election in 1928 (David Fitzpatrick, 'Yeats in the Senate', *Studia Hibernica*, vol. 12 [1972], p. 23 and p. 24).

solution was 'tyrannical ... Those who disapprove of divorce should abstain from divorce, but I do not think that they ought to try and coerce others ... what good, material or moral, is it going to do this country to do away with facilities for divorce?'[50] Douglas, claiming that he would have refused the chair of the committee if he had known that it would consider divorce, maintained that the proposed motion protected majority rights.[51] More uncompromising comments affirmed Yeats's avowal of an ill-placed sense of superiority: divorcees were allegedly homewreckers and divorce was proclaimed as so commonplace in Britain that 'next to Association football, it has become the most popular pastime' allowing those 'laden with money to spend, to spend it unwisely in sexual frivolities. . . . Do we want that here? . . . we do not.'[52]

Some debate on the sexual double standard ensued, but Senator Jenny Wyse Power misunderstood the implications of dependent domicile and reaffirmed that divorce was not always a feminist concern:

Speaking as a woman I stand for the protection of women. A woman cannot get a divorce in the same way as a man. I understand that a woman wanting a divorce will have to leave this country and take up residence abroad. A man need not do that. It is difficult for a woman to do that. Granted that a few will do so, I think the majority of women will be protected, their homes made permanent, and the children kept there, and that if a few women suffer – and there will be very few – they will suffer in a very good cause.[53]

This long-standing notion of female forbearance was strongly refuted by the Countess of Desart, yet she also aligned divorce with Protestantism:

In the name of woman I protest against the idea that it is divorce that destroys the sanctity of the home ... to anchor the guilty man irremovably to the hearth he violates, or to cast the guilty woman on to the streets, cannot make for morality or for a high standard of virtue. It would be a hideous injustice to the women of this country. . . . We protest against the taking away from the minority of a right which it has enjoyed for nearly two hundred years ... the right the minority claims has never been abused.[54]

These misapprehensions were not the only inaccuracies; Senator Maurice Moore wrongly stated that there were only five applications for divorce in the preceding century. There was also erroneous optimism that no church would influence social policy while the limited demand for divorce in Northern Ireland was used to support a suggestion that if hardship was

[50] Bagwell, Seanad Éireann debates, 11 June 1925, cols. 450–2.
[51] O'Sullivan, *Irish Free State*, cited p. 168.
[52] The American divorce rate and the existence of mutual divorce in Denmark were also criticised, the latter being blamed for high illegitimacy rates (O'Farrell, Seanad Éireann debates, 11 June 1925, vol. 5, col. 471).
[53] Ibid., col. 463.   [54] Desart, ibid., cols. 463–4.

caused by the non-availability of divorce 'an exceedingly small number of people' would be affected. The fact that such limited demand was a consequence of the trials of parliamentary divorce was not considered.[55]

The Douglas motion proved problematic: legal practitioners like Samuel Brown affirmed that the definition of private bills included divorce bills and it was unconstitutional to rule otherwise; bills should therefore be brought to either the upper or lower house where they would likely be rejected.[56] The Seanad vote on Douglas's compromise was close: fifteen, including Yeats, voted for the motion; thirteen, including Jenny Wyse Power, opposed it with ten (eight of whom were Catholic) abstaining. The latter inferred that not all were willing to abide by clerical instruction to defeat divorce.[57] Cosgrave's opposition was emphatic when the motion came before the Dáil in June 1925. Smarting from the Glenavy motion which he believed was 'wrong' and effectively led to 'having the door slammed on my method', he now contended, with justification, that divorce should not be countenanced as possible when the opposite was true; either the Dáil or Seanad was likely to defeat divorce bills on their first reading. This was a *volte face* on what Cosgrave earlier proposed to the archbishop of Dublin, but he was now aware that even an assembly rejecting all divorce cases which came before it was unpalatable to the church.[58] Individual bills, replete with 'unsavoury details', would consequently be discussed without due cause as 'there is no intention of granting relief'.[59] Cosgrave's use of the term 'relief' indicated some empathy for the hardship of marital breakdown and the respite that divorce could bring. Yet, he overlooked the fact that debate never followed the first reading of any bill in the Seanad; the Dáil's standing orders allowed the speaker to put the question following a brief statement from the member introducing the bill and another from a member who opposed it. Only in the second reading, which acted as the trial of the case, could private details be aired. Glenavy's original objection, that standing orders could not be used to prohibit divorce, was also marginalised in the Dáil debate. Thomas Johnson was the only member to make public his desire to uphold the right for persons to introduce legislation by use of private bills. Although Ernest Blythe, the minister for finance admitted a 'general validity' to this argument, Cosgrave saw this solely as a means to facilitate divorce.[60] The motion refusing to adopt the Seanad's resolution was carried without division and

[55] Ibid., col. 472.   [56] Brown, ibid., col. 465.   [57] Murray, *Oracles of God*, p. 113.
[58] Archbishop Byrne told Cosgrave that although 'he would not oppose the course . . . he did not like it' (Cosgrave to Downey, 21 September 1925 [NAI, MS TAOIS/3/S4127]).
[59] Cosgrave, Dáil Eireann debates, 25 June 1925, vol. 10, col. 1567.
[60] Johnson, ibid., cols. 1569–72; Nolan, 'Influence of Catholic nationalism', cited p. 135.

was formally rescinded in the upper house on 7 July 1925. This did not ban divorce but prevented any parliamentary process to allow divorce bills to be heard.

This impasse did not end the 'sectarian bear pit' which divorce engendered.[61] Those supporting the Douglas motion were lampooned and the impact was palpable in the September 1925 election. Seanad clerk Donal O'Sullivan rightly saw this as a 'campaign of vilification'. Thomas Foran and J. T. O'Farrell, two Catholic Labour senators, were branded pro-divorce and a 'black list' was published of members who voted for the motion and sought re-election. Abstainers were also named and shamed as 'defaulters'. By comparison, those who voted against the motion were 'specially commended' and the electorate was instructed that 'the Catholic's duty is plain'.[62] Much of this campaign was conducted by the Catholic press; Douglas had to defend himself to Archbishop John Harty of Cashel, president of the Catholic Truth Society, to counter press claims that he was 'prominently associated' with attempts to introduce divorce.[63] Harty was unmoved: he accused Douglas of authoring a resolution that 'merited condemnation' as it would have allowed 'the State to exercise immoral power' contrary to 'catholic principles'.[64] Douglas also contacted Cosgrave, alleging attempts to bar him from public office by misrepresenting his actions as antagonistic to the Catholic Church and labelling him 'an anti-catholic bigot'.[65] Archbishop Harty and Bishop Downey similarly wrote to Cosgrave regarding Peter de Loughrey's abstention from the divorce vote. Downey deemed de Loughrey 'a less than satisfactory Catholic' who would not be supported in the election despite the Taoiseach's patronage. Cosgrave, 'very much pained' at his judgement being questioned, stated that although valuing 'most highly their good opinions[,] I should very much like to retain their confidence'; he stood by de Loughrey. Producing a seven-point summary of the Douglas motion, Cosgrave admitted that Catholic members of the Dáil and Senate had 'made mistakes in the matter of Divorce ... [but] were innocent in so far as the persons who made them were unaware of the facts ... much, if not all, of the difficulty would have been avoided had the Catholic members ... had better knowledge of Catholic teaching on the subject matter.' He was similarly frustrated by the scapegoating of those like de Loughrey: 'blame in the matter of divorce, if there be any, was not fairly

---

[61] Ferriter, *Transformation of Ireland*, p. 339.   [62] O'Sullivan, *Irish Free State*, p. 171.
[63] Douglas to Archbishop Harty, 14 September 1925 (NLI, MS 49,581/34, folio A5).
[64] Archbishop Harty to Douglas, 18 September 1925 (ibid., folio C7A).
[65] Douglas to Cosgrave, undated (ibid., folio C72).

apportioned . . . the whole question from the earliest period was not fairly discussed and criticised'.[66]

Some Catholic clerics also collectively rallied against Seanad members who might support an 'unCatholic measure', noting 'a certain number of Protestants . . . endeavouring, in the name of civil rights, to force on us Catholics legislation or permission of divorce'.[67] Foran and O'Farrell were re-elected but of the eight senators who supported the Douglas motion and whose term of office was over, five were not re-elected including Douglas Hyde who the Catholic Truth Society wrongly branded pro-divorce. Douglas was also defeated; he was elected to the Dáil in 1927 although his rehabilitation did not signal any accommodation of divorce or divorcees. Major Bryan Cooper of Markree Castle, Co. Sligo, for example, having earlier divorced his wife in Westminster and remarried a divorcee in 1925, unsurprisingly supported the provision for divorce in the Irish Free State but, standing as a Cumann na nGaedheal candidate in 1927, was challenged at church gates and lambasted by clerics as 'an expert on divorce . . . a danger to nationality . . . [and] the sacred truths that every Catholic holds in reverence'.[68]

The Bishop Morrisroe of Achonry's Lenten pastoral of 1929 on the horrors of dance halls can therefore be more widely applied: 'Though not formally Catholic, our Government at the same time legislates for Catholics in the main, so that its laws . . . should take special account of the needs of the overwhelming portion of the subjects.'[69] Papal encyclicals also effectively conveyed an anti-divorce message to the masses.[70] From the late nineteenth century, the encyclical gaze was increasingly on Catholic moral teaching and this continued into the next century:[71] Pius Xi's *Casti Connubii, on Christian Marriage*, issued in 1930, took Pope Leo III's papal encyclical *Arcanum* of half a century earlier as inspiration, seeking to defend the 'divine institution' of marriage which was 'often scorned and on every side degraded': 'The advocates of the neo-paganism of today . . . continue by legislation to attack the indissolubility of the marriage bond, proclaiming that the lawfulness of divorce must be

[66] James Downey to Cosgrave, 15 September 1925 and Cosgrave's reply, 21 September 1925 (NAI, MS TAOIS/3/S4127). De Loughrey denied the Douglas motion would encourage divorce and reaffirmed his opposition to divorce in the local press.

[67] Murray, *Oracles of God*, cited p. 116.

[68] Ibid. cited p. 276. See also PA, HL/PO/PB/1/1920/10&11G53.

[69] Less convincingly Bishop Morrisroe claimed such laws were 'not oppressive to any section' (John H. Whyte, *Church and state in modern Ireland, 1923–79* [Dublin, 1984], cited p. 50). The diocese of Achonry included parts of Mayo, Sligo and Roscommon.

[70] *The Statesman* ceased publication in 1930.

[71] Perreau-Saussine, *Catholicism and democracy*, p. 68.

recognized, and that the antiquated laws should give place to a new and more humane legislation.' *Casti Connubii* therefore indicated it was 'hardly necessary to point out what an amount of good is involved in the absolute indissolubility of wedlock and what a train of evils follows upon divorce'. Divorce was repeatedly blamed for destabilising marriage, inducing infidelity and harming children.[72]

This generated legislation to control the spread of material that was deemed morally suspect. The 1929 Censorship of Publications Act, best known for banning literature deemed obscene and limiting contraceptive advertisements, also prohibited the publication of reports on cases of divorce, separation, restitution of conjugal rights and nullity. A concern for the allegedly unseemly content of this legal material was accompanied by a virulent anti-Englishness. As Rev. Richard Devane, a Jesuit priest and member of the Irish Vigilance Association, wrote to Fr James Dempsey, member of the Committee on Evil Literature, in 1926: the Irish 'legal mind is still dominated by English tradition and practice'.[73] The British Sunday papers were singled out for particular reproach with their coverage of crime and divorce alleged to incite passions and portray 'wholly distorted pictures of social life',[74] but these assertions of immorality were ill founded: England limited press coverage of divorce cases in 1923.

Foreign jurisdictions soon asked questions on the country's divorce provision. As early as 1926, the Belgian ambassador sought information on divorce and judicial separation in the Free State and the governor general's draft response implied some unease; disregarding the fact that it was impossible to have a divorce bill passed in the Oireachtas, a substantial memorandum, subject to several revisions by the Department of Justice, claimed the following:

[N]o change has been made in regard to these matters ... with exception that the former procedure for obtaining divorce a vinculo matrimonii, namely, the passing of a private Bill through the British Parliament, is now superseded and such divorce can only be obtained by means of an act of the Oireachtas.[75]

The first conference for the Codification of International Law in 1930 also discussed the effects of marriage and its dissolution on nationality.

---

[72] *Casti Connubii*, 31 December 1930 (www.papalenclclicals.net). Dating to 1880, *Arcanum* similarly dealt with the subject of Christian marriage.

[73] Devane to Fr James Dempsey, 21 April 1926 (NAI, JUS7/2/9).

[74] De Bruca to Committee on Evil Literature, 28 April 1926 (NAI, JUS7/2/5).

[75] Draft dispatch from the Governor General to the Secretary of State for Dominion Affairs, 29 November 1926 and Sean Lester, Department of External Affairs to Secretary of the Executive Council, 13 January 1927 (NAI, TAOIS/3/S4680).

An Irish delegation was invited, and in the view of the Department of External Affairs' J. P. Walshe, attendance was essential:

We have already ... taken a definite point of view. The whole question of the status of our nationals is of 1st rate importance, and the issues of diplomatic protection of nationals and the relationship between States with regard to nationality law concerns us fundamentally at the present time.[76]

The international engagement did not stall successive administrations embedding the conservatism of independent Ireland. Eamon de Valera's Fianna Fáil government, acceding to power in 1932, was even more accommodating of Catholic moral teaching than its predecessor. Elected on a decidedly Catholic card, de Valera highlighted that 'the majority of the people of Ireland are Catholic and we believe in Catholic principles ... it is right and natural that the principles to be applied by us will be principles consistent with Catholicity'.[77] In 1934, he responded to Westminster's secretary of state for dominion affairs' request for information regarding amendments made to the law regarding marriage, divorce as well as the legitimisation of children since 1906. In a statement of unapologetic brevity, de Valera was more forthright than his predecessors: 'No change has taken place in the law relating to divorce since the establishment of the Irish Free State. No Standing Orders have been devised in connection with Private Bill procedure for the facilitation of divorce a vinculo matrimonii by Private Bill.'[78] His 1935 St Patrick's Day broadcast to the United States confirmed the church embrace; he addressed a 'Catholic nation'.[79]

It was therefore preordained that divorce would feature in any revised constitution under de Valera's command. As Seanad clerk O'Sullivan ascertained, a constitutional ban on divorce only formalised 'what has been the de facto position since the beginning' of the state.[80] O'Rahilly's earlier draft constitution article was influential, but John Charles McQuaid, a future Catholic archbishop of Dublin and authority on papal encyclicals, was instrumental. McQuaid thought it 'hardly possible to describe how great are the evils that flow from divorce':

Matrimonial contracts are by it made variable, mutual kindness is weakened, deplorable inducements to unfaithfulness are supplied, harm is done in the education and training of children, occasion is afforded to the breaking up of homes, the seeds are sown of dissension among families, the dignity of

---

[76] J. P. Walshe, Dept. of External Affairs to Secretary of the Executive Council, 17 February 1930 (NAI, S5175).
[77] Murray, *Oracles of God*, cited p. 262.　[78] NAI, DFA/3/131/23.
[79] Whyte, *Church and state*, cited p. 50.　[80] O'Sullivan, *Irish Free State*, p. 496.

womanhood is lessened and brought low, and women run the risk of being deserted after having ministered to the pleasure of men.[81]

A 1936 draft of the constitution included an article by McQuaid declaring: 'No law shall be enacted authorising the dissolution of a valid consummated marriage of baptised persons.' Other clerics made similar submissions: Jesuit Fr Edward Cahill, for example, stated 'The Civil Powers cannot dissolve a marriage validly contracted and betrothals and marriages of Catholics shall be identical with those laid down in the Code of Canon Law of the Catholic Church.' The final version of Article 41.3.2 was even starker: 'No law shall be enacted providing for the grant of a dissolution of marriage.' De Valera impressed on the Dáil that such a ban was not due to religious conviction but, echoing McQuaid, 'was justified having regard to the obvious social evils caused by the availability of a divorce jurisdiction'.[82] Trinity teachta dála (TD) Dr Robert Rowlette was a lone protester in the Dáil, highlighting instances where divorce 'would conceivably give an opportunity for establishing a happy home which would be useful to society' but de Valera claimed the debate 'lacked "useful purpose"'.[83]

Individuals also tried to impress upon de Valera the personal cost of a constitutional ban on divorce and the potential for the non-recognition of foreign divorces enshrined in Article 41.3.3:

[A] person whose marriage has been dissolved under the civil law of another State cannot validly re-marry in this country if the marriage so dissolved is still regarded as subsisting valid marriage under the law in force in this country. . . . Conversely, if our law regards a marriage dissolved in another country as properly and validly dissolved, then the subsection does not prohibit the re-marriage of the parties thereto in this country.

Kathleen Liddell from Galway thus described her marriage to a non-Catholic in a Manchester Catholic Church in 1919 after which she parted 'immediately' from her spouse. The marriage was unconsummated, and a divorce was granted to her husband in Chicago on the ground of desertion. Liddell's petition for a church annulment was before Rome: 'Should my petition for annulment be successful it is my intention to marry again immediately but under the new Constitution it will not be possible. . . . I am sure it was never intended to have such effect.' Only

---

[81] McQuaid was archbishop of Dublin from 1940 to 1973 (Dermot Keogh and Andrew J. McCarthy, *The making of the Irish constitution, 1937* [Dublin, 2007], cited pp. 112–14).

[82] G. W. Hogan, 'Law and religion: church-state relations in Ireland from independence to the present day', *American Journal of Comparative Law*, vol. 35, no. 1 (Winter 1987), p. 55. Members of Dáil Éireann are also known as deputies.

[83] Fitzpatrick, 'Divorce and separation', cited p. 194.

a draft of Article 41.3.3 was sent to Kathleen Liddell in reply.[84] Others vented their frustration in the press. Considering minority rights, Dublin's Enda Fitz Henry explained the popular reticence to openly challenge the divorce ban:

> To object to this is to lay oneself open to misinterpretation; the reason, I suppose, why many Catholics and Non-Catholics who have privately expressed disapproval of it have hitherto hesitated to do so publicly.
>
> To include such a clause in a Constitution professing to uphold freedom of conscience is to embody in civil law a law of the Catholic Church, and therefore to impose the discipline of that Church upon citizens who are not members of it. It is an injustice which affects a minority in this country, but the quality of an injustice does not vary in proportion to the number of people affected.[85]

The constitution passed in the Dáil with little debate by 748 votes to 62. Indeed, at the committee stages when divorce was discussed, the required quorum of twenty deputies twice necessitated a headcount.[86] The tacit opposition that Fitz Henry referred to was borne out in the subsequent referendum which passed by 685,105 (54.8 per cent) votes to 562,945 (45.1 per cent). Despite the high numbers rejecting the constitution, Very Rev. Canon Boylan professed a Catholic victory: 'The Catholic Church is more favourably placed in Ireland than it is in even the most Catholic countries of the continent.'[87] This bred a heightened censure of divorcees: in 1938, Dr Joseph Walsh, then auxiliary bishop of Tuam, advised Catholics not to associate with divorcees.[88] Akin to Cullen's covert surveillance of Catholic MPs' voting patterns during the 1857 Westminster divorce debates and the victimisation of those believed to support divorce in the Oireachtas in the 1920s, those challenging the state came under increased scrutiny. 'Repugnancy to the Constitution', a government file, collated information on liberal organisations like the Irish Secular Society. Formed in 1933, it condemned theology 'as superstitious ... mischievous, and ... as the historic enemy of progress'. Its immediate objects included divorce reform and the cessation of gendered inequality. It later called for a removal of the constitutional ban on divorce. However, even before that pronouncement, its London counterpart was considered suspect by the Irish government: its membership form was included in a file labelled 'The Freethinkers' under the collective title of

---

[84] Liddell to de Valera, 5 June 1937 and reply from M. O. Muimhneachain, 16 June 1937 (NAI, S12952).

[85] *Irish Independent*, 13 May 1937.

[86] William Duncan, *The case for divorce in the Irish Republic* (Dublin, 1979), p. 7.

[87] Paul Blanchard, *The Irish and Catholic power. An American interpretation* (Boston, 1953), cited p. 49.

[88] Whyte, *Church and state*, p. 172 and see *Irish Weekly Independent*, 3 February 1938.

'Objectionable Articles'.[89] The Irish branch also faced discrimination, finding it 'difficult to reach the public and denied access to meeting rooms'.[90]

Censoring the publicity afforded to divorce also continued. In the 1940s, for example, the censor changed the name of the American film *I Want a Divorce* to *The Tragedy of Divorce*.[91] To writer Frank O'Connor, this was evidence that Ireland 'used her new freedom to tie herself up into a sort of moral Chinese puzzle from which it seems almost impossible that she should even extricate herself'.[92] Sean O'Faolain's *The Irish*, published in 1947, was similarly courageous; he accused the Irish Catholic Church of being 'licked' in the 'imperious tradition, ruling by command' and 'unable or unwilling to admit that its flock has been developing ahead of it'.[93] The same disconnect between the moral ideal and marital reality was acknowledged in Pope Pius XII's 1947 address to the Congress of the International Union of Catholic Women's Leagues in Rome: '[In] sorrow and ... shame ... even among Catholics, false doctrines on the dignity of woman, on marriage and the family, on conjugal fidelity and divorce ... have stealthily infiltrated souls, and like gnawing worms have attacked the roots of the Christian family and of the Christian ideals of womanhood.' This inching immorality reaffirmed that despite the efforts of the church, state and censor, marriages broke down. Yet, any 'generous tendency that makes us sympathize with others, and share in their sorrows, their joys and their hopes' was discouraged as a 'misleading sentimentality which offers divorce as a remedy to unhappy wives'.[94]

This was cogently applied later in the same year when the Galway Blazers' hunt appointed Mrs James Hanbury, a remarried Protestant divorcee, as joint master.[95] More than sixty Catholic farmers subsequently denied the hunt access to their land, issuing verbal and written protests. One sign on farmland read: 'On Catholic principle and in the interest of good morals the right to hunt over these lands is now withdrawn', bringing the Victorian notion of moral contagion to a new high.[96]

---

[89] 'The Freethinkers', Objectionable articles file (NAI, S6522).

[90] Evelyn Mahon, 'Women's rights and Catholicism in Ireland' in *New Left Review* (November–December 1987) p. 57.

[91] Kevin Rockett, *Irish film censorship: a cultural journey from silent film to internet pornography* (Dublin, 2004), p. 92.

[92] Frank O'Connor, 'The future of Irish literature' in *Horizon*, January 1942, p. 57.

[93] Sean O'Faolain, *The Irish* (1947, revised edition, London, 1969), p. 119.

[94] *Papal directives for the woman of today*, 11 September 1947 (www.papalencyclicals.net).

[95] The County Galway Hunt dates from the mid-nineteenth century and is known colloquially as 'The Blazers'. The Joint Master is an abbreviation for Joint Master of the Foxhounds, a role which typically involves the management of the hunt, its paid staff and the care and breeding of the hunt's dogs.

[96] *Irish Times*, 23 December 1947.

The protests were bolstered by a muscular statement from local bishops; Archbishop Walsh of Tuam, Bishop Dignan of Clonfert and Bishop Brown of Galway stigmatised those who supported divorce but shied away from labelling them as Protestant:

It has been contended on the other side that divorce and remarriage are entirely the private affair of the individuals concerned; that no one has a right to show disapproval of such conduct. ... Such a contention shows gross ignorance or contempt for the religious convictions and feelings of a Catholic people.[97]

After trying to defend her marital status as acceptable to her church, Hanbury resigned in 1948.

The aggressive Catholicism so readily on display in Galway often conjoined divorce to an array of presumed 'evils' like contraception. As Fitz Henry earlier indicated, this deterred many reformers from publicising their views: 'The question of the right of divorce is never raised in public, and no one dares suggest an impartial survey to discover what are the actual facts concerning marital discord in the country.'[98] The majority view, so often cited in justification for divorce's prohibition in independent Ireland, is therefore partially illusionary. By comparison, opposition to reform was readily expressed. The British Medical Association's special committee's proposition that a Royal Commission should consider divorce reform met public resistance when meeting in Dublin in 1953. Led by the British Guild of Catholic Doctors, even making this suggestion in Ireland was deemed odious: the committee's recommendation was withdrawn. As the Most Rev. Dr O'Callaghan, bishop of Clogher, vividly reaffirmed, divorce was portrayed as an unwelcome import: 'British law has legalized divorce. We will speak against that as long as there is life in us. Let them know that we are prepared to lay down our lives rather than be traitors to Almighty God or his Divine law.'[99] Such defensive rhetoric, however, intimated that the consensus between the Irish Catholic church and the state was beginning to strain.

---

[97] Ibid., and Whyte, *Church and state*, cited p. 172.
[98] Blanchard, *The Irish and Catholic power*, p. 159.   [99] Ibid., cited p. 159.

10 Marriage Law 'in This Country Is an Absolute Shambles': The Reform Agenda

Irish divorce reform began in an opaque area of the law: the recognition of foreign divorces. Described as a 'legal exercise ... based on fiction', the Irish government reviewed the impact of the 1937 constitution with a committee from the Office of the Attorney General and Department of External Affairs in 1940.[1] The ambiguous wording of Article 41.3.3 regarding the recognition of foreign decrees of divorce in Ireland had already prompted several personal approaches to the Department of Local Government and Public Health. An earlier draft of this article, banning the remarriage of foreign divorcees, would have provided much-needed clarity, but aligning this with Article 50, recognising laws which predated the constitution, proved too taxing. There was also confusion amongst Irish civil registrars who, according to the committee, 'seem to have conceived the idea that ... [Article 41.3.3] had the effect of confining the prohibition against the marriage of divorced persons to those whose marriages were celebrated in this State, but that they do not prohibit the re-marriage here of persons married and divorced in other States'.[2]

Irish case law relating to domicile was almost wholly absent. In consequence, English law predating independence was often cited. The 1895 case of Le Mesurier versus Le Mesurier, with its emphasis on domicile to determine the jurisdiction to dissolve a marriage, was especially significant. Thus, only permanent domicile rather than residency allowed a foreign court to grant a divorce which would be valid in England. Judge Warren's ruling in the 1896 case of Sinclair versus Sinclair (with a husband domiciled in Ireland) gave similar weight to domicile; a divorce granted in England to parties who were not domiciled there was only valid

The quote in the chapter title comes from the *Irish Times*, 20 June 1975.
[1] Kathleen O'Higgins, *Marital desertion in Dublin. An exploratory study* (Economic and Social Research Institute, Broadsheet, no. 9) (May, 1974), pp. 3–5. Some Irish citizens living abroad also struggled to divorce. From 1925, Lord Leitrim, pursuing a divorce in France, failed to convince either his spouse or the French court of his domicile. See the Leitrim papers (NLI, MS 33,888 [4]).
[2] International law, specifically Private International Law, also known as the Conflict of Law, applied to both Ireland and England.

in the country where the divorce decree was made: 'for this purpose, as regards English decrees, Ireland is a foreign country'.[3] The rule of English law on the validity of foreign divorces had also recently been called into question in Northern Ireland: a 1937 case in the Northern Ireland Court of Appeal, Lyons re. Infant, adhered to the Le Mesurier ruling.[4] The complexity of many of these decisions resulted in legal limbo as epitomised by the Gibson versus Patterson case. Heard in Dublin's High Court in 1939, Justice Gavan Duffy held that a woman who divorced in England where her husband was domiciled neither died 'unmarried' nor left a surviving husband, although her former spouse was alive. There was no Irish legislation to invalidate this divorce and this woman died in 1937 before the constitution was implemented.[5]

The 1940 committee concluded that Article 41.3.3 did not change pre-existing law 'that where a person obtains a divorce not valid according to the law in force in this jurisdiction, he should be prosecuted for bigamy if he attempted to re-marry during the lifetime of his former spouse'. They conceded, however, that the article was 'open to doubt and cannot be stated with any approach to certainty'. Yet, the abstruseness of the constitutional wording facilitated a welcome 'elasticity ... and enables legislation on the subject to be enacted giving effect to whatever intention the Government may desire to give effect to'. Foreign domicile and a valid divorce according to the law of the country of domicile should therefore be recognised as a divorce in Ireland and allow either of the parties to remarry.[6] Despite this, the recognition of foreign divorces remained vexing. The 1958 Mayo-Perrott case heard in Dublin's High Court brought the issue of whether an English female divorcee was entitled to recover costs against a former spouse awarded by the English courts to the fore. Helen Mayo-Perrott of Co. Wicklow claimed £339–1-5d against her former spouse, Major John Perrott of Co. Dublin as the residue of costs awarded when she divorced on the ground of cruelty in England. The couple married in London in 1945 and moved to Ireland. In 1951, Mrs Mayo-Perrott petitioned for divorce and a decree was granted in 1953. Major Perrott, who remarried, was ordered to pay taxed costs. The Irish proceedings, listing Mrs Mayo-Perrott 'as a single woman' and 'suing on a foreign judgment', questioned the recognition of foreign divorces.[7] The

---

[3] This case went to appeal in Ireland and to the House of Lords where a private divorce bill was passed in 1897; see Chapter 6. See also the Malone Divorce (Validation) [Ireland] Act which passed in 1905.
[4] Irish Law Times Review, vol. 72, p. 86.   [5] Irish Times, 22 July 1939.
[6] Memorandum on the position of foreign decrees of divorce in Ireland, 27 October 1940 (NAI, S12506).
[7] Irish Independent, 19 November 1958.

High Court, departing from the usual practice of recognising a judgement for a specified amount, disallowed this case: Mr Justice Murnaghan refused to separate the claim for unpaid costs from the original divorce proceeding: '[T]he public policy of this country on the question of divorce was quite clear and in his opinion was incompatible with the prevailing law in England and therefore the plaintiff could not succeed.'[8] Murnaghan was not alone in regarding divorce as 'repugnant';[9] his ruling was upheld in the Supreme Court but the case added to the growing debate on the interpretation of Article 41.3.3.[10]

By the mid-1960s, with more cases concerning foreign divorce being heard, mostly seeking maintenance, custody or inheritance, the flexibility in interpreting Article 41.3.3 which the 1940 commission lauded, unsurprisingly continued to produce conflicting legal decisions. A Constitution Review Group recommended the removal of Article 41.3.3 in 1967 but this did not effect any change in the law, and Ireland was not a signatory to the 1970 Hague Convention on the Recognition of Divorce and Legal Separations. In the case of Caffin deceased: Bank of Ireland versus Caffin in 1971, the High Court ruled in favour of a second wife of an English divorcee receiving half of the deceased's estate, but in C. versus C. in 1973, as the husband had Irish domicile, a 1972 English divorce was not recognised and the second wife's claim for maintenance failed.[11] The balance of these rulings pivoted on domicile, the intention to reside in a country permanently, which was challenging to test and still dictated by a husband's domicile.

This was reinforced by Kathleen O'Higgin's pioneering work on marital desertion in Dublin. Based on interviews with forty women, including divorcees, with no facilities for divorce in Ireland, a 'deserted wife remains a deserted wife'. The exception was when a woman was deserted and then divorced by her husband in another jurisdiction; she would be excluded from the means-tested deserted wives' allowance introduced to Ireland in 1970 as 'in the eyes of the law and of the Department of Social Welfare, [she was] no longer married'. This would only apply if the parties of the divorce were domiciled in the country granting the divorce; more temporary residence would cause the divorce to be unrecognised. The reality of this situation was that 'If the husband deserts to England, the law

---

[8] *Irish Times*, 3 December 1955.

[9] William Binchy, *A casebook on Irish family law* (Abingdon, 1984), cited p. 227.

[10] Murnaghan admitted that Article 41.3.3 did 'not lend itself to easy interpretation' (*Irish Times*, 26 December 1958). For a more moderate interpretation, see Cedric Jones, 'The non-recognition of foreign divorces in Ireland' in *The Irish Jurist* (1968), pp. 299–321.

[11] Binchy, *Casebook on Irish family law*, pp. 236–7. In the Caffin case, the 1965 Succession Act was called into play.

presumes that both parties are living there, whereas in fact she has been deserted and is still living in Dublin . . . Domicile "legally" distorts the real position.'[12] The attorney general acknowledged this as fact by ruling that divorce did not automatically exclude a woman from receiving a deserted wife's allowance in 1973 and the critique continued: Senator John Kelly called in 1971 for a commission on divorce as the exiting provision was 'unfair and potentially cruel . . . it is no credit to our civil institutions'.[13] Moreover, the 1975 case of Gaffney versus Gaffney in the Supreme Court led to a warning from Justice Walsh that married women's dependent domicile may be unconstitutional. The patience of the attorney general was also wearing; he described dependent domicile as 'medieval' and one of the 'last relics of slavery' in the same year.[14] This found support in some unlikely places, including the Committee of Catholic Bishops Council for Social Welfare which sought to halt the spectre of Irish women being divorced by their spouses in foreign jurisdictions.[15]

A Committee on the Law of Domicile was established in 1976, but it was a decade before legislation amended this legal anomaly.[16] In the interim, cases such as C. M. versus M. C. in 1985 saw Justice Barr deny the validity of requiring both spouses to be domiciled in the country granting a divorce. This was enshrined in the Domicile and Recognition of Foreign Divorces Act of 1986 which ended married women's dependent domicile and recognised foreign divorces passed in the post-October 1986 period where either spouse was domiciled, with at least one of the parties normally domiciled in the foreign jurisdiction when the divorce proceedings were instituted.[17] Defining domicile rather than residency, however, remained complex; the former's definition derived not only from the 1986 legislation but also case and common law and the constitution. David Andrews, the minister for foreign affairs, offered one of the clearest explanations which also highlighted the primacy of men's legal status:

[F]or the purposes of Irish law an adult individual is domiciled in the country where he or she is resident and intends to reside permanently or indefinitely. If the

---

[12] O'Higgins, *Marital desertion in* Dublin, pp. 3–5.
[13] Kelly also sought contraceptive reform (*Irish Times*, 25 March 1971).
[14] *Irish Times*, 31 December 1975. In the Gaffney case, the Supreme Court supported the first wife who divorced in 1959 as the lawful widow as opposed to a second wife. An appeal was dismissed.
[15] Ibid., 20 August 1974.
[16] The LRC's Report: Recognition of Foreign Divorces and Legal Separations (LRC 10–1985, April 1985) recommended residence as a basis for recognition rather than domicile, pp. 23–7.
[17] This came in the wake of similar international reforms, for example, in England and New Zealand in 1973 and 1976, respectively.

individual has no fixed intention he or she is domiciled in his or her domicile of origin; an individual's domicile of origin is generally dependent on the domicile held by his or her father at the time of his or her birth.[18]

By 1991, 8.9 per cent of separated women and 14.5 per cent of separated men in the Republic of Ireland were recorded as securing foreign divorces. The practice of forum shopping, whereby the most favourable jurisdiction in which to secure a divorce was selected by Irish citizens of sufficient means, subsequently emerged to create 'a lawyer's paradise and a social nightmare'.[19] In addition, a disparity between the court rulings on foreign divorce and the revenue commissioners persisted. The latter, for income and capital gains tax purposes, recognised second marriages which were not legally valid and therefore bigamous.[20] The Irish Supreme Court ruling of W. versus W. in 1993 led to the recognition of foreign divorces granted before October 1986, but applying for maintenance, inheritance and barring orders remained difficult.[21]

The Family Law Act of 1994 helped clarify the situation by allowing those divorced in foreign jurisdictions to apply for maintenance orders and other support under certain circumstances.[22] This slow and, at times, convoluted reform of the recognition of foreign divorce was part of a broader process of Irish family law reform which reflected changing social mores. The state, passing legislation such as the 1964 Guardianship of Infants Act, which granted joint guardianship to parents and the 1965 Succession Act, which reformed widows' inheritance rights and introducing an Unmarried Mothers Allowance in 1973, recognised that the reality of family life could fall short of the constitutional ideal. Attitudes regarding wifely perseverance were patently transforming. Kevin Kearns's collection of oral testimony from residents in tenements in 1950s Dublin revealed the following: 'He was your husband and when you married him you had to do what he *told* you . . . Or you'd get a few punches. That was always battered into you from your *own* parents when you'd be getting married.'[23] Yet, Kathleen O'Higgins's interviews on

---

[18] Dáil Éireann debates, 13 May 1998, vol. 491, col. 173.

[19] Muriel Walls and David Bergin, *The law of divorce in Ireland* (Bristol, 1997), p. 215 and cited p. 153.

[20] Shannon, *Divorce act*, p. 2.

[21] Ireland signed an EU convention relating to the recognition of foreign divorces, separation and annulments in 1998 and recognised EU member state divorces, with the exception of Denmark where mutual divorce was permissible, from 2000 with new member states added in the following year (Dáil Éireann debates, 12 June 2001, vol. 537, col. 1396).

[22] Dervla Browne, 'Legal changes in the law covering marital breakdown in Ireland' in Mags O'Brien (ed.), *Divorce? Facing the issues of marital breakdown* (Dublin, 1995), p. 65.

[23] Kevin C. Kearns, *Dublin tenement life. An oral history* (Dublin, 1994), cited p. 51.

marital desertion in Dublin in the early 1970s highlighted that the desire to remarry was strong especially amongst younger deserted wives. Others wanted divorce for protection and 'to be free of the man through whom they had suffered so much. These women felt that divorce ... would be a more secure way of ensuring that their husbands did not harass them in the future.'[24] There was therefore some latent demand for divorce but mobilising this was exacting. Anxiety regarding the position of the Catholic Church in the Irish state was also emerging. The Dublin Synod of the Church of Ireland, the Ad Hoc Committee on the Status of Women and the Irish Council of Churches, representing all the major non-Catholic denominations in Ireland, averred to unease at the state's long engagement with Catholic moral teaching. A monolithic Catholicism should not, however, be presumed. Some more liberal Irish priests emerged in the 1960s as evidenced by the writings of Fr Peter Connolly of Maynooth and Fr John Kelly, SJ, in *Studies* and the *Furrow*. Yet, more effective in prompting a reassessment of the position of the Catholic Church was the Vatican Council Decree on Religious Liberty. Popularly known as Vatican II, it deliberated from 1962 to 1965, giving 'explicit, albeit measured and conditional, recognition' to democracy and liberalism. Attachment to a confessional state also fell; the council's final document, 'The Pastoral Constitution on the Church in the Modern World' (*Gaudium et spes*) separated church from state. Vatican II thus moved the church away from the idea that politics should be modelled on an alliance between civil and ecclesiastical powers.[25] This encouraged Taoiseach Sean Lemass to seek clarification on the implications for Irish divorce, asking Minster for Justice Brian Lenihan whether a change in the law 'so as to allow divorce and remarriage for those of our citizens whose religion tolerates it' might be introduced. Although circumventing the rights of religious minorities and the need for church sanction, Lemass still sought guidance from the Catholic hierarchy: '[Y]ou might institute informal consultations with some members of the hierarchy for the purpose of getting their views as to implications of the Vatican Council Decree in respect of our legislation in this matter generally.' Lenihan subsequently 'sounded' Monsignor Rev. Dr Gerard Sheehy, chancellor of the Dublin archdiocese, who previously assisted the Department of Justice with aspects of the 1965 Succession Bill. Sheehy 'agreed to have an informal talk on the implications after he has had time to consider the matter' and consult more widely, most notably with Archbishop

---

[24] O'Higgins, *Marital desertion*, p. 128.
[25] Vatican II also revived the Gallican attachment to the laity having political power (Perreau-Saussine, *Catholicism and democracy*, p. 2 and p. 117).

McQuaid whose reaction to Vatican II was far from favourable.[26] That meeting in early 1966 confirmed the immovable Irish hierarchical stand on divorce: '[T]here would be "violent opposition" from the Hierarchy to any proposal to allow divorce in the State. Whether or not there was divorce did not . . . affect the question of religious liberty . . . an informal discussion . . . would not achieve anything.'[27]

Despite this, the impact of the constitutional ban was more openly discussed as part of broader secular and clerical conversations on the ethos of the state from the mid-1960s. Indeed, as Fanning avers, there was a gradual move away from a solely 'ethno-Catholic conception of national identity'.[28] An *Irish Times* series on divorce publicised that a considerable number of Irish citizens were pursuing divorce in the English courts 'with a seeming disregard' for the fact that it would not be recognised in the Republic of Ireland. Written by an anonymous barrister, the 'ostrich-like attitude' to the legal consequences of securing a divorce in England was aligned to an alleged 'happy-go-lucky attitude to life' and, more convincingly, to the rarity of prosecutions and the minimal sentences for bigamy in the Republic of Ireland.[29] Cases where both parties were aware of a previous marriage that was dissolved and some question remained regarding the validity of the divorce would probably not result in prosecution, but remarriage following an invalid divorce was bigamous wherever it was celebrated. However, only Irish citizens could be guilty of bigamy in the Republic and the prosecution rate was low. Indeed, there were claims that this was tantamount to a 'public policy . . . not to prosecute' in the thorny realm of church-state relations which generated a 'lack of respect for the civil law'.[30] As Judge O'Briain noted in The People (Attorney General) versus Ballins in the Circuit Court in 1964:

The position of a Judge who is called upon to administer the civil law that for historical reasons conflicts with the canon law which is binding upon the majority of people of the state is . . . unenviable . . . after 40 years of independence, it should be possible to amend the law here which for historical reasons now raises a grave problem of conscience among the majority of Irish citizens. It should be possible to amend the law without in any way creating a new problem of conscience for the majority, Protestants or otherwise.[31]

---

[26] Taoiseach Sean Lemass to Brian Lenihan, minister for justice, 25 September 1965 and reply 16 November 1965 (NAI, 96/6/364). On McQuaid's reaction, see John Feeney, *John Charles McQuaid. The man and the mask* (Dublin, 1974), pp. 45–53.
[27] Lenihan to Lemass, 17 February 1966 (NAI, 96/6/364).
[28] Bryan Fanning, *The quest for modern Ireland: the battle of ideas, 1912–86* (Dublin, 2008), p. 222.
[29] *Irish Times*, 26 December 1966.
[30] New Ireland Forum submission case file: John O'Connor, Divorce Action Group, Dublin (NAI, 2004/40/133).
[31] Binchy, 'Divorce', p. 101 and cited p. 106.

Difficulties also arose for children of bigamous unions; the 1965 Succession Act's provision for widows and children did not apply in the case of a second union as they needed to be fully named in a will and 'not merely as "my darling wife" or "my son Sean."' This not only applied to Irish citizens but anyone with Republic of Ireland domicile.[32]

The legal reticence to engage with divorce was further highlighted by a 1962 request from the German Fourth Civil Court of the Federal Republic that the Irish High Court take the evidence of an Irish female respondent in a divorce case made under the Foreign Tribunals Evidence Act of 1856 which by this juncture was regulated by the rules of the Supreme Court. The High Court judge refused the request on the ground that it would be repugnant to Article 41 of the constitution as it related to divorce. This came before the Supreme Court on appeal on behalf of the minister for external affairs:

[I]f a letter of request came before a court through the proper channel the court should make the order without inquiring too deeply into the nature of the action. ... The court ... was not considering a decree of divorce in this case and in principle, the evidence of a respondent in a divorce case should not be calculated to lead to divorce, it should have the contrary effect.[33]

The Supreme Court agreed to the request for evidence, but this did not establish inalienable precedent: in a 1978 case, reminiscent of Mayo-Perrott in 1958, the High Court judge refused to accede. In 1987, however, the Supreme Court again enforced an English court order for a wife's maintenance following a divorce on the basis that Irish law also demanded maintenance for dependent spouses. Such inconsistent legal rulings, Vatican II and an emergent secularisation inspired Lemass to establish the first Constitution Review Group in 1966. Chaired by Minister for Industry and Commerce George Colley, it was composed of TDs and senators from the three main political parties to review the constitutional, legislative and institutional aspects of government. Indicating the distancing of church and state, there was no hierarchical involvement. For Sean O'Faolain, the committee's creation was 'a healthy sign of the times', but the lack of public discussion it engendered was troubling: 'no one ever discussed divorce per se' and the issue remained clouded by considerations of religious and minority rights.[34] The committee also seems not to have consulted Protestants and lacked Protestant membership. Much of its attention focused on divorce and, after seventeen meetings, hearing evidence from both individuals and organisations, assessing foreign constitutions and considering various

[32] *Irish Times*, 26 and 29 December 1966.   [33] *Irish Press*, 25 July and 1 August 1962.
[34] O'Faolain, *The Irish*, p. 121.

written expressions of opinion, its December 1967 report was unanimous and valiant: the ban on divorce was 'coercive ... unnecessarily harsh and rigid [and] a source of embarrassment' for those seeking to improve relations between the north and south of the country.[35] The report was not, however, binding on the government; there was no compulsion to implement its recommendation to revise the constitution regarding divorce on the following lines: 'In the case of a person who was married in accordance with the rites of a religion, no law shall be enacted providing for the grant of a dissolution of that marriage on grounds other than those acceptable to that religion.'[36] The inclusivity of the constitution was questioned as it was 'intended for the whole of Ireland and that the percentage of the population of the entire island made up of persons who are Roman Catholic though large, is not overwhelming ... there are other predominantly Catholic countries which do not in their Constitutions absolutely prohibit the enactment of laws relating to the dissolution of marriage'. The constitutional ban was also deemed at variance with Vatican II. Moreover, church annulments made the Republic's divorce ban appear obtuse, as it imposed 'regulations more rigid than those required by canon law'.[37]

The report 'created a sensation'.[38] Cardinal Conway was the first member of the Catholic hierarchy to respond: critical of the lack of church consultation, he inflated the impact of enacting the report's recommendations: '[T]he proposal would involve the setting up of divorce courts in the Republic ... this would only be the first step. Everyone knows how these things spread once the gates are opened. Already, within 24 hours, one national newspaper has suggested that there should be divorce for all.' The suggestion that other faiths might seek divorce was also questioned, countering the connection often made between divorce and Protestantism: '[C]omparatively few believe in divorce, and fewer still of them want it. Even these few have little difficulty in securing a divorce elsewhere, and many of them have done so.'[39] McQuaid's charge followed: downgrading the report to the mere workings of an 'informal committee', his 1968 Lenten regulations portrayed divorce as 'contrary to the law of God' and responsible for 'the gravest evils in society'. Bishop of Cork Dr Lucey's reference to divorcees as 'the wayward and the

---

[35] *Report of the Committee on the Constitution* (Dublin, 1967), pp. 43–4. As previously noted, the committee recommended the removal of Article 41.3.3 on foreign divorce.
[36] Ibid., p. 44.
[37] Extract from *Report of the Committee on the Constitution* (Dublin, 1967), pp. 43–5 (NAI, 96/6/364).
[38] Eilis Bean Ui Sheoighe, Malahide to Jack Lynch, 8 January 1968 (NAI, 96/6/364).
[39] *Irish Times*, 15 December 1967.

wanton' was highly derogatory but paled in comparison to Bishop of Elphin Dr Hanly's denial of state authority to dissolve 'even the marriage of pagans'. He reminded all Catholics of their 'solemn duty ... to ... vote against the provision of divorce'.[40]

Although Fianna Fáil's university Cumann (association) called for the 'rights of conscience of religious minorities' to be legally guaranteed,[41] there was considerable popular opposition to the report. Graduate, teacher and lifelong Fianna Fáil supporter Eilis Bean Ui Sheoighe, from Malahide, wrote to Taoiseach Jack Lynch:

[E]ven Protestants, or other faiths do not want it and have said they would not again vote for your party. ...

The family is the most important unit in a Nation – it is the Nation – and if broken up creates all sorts of tensions, emotional disturbances. ... Children cannot be properly reared or educated, both parents are really necessary to the Children's welfare.

Some of the newly young inexperienced parents, some of them only 6 months married would separate in the morning if the bill went through. Difference of opinions, rows and petty quarrels can as we all know be patched up, once there is no way out ... what kind of example is this Catholic Country of ours giving to the world. ... The unification of Ireland would never be worth the passing of this bill. We cannot understand why a man of your ability, a good Catholic and Corellonian could for a single instance stand over this bill. Save your party and think about it a second time.

A prompt response proffered assurance that the government did not plan to introduce divorce legislation and any constitutional amendment would have to be passed by both the Dáil and the Seanad before being put to referendum.[42] Lady Gwendolene Hort, president of the Mothers' Union in Ireland, also recorded her organisation's 'grave concern':

Our society aims to help parents build Christian homes, and we believe this can best be done by holding to Our Lord's teaching that marriage is a life long union. We deplore that the Government of Eire who have always stood for the permanencies of the marriage bond, should now propose to lower its standard ... although I live in the north, I speak for the whole of Ireland, and our membership is 17,500 strong.[43]

---

[40] Whyte, *Church and state*, cited p. 348 and p. 349 and John Cooney, *John Charles McQuaid* (Dublin, 1999), p. 36. See also *Irish Times*, 15 December 1967 and *Irish Independent*, 26 February 1968.

[41] Resolutions were received from Trinity College Cumann and the Kevin Barry Cumann of University College Dublin (NAI, 96/6/364).

[42] Eilis Bean Ui Sheoighe, Malahide to Jack Lynch, 8 January 1968 and reply from H. S. O'Dubhda, 10 January 1968 (NAI, 96/6/364).

[43] Lady Gwendolene Hort, Omagh to Jack Lynch, 29 February 1968 and reply from H. S. O'Dubhda, 14 March 1968 (ibid.).

Alice Crabb of Wicklow, who shared these sentiments, contacted the minister for justice describing her 'bitter disappointment, sadness and grave misgivings':

> Broken marriages may sometimes be inevitable, the social crime divorce is not. . . . Why . . . legalise divorce which all Christian people know is wrong. By legalising divorce we would be condoning (a) broken marriage vows, (b) the seducing by unscrupulous person's [sic] of someone else's husband or wife, (c) the desertion of family responsibilities. By the passing of one Act we could undermine all that goes to make a nation great. . . . Happy, secure homes are the bulwark of a nation. Please do not endanger your immortal soul by becoming the person responsible for striking a damning blow on Irish home life. . . . I have seen the drastic, unhappy results of divorce. A wife, heart-broken having relinquished her husband to another woman. A young girl of nineteen haunted by the black shadow of her parent's divorce.
>
> As long as divorce is unobtainable in Ireland, unthinking, greedy, selfish people will be deterred from stealing other people's marriage partners.

Crabb, however, acknowledged the reality of marital breakdown in Ireland, suggesting that 'time, brains and money to be . . . directed into the setting up of marriage advisory clinics and used to keep homes together'.[44] Joseph Cole's articles on deserted wives in the *Evening Press* in 1967 made public the hardships of broken marriages that Crabb referenced. Cole castigated desertion as a form of *de facto* divorce where men

> simply walk[ed] out on the wives and families and disappear[ed] in the large industrial centres of Britain. This has become known as Divorce – Irish Style – nobody has dared publicly to put a name on it. The name is divorce. The Vatican, in trying to keep the family as the most important social unit in society by forbidding divorce, has unwittingly achieved the opposite in Ireland for here, families are being broken up every day.[45]

Two years later, Dorine Rohan's *Marriage Irish Style* sought to answer what she classified as the 'great unknown . . . [the] number of Irishmen and women who would end their marriages if they were permitted to'. Estimates of unhappy Irish marriages varied widely from 70 per cent to 1 per cent, but a quarter of women and even higher numbers of men in Rohan's sample supported divorce: 'Women feel that a bad marriage is better than a divorce, but on the whole their fears are economic rather than emotional.'[46] The failure of Irish family law to address the realities of

---

[44] Alice Crabb to Minister for Justice, 16 January 1968 and Sean Flanaghan, Minister for Health's reply, 28 February 1968 (NAI, 96/6/364).

[45] Cole's articles were published in April 1967; Rohan, *Marriage Irish style*, cited p. 27 and p. 41.

[46] Rohan, *Marriage Irish style*, p. 54.

the situation, so graphically described by Rohan and Cole, depressed legal authorities like William Duncan: 'The dominant theme is one of neglect. . . . The law has failed to react to the increasing problems raised by modern matrimonial breakdown. . . . The charge of hypocrisy must be laid.'[47]

For those seeking a release from a broken marriage, the committee's report was a false dawn: it was declared 'dead' in 1968.[48] Once this became more popularly known, there were written appeals for help: Frances Foy-Wyse of Dublin wrote to Lynch pleading to end her marriage. Her testimony revealed both shame and fear:

[W]e are living very much a dirty game[,] we are only mocking God the Church included.

The state declares a man married . . . can live with who he likes as long as he supports his wife.

The Church states a man can break the sacrement [sic] of marrage [sic]. And can live with another woman married, widowed or single, in sin or what ever [sic] he likes as long as he is seen going to his duties how is that for a laugh but his wife and family must stand by watching him living with a widow in the same Parish and what fear and dread for them as long as he can't marrie [sic] again I and his family are in great danger as we are living in his House and the widow has a grown daughter and son.

Many have been got rid of in a way nobody knows which he has often treathned [sic] to us in those words.

If you make [a] law that anyone who wants to marrie [sic] again wheather [sic] they be Catholic or not can do so by going to court I will be the first to do so maybe the people in the north will be glad of this law . . . be a sport and grant my Request like a good man for I don't intend to copy my Husband in his way Marriage was suppose[d] to last and the Church tied us together now freedom for the Husband but not for the wife when are the women of Ireland going to be respected may one ask[?]

A postscript underscored her desperation: 'If you can't pass the divorce Law for all grant me one and tell me which court. Please.' A reply offered no solution and little solace: '[T]he Government have no proposals under consideration for legislation to permit divorce. It is suggested that your personal problem is one which you might wish to discuss with a Solicitor or with your Parish Priest.'[49]

A Dublin symposium on Constitutional Changes on Divorce in Ireland, organised by the Forum Discussion Group in 1968, saw clerics join with medics and legal practitioners which in itself was revelatory of

---

[47] Duncan, 'Desertion and cruelty', p. 237.
[48] Liam Cosgrave, Dáil Éireann, 8 February 1968, vol. 232, col. 797.
[49] Frances Foy-Wyse to Taoiseach Jack Lynch, 27 August 1969 and reply from R. S. Dubhda, 29 August 1969 (NAI, 96/6/364).

a more pragmatic approach, but there was little consensus. There was, however, a recognition of the considerable marital strife especially in lower-income groups which revived the earlier correlation between class and marriage breakdown as well as the 'great deal of psychological disturbance ... caused in the children of these homes'. E. Garrett Gill of the Brothers of the Sacred Heart (SC) was more forthright and epitomised liberal Catholicism by calling for constitutional amendment particularly of Article 41: 'It was undesirable that people who could not live amicably together should be forced to continue in an unnatural partnership and prevent them from re-marrying or forced into getting a divorce in other countries.'[50] Gill could make such a pronouncement due to the growing, if not universal, attachment to the practice of informed conscience which allowed church teachings to be questioned. Moderation was also evident at the Catholic bishops' 1971 spring meeting where it was suggested that legislators should accept the will of the people who voted for them.[51] This riled conservatives like McQuaid. Coming near the end of a long tenure as archbishop of Dublin, his Lenten regulations of that year defensively depicted an assault 'by public pleas' for 'evil' divorce, which, by its association to minority rights, 'gave a false appearance of reason and morality to the debate'.[52]

The removal of Article 44 of the constitution on the special position of the Catholic Church in 1973 was a significant recasting of national identity, but this distanced rather than terminated the church-state connexion. Aspirations for Irish unity partly fuelled this reinvention and letters from the Irish Embassy to the Holy See intimated that the church would not oppose legislative reform including divorce 'in the context of a united Ireland [and] nor would the people'.[53] This laid the foundation for a 1973 Helsinki meeting between Minister for Foreign Affairs FitzGerald and Monsignor Agostino Casaroli, secretary of the Council for the Public Affairs of the Church at the Vatican. Secret correspondence revealed that 'a number of ... problems' in the context of Irish unity were discussed, including divorce. Rather than focusing on the increased instance of marital breakdown, FitzGerald stressed the negative impact of the divorce ban on the government's overarching priority – Irish reunification – as well as the possibility of a pogrom against northern Catholics if tensions in Northern Ireland reached a 'flashpoint'. The constitution's all-island reach and ban on divorce was portrayed as

---

[50] *Irish Press*, 1 February 1968.   [51] *The Furrow*, vol. 22, no. 4 (April 1971).

[52] Contraception was also deemed 'evil' (Cooney, *John Charles McQuaid*, cited p. 341. See also *Irish Times*, 12 March 1971). McQuaid resigned in 1971.

[53] Irish Embassy to the Holy See, Cardinal William Conway, Archbishop of Armagh, 24 May 1972 (NAI, 2008/81/4).

endangering existing divorce provision in Northern Ireland if reunification occurred. FitzGerald thus suggested that a 'strong case' could be made for a new constitution without the ban to help accommodate Protestants and build a pan-Christian alliance between the north and south of the country. Even after reassurances of 'only limited support' for divorce reform,[54] Casaroli countered the earlier suggestion that reform would be palatable; as unity was not imminent, the various changes which would unsettle the Republic 'would not in themselves' bring unification and therefore could not be pursued.[55] The price of allowing individualism to triumph was evidently still too great.

The more reformist spirit evident in FitzGerald's approach did not include a strong feminist element. Second-wave feminism emerged in the 1970s but was a complex and sometimes disparate movement. As in feminism's earlier incarnation, issues like divorce did not always automatically fall under its remit. Fissures over tactics also spawned a myriad of organisations. The radical, confrontational and ideologically inspired Irish Women's Liberation Movement (IWLM) was active in 1970–71 and sought to challenge the state rather than work within its parameters. Moderate, liberal Irish feminism was exemplified by the Council for the Status of Women (CSW), established in 1970 after several years of campaigning, and the Action, Information, Motivation (AIM) group, founded by Nuala Fennell and Bernadette Quinn in 1971 to co-ordinate a campaign for legal reform including social welfare and maintenance payments.[56] Irish feminism would later engage fully with the issue of divorce, but the abolition of the criminal conversation suit first captured its attention.[57] After a nine-year campaign which aligned AIM, the liberal press, the newly formed Divorce Action Group (DAG), the Irish Countrywomen's Association (ICA), the single parents' association Gingerbread, legal practitioners, the Church of Ireland's Law Advisory Committee, the Committee of Catholic Bishops' Council for Social Welfare and some cross-party support, the Family Law Bill, which included criminal conversation's abolition, was passed in

---

[54] Education, mixed marriages and contraception were also discussed (Garret FitzGerald, Department of Foreign Affairs to A. Ward, Department of Justice, 14 August 1973 [NAI, 2004/27/12]).

[55] Views of the Nuncio in Dublin on meeting between FitzGerald and Casaroli, 12 September 1973 (ibid.).

[56] Indeed, Fennell formed AIM after resigning from IWLM in protest that it was too left wing. See Linda Connolly, *The Irish women's movement from revolution to devolution* (Basingstoke, 2002), pp. 145–54. IWLM was largely defunct by 1972. CSW was later state sponsored and is now known as the National Women's Council.

[57] See Diane Urquhart, 'Ireland's criminal conversations', *Études Irelandaises*, vol. 37, no. 2 (2012), pp. 65–80.

1981.[58] However, support for criminal conversation's tardy termination, having been abolished in England in 1857 and in Northern Ireland in 1939, did not prompt a universal feminist call for divorce law reform. AIM, for example, was not wholly pro-divorce; 'its members . . . [were] divided on the issue and anxious to avoid a further split'. It, however, most clearly linked criminal conversation to the need for further reform and called for a divorce referendum.[59] Such an association should not be presumed. In Italy, the most recent European country to introduce divorce in 1970, divorce reform was not equated to women's issues.[60] The 1971 *Chains or Change* pamphlet produced by the radical IWLM also tellingly omitted divorce from its reform programme. Irish Women United's manifesto of 1975 did likewise but revised this in the following year.[61] As feminist Nell McCafferty highlighted, it was 'a measure of our utter innocence. . . . It just did not occur to us that marriage could or should be legally terminated'.[62] McCafferty and AIM's Nuala Fennell presented reports on divorce, contraception, criminal conversation and women's legal status in Ireland to an international tribunal on crime against women held in Brussels in 1976. Yet, Fennell, standing as an independent candidate in the election of the following year, did not include divorce reform in an otherwise liberal manifesto, underscoring the controversy the issue still aroused.[63]

Ireland's membership of the EEC in 1973 provided a wider platform to publicise the inequalities of Irish law. The European court fast emerged as a site for legal challenges to the Irish state which illuminated a level of frustration with the conservatism of the Irish judiciary: Josie Airey's 1977 successful challenge that legal aid's availability for only criminal cases breached Articles 6 and 8 of the Convention of Human Rights opened legal aid to all civil cases.[64] Like several earlier reformers, Airey experienced the law's limitations at first hand: her marriage was blighted by alcoholism and abuse but with estimated separation costs of £1,000 she was unable to proceed. Even with fewer than ten cases for judicial separation per annum in the Republic from 1972 to 1976, the court

---

[58] This act also abolished tort of enticement, harbouring a spouse and the breach of promise action and was part of a wider reform of Irish family law.

[59] Mahon, 'Women's rights', p. 60.

[60] Michelle Dillon, *Debating divorce* (Lexington, KY, 1993), p. 71. Italian divorce law, based on no-fault divorce after five years of separation, was unsuccessfully challenged by referendum in 1974.

[61] Yvonne Scannell, 'The constitution and the role of women', Brian Farrell (ed.), *De Valera's constitution and ours* (Dublin, 1988), p. 129.

[62] Ferriter, *Occasions of sin*, cited p. 441.   [63] *Irish Times*, 16 June 1977.

[64] Free legal aid advice centres were operative in the Republic of Ireland from 1969 and family law, especially marital breakdown, comprised the largest (39 per cent) caseload from 1974 to 1975 (Duncan, *The case for divorce*, p. 15).

acknowledged that hers was not an isolated problem.[65] Airey's legal challenge impacted Ireland and all signatory states to the EU Convention on Human Rights. It also allowed her to separate in the Irish High Court in 1979; she received £3,140 damages. Of similar import was the 1986–87 test case of Johnston versus Ireland in the European Court of Human Rights. Represented by Mary Robinson, this called Articles 8 and 12 of the European Convention on Human Rights into question and challenged the Irish constitutional definition of a family being bound by marriage. That the right to marry implied a right to break that union was not upheld and Article 8 of the constitution relating to family life was deemed to not compel the state to introduce divorce.[66]

Other states with a ban on divorce or restricted divorce provisions often had high levels of collusive annulments and foreign divorces as well as extended grounds for civil nullity. By comparison, in 1970s Ireland there was allegedly 'no evidence' of collusion or for 'Irish couples . . . obtaining foreign divorce in any large numbers' although these were always difficult to detect unless followed by a legal challenge. However, in 1975 fewer than 50 marriages in Ireland involved one party who was divorced although many of these were foreign nationals. The grounds for civil nullity were not radically augmented, but the consideration of mental incapacity impeding the ability to consent to marriage became more nuanced as psychiatry developed.[67] Although only 'a handful' of annual nullity petitions were presented to the civil courts,[68] c. 800 annual petitions were presented for church annulment in the mid-1970s, a figure which, although subject to significant increase, was still comparatively small.[69] Limited civil and church annulments as well as separations (255 separation cases were heard in the Irish High Court from 1972 to 1978) were often used as evidence for a lack of demand for divorce, but there was no comprehensive analysis of the level of marriage breakdown or a consideration that the majority simply could not afford to pursue these

---

[65] Minutes of Irish Parliamentary Labour Party, 16 April 1980 (NLI, MS 49,494/369).

[66] The non-recognition of some foreign divorces was ruled non-discriminatory. The Status of Children Act followed in 1987 to remove the illegitimacy label (James, 'Céad Míle Fáilte?' pp. 198–200). See also Kathleen M. Dillon, 'Divorce and remarriage as human rights: the Irish constitution and the European Convention on Human Rights at odds in Johnston v. Ireland', *Cornell International Law Journal*, vol. 22, no. 63 (1989), pp. 63–90.

[67] Report: Nullity of Marriage (LRC 9–1984, October 1984), p. 89.

[68] There were twenty to thirty civil annulments per year in the mid-1990s but with the cost estimated at £6,000–£10,000, this was not a viable option for many. The most common grounds for civil annulment were insanity, non-consensual marriage or the sexuality of one spouse (O'Brien, *Divorce?*, p. 117).

[69] A total of 751 applications were made for church annulment in Ireland in 1976, rising by 15 per cent to 884 in 1977 (Duncan, *The case for divorce*), p. 12. Church annulments were the subject of increased public debate at this juncture.

means to end a marriage. However, the rising number of women in receipt of deserted wives' allowances – 4,785 in 1976 – indicated a level of marital breakdown that became harder to disregard.[70]

The Law Reform Commission, established in 1975, evidenced a state cognisance that far-reaching legal reform was required which was in itself indicative of a growing, if not absolute, liberal consensus.[71] The commission considered a gamut of issues including those relating to sexual morality and the family and admitted to a lack of public discussion on marriage dissolution.[72] Initially favouring a continuation of laws to protect marriage and displaying a sense of moral arbitration which constrained reform, it was, at times, criticised for timidity inspired by a desire not to alienate the Catholic Church.[73] However, support for Irish divorce reform increased. A proliferation of polls on divorce began in the mid-1970s. A 1974 Market Research Bureau Ireland (MRBI) poll suggested 50 per cent of Catholics believed that divorce should never be legalised, 45 per cent thought it should be permitted under certain circumstances and 5 per cent expressed no opinion. Ninety-four per cent of non-Catholics polled supported divorce, with 3 per cent expressing no opinion whilst younger, unmarried, urban and higher–social strata respondents supported divorce. Older, rural, married and less wealthy respondents opposed divorce. With 51 per cent of men and 45 per cent of women supporting divorce, this corroborated Rohan's previous findings. Another poll in 1977 showed 65 per cent supporting divorce reform and 26 per cent in opposition with similar age and regional differentials as its predecessor.[74]

The government, however, remained timorous of far-reaching social reforms especially if they entailed morality. In consequence, it initially considered civil nullity as an alternative to divorce. In 1976, the Office of the Attorney General published the discussion paper 'The Law of Nullity in Ireland'. As Cosgrave earlier highlighted,[75] the lack of provision for civil annulments to follow ecclesiastical nullity to facilitate non-bigamous

---

[70] O'Brien, *Divorce?* p. 101. From 1986 to 1991, applications for this benefit increased by 66 per cent. Benefits to deserted wives were known as Lone Parents' Allowance from 1991 (Finóla Ó Raigáin, 'Reasons for marital instability and separation' in O'Brien, *Divorce?*, p. 27 and p. 32).

[71] See Fanning, *The quest for modern Ireland.*

[72] Report: Recognition of Foreign Divorces and Legal Separations (LRC 10–1985, April 1985, p. 1).

[73] Noel Brown, *Irish Times*, 18 June 1980.

[74] William Binchy, 'Divorce in Ireland: legal and social perspectives', *Journal of Divorce*, vol. 2, no. 1 (1978), pp. 102–3.

[75] Cosgrave claimed that Byrne 'admitted' that remarriage after a church annulment could cause prosecution for bigamy 'but stated that we could not be expected to legislate for the individual' (Cosgrave to Archbishop Byrne, 21 September 1925 [NAI, MS TAOIS/3/S4127]).

subsequent unions was problematic, but the focus was on extending the grounds of civil nullity to include a wider definition of mental disorders.[76] This was controversial but garnered support, particularly from the Catholic Church. An acknowledgement that marriages could end by means other than death was evident in other denominations and led some to call for divorce. As the Dublin Methodist synod noted, 'Valid marriages do break down and there ought to be facility for divorce' in the Republic, correctly deeming nullity 'a convenient ecclesiastic term used to avoid accepting the reality of divorce'. Dublin's Society of Friends also believed that divorce as opposed to nullity would be a more compassionate response to those experiencing marital breakdown,[77] while the Presbyterian Church in Ireland called for divorce to be made available in the following year as the 'only equitable and acceptable solution' to permanent marital breakdown.[78] Some support for divorce reform was also apparent in the Catholic Church: Bishop of Cork and Ross Rev. Dr Cornelius Lucey was a controversial Catholic commentator who publicly backed the right of the minority to divorce:

Obviously if the majority do not regard it as of a natural right then it shouldn't be made available for all in the community. If the minority demanding it, however, is a religious one and a sizeable one, the State may provide it for that particular group ... but most emphatically not to the extent of providing these facilities for everybody regardless of their religion.[79]

Government ministers like Dr Conor Cruise O'Brien, who claimed English domicile to secure his own divorce, and Garret FitzGerald, whose pluralism shocked many in the Catholic hierarchy, as well as officials like Dr John Kelly, parliamentary secretary to the Taoiseach, now also declared their support for divorce.[80]

By the late 1970s, court rulings, piecemeal family law reform, polls and sociological investigations collectively proved that Irish marriages broke down with increased regularity despite the constitutional ban on divorce. With an estimated 17 per cent of second marriages in Dublin involving divorcees who had established English domicile to divorce, Labour chief whip Mervyn Taylor made headlines, reminiscent of the nineteenth century, in declaring that the present law favoured the rich.[81] William Duncan therefore made a convincing case: the constitutional ban on divorce was giving 'rise to the practice of evasion and avoidance' which

[76] Bruce Arnold papers, 22 December 1976 (NLI, MS 41,430).
[77] Binchy, 'Divorce in Ireland', cited p. 104.   [78] *Irish Times*, 20 January 1977.
[79] *Cork Examiner*, 6 May 1976.   [80] *The Observer*, 2 May 1976.
[81] *Irish Press*, 20 May 1986.

was common in Italy in its pre-divorce era.[82] The divorce ban served the purpose of creating an unwarranted portrayal of familial stability when the state could not control private lives in actuality: '[T]he manner in which the law deals with marital breakdown, whether it be strict or liberal in its approach, has very little influence on marital stability generally.'[83] Charles Haughey, Taoiseach from 1979, would initially not be drawn into the emergent debate, which formed part of his wider schema to avoid colliding with the Catholic Church's moral teachings.[84] However, a year after Haughey's accession to power, Dr Noel Browne unsuccessfully attempted to repeal the constitutional ban on divorce with the ninth amendment of the constitution bill prepared by Senator Mary Robinson. Conservative and evoking the language of protectionism, the bill inverted many of the popular tropes concerning divorce; it pledged to guard the institution of marriage and seek reconciliation between parties experiencing marital problems.[85] Its supporters met at Dublin's Liberty Hall to establish the Divorce Action Group but believed, with justification, that 'it could take twenty years to achieve their goal'.[86]

By 1981, the question of church nullity constituting 'a type of Catholic divorce' with the number of annulments claimed to have risen 2000 per cent in the past five years, was posited as further evidence for the need to consider civil divorce in the Dáil. Haughey was still resistant; he would only state that the recommendations of the 1967 committee on the constitution were 'unacceptable' as they proposed to introduce varying provisions for different religions which would undermine legal equality. Thus, whilst acknowledging the anomalies of the law, he suggested that an all-party committee was the only way to counter 'a situation which is now very much entangled'. This proved that although Ireland was changing, it was not yet transformed, and Browne was incredulous: 'Just like your predecessor you are afraid of getting a belt of a crozier.'[87]

The praise of Irish exceptionalism meted by Pope John Paul II on his 1981 visit to Ireland bolstered Haughey's torpor: women were encouraged to stay at home and contraceptive and divorce reform were to be resisted. In the same year, Haughey, in the wake of his first summit with

---

[82] W. R. Duncan, 'Supporting the institution of marriage in Ireland', *Irish Jurist*, vol. 2 (1978), p. 227.

[83] Duncan, *The case for divorce*, p. 9.

[84] The 1979 Health and Family Planning Act, which restricted access to contraceptives to married couples on prescription, is a classic example of Haughey's approach.

[85] The bill also noted the state would take measures to encourage preparedness for marriage and provide economic and physical protection for vulnerable family members (Minutes of the Irish Parliamentary Labour Party, 16 April 1980 [NLI, MS 49,494/369]).

[86] Ferriter, *Transformation of Ireland*, p. 718.

[87] Dáil Éireann, debates, 8 July 1981, vol. 329, cols. 226–7.

Margaret Thatcher, confirmed that reform was not on the agenda by declaring that 'separate constitutional arrangements might be necessary for the two parts of the island in matters such as divorce'.[88] FitzGerald's accession to power with a Fine Gael/Labour coalition in mid-1981, however, gave the nascent divorce reform campaign an impetus that was previously lacking. This formed part of FitzGerald's self-proclaimed 'constitutional crusade' to change both Irish society and the Republic's relationship with Northern Ireland. Workers' Party TD Proinseas De Rossa subsequently moved a bill to amend the constitution to facilitate divorce in 1983, believing its lack of provision now sullied parliament: '[T]his problem exists, and if this House is to have any relevance we must sit down and tackle it. ... Marital breakdown is a fact of life and a ban on divorce does nothing to protect family life.'[89] The government again acknowledged that marriages broke down but, committed to all-party talks to find a balance 'between the interests of individuals ... [and] society as a whole', declared the bill premature and it subsequently failed.[90] This was part of wider reactionary recoil against liberalism which was, in many ways, typified by the successful 1983 eighth amendment of the Irish constitution on the right to life of the unborn.

However, the sectarian divorce divide of Yeats's imagining never emerged. Whilst support for divorce reform was forthcoming from the leaders of the Presbyterian, Quaker, Jewish, Baptist, Methodist and Anglican Churches in the 1980s,[91] the emergent divide was with the more conservative elements of the Catholic hierarchy and Catholic lay organisations such as Family Solidarity, an advocacy group formed in 1984 in the aftermath of the successful fight for the right of the unborn to be protected in the eighth amendment to the Irish constitution. A delegation, including Catholic Archbishop of Dublin Dr Kevin McNamara, for example, in 1985 presented FitzGerald with a twenty-two-page document which claimed that divorce damaged marital stability: '[B]eing a permanent contract, marriage tended to be seen as a temporary thing once divorce legislation was introduced.' Cardinal Ó Fiaich also rejected the idea that divorce reform could ease relations with Northern Ireland and made clear 'that the Catholic bishops will not be deflected for their opposition to divorce'.[92]

---

[88] *The Tablet*, 21 March 1981.
[89] De Rossa, Dáil Éireann debates, 15 February 1983, vol. 340, cols. 202–3.
[90] Speech by Nuala Fennell, Minister for State for Women's Affairs and Family Law Reform, 15 February 1983 (NAI, 2013/100/72).
[91] The Presbyterian General Assembly, for example, called for a referendum on divorce in the Republic of Ireland in 1981 (*Irish Independent*, 24 April 1986).
[92] *Irish Times*, 8 April 1983.

This contradicted the 1984 'Irish values and attitudes' survey, part of the European Value Systems study, where only 'mild disapproval' of divorce emerged.[93] Yet, De Rossa's introduction of another bill to allow the tenth amendment to the constitution to facilitate divorce was quickly rejected in what he depicted as

an indication of the kind of double standards which various Governments have applied in reaction to social issues in the country . . . the need for divorce is beyond dispute . . . there are 7,000 deserted wives at present in receipt of either a deserted wife's benefit or allowance. I suppose that can be termed an Irish solution to an Irish problem. There are many thousands more who, because they are in a different economic income bracket, have agreed to separate and make various financial arrangements. There are others in a higher bracket still who can afford to go abroad and get [a] foreign divorce. . . . To argue . . . that there is no need for divorce in Ireland is to ignore all the evidence which exists and which any of us who are active in constituency advice centres can see every week.

De Rossa was supported by both Fine Gael and Labour (the latter of which called for family law reform, including divorce, in its most recent manifesto), but there was no sustained debate: the Dáil had not discussed the question of divorce at length since 1937.[94] Nuala Fennell, formerly of AIM and now minister for state at the Department of Justice, defended the government's opposition in terms of waiting for a mooted joint committee report on marital breakdown, but admitted the following:

[T]he question of whether to legislate for divorce . . . has now definitely entered the arena of public debate in our country. . . . We live in changing times in which traditional answers no longer provide an adequate response. As politicians, we are all aware that public opinion has moved in the direction of a more flexible and human approach to marriage breakdown.[95]

The 1983–4 New Ireland Forum, aiming to reconcile nationalist opinions in the north and south of the country, was a more public test of the plurality which Fennell identified.[96] The forum heard 200 submissions, including one from the Divorce Action Group. Its seven-page submission, composed by chairman John O'Connor, called for a referendum on

---

[93] Mahon, 'Women's rights', p. 56.
[94] De Rossa, Dáil Éireann debates, 15 May 1984, vol. 350, cols. 1009–10. By comparison, the Seanad discussed divorce in 1983.
[95] Fennell, ibid., col. 1012.
[96] Non-nationalist parties abstained although the Ulster Unionist Party's Chris and Michael McGimpsey made a submission to the forum. Sinn Féin was excluded from the forum. The forum's steering committee was composed of the following party leaders: Garrett FitzGerald (Fine Gael), Charles Haughey (Fianna Fáil), Dick Spring (Labour) and John Hume (SDLP). The forum made three proposals for the future of Ireland: a unitary thirty-two-county state, a federal/confederal state or joint authority for Northern Ireland from the British and Irish governments.

divorce to cease the 'suffering' of those whose marriages broke down 'without any proper means of re-establishing themselves in society'. An equalisation of the law between the north and south of the country was also necessitated by the existence of diocesan boundaries which predated partition: 'Catholics who live North and South of the Political border in the same diocese live under totally conflicting rule of Church and State.'[97]

More highly anticipated was the Catholic hierarchy's forty-five-page submission and subsequent oral evidence which came under such scrutiny that Cardinal Ó Fiaich claimed media distortion and unfair treatment.[98] Its written submission was anti-pluralist, claiming 'a Catholic country or its government ... [or] its legal system ... reflects Catholic values'. Divorce was therefore portrayed as detrimental to the stability of marriage, family and society. Drawing parallels to Britain's non-tolerance of polygamy when some citizens believed in the practice, defending the 'principles of the majority' required the 'sacrifice of minorities in the interests of the common good'. Although denying that this was a demand for Catholic teaching to inform the constitution,[99] it was lambasted as 'a damned disgrace' by the forum and its 'defensive and negative tone' was disappointing to many.[100] The Northern Irish reaction was ecumenically hostile: the SDLP, Sinn Féin, OUP and DUP collectively opposed the emphasis on an all-embracing Catholicism. Indeed, SDLP chair Sean Farren questioned the definition of a greater good, intonating that this should be for the 'whole community' and take account of minority rights. Sinn Féin president Gerry Adams went further, accusing the hierarchy of attempted political interference; he called for both divorce and contraceptive reform in the Republic: 'The catholic Hierarchy's past success in stamping its ethos on the Free State is grist to the propaganda mill of Loyalist claims of Rome Rule, and is highly offensive to non-Catholics.'[101] A *Belfast Telegraph* editorial proved his point; the hierarchy's submission was deemed to nullify the reconciliatory aim of the forum.[102]

The Catholic Church's refusal and then delay in appearing before the forum was interpreted by some as a tactic to overcome internal fissures, but Cardinal Ó Fiaich only admitted to 'different nuances and emphasis'.[103] The church's oral submission of February 1984 came

---

[97] New Ireland Forum submission case file: John O'Connor, Divorce Action Group, Dublin (NAI 2004/40/133). O'Connor was also secretary to the Irish Labour Party's Lawyers' Group. The submission of the Belfast-based Women's Law and Research Group also called for divorce reform.
[98] *Irish Times*, 16 January 1984.
[99] Anon. forum member, *Irish Times*, 13 January 1984.
[100] Maurice Manning, ibid., 14 January 1984.   [101] Ibid.
[102] *Belfast Telegraph*, 13 January 1984.   [103] *Irish Times*, 16 January 1984.

from a panel of six composed of bishops, priests and laypersons. Minority rights were given more prominence than in the written submission. Indeed, the contribution of the Bishop of Down and Connor Dr Cathal Daly, highlighting individual conscience, was markedly more measured than the church's written submission. When pressed on the possible church reaction to a referendum on divorce, he stated, 'I don't want to cop out by saying this is a political question. I don't think the Church should have to say whether there should or should not be a constitutional amendment on divorce ... as pastors we would express our view but respect the conscience of the legislators.' The separation of church and state was a key recommendation of the forum's report: 'The criteria which relate to public legislation may not necessarily be the same as those which inform public morality ... public legislation must have regard for the conscientious beliefs of different minority groups.'[104] This initially appeared palatable to many but, when steps were taken to put this into practice, divorce was again decried as a destructive liberalising force that could subvert society.

[104] Ibid., 10 February 1984. Dr Daly was archbishop of Armagh from 1990 to 1996.

11   A 'Curiosity [and] . . . an Oddity': Referenda in 1986 and 1995

The period from 1969 to 1984 saw divorce reform in the majority of Western countries. In 1969, for example, in the United States, California introduced the first no-fault grounds for divorce in Western society with English reform coming in the same year when a marriage could be proven to have permanently broken down by separation, mutual consent or the fault of a spouse. Sweden, West Germany, the Netherlands and nineteen American jurisdictions also moved to no-fault processes. Civil divorce was implemented in Italy and Spain in 1970 and 1981, respectively, and extended to Catholic marriages in Portugal in 1975,[1] but Ireland remained in the unique position of Western European countries with no provision for divorce, finding an ally only further afield in Malta.[2] The establishment of the Oireachtas Joint Committee on Marital Breakdown in 1985 was, however, an admission by the state that increasing numbers of marriages ended before the death of a spouse. Receiving 700 written submissions and hearing oral evidence from twenty-four organisations, testimony revealed that the practice of some of the deserted or separated was to take a second partner's name via deed poll as they could not remarry.[3] All the minority churches, with the exception of the Church of the Latter Day Saints, popularly known as the Mormon church, also declared support for divorce reform to the committee. The subsequent report tentatively recommended a referendum to facilitate a constitutional reworking of divorce provision but, anticipating an antagonistic debate, made no comment on whether such a move was desirable. Fianna Fáil members of the committee also opposed holding

---

The quote in the chapter title is from Dillon, *Debating divorce*, p. 2.

[1] Mary Ann Glendon, *Abortion and divorce in Western law. American failures, European challenges* (Cambridge, MA, and London, 1987), pp. 66–9. Italian divorce was challenged by referendum in 1974, but 68 per cent voted to keep divorce. See Allesandra de Rose, 'The Italian experience of divorce' in Gabriel Keily (ed.), *In and out of marriage. Irish and European experiences* (Dublin, 1992), pp. 19–32.

[2] Malta introduced divorce in 2011.

[3] A deed poll is a legal document that provides evidence of a name change.

a referendum and the report was defeated in the Dáil by sixty-three to thirty-seven votes.[4] This was replicated in successive parliamentary sittings where, despite more sustained efforts to introduce divorce reform, including a motion to hold a divorce referendum, any furthering of the liberal agenda was rejected. A bill to amend the constitutional ban and a divorce bill also 'died in the Dáil' after failing to muster the required support of at least ten TDs.[5]

Although many divorce polls looked increasingly encouraging, an Irish Countrywomen's Association (ICA) questionnaire on a divorce referendum saw a two-to-one majority of the organisation's guilds oppose constitutional change to allow divorce in 1984. With an additional 11 of 428 guilds abstaining, it was clear that majority support for reform was far from secured. Some guilds expressed sympathy for the victims of domestic abuse and support for divorce if accompanied by a church annulment as a last resort, but there was also outright opposition: 'The best interests of society would not be served by introducing divorce. . . . Divorce in other countries has not solved the problem.' The ICA could only conclude that this was still a 'divisive issue'.[6] A later *Irish Times*/MRBI poll of February 1986 conversely suggested 52 per cent favoured removing the constitutional ban; 42 per cent opposed such a move and 77 per cent favoured divorce in some, unspecified, circumstances.[7] In the same month, the Labour Party introduced another divorce bill which met a similar fate as its predecessor, being defeated by fifty-four to thirty-three votes, but the push for reform continued. In April 1986, Taoiseach Garret FitzGerald met the Catholic hierarchy; whilst they did not oppose a referendum, their stand on divorce was fixed. Cardinal Ó Fiaich reiterated the New Ireland Forum stance, defending the church's right to comment on moral questions, but the issue of a referendum was off limits as 'strictly a political question and the hierarchy was not entitled to tell Dr FitzGerald what to do'.[8] FitzGerald also met with Protestant church leaders who all favoured divorce reform and in April government plans for a referendum were made public.[9] FitzGerald was personally opposed to divorce, dismissing claims of it as a civil right as 'A nonsense. You can't have a civil right to break a contract that was indissoluble. That's

---

[4] Richard B. Finnegan and James R. Wiles, *Women and public policy in Ireland. A documentary history, 1922–97* (Dublin, 2005).

[5] Nick Lowry, 'Garret's loaves and fishes: the defeat of the divorce amendment' in William Binchy, Kevin Doran, John O'Reilly and Nick Lowry, *Fusion or fission. Ireland's option for the family* (Dun Laoghaire, 1988), pp. 52–3.

[6] A total of 2,844 favoured constitutional change; 4,171 opposed it and 1,205 abstained, 24 March 1984 (NLI, MS 39,373).

[7] *Irish Times*, 2 February 1986.   [8] *Irish Independent*, 8 April 1986.

[9] Lowry, 'Garret's loaves', pp. 53–4.

a contradiction in terms.'[10] He therefore led the 1986 referendum campaign on the ground that second unions that were unrecognised by both church and state undermined the institution of marriage. Thus the referendum was, as Meehan observed, 'a liberal measure conceived within a conservative framework'.[11] Divorce's association with north-south reconciliation was well established. However, Senator Catherine McGuinness's assertion that a no vote for the referendum was 'a blow in the face to all moderate Protestants who are trying to make the Anglo-Irish Agreement work'[12] led Catholic Coadjutor Bishop of Kildare and Leighlin Lawrence Ryan to call for a cessation of issues being presented 'as Church and State confrontations for polemic purposes'.[13]

At the start of a nine-week campaign, Senator Mary Robinson, a stalwart of liberal reform, presented divorce as an acknowledgement of fact: 'a death certificate for a marriage that has totally broken down'.[14] Parties quickly began to side: Fine Gael, Labour, the Progressive Democrats, the Workers' Party and Sinn Féin in addition to the Irish Trade Union Congress were pro-divorce. They mostly worked separately towards the same end which was indicative of the lack of unity in the wider pro-reform lobby, but Labour, although running an independent campaign with the slogan of 'Put Compassion in the Constitution', collaborated with trade unions and DAG in the constituencies.[15] In terms of party, although Bishop of Limerick Dr Newman claimed pressure was being exerted on party members to support divorce, only Labour fully backed the reform and even some of its rural TDs were reticent to comment, fearing doing so could cost votes in the next election. Free votes were afforded to Fianna Fáil, which remained officially neutral, and to Fine Gael; the majority position in each party opposed and supported the reform, respectively.[16] Support from the Jewish and Protestant churches was more cohesive, a commitment reinforced by their recent pledge at the New Ireland Forum to aid reconciliation with the north of Ireland. As the Irish Council of Churches' June 1986 statement averred, divorce should not be easy but was needed as a solution for broken

[10] Kennedy, *Cottage to crèche*, cited p. 236. FitzGerald's view was at odds with the Council for Civil Liberties and the Irish Trades Union Congress which supported divorce as a civil right in 1986.
[11] Meehan, *A just society*, pp. 3–4.   [12] Dillon, *Debating divorce*, cited p. 65.
[13] Louise Fuller, *Irish Catholicism since 1950* (Dublin, 2004), cited p. 245.
[14] *Irish Times*, 23 May 1986. Robinson previously referred to the constitutional ban as cruel. See *Irish Times*, 14 October 1983.
[15] Ibid., 13 November 1985. See Minutes of the Irish Labour Party Administrative Council, 22 April 1986 (NLI, MS 49,494/174) and minutes of the National Referendum Committee, 6 May 1986 (NLI, MS 49,494/925).
[16] A free vote, also known as an unwhipped vote, allows a vote without the influence of party whips.

marriages.[17] Yet, even here there were gradations of opine and not all agreed with Church of Ireland Primate Robin Eames's view that divorce was required to allow remarriage.[18] The national press was also pro-reform, leading to a considerable disparity in the coverage afforded to the campaigns: Logan and Hamilton's measurement of column inches given to the pro- and anti-camps between 24 April and 24 May 1986 revealed 73 per cent of the *Irish Press*, 71 per cent of the *Irish Independent* and 68 per cent of the *Irish Times* coverage supported reform.[19] The Catholic hierarchy censured such partiality,[20] but Labour also believed that the national media focus was on Fine Gael and intra-church disputes rather than on the reform per se. In the provincial press, letters to the editor pages provided a key forum for debate, but claims that divorce caused anorexia, depression, delinquency and sexual abuse by stepfathers indicate the fear and misapprehension that the issue of divorce engendered.[21]

Support for the pro-reform lobby initially appeared buoyant. An *Irish Times*/MRBI poll of 5 May found 57 per cent were pro-amendment; 36 per cent opposed it and 7 per cent gave no opinion. Even in the week before the referendum, a *Sunday Independent*/Irish Market Survey poll suggested a 56 per cent yes vote. This lulled the pro-divorce lobby into a false sense of security. Its key body, the Divorce Action Group, was small, especially outside of Dublin. It was also 'comparatively poor' and relied on fundraising rather than donations. DAG lacked campaign experience, but many of its members were separated and thus had invaluable first-hand knowledge of the law's limitations.[22] Feminist and Labour Party member Jean Tansey was to the fore as well as William Duncan who repeatedly challenged the idea that divorce's very existence caused marriages to break down, drawing a parallel to 'forbidding funerals in the hope of eradicating the problem of death'. Duncan also doubted the law's protectionist ability on both an individual and a national level: 'to influence conduct in the sphere of intimate human relationships' whilst 'a rising tide of marital breakdown . . . suggests the ban on divorce has in fact done little to prevent marital instability'.[23] Peter Ward was more derisive: 'The belief that the retention of the constitutional ban on divorce in some ways renders us immune from the deleterious financial consequences of

[17] *Irish Times*, 6 June 1986.   [18] Ibid., 21 May 1986.

[19] Michael J. Breen, *The influence of mass media on divorce referenda in Ireland* (Lampeter, 2010).

[20] Lowry, 'Garret's loaves', cited p. 59. The hierarchy alleged unfair media coverage in the 1985 pastoral *Love is for life*.

[21] Report by Labour Press Officer Kathleen O'Meara on the divorce referendum, 2 July 1986 (NLI, MS 49, 494/925).

[22] Jenny Beale, *Women in Ireland. Voices of change* (Basingstoke, 1996), cited p. 83.

[23] Duncan, 'Supporting the institution of marriage', pp. 226–7.

marriage breakdown raises our capacity for self-deception to new and dizzying heights.'[24] DAG thus found allies in organisations like AIM, Gingerbread and the Irish Council for Civil Liberties[25] as well as liberal Catholic clerics like Fr Pat O'Brien who claimed that his church 'will only come into maturity in a secular society': 'Only when it slips its hand from the glove of the State can it recover its real energy and its truly critical role in our future ... the most important element ... the root of all morality and law – is human freedom.'[26]

The proposed grounds for divorce – no-fault divorce after a period or periods which cumulatively amounted to five years' separation with no prospect of reconciliation and provision made for any dependent spouse or child – proved too progressive for a state without any divorce provision.[27] Fault-based divorce was criticised: the archbishop of Canterbury's review group and the English Law Commission in 1966 rightly suggested that it allowed marital difficulties to be tailored to fit the grounds for divorce, increasing the likelihood of collusion and acrimony. However, many equated no-fault provision with easy divorce and more conservative reformers were deterred. Conversely, the long gestation proposed between separation and divorce was criticised from the perspective of those living in the immediate aftermath of marital breakdown who feared that they would have to wait for a bill to pass and an additional five years to finally divorce.

The wider implications of the reform concerning benefits, property, pension and inheritance rights always seemed ill considered. The government, for example, republished its intentions in April 1986 in response to key questions regarding maintenance, spousal pension and succession rights, family homes, social policy and children's rights.[28] Given the centrality of the family in Irish society, these areas were pivotal in encouraging opposition. Furthermore, the long-standing assertion that divorce's very existence would increase its frequency forcibly re-emerged. Although DAG and FitzGerald argued that divorce protected women, Fine Gael's Alice Glenn's comment that 'any women voting for divorce is like a turkey voting for Christmas'[29] and the 'Divorce impoverishes

---

[24] Peter Ward, *Divorce in Ireland. Who should bear the cost?* (Cork, 1993), cited p. 3.
[25] Founded in 1976, the Irish Council for Civil Liberties is a non-government organisation committed to civil rights.
[26] *Irish Times*, 29 May 1986. DAG had branches in Dublin, Cork, Dundalk and Drogheda (Linda Connolly and Tina O'Toole, *Documenting Irish feminism. The second* wave [Dublin, 2005]).
[27] Part II of 10th Amendment to the Constitution Bill, 1986 (NAI, 2016/51/1361).
[28] Statement of Government's Intention with regards to Marriage, Separation and Divorce, 23 April 1986 (ibid.).
[29] *Newsweek*, 7 July 1980. Women were also portrayed as victims of divorce in the United States. Mary Harney of the Progressive Democrats was 'insulted' by Glenn's analogy,

women and children' slogan of the 'antis' were persuasive.[30] Considerable emphasis was also placed on international research, particularly from the United States, for the same purpose. This included Weitzman's now discredited 1985 analysis of divorce in California which showed a significant (70 per cent) decline in women's living standards in the first post-divorce year, an associated 40 per cent rise in men's standard of living and only 13 per cent of women with children younger than age six being awarded alimony. Lack of Irish research on the economic effects of desertion and separation made it difficult for the pro-divorce lobby to prove that marital breakdown rather than divorce caused financial hardship.[31] Indeed, by May Labour's National Women's Committee was concerned by the gender-based scaremongering: '[T]his campaign aimed at planting worries in people's (especially women's) minds has been very successful, since the arguments are emotional ones, aimed at creating a level of fear and insecurity.'[32]

The Anti-Divorce Campaign (ADC), established only when the referendum was announced in 1986, was masterminded by the lay-led, conservative lobby Family Solidarity. This provided a ready-made parish point of contact for the anti-divorce campaign.[33] ADC was non-party but drew some members from the pro-life movement and Catholic right-wing groups such as Opus Dei, the League of Decency, the Knights of Columbanus and the Responsible Society.[34] Such bodies, labelled 'lay fundamentalists' by *The Tablet*, were supported with finance and literature from similar bodies in Northern Ireland, Britain and the United States.[35] This provided the £60,000 required to send an anti-divorce leaflet to every Irish home, a sum which amounted to the total campaign budget of their opponents.

---

describing it as 'degrading ... offensive ... insulting to Irish women' (Dillon, *Debating divorce*, cited p. 85).

[30] Ward, *Divorce in Ireland*, p. 1.

[31] Dervla Brown, 'Divorce in other jurisdictions' in O'Brien, *Divorce?* pp. 76–7. Willam Binchy, *Is divorce the answer?* (Dublin, 1983) considered the financial and child custody implications of divorce in detail as well as the supposed impact that divorce would have on the stability and longevity of marriage.

[32] Proposal from Labour Women's National Committee to the National Referendum Committee, 21 May 1986 (NLI, MS 94,494/925).

[33] Dillon, *Debating divorce*, p. 32. ADC was chaired by Fianna Fáil Senator Des Hanafin with barrister William Binchy as its legal spokesperson and Mary McAleese as legal advisor.

[34] Founded in Spain in 1928, the Prelature of Holy Cross and Opus Dei is a Catholic body, mainly composed of lay people, with a belief that everyone is called to holiness; established in 1933 the Catholic League of Decency initially identified objectionable material in US films; the Knights of Columbanus is an Irish national Catholic fraternal benefit organisation established in 1915; the Responsible Society is a moral conservative pressure group established in Britain in 1979 which became active in Ireland in the following year.

[35] Dick Walsh, 'New horizons for the new Ireland', *The Tablet*, 13 March 1999.

The anti-divorce campaign did not place much emphasis on the church's moral teachings on divorce, preferring to present divorce as endangering all marriages. It also adopted a tailored regional approach: areas with high unemployment were targeted with 'We Want Jobs, Not Divorce' posters; others cited 'Divorce Kills Love' and parodied the 'Ulster says No' opposition to the Anglo-Irish Agreement with the words, 'God Says No'. A suggestion that divorce would be financially detrimental to all taxpayers was similarly effective. As one leaflet claimed: 'Taxpayer pays all – Divorce will cost IR£200 million p.a., IR£17 per week extra out of each taxpayer's pocket.'[36] That figure was inflated: Justice Brian Walsh of the Irish Supreme Court noted a more realistic annual figure of £1,200 but this came too late to offer reassurance and change opine.[37]

A preliminary statement by the hierarchy emphasised its non-interventionist intent and Bishop of Clonfert Joseph Cassidy, the Catholic hierarchy's official spokesman, denied that it was instructing people how to vote as informed conscience would be the deciding factor, but that very term implied the need for guidance.[38] This vexed those like DAG member Conor Cruise O'Brien who accused the hierarchy of hypocrisy: '[Y]ou don't know what you are talking about. You are a group of celibates, assuming yourselves to be authorities on married life: the condition which you are unanimous in having rejected for yourselves.'[39] Cassidy's claim was also undermined by the more emotive aspects of the anti-reform campaign: Catholic Archbishop of Dublin Dr McNamara was at the extreme end of clerical censure. His comparison of divorce to the Chernobyl disaster and his arranging for schoolchildren 'to speak against divorce, wearing tee-shirts and stickers with such slogans as "Save the Family" and "Protect the Family"' made headlines. The Prayer Life Movement also asked of children, 'Would you like your daddy to walk away forever and leave you an orphan crying in the night?'[40] whilst ADC's William Binchy claimed child sexual abuse was more prevalent amongst stepfathers than natural fathers.[41] Catholic sermons on the family and the evils of divorce proliferated. An address by Cardinal Ó Fiaich further alleged that Northern Irish divorce rates were of 'epidemic' proportion in consequence of the no-fault provision even though a mixed fault and no-fault system prevailed there.[42]

The Irish hierarchy's 1986 *Marriage, the Family and Divorce*, an abridged version of the *Love Is for Life* pastoral of the previous year, acknowledged the 'unprecedented pressures' of modern marriage and

---

[36] Ferriter, *Transformation of Ireland*, cited p. 719.   [37] *Irish Times*, 4 March 1987.
[38] Fuller, *Irish Catholicism*, p. 245.   [39] Dillon, *Debating divorce*, cited pp. 123–4.
[40] O'Brien, *Divorce?* cited p. 16.   [41] *Sunday Independent*, 8 June 1986.
[42] Ibid., 24 January 1986. Ó Fiaich later averred that divorce would have to be available in a united Ireland.

the 'worrying picture' of Catholic marriages breaking down at a 'considerable' and 'increasing' rate in both the north and the south of the country. Increased urbanisation, industrialisation, a lessening attachment to the extended family, partly caused by the dispersal of inner-city communities, migration, feminism, higher levels of working married women and heightened expectations of marriage were all cited as causal factors. Young age at marriage, which re-emerged in the mid-1960s for the first time since the famine, and the subsequent lengthening of marriages as well as the imprisonment of mainly young men as a result of the Troubles in Northern Ireland also increased the likelihood of marital breakdown. Gambling, alcoholism, poor financial or household management might similarly put a marriage under duress; however, unlike in the nineteenth century when an errant wife was more highly criticised than an adulterous husband, infidelity on the part of either the husband or the wife was now more equitably conveyed as 'the gravest blow to the happiness of a marriage'.

The church stressed its toleration of separation and spouses living apart but rescinded the claim of rights over all Christian marriages: 'We do not ask that Catholic doctrine as such be enshrined in law. We recognise that morality and civil law do not necessarily coincide', but 'we as pastors have a responsibility to offer moral guidance to Catholics . . . as legislators or as voters'.[43] It refused, however, to align the number of broken marriages to a demand or need for divorce, alleging many deserted spouses sought reconciliation rather than divorce 'to remain faithful to their marriage vows'.[44] The church therefore offered no hope of divorce and remarriage to 'those . . . who accept the teaching of the Catholic Church . . . it is impossible'. Moreover, the remarriage of a civilly divorced person was 'not a real marriage in the eyes of God. God's law continues to bind, no matter what the civil law says.' It also refuted the idea that the impact of divorce would be minimal, citing women and children as its victims and the United States and England as examples where reform led to a fast acquiescence that divorce was 'socially acceptable, even fashionable . . . marriage . . . becomes, in legal principle, a temporary union . . . commitment is weakened. . . . Once divorce is introduced, it does not seem possible to restrict it.'[45] The pastoral, however, failed to assess international divorce statistics against the backdrop of a decline in marriage rates and the variances in relative populations: 'The result was that people felt that one in every two marriages would end in divorce and this terrified them . . . the poverty of families headed by single female parents in the

---

[43] Ibid., p. 55.   [44] Ó Fiaich et al., *Love is for life*, pp. 45–51.
[45] This replicated the Second Vatican Council's castigation of divorce as 'a plague' (ibid., cited p. 67).

USA was also used as an example of what might befall women if divorce was introduced.'

The government failed to effectively counter these claims.[46] The lack of publicity it gave to the intersectionality emerging between civil divorce and church nullity was especially marked. An English case, reported in the Irish press in 1986, saw a contested church annulment considered in court, leading the Catholic Church to require that a civil divorce precede an annulment. Although there was some distancing from this in Ireland, it was commonplace in US annulments where it was used to prove that there could be no reconciliation between the parties.[47] This was a lost opportunity to demonstrate that divorce was not wholly objectionable to the Catholic Church.

Ultimately the tenor of the referendum campaign, based on apprehension of societal dislocation and the consequences of letting the individual decide whether to stay married,[48] was 'shrill, bitter, sectarian, divisive and unpleasant'. Even supporters of the amendment, including some government ministers, endeavoured to disassociate themselves: 'Television and newspaper debates were conspicuous by the absence of established political figures, even those still active in the campaign. As soon as most politicians had ducked for cover, those who did not were marginalized ... a spiral of silence among elites on both sides of the issue' generated distrust amongst voters.' Criticism of President Mary Robinson's pro-divorce comments on US television further accelerated this process.[49]

Votes were cast on 26 June 1986. The turnout of 62.7 per cent was relatively high (and above that of the 1983 abortion referendum): 36.3 per cent were pro-amendment; 63.1 per cent opposed it. The Pearson correlations between voting patterns in the 1983 abortion and 1986 divorce referenda in Ireland further accentuate the anti-liberal agenda of the opposition. The geographical split, for example, was a stark replica of the abortion referendum: only six of forty-one constituencies, mainly in Dublin, supported the divorce amendment. Outside Dublin, urban support was low in areas such as Cork, Limerick, Galway and Waterford. The rural rejection ratio, apparent from the outset of the campaign and not subject to serious fluctuation, was 3:1, including Monaghan, Donegal and Cavan with their sizeable Protestant communities.[50] Support in the middle ground, however, collapsed,

---

[46] Mahon, 'Women's rights', pp. 69–70.   [47] *Irish Times*, 26 May 1986.
[48] Jenny Burley and Francis Regan, 'Divorce in Ireland: the fear, the floodgates and the reality', *International Journal of Law, Policy and the Family*, vol. 16 (2002), cited p. 208.
[49] Brown, 'Divorce in other jurisdictions', pp. 76–7.
[50] Lowry, 'Garret's loaves', pp. 63–4. See also John Coakley, 'Moral conservatism in a secularizing society: the Irish divorce referendum of 1986', *West European Politics*, vol.

especially amongst female voters; their predicted level of support declined by 27 per cent from April to June 1986. This is more striking when compared to a fall in male support of 8 per cent which was indicative of 'the fear of the unknown which frightened many women voters'.[51] The emotive use of children, epitomised by the 'Hello Divorce, Bye-bye Daddy' billboards, also nurtured a protectionist mentality amongst many 'no' voters whilst ignoring the hardships of separation and desertion.[52] Mags O'Brien, separated for fifteen years and a stalwart of the 'yes' campaign, recalled that slogan 'was like a stab'.[53] Protectionism was also central to fears that divorce would disinherit a first wife and children from family farms; FitzGerald rightly suggested this inspired more opposition than any other factor: 'Property was the fact that defeated the divorce referendum. No doubt about that.'[54] However, the specifics of the proposed reform were also key to its defeat. Indeed, the *Belfast News-letter* censured not the referendum result, but the 'unprincipled liberalism' of the no-fault proceeding which held little attraction 'to the great mass of people in Northern Ireland – any more than it appealed to those in the South ... they share the common respect for people of sound principles and patent integrity'.[55]

Despite the referendum result, a significant and overdue era of Irish family law reform followed which laid the foundations for a second divorce referendum and ultimately the removal of the constitutional ban. It was indicative of the extent of required reform that the Law Reform Commission dedicated three of its first ten reports to marriage dissolution.[56] The 1988 Family Law Act ended restitution of conjugal rights proceedings which could force a spouse of either sex to return to the marital home; the 1989 Family Law Reform and Judicial Separation Act, introduced as a private member's bill by Alan Shatter and the first such bill to pass in three decades, legislated for separation when one party proposed it and was not guilty of misconduct.[57] This replaced Section 7

10, issue 2 (April 1987), p. 294. The cost of the referendum was estimated at £1 million (John Bruton, Minister for Finance, Dáil Éireann debates, 18 June 1986, vol. 368, col. 337).

[51] Democratic Left, 'Divorce providing a second chance', undated [1992] (NLI, MS 49,807/35).

[52] Burley and Regan, 'Divorce in Ireland', pp. 211–3.   [53] *Irish Times*, 19 January 2015.

[54] Kennedy, *Cottage to crèche*, cited p. 236.   [55] *Irish Times*, 30 June 1986.

[56] See Report: Divorce a Mensa et Thoro and Related Matters (LRC 8–1983, 16 December 1983); Report: Nullity of Marriage (LRC 9–1984, October 1984); Report: Recognition of Foreign Divorces and Legal Separations (LRC 10–1985, April 1985).

[57] Kennedy, *Cottage to crèche*, p. 235. The Judicial Separation and Family Law Reform Act in 1989 allowed both fault and no-fault grounds for separation after a year with jurisdiction for maintenance, custody and property and required confirmation of mediation.

of the Matrimonial Causes (Ireland) Act and increased the grounds for separation to include desertion, separation without consent for a minimum of three years or with consent, unreasonable behaviour, adultery and marriage breakdown. This was another tacit acknowledgement on the part of the state that marriages broke down and often left women and children in need of legal protection. This was reinforced by application of the act; marriage breakdown became the most-cited ground for separation.[58] In the same year, the Maintenance Act overhauled processes for recovering maintenance payments from outside of Ireland and the 1995 Family Law Act raised the minimum age of marriage from sixteen to eighteen, required three months' notice before a marriage could legally take place, ended jactitation (falsification) of marriage proceedings and provided for ancillary orders after separation or foreign divorce.[59] This act also gave substantial court powers in regards to maintenance, inheritance and property to deal with the financial impact and the tax and social welfare implications of marital breakdown and thus removed one of the major obstacles which helped defeat the first divorce referendum.

These reforms were symptomatic of changing social mores and a growing awareness of the level of marriage breakdown. This was also evidenced by the census including a category of 'other status' in the marital classifications in 1979 although it took officialdom some time to reflect this: the Central Statistics Office recorded as 'married' those who returned themselves as 'other' in this census.[60] From 1979 to 1981, this category increased by 85 per cent and from 1981 to 1986 by 164 per cent. This was, however, a low estimate as the figures for marital breakdown may underestimate the scale of problem by a 'factor of two or more'.[61] The 1986 census was the first to include a category for separated persons which the Divorce Action Group had lobbied for since 1981: 37,245 (14,638 men and 22,607 women) were subsequently recorded as separated with a prevalence in urban areas. An additional 11,622 were listed as deserted with the rate for women three times that of men. A total of 983

Separation remained expensive, even for middle-class budgets and a lack of law centres in rural areas and long delays for both court dates and legal aid caused problems. The last Irish case for restitution of conjugal rights was Hood v. Hood in 1959. In the UK, restitution of conjugal rights decrees became less common after the Matrimonial Causes Act of 1950. A case was brought by a wife in 1968 (Nanda v. Nanda), but the process was abolished in the UK in 1970 (see Harding, 'The definition of marriage in Irish law', vol. 1, pp. 237–8).

[58] Walls and Bergin, *Law of divorce*, p. 4.
[59] Burley and Regan, 'Divorce in Ireland', p. 219.
[60] Connolly and O'Toole, *Documenting Irish feminism*, p. 72.
[61] Ó Raigáin, 'Reasons for marital separation', p. 35.

annulments and 4,391 foreign divorces were also recorded.[62] The number of judicial separations, always an ill indicator of the actuality of marriage breakdown, however, remained moderate. The years 1983–5 saw 393 applications with a relatively low success rate. In 1983, for example, of 53 applications to the Circuit Court, 14 (26 per cent) were granted. In the following year of 115 applications, 51 (44 per cent) were granted.[63] Even after the 1989 reform, separation remained financially inaccessible, trying and even when granted often proved an incomplete remedy for marital breakdown. Applications for deserted wives' allowances were also higher than the numbers recorded in the census, suggesting that the stigma surrounding marital breakdown still prevailed.

Holding a second referendum on divorce to coincide with the European elections was unsuccessfully mooted in 1989, but a poll of the following year predicted that 56 per cent of the population would support legalising divorce. This led to some clerical criticism in the press; Rev. Leo Donnelly of Limerick doubted the poll's veracity and avowed that Ireland should not follow the liberal road 'like Gadarene swine, down the slope to destruction. . . . Divorce is the deadly enemy of the family. . . . When large numbers of families break down, the nation eventually breaks up.'[64] Donnelly's alignment of divorce to abortion, contraception and euthanasia stands as another example of the continued collective consideration of moral issues which was commonplace not only in the church but also in the press and polity. This muted demands for single-strand reform. As an earlier thirty-page memorandum prepared for the government on contraception noted, '[T]here is . . . a campaign for divorce and a growing use of argument for contraception that, if accepted, would make divorce inevitable.'[65]

There was some expectation that a referendum on divorce would be held alongside with the Maastricht referendum in 1992 and various draft amendments to the constitution were published in the 'White Paper on Marital Breakdown' in the same year.[66] The latter, initiated by Taoiseach Charles Haughey, was a marker of acceptance that the constitutional ban could not safeguard marriage. This highlighted that instances of

---

[62] Ward, *Divorce in Ireland*, p. 12.

[63] Dáil Éireann debates, 5 June 1986, vol. 367, col. 1281 and 4 March 1986, vol. 364, col. 691.

[64] *Irish Times*, 22 December 1990.

[65] Ferriter, *Occasions of sin*, cited p. 409. The memorandum was submitted to Jack Lynch in 1970.

[66] Formally known as the Treaty on European Union, the Maastricht Treaty created the European Union, enhancing its authority and establishing plans for a single currency. In the Republic of Ireland, debates over the treaty were conjoined with demands that the country's ban on abortion would be maintained.

separation had doubled since 1986 and the number of deserted wives claiming social welfare trebled from 1982 to 1992. Various divorce options were presented, and one of the major failings of the earlier referendum campaign was redressed by drafting the bill that would be introduced if the constitutional ban were removed. The suggested grounds for divorce were not far reaching in an attempt to win more widespread support[67] and, as O'Brien notes, 'its language [was] of strict regimes', emphasising blame and spousal guilt.[68] The minister for equality and law reform would also examine property and maintenance considerations, which were central to the defeat of the first divorce referendum. A second referendum was recommended to be held before the end of 1993.

Considerable material supported the White Paper's suggestion that marriage breakdown was commonplace in Ireland. Within a year of the passage of the Judicial Separation and Family Law Reform Act in 1989, the number of applications to separate trebled from 207 in 1988–9 to 623 in 1989–90.[69] The 1991 census included a category for foreign divorce for the first time and recorded more than 2,000; 3,858 persons had also remarried after a foreign divorce or an annulment. In addition, 55,143 persons were separated, a 45 per cent increase from 1986.[70] This included 12,000 more women than men, the lower male figure was again due to men leaving the country or claiming tax allowances as married men.[71] The census, however, highlighted that informal means of ending a marriage endured: 43 per cent were deserted, 24 per cent lived apart without any legal proceeding having been instituted whilst 20 per cent were legally separated, 11 per cent were divorced and 2 per cent had annulments.[72] By 1993, the number of separated persons further increased to 75,000 and an estimated 2,700 marriages broke down annually.[73] The figures were disputed, and this was still the lowest rate of marital breakdown in Europe,[74] but political pressure for a second divorce referendum mounted.

---

[67] Burley and Regan, 'Divorce in Ireland', p. 206. The report of the second commission on the Status of Women also called for the removal of the constitutional ban on divorce in 1993.

[68] O'Brien, *Divorce?* p. 22.

[69] Dáil Éireann debates, 27 June 1996, vol. 467, cols. 1773–5.

[70] O'Brien, *Divorce?* p. 7.

[71] Carol Coulter, '"Hello divorce, goodbye Daddy": women, gender and the divorce debate' in Anthony Bradley and Maryann Gialanella Valiulis (eds.), *Gender and sexuality in modern Ireland* (Amherst, MA, 1997), p. 278.

[72] O'Brien, *Divorce?* p. 27.

[73] Dáil Éireann debates, 27 June 1996, vol. 467, col. 1811. The 75,000 figure represented 6 per cent of all married persons in Ireland.

[74] Binchy et al., *Fusion or fission*, p. 3.

The Fianna Fáil–Labour coalition government of 1993, especially Labour's insistence that divorce feature on the government's agenda, led to the *Programme for Partnership Government* which included plans for an overhaul of family law and a referendum on divorce. The policy document *A Government of Renewal* committed the government to a referendum on divorce in 1995 with the precondition that, in an embrace of the 1992 White Paper's recommendation, a draft bill be circulated. The Progressive Democrats were most vocal on the human cost of further delaying a referendum: Liz McManus twice asked for a timetable for reform in 1993: '[I]t is like asking how long is a piece of string. ... We are going in circles. If there some kind of mating dance going on between the Government and Fine Gael we should know. ... If there is not, it is simply an excuse for lack of clarity and direction.'[75] Fine Gael deputy and family law expert Alan Shatter also accused the coalition of keeping its approach to divorce reform 'a national secret'.[76]

The issue of a second divorce referendum took up increasing amounts of Dáil time from 1994, especially the possibility of holding the referendum to coincide with the European elections in June. The unsuccessful 'F' case before the High Court in July 1994 which was then heard in the Supreme Court, challenging the constitutionality of the provisions of the Judicial Separation and Family Law Reform Act of 1989, however, delayed progress. The resultant frustration was again particularly evident amongst the Progressive Democrats: 'We have a fiasco in terms of family law ... women in particular have expressed deep concern' at the referendum's delay.[77] This deferral was cold comfort for some in the Catholic hierarchy. Archbishop of Dublin Dr Desmond O'Donnell's defensive denouncement of divorce as damaging 'the foundation on which Irish family tradition depends ... society would promote its own disintegration by removing the requirement in law of life-long fidelity in marriage' in 1994 was widely reported but much Catholic commentary now focused on women being made vulnerable by divorce.[78] However, 'Against Divorce', an article by Seamus Murphy SJ, revealed a different concern – the availability of marriage partners for men: 'Divorce adds a new dimension to inequality ... enabling wealthy successful men to enjoy a series of wives, thereby reducing the pool of women available to poorer men.'[79] Yet, as DAG's Mags O'Brien's survey of church attitudes to divorce

---

[75] McManus, Dáil Éireann debates, 1 June 1993, vol. 431, col. 1225 and ibid., 3 November 1993, vol. 435, col. 1228.

[76] Shatter, ibid., 1 June 1993, vol. 431, col. 1229.

[77] Helen Keogh, ibid., 24 May 1994, vol. 433, col. 28.

[78] These comments were made on 15 May 1994 (O'Brien, *Divorce?* cited p. 127).

[79] Seamus Murphy, SJ, 'Against divorce', *Studies*, vol. 84, no. 333 (Spring, 1995), p. 14.

revealed, such views were increasingly limited to more conservative Catholics.[80]

By comparison, many other churches still saw lifelong marriage as a 'Divine ideal' but supported, with varying degrees of accommodation, those whose marriages broke down. The Church of Ireland, the Church of Jesus Christ of the Latter Day Saints, the Islamic faith, the Lutheran Church, the Jewish faith, the Presbyterian Church and the Society of Friends all permitted the remarriage of divorcees.[81] The Baptist Church, although having mixed views on the remarriage of divorcees in church, upheld that the state's responsibility was to legislate for the welfare of all its citizens: '[T]here is an infringement of civil liberties where a substantial number of people are "legally imprisoned" in marriage contracts when in fact the marriage is already dead. Provision for limited civil divorce is a necessity in modern Irish society.' The Islamic view was analogous, seeing the constitutional ban on divorce as 'an infringement of... rights' for its community and Lutheran Pastor Paul Fritz concurred: '[In the] present circumstances it would prevent him [Fritz] from applying for Irish citizenship.'[82]

The government, now committed to removing the constitutional ban on divorce, established a Constitution Review Group in 1995. Embodying the spirit of Lemass's earlier committee, its interim reports were an important forerunner to the establishment of an all-party committee to consider constitutional reform, including divorce. Government confidence was bolstered by poll results. Minister for Equality and Law Reform Mervyn Taylor contacted Tánaiste and Minister for Foreign Affairs Dick Spring in 1995 with details of another MRBI poll on divorce which suggested that 66 per cent would support constitutional change: '[T]here are now more intending yes voters than no voters in every geographical area, in every age group, in every category defined by marital status, and in every socio-economic category ... useful confirmation that we are broadly on the right course.' Taylor believed it would still be

---

[80] There was no discussion of the Pauline or Petrine privileges which allowed a Catholic who was married to a non-Christian to remarry in the Catholic Church or of a non-Christian converting to Catholicism and seeking to marry a Catholic which permitted any previous marriage to a non-Christian to be dissolved by the Catholic Church (O'Brien, *Divorce?*, pp. 118–22).

[81] The 1994 Church of Ireland synod opened the possibility for divorcees to remarry in church provided they performed an act of penitence. In the Lutheran Church, like the Anglican Church, a pastor could refuse to remarry divorcees. In the Jewish religion, the *ketuba* given to a bride at her wedding detailed what she would receive if the couple separated. A Jewish husband is required to grant a *gett*, a religious divorce, to allow a civilly divorced Jewish woman to remarry (*Divorce – the new law in Northern Ireland*, p. 19).

[82] O'Brien, *Divorce?*, p. 22.

necessary to court Fianna Fáil's 'minimal enthusiasm', which, along with the Catholic Church, he blamed as 'key players' in the earlier defeat. He thus considered four years' separation before divorce proceedings could begin to counter claims of easy divorce: 'There is nothing we can do about the Church ... the referendum result will be very tight. ... We will need every vote we can get.'[83] Many of Taylor's Labour Party colleagues were similarly determined, initiating a letter-writing campaign, distributing leaflets, holding daily media briefings and nightly legal advice hotlines as well as regional public meetings with its Women's National Council particularly seeking to allay women's fears of divorce. Large public meetings were, however, abandoned after a Cork assembly which Taylor addressed was packed with anti-divorce supporters.[84]

In a clear departure, government funding was promised to support the 'yes' campaign in the referendum whilst the government was not duty bound to provide any finance for the anti-divorce lobby. Richard Humphrey, Taylor's special advisor, however, recommended equilibrium to minimise legal challenges: 'There is merit in justness and fairness in giving a facility to the other side in a referendum campaign. ... To exclude these would be discriminatory and could give rise to challenge ... trying out fly-by-wire ad hoc administrative solutions is really the equivalent of digging for fire.'[85] The financial implications of social welfare, particularly on a spouse's contributory pension if divorce was implemented, were additional early concerns; Minster for Social Welfare De Rossa intimated that a £1 million shortfall over a period of five years might follow the introduction of divorce in extending entitlement to survivors' pensions to divorcees who had not remarried on the death of former spouses. The Social Welfare (No. 2) Act of 1995, however, determined that no spouse would be disadvantaged in terms of their entitlement to social welfare benefits because of a change in their marital status from married to separated, deserted or divorced. In context, the figure of £1 million was less than 0.3 per cent of the cost of survivors' pensions, estimated at a total of £342 million in 1995.[86] More research on the economic impact of marital breakdown was also available than for the preceding referendum. In relation to deserted wives' benefits, women would be better off on social welfare than in receipt of maintenance:

[83] Notes of Mervyn Taylor, 8 August 1995 (NLI, MS 39,373).
[84] Minutes of Irish Labour Party General Council, 22 February 1995 (NLI, MS 49,494/428) and 11 October 1995 (MS 49,494/430).
[85] Humphrey to Taylor, 12 July 1995 (NLI, MS 46,455/3).
[86] De Rossa cited estimates from the Central Statistics Office noting that of the 55,000 separated persons, 75 per cent were predicted to avail of divorce once implemented and 50 per cent would remarry (Dáil Éireann debates, 13 June 1995, vol. 454, cols. 516–8). The total social welfare costs were £4.18 billion in 1995.

a 1993 survey revealed that only 9 per cent of maintenance orders were not in arrears which countered claims of women's economic vulnerability being caused by divorce: '[I]n "divorce-free" Ireland, families are suffering the same economic effects . . . as those suffered by families in other countries after divorce. Divorce does not cause poverty; on the contrary, divorce legislation, if properly drafted, can alleviate it.'[87]

Smaller bodies like the Muintir na hÉireann (Family of Ireland) Party, the Irish Christian Centrist Party, the Family Prayer Movement, committees of teachers and lawyers against the amendment and regional anti-divorce groups embraced a common claim that all marriages would be affected if the referendum were carried: marriage would no longer be legally defined as a lifelong union and more marriages would consequently end, causing children and former wives distress and increasing reliance on social welfare.[88] It was also predicted that serial divorcees would emerge, destabilising second unions whilst a 'guilty' spouse divorcing against the will of their partner was deemed 'fundamentally unjust'. Even less convincing was the assertion that the constitution 'guaranteed . . . a mutually binding lifelong commitment' when, as Duncan averred, it could never curb individual will. Counter-arguments now more effectively emphasised that many Irish marriages already ended without divorce and allowing those who were currently separated to remarry would fortify rather than diminish the institution of marriage. An important distinction was also made between the harm caused to children by marriage breakdown and divorce.[89]

Unlike its predecessor, there was all-party support for the amendment although, as Taylor predicted, some Fianna Fáil members provided considerable opposition. This caused political casualties: Fianna Fáil whip, Michael J. Noonan was expelled from the party for not voting after pledging to his Limerick West constituents that he would 'let the people decide'.[90] Although divorce reform could never singularly reunify the north and south of the country, it might, as had been mooted since the early 1920s, improve relations. Taoiseach John Bruton certainly presented the referendum as symbolic of minority rights, requiring a balance of personal opine 'against those of others and to take account

[87] Browne, 'Divorce in other jurisdictions' in O'Brien, *Divorce?* pp. 77–8.

[88] The small Irish political party Muintir na hÉireann was founded in 1994 with a socially conservative manifesto; the Christian Centrist Party was established in 1991 but changed its name to the Christian Solidarity Party in 1994.

[89] The Ad Hoc Committee on the Referendum produced a statement of the case for [and against] the proposed amendment to Article 41.3.2 of the constitution. Two senior counsels prepared the statement: Gerard Durcan for the pro-divorce statement and John Finlay for the anti-statement.

[90] David Andrews, *Kingstown Republican* (Dublin, 2007), cited p. 154 and p. 156.

of the views of minorities. These considerations are important in the context of relationships on this island.' Yet, he refused to comment on the Rev. Ian Paisley's promise to 'celebrate' a 'no' vote as they 'do not wish to adhere to the principle that minorities have rights in any civil society and continue to maintain a majoritarianism approach which they have always demonstrated in Northern Ireland'. Moreover, one of the recommendations of the New Ireland Forum was now an actuality; Bruton drew a distinct line between church and state:

A church is a voluntary association. The State is a compulsory association and people have no choice but to follow the rules laid down by it. ... You cannot transpose the teaching of any church into State law. There is a clear distinction between the function and role of the two institutions. Though equally important they are different.[91]

Although Irish poet Paul Durcan urged, 'Do not bring ideology into my house of prayer',[92] much of the anti-divorce propaganda was religiously inspired. The Catholic hierarchy issued a statement from its episcopal conference in November 1995, praising the deserted as 'an authentic witness of fidelity of which the world today has great need'.[93] Pope John Paul and Mother Theresa both urged a 'no' vote in the referendum and posters read, 'Jesus has already said NO to Divorce. Now it's up to you!'[94] This provoked Church of Ireland critique; Rev. John Marsden called for 'greater compassion and an increased readiness to come to terms with the realities of human life ... the frailty of human nature makes provision for divorce a sad necessity' whilst holding the deserted as altruistic paragons burdened the victims with unfair societal pressure.[95] The views of hierarchy spokesman Bishop Flynn of Achonry that if divorced or in a second union, the sacraments would be denied were also not wholly representative.[96] Indeed, Fr Gabriel Daly challenged Flynn outright: '[T]here are many priests in Ireland and abroad, who would take a much more positive and pastoral view.'[97]

Taylor continued to meet various interest groups such as the Irish Countrywomen's Association which discussed divorce from 1980 and gave members a free vote in the referendum, the Council for the Status of

[91] Dáil Éireann debates, 22 November 1995, vol. 458, cols. 1222–4.
[92] Paul Durcan, 'The Divorce Referendum, 1986'.
[93] *The Furrow*, 4 September 1996 and *Irish Catholic*, 9 November 1995.
[94] Irish Labour Party archive (NLI, MS 49,494/925).
[95] *The Furrow*, 4 September 1996.
[96] It later emerged that this statement followed a letter from the Vatican's Congregation for the Doctrine of the Faith which stated that divorcees and those who remarried without a church annulment should not receive Holy Communion (Tom Inglis, *Moral monopoly. The rise and fall of the Catholic Church in modern Ireland* (2nd ed., Dublin, 1998, p. 221).
[97] Ibid.

Women, AIM, the Divorce Action Group as well as political parties.[98] The government clearly believed it could not afford to lose this vote, thrice commissioning the MRBI to conduct research for the cabinet sub-committee on divorce[99] Summer polls showed declining support, but this was countered by a government-financed propaganda campaign. A Department for Equality and Law Reform leaflet emphasised familial protection and provision for divorcees: 19,000 copies were printed, including 1,000 in the Irish language, at a cost of £2,136.[100] This was small change when compared to the government expenditure on the divorce referendum: this totalled £493,953, but some estimates were as high as £3.5 million. Most expenditures (£182,585) were on newspaper advertisements, advertising agency costs (£47,497) and postal costs (£40,893).[101] Every household received a leaflet setting out the main points of the case for and against reform at a cost of £151,000 and a reminder to vote cost an additional £57,000.[102] This expenditure, particularly advocating a 'yes' vote, led to an unsuccessful High Court action brought by pro-divorce reformer and Green Party MEP Patricia McKenna. McKenna then appealed to the Supreme Court which agreed that government partiality was unconstitutional. The government's advertising campaign was subsequently withdrawn, but only in the week before the referendum. Some advertisements in the *Sunday World* had already gone to press so the immediate impact of this ruling was minimal. Indeed, the legal challenge may have inadvertently enlivened the campaign in its dying phases.[103]

Last-minute polls suggested that an estimated 55 per cent of men and 49 per cent of women supported the removal of the constitutional ban.[104] The amendment passed by 50.28 per cent to 49.72 per cent on 24 November but with only a 9,000 (0.6 per cent) vote majority. The result was so close, 'the narrowest margin of any of the constitutional amendment referenda to date', that a recount was held. Anti-divorce campaigner Úna Bean Mhic Mhathúna's reaction to the count in

---

[98] See ICA report, 11 October 1980 (NLI, MS 39,362); ICA minutes, 11 September 1985 (NLI, 39,383/2) and ICA press release, 1985 (NLI, MS 39,744/5).
[99] Minister for Equality and Law, Dáil Éireann debates, 6 December 1996, vol. 459, col. 663.
[100] Ibid., 30 May 1995, vol. 453, col. 1363 and col. 1365.
[101] Ibid., 11 June 1996, vol. 466, col. 1549. The first divorce referendum cost an estimated £1 million.
[102] Ibid., 23 January 1996, vol. 460, col. 317.
[103] *Irish Times*, 8 February 1996. This ruling led to the establishment of the Referendum Commission. The ITUC Executive Council was also very active in the pro-reform campaign, circulating 150,000 handbills.
[104] John Coakley and Michael Gallagher (eds.), *Politics in the Republic of Ireland* (3rd ed., London and New York, 1999), p. 312.

Dublin, directed at members of the Divorce Action Group, of 'G' way, ye wife-swappin' sodomites' elucidates the vitriol of much of the campaign.[105] The result, however, only partially revived the urban/liberal and rural/conservative fault lines of the 1986 referendum: 39 per cent of urban dwellers and 42 per cent of those in rural constituencies supported the reform. The highest number of 'yes' votes occurred in Dublin and its environs of Kildare, Louth and Wicklow.[106] With 1.6 million votes cast, one in six voted. Dublin's turnout of 64.56 per cent was the highest in the country, but the rest of Leinster saw 61.98 per cent, Munster 62.8 per cent, Connaught 58.03 per cent and Ulster 54.79 per cent. Excluding undecided voters, an *Irish Times*/MRBI poll taken at the time of the referendum found 66 per cent of all voters under age 34, 55 per cent age 50–64 and a third in the 23–34 age range supported reform. By comparison, three-quarters of those older than age 64 opposed it. In relation to gender and marital status, women and married couples were equally divided on the issue, but the unmarried favoured the change by a 38 per cent margin. Opposition from farmers was high with 70 per cent of larger farmers and 69 per cent of smaller farmers voting against reform which is indicative of the continued centrality of property rights on voting patterns. Middle-class voters were most in favour at 37 per cent, but working-class support was considerable; 33 per cent of those surveyed voted 'yes'. A party divide was also evident: 49 per cent of Fianna Fáil voters opposed divorce which, given the party's determination to pass this amendment, was a less than wholesale endorsement. By comparison, Fine Gael was nearly evenly divided on the issue, 44 per cent for and 43 per cent against with Labour in favour by a margin of 2:1.[107] Ireland now faced the challenge of introducing legislation on an issue long held as the pinnacle of liberalism where many remained resistant to reform.

---

[105] *Irish Times*, 19 January 2015.
[106] The referendum passed by 818,842 to 809,728 votes. Dublin's 'yes' votes amounted to 63.56 per cent; the rest of Leinster 49.42 per cent, Munster 43.88 per cent, Connacht 40.55 per cent and Ulster 39.14 per cent.
[107] *Irish Times*, 3 January and 14 June 1996.

12 The 'Last Stretch of a Long Road': The Family (Divorce) Law Act of 1996

Hopes of a swift reform in the aftermath of the second divorce referendum were negated by further legal challenges to the government's pro-divorce stance. The award of the government's advertising contract to Quinn McDonnell Pattison (QMP), with Conor Quinn, brother of the minister for finance, on its board led to Dáil questions on propriety. The amount of government funding given to bodies active in the pro-divorce lobby such as the Divorce Action Group, the Right to Re-marry Campaign, AIM, the Irish Countrywomen's Association and the Council for the Status of Women were also controversial even though only the latter had been funded in relation to the divorce referendum: £20,969 were granted for the referendum in 1994 and £7,895 in the following year.[1] Chair of the anti-divorce campaign Des Hanafin brought the first action under the 1994 Referendum Act, filing an official complaint in the High and Supreme Courts alleging that the use of public monies to fund the government's 'yes' referendum campaign influenced the vote by between 3 per cent and 5 per cent – and was therefore sufficient to have impacted the close result – and that the government continued to advertise online and in the press after the McKenna ruling. Hanafin wanted the referendum declared null and another to be held. This was unsuccessful although in the Supreme Court Mr Justice Murphy acknowledged that the government spending was unconstitutional, but this did not equate to 'an electoral wrongdoing'.[2] These proceedings delayed the divorce bill's introduction[3] and revealed the nature of QMP's advice to the government: 'They must learn from the 1986 vote and accept that public opinion could be fickle and prone to sudden change on divorce.' It advised a confident but non-arrogant

---

The quote in the chapter title is from Mervyn Taylor, Dáil Éireann debates, 27 June 1996, vol. 467, col. 1755.

[1] Dáil Éireann debates, 13 December 1995, vol. 459, col. 1476.

[2] The Referendum Act only applied to the referendum and not to accompanying campaigns (*Irish Times*, 8 February 1996).

[3] Fianna Fáil Deputy Willie O'Dea claimed that 'the Government played Russian roulette with the referendum' (O'Dea, Dáil Éireann debates, 27 June 1996, vol. 467, cols. 1803–4). See also the criticism of N. Ahern, ibid., cols. 1823–4 and col. 1827.

approach; more damaging was the revelation to be 'a bit liberal with the truth' regarding the implications of reform.[4]

Much of the debate on the subsequent Family Law (Divorce) Bill revealed a country coming to terms with the reality of marriage breakdown. Debate from Fianna Fáil was particularly muted, but this was a common-sense acquiescence of what was agreed in the referendum and confirmed in court. Taoiseach John Bruton adopted a similarly non-confrontational approach when meeting the Vatican Secretary of State Cardinal Angelo Sodano in January 1996, re-emphasising the 'complimentary but necessarily separate function' of church and state.[5] In the same month, the Irish Catholic hierarchy's fifteen-page submission to the Forum for Peace and Reconciliation claimed no political authority on the part of the church, but a continued commitment to teaching marriage as a sacrament in a pluralist society.[6] In the New Catechism divorce was thus denoted as 'immoral ... because it introduces disorder into the family and into society ... brings grave harm to the deserted spouse, to children traumatised by the separation ... its contagious effect ... makes it truly a plague upon society'.[7] Wicklow priest Fr Arthur O'Neill also warned that the now divergent views of marriage held by church and state could impact the clerical regulation of Catholic marriage.[8] Relations were further soured by the Minster for Social Welfare Proinsias De Rossa's calling the Archbishop of Cashel Dr Dermot Clifford a liar due to his citation of divorce statistics during the referendum campaign:[9]

[I]t would have been unthinkable even ten years ago for a left-wing minister in a Fine Gael–led coalition to call a Catholic Archbishop a liar, and get away with it – without either any Fine Gaeler repudiating his remark or the other bishops rallying in outrage in their colleague's defence.[10]

In the larger Protestant denominations, however, preparations were made to accommodate both divorce and divorcees. The Presbyterian Church, for example, produced divorce guidelines for its clergy; if they wished to divorce they were required to inform the presbytery and have their grounds for divorce considered. Although divorce should not cause removal from office, approval was required if they wanted to retain their ministry. There was no accompanying advice for their spouses and an unsuccessful amendment that adultery or desertion on the part of either spouse and where the cleric initiated the divorce and married another

---

[4] *Irish Times*, 17 and 20 January 1996. The Hanafin case was unanimously rejected by the Supreme Court in June 1996.
[5] Ibid., 18 January 1996.   [6] Ibid., 17 and 20 January 1996.   [7] Para. 2385.
[8] *Irish Times*, 2 March 1996.   [9] Ibid., 10 Feb .1996.
[10] Inglis, *Moral monopoly*, cited p. 223.

should lead to resignation highlighted a continued moral conservatism.[11] This was also evident in the creation of a new National Party, headed by Nora Bennis, in 1996. Conservative and pro-family in ethos, it aimed to rally those who opposed divorce reform, but neither this nor the anti-divorce Christian Solidarity Party polled well in the 1997 election. The ADC also continued post-referendum. Chaired by former High Court judge Rory O'Hanlon, it produced twenty-six points on the wrongs of divorce with an emphasis on alleged augmented taxes, increased marital breakdown and the moral fallout, especially for children.

The preceding decade of family law reform which saw eighteen bills passed, more than had been collectively enacted since the 1937 constitution, especially the Family Law Act of 1995, laid much of the legal framework for divorce.[12] This piecemeal approach acclimatised many to the fact that the availability of legal remedies to marital breakdown did not cause these unions to end. International changes such as the United Nation's broad definition of the family were also adopted in Ireland's social welfare system and recognition that Ireland, with marriage breakdown, a falling rate of marriage and rising illegitimacy, looked very like its European counterparts, also impacted. The provision of divorce was gradually perceived as a mark of maturity in a state which 'should not institutionalise misery. That happened to a degree over a number of years. ... There is no evidence that society in Northern Ireland or in Europe is any better or any worse as a result of the availability of divorce.'[13]

However, any proposition that divorce reform marked the end of the country's liberalisation was premature: Ireland still had to negotiate a myriad of social issues including abortion.[14] Furthermore, not all were ready to accept the inevitability of the divorce bill's passage. The idea of a pent-up demand for divorce that characterised the referenda debates, much of the Northern Irish reform agenda and the 1857 English reform, led to suggestions that 'some 10,000 to 15,000 ... will wish to obtain a divorce as soon as that possibility exists'. Enhanced funding for mediation and legal aid, a fear that divorce would be a wealthy domain, the increased need for judges with family law expertise as well as improved court accommodation constituted the crux of

---

[11] *Irish Times*, 22 May 1996.
[12] Taylor, Dáil Éireann debates, 31 January 1995, vol. 448, col. 593 and cols. 595–6. See, for example, the Judicial Separation Act (1989), the White Paper on Marital Breakdown (1992), the Maintenance Act (1994), the Civil Legal Act (1995) and the Domestic Violence Act (1996).
[13] John Dardis, Seanad Éireann debates, 10 October 1996, vol. 148, cols. 1665–6.
[14] The eighth amendment of the Irish constitution on the right to life of the unborn was only removed in 2018.

the parliamentary debate.[15] Some politicians, although deferring to the democratic will of the country, remained concerned by remarriage, especially that of mentally or physically abusive spouses which may 'result in more lives being damaged ... many people will be hurt by this fateful step'.[16] Less compliant were those, like Fianna Fáil's Noel Ahern, who claimed that the 'cult of individualism' had triumphed:

Had the gods been with the anti-divorce people and the weather been better in the west but not so kind in the east, there might well have been a different result ... the country will not fall apart overnight. It will take five, ten or 15 years before we realise the mess we have foisted upon ourselves. ... I wonder if divorce is being introduced to give genuine people a second chance or to create another bonanza for the vultures who fly around society willing to pick on the bones of other people's misery.

Yet, even he assented that, in consequence of annulments and the recognition of foreign divorces, the ban could not have remained indefinitely: 'With the benefit of hindsight we probably should have done something earlier to resolve the problem legally before it came to the matter of divorce.'[17]

The divorce bill, bar minor and technical amendments, mirrored the draft bill presented to the country prior to the second referendum. At the date of instituting divorce proceedings, spouses were to have lived apart for periods of, or amounting to, four of the preceding five years; be without any prospect of spousal reconciliation; and any dependants be provided for under terms decided by the Circuit Court. Cases where property had a rateable value of more than £200 would be heard in the High Court. The courts would also, under Section 11 of the Guardianships of Infant Act, 1964, direct child welfare, custody and access and had the authority to make financial, property and pension adjustments in addition to any order required to ensure justice to both parties and any dependants.[18] Property, as in separation cases, was not

[15] See also Deputy Alan Shatter's call for costs to be kept to a minimum, Dáil Éireann debates, 27 February 1997, vol. 475, col. 1203–4. This was also emphasised by the Progressive Democrats. Demand on the court system was another Fianna Fáil concern, with current waiting lists in the Circuit Courts averaging between twelve and eighteen months, partly due to the limit of civil litigation doubling to £30,000 in 1991 (Dr Michael Woods, ibid., 27 June 1996, vol. 467, cols. 1780–2).

[16] D. Wallace believed that the grounds for divorce were too lax, too reliant on the will of one spousal party and downgraded the status of marriage (ibid., 27 June 1996, vol. 467, cols. 1816–20). See also the comments of Neville, Seanad Éireann debates, 10 October 1996, vol. 148, cols. 1637 and 1640 and O'Farrell, ibid., col. 1658. O'Farrell also criticised the country's 'á la carte society where people can pick what suits them and ignore what they do not like' (col. 1653).

[17] Ahern, ibid., 27 June 1996, vol. 467, cols. 1823–4 and col. 1827.

[18] Taylor, ibid., col. 1761.

limited to the family home. Rather, it referred to any property or business, shares or monies. Section 13 of the bill also made it possible for the court to order that one spouse remain in the family home to the exclusion of the other or to order the sale of the home. Spousal rights of succession would terminate on divorce, but this would be compensated as the court saw fit. Mediation and reconciliation, which were much discussed in the Dáil, formed key parts of Sections 5 and 6 of the bill.[19]

The act's provisions were partially liberal. Separation, as defined by the 1989 Judicial Separation Act, rather than fault, provided the sole ground for divorce. More conformist was the separation period which was longer than the two years common to much of Europe. Indeed, bodies like the Democratic Left earlier remonstrated that this was excessively long and could 'encourage unnecessary and sometimes mischievous delay in dealing with problems of finance, [and] custody'.[20] Again, in contrast to much divorce provision elsewhere, there was no principle of a clean break. The financial settlement made at the time of the divorce could be subsequently adjusted which later proved unpopular with many divorcees, the legal profession and the judiciary and deterred divorce in some instances.[21] Moreover, all divorce cases were to be heard *in camera* which negated the long-held concern for the allegedly corrupting influence of publicising details of marital wrongdoings. The *in camera* ruling effectively continued the precedent set in the 1920s of censoring the publication of cases of marital breakdown and denied the public any sense of the reality of divorce or its frequency. As Earner-Byrne highlights, this 'increased the cultural tendency to see the family as a site of inviolate privacy about which no tales could be told'.[22] Widening the grounds for divorce would also require another referendum. Divorce was therefore never as easy as the anti-reformers claimed and ultimately, although divorce was available in Ireland, 'the law prefers marriage'.[23]

Regardless of its shortcomings, the government was right to present this as 'a significant turning point', ending a 'harsh, unbending and uncaring' ban:

---

[19] Mediation and counselling dominated the committee and report stages of the debates. The international precedent for solicitors to certify mediation and counselling procedure was the Australian Family Law Act of 1975. Sections 27 to 32 of the bill provided for changes to be made to the tax code for income and capital taxes for divorced couples. This covered capital acquisitions tax, capital gains tax, probate tax and stamp duty.

[20] They favoured divorce with consent after two years without a 'normal marital relationship' and three years without consent (Democratic Left, 'Divorce providing a second chance', undated [1992] [NLI, MS 49,807/35]).

[21] See Aide-Memoire from the Office of the Minister for Finance to Mervyn Taylor, Minister for Equality and Law Reform, 1 March 1994 (NLI, MS 46,455/1).

[22] Earner-Byrne, 'The family in Ireland', p. 650. Incest cases were also heard *in camera*.

[23] Spreng, *Abortion and divorce*, p. 208.

It brought the law into disrepute because it was unable to address properly the position of those tens of thousands of persons whose marriage had ended, many of whom had entered second relationships and wished to remarry. . . . [I]n time many people will come to terms with the fact that our law on divorce and the right to remarry gives legal options which must be available to members of society, as is the case in other jurisdictions throughout the world, many of which have a strong family ethos and cultural traditions not unlike our own.[24]

Reiterating the words nineteenth-century divorce reformer William Brooke, Helen Keogh of the Progressive Democrats reflected on the 'tortuous' pace of Irish divorce law reform and the fallacy of a morally superior land: 'There was no idyllic Ireland. We are living in a complex society where the pressures are intense. . . . The introduction of divorce and the right to remarry for many thousands of people is a humane and necessary reaction to reality within society.'[25] David Norris debunked the same ideal: '[W]e liked to delude ourselves that we lived in a specially ordered, neat little corner of the world which was unlike those jurisdictions where divorce was possible. I like to think we have now grown up.'[26] Indeed, Senator Maurice Manning could now air his personal experience of divorce without fear of censure:

The fact that I was married in a different domicile meant I was able to get a divorce in another domicile and remarry legally. That process enabled me to maintain a relationship of great civility and courtesy with my former spouse which might not have been the case had we to go through the then existing Irish process. It gave me an opportunity to remake my life, as it did my former spouse.[27]

After a sixteen-year campaign, the divorce bill passed its final Seanad stage without a vote in September 1996.

Little fanfare hailed the Family (Divorce) Law Act of 1996 which came into operation on 27 February 1997.[28] The Catholic Church accommodated the reform as part of a broader process of moral and legal distancing: 'No change in State law can change the moral law.'[29] Popular opposition to the legislation was subdued, despite Dr Gerard

---

[24] Taylor, Dáil Éireann debates, 27 June 1996, vol. 467, cols. 1755–7.

[25] Keogh, ibid., 27 June 1996, vol. 467, col. 1785 and col. 1795.

[26] Norris, ibid., 10 October 1996, vol. 148, col. 1684. Minister for Equality and Law Reform, Taylor also refuted the anti-divorce lament, apparent since the mid-nineteenth century, that divorce fostered marriage breakdown and a 'divorce culture': 'The law can only deal with reality, not some idealistic dream. I suspect that there were problems even in the old days. People might not have been as upfront as they are now but the problems were there' (Taylor, Seanad Éireann debates, 10 October 1996, vol. 148, col. 1690).

[27] Manning, ibid., col. 1661.

[28] The bill also removed coverage of divorce, separation, restitution of conjugal rights and nullity from the remit of the 1929 Censorship of Publications Act.

[29] Fuller, Irish Catholicism, cited p. 247.

Casey, vice-chair of the No-Divorce Campaign's vow: 'We have not yet begun to fight. We will torment people for the next 40, 50, 60 years.'[30] Catholic Archbishop of Dublin Dr Desmond Connell's sermon for the Feast of the Holy Family also emphasised divorce as delivering 'a most serious blow' to Irish family life which was at variance with that promoted by the church.[31] The responses of the Catholic Church's official newspaper, *L'Osservatore Romano,* as well as that Vatican Radio, were more broadly based, lamenting the reform as a 'defeat for Catholicism' which, coinciding with the election of a Polish communist government, dealt 'a double blow for the Church in Europe'.[32]

There was no flood of applications to divorce as many had predicted in the anti-divorce campaign. Feminist publications like *The Women's Watch* estimated 15,000 divorces in the first post-reform year.[33] The first petition for divorce came on 15 January 1997 from a terminally ill man in his sixties in Dublin petitioning to divorce to allow him to remarry his long-term partner with whom he had a child. He petitioned the High Court which, in a compassionate ruling, allowed the divorce before the legislation was enacted; he died on 1 February 1997 just ten days after remarrying.[34] Divorce was legalised later that month with the first divorce, R. C. versus C. C., heard in a two-and-a-half-hour hearing in Castlebar Circuit Court in March. In June, the chair of the Divorce Action Group and her spouse represented themselves in Dublin's Circuit Court to divorce after a twelve-year separation, at a cost of less than £15, but only 95 divorces were granted in 1997, which did not indicate any pent-up demand or similar pattern to post-reform divorce figures in England or Northern Ireland.[35] Few of the 60,000 citizens who had been separated for at least four years and could now divorce came forward. Legal Aid, however, advised 1,863 people on divorce in 1997, which evidences that many sought information but did not proceed to court. The decisive factor was often a successful legal aid application which could reduce the cost of divorce from thousands of pounds to £23. The quest for information on legal aid was also evident in the 'overflowing attendances' at the Law Society and Bar

---

[30] James, 'Céad Míle Fáilte?' cited p. 218.   [31] *Irish Times,* 30 December 1996.
[32] Ibid., 12 October 1996.
[33] *The Women's Watch,* vol. 10, no. 2 (December 1996), p. 7.
[34] James, 'Céad Míle Fáilte?' p. 221.
[35] Dáil Éireann debates, 29 May 2001, vol. 537, question 99. Circuit Court Office figures provide no information on the social standing of those seeking to divorce, a situation, which although partially justified by Minister for Justice, Equality and Law Reform John O'Donoghue on the need for confidentiality, was at odds with the international standard and caused the censure of the National Statistics Board.

Council's seminars for solicitors on divorce[36] and demand for the Citizen's Information Centre's booklet *Separation and Divorce Explained* was 'phenomenal'.[37] *Divorce. A Practical Guide for Solicitors* was also published by two Dublin law firms and the Irish Progressive Building Society produced a guide to life insurance and pension rights for those who were married, separated and divorced.

Regional analysis of the 1997 divorce figures revealed a clustering of applications in Dublin, accounting for 216 of 431 applications received and 51.5 per cent of divorces. Cork ranked second with 44 applications submitted but only 4 divorces granted. Waterford, Naas, Galway and Wicklow followed with 20, 18, 14 and 14 applications and 0, 1, 7 and 3 divorces granted, respectively; the success rate was therefore low which is suggestive of an initial lack of familiarity with the new law's provisions. Seven divorce applications were also awaiting hearings in the High Court, the location for more complex suits often involving extensive wealth.[38] The time to secure an uncontested divorce was estimated at eight weeks, whereas a contested divorce could take six months or more depending on the intricacies of the hearing. In 1998, the number increased to 1,421 divorces and this upward trajectory continued: 2,333 and 2,623 divorces were granted in 1999 and 2000, respectively.[39] Alarmist concerns that Cork was turning into a divorce capital emerged by the latter juncture, but Cork had earlier produced a high number of parliamentary divorces, many involving military personnel, and its divorce rate later levelled.[40] Cost, estimated at a minimum of £1,000 to £1,500 per client in 2002, as well as the lingering stigma attached to divorce remained important considerations and helped curb the predicted divorce deluge.[41]

Alternatives to divorce were, however, in decline post-1997. Civil nullity suits were never popular as they could cost an estimated £10,000 but their number fell after divorce was introduced.[42] The number of separations followed a similar pattern, declining from 1,413 in 1997 to 703 in 2014. The frequency of church nullity suits was slower

---

[36] Walls and Bergin, *Law of divorce*, forward.   [37] *Irish Times*, 6 May 1998.

[38] Dáil Éireann debates, 5 October 2000, vol. 523, col. 1526.

[39] Ibid., 29 May 2001, vol. 537, question 99.

[40] See question by Stanton in ibid., 8 June 2000, vol. 520, col. 1374.

[41] Burley and Regan, 'Divorce in Ireland', p. 217.

[42] Only thirty decrees of civil nullity were granted, for example, from 1989 to 1990. Briefing notes from Mervyn Taylor to Department of Social Welfare, 24 January 1994 (NLI, MS 46,455/6). On civil nullity, see Maebh Harding, 'Religion and family law in Ireland: from a Catholic protection of marriage to a "Catholic" approach to nullity' in E. Orucu and J. Mair (eds.), *The place of religion in family law: a comparative search* (Antwerp, 2011), pp. 161–85. Nullity was under review by the LRC from 1976 (see Report: Nullity of Marriage [LRC 9–1984, October 1984]). The 1984 report did not suggest that the state should recognise church annulments (ibid., p. 88).

to decrease; their number peaked with 499 applications submitted in 2004. This indicated that some opposition to divorce remained. Although few paid the full £600 cost for a church annulment, this could take four years to secure. The church could, and did, revoke the right of one or both of the parties to remarry in the Catholic Church by the use of *vetitum* (prohibition) which was applied in an estimated three-quarters of church annulments.[43] Presenting evidence to two church tribunals, one regional in Armagh, Dublin, Cork or Galway as well as the National Appeals Tribunal, which had to concur for a marriage to be annulled, was also a trying and emotional experience for many.[44] Only 244 began this process in 2012.[45] Separations and church and civil nullity actions were therefore previously used as a partial substitute for divorce for those of financial means, but the permanency that divorce afforded saw it become an increasingly attractive option to those whose marriages had ended.

The granting of the first divorce in independent Ireland on compassionate grounds before the bill's formal enactment supports some of the claims made of this reform as 'a milestone in the creation of a more … tolerant and caring society. … It sure is changed times.'[46] Yet, divorce was contested after its implementation with legal challenges acting as a backlash to the reform: in March 1997 the High Court ruled that the minister for the environment was wrong to claim he had no authority to change the regulations to allow anti-divorce campaigners to monitor the counting of votes in the 1995 referendum.[47] In the following month, a complaint brought against the Irish broadcaster RTÉ for a repeat broadcast by the Right to Remarry group was upheld by the Broadcasting Complaints Commission.[48] The High Court's jurisdiction to grant divorce also had to be confirmed by the first case of divorce heard in the Republic. Other legal challenges, like John Corway's 1999 High and Supreme Court cases claiming that Helen Shea's 1995 *Sunday Independent* cartoon, punning the former byline of the 'antis' and depicting

---

[43] L. L. Abbate, 'What God has joined "let" man put asunder: Ireland's struggle between canon and common law relating to divorce', *Emory International Law Review*, vol. 16, no. 2 (2002), pp. 583–637. The decisions of church annulments are not publically available.

[44] Wood and O'Shea, *Divorce in Ireland*, p. 116.

[45] Figures from www.irishcatholic.ie, accessed 3 March 2017.

[46] *Irish Times*, 26 September 1996.

[47] The case was brought by Fionnuala Sherwin who worked for the 'no' campaign.

[48] The case was brought by Anthony Coughlan. In 1998, RTÉ's referendum broadcasts were also criticised as too biased towards the 'yes' campaign. In one week, for example, an estimated forty-three minutes of airtime were granted compared to ten minutes to the opposition. A 2000 Supreme Court appeal was unsuccessful (*Irish Times*, 15 October 1996).

Figure 12.1 Helen Shea cartoon, 'Hello, Progress – Bye-Bye Father?'
Sunday Independent, 26 November 1995
(image reproduced courtesy of the Irish News Archive,
www.irishnewsarchive.com).

Proinsias De Rossa, Ruiri Quinn and John Bruton, was blasphemous
as it insulted the Eucharist, were unsuccessful (see Figure 12.1).[49]

This was symptomatic of a continued, albeit minority, resistance to
divorce, but there was also conciliation: Fianna Fáil reinstated Noonan as
a party whip and Archbishop of Cashel and Emly Dr Clifford accepted
outgoing Minister for Welfare De Rossa's apology for his previous accu-
sation of lying. Support groups like the First Wives' Club also emerged to
counter isolation amongst female divorcees and help those lacking professional advice. Various Protestant denominations permitted divorcees
to remarry in church; the Church of Ireland, after two year's deliberation,
accepted this in 1996 whilst allowing clergy to opt out of performing such
ceremonies as encompassed in the 1857 divorce act. The Presbyterian
and Methodist Churches similarly allowed this with Baptists leaving
individual churches to decide. As in the lay population, church

---

[49] Barbara Hyland's charge that the government's failure to inform the country of the
possibility of remarriage under the laws of nullity was misleading was struck out by the
High Court in 1996; Denis Riordan's case that divorce was repugnant to the constitution
was similarly rejected in 1997 and its revival in the Supreme Court was ruled as an abuse
of court process in 2000. He appealed and was jailed for a week for contempt of court in
2001.

accommodation of divorcees was not universal: divorcees cannot marry in a Free Presbyterian Church or be married by a Free Presbyterian minister and in the Catholic Church divorcees cannot remarry or receive communion.[50]

By the late 1990s, the Irish divorce rate moved towards Western European norms with an estimated 10 per cent of families having one parent compared to a European average of 11 per cent. The Irish figures were below the UK and Danish rates of 15–17 per cent, but higher than the Greek, Italian and Spanish rates of 5–6 per cent.[51] The Irish divorce rate peaked in 2007 with 3,684 divorces; numbers declined thereafter in consequence of the post–Celtic Tiger recession which saw an Irish banking crisis and rapidly rising rates of bankruptcy and unemployment from 2008. Thus, as in the parliamentary divorce era, economics rather than morality often stymied Irish divorce rates. By 2013, the Republic's divorce rate was the lowest in the EU: 0.6 per 1,000 of the population compared to 2 in the UK.[52] The 2014 divorce rate was 2,629, a decline of 230 on the 2013 figure.[53] It also became quickly apparent that, akin to Northern Ireland and Britain, Irish women were in the majority as divorce petitioners. Initially, an estimated three out of four applications in the Republic of Ireland were brought by women but by 2000 the ratio of women to men was 2:1. From 2008 to 2014, women remained in the majority which further evidences a diminishing rate of female forbearance: 14,092 (55 per cent) female divorce applications compared to 11,490 (45 per cent) brought by men. Divorce rates were also higher in more populous urban areas. This was especially marked in Dublin which averaged 101 divorces per annum from 2008 to 2014; Waterford averaged 88, Carlow 86, Cork 83, Galway 81 and Limerick 78. The lowest annual instances of divorce were in Kildare (55), Cavan (56) and Donegal (57) and the larger Protestant populations in the latter two counties reiterate that aversion to divorce was not solely a Catholic domain.[54]

Divorce, as the anti-reform campaigners predicted, put pressure on the legal aid budget and services; by 1998, there were ten-month delays to consult a legal aid solicitor with almost half of the 2,175 people seen in the previous year seeking to divorce; by 2000, half of all divorces were financed by legal aid.[55] The introduction of divorce in the Republic of

---

[50] See www.freepress.org, accessed 12 May 2015.   [51] Ward, *Divorce in Ireland*, p. 7.
[52] Figures from www.cso.ie, accessed 25 July 2017.
[53] This is a combined circuit courts and high court figure: in 2014, 2,603 divorced in the circuit courts, 26 in the High Court (ibid.).
[54] Figures from www.rte.ie.iu.divorce, accessed 18 July 2016. A gender breakdown was only possible from 1998.
[55] Legal Aid annual report, 1997 (*Irish Times*, 21 October 1998).

Ireland provided a welcome yet tardy remedy for those deserted, abused and left fearful in unions which were irretrievably broken. Of equal import was the facilitation of remarriage and the associated more liberal redefinition of what constituted a family. And, as Irish divorce rates stabilised, they proved that most of the qualms which both delayed divorce law reform and fuelled preoccupations with the 'common good' over the needs of the individual were inexorably flawed.[56]

[56] Article 41.2, 1937 Irish constitution.

Conclusion

At the turn of the twentieth century, writer Katharine Tynan lamented 'the extraordinarily loveless marriages which still obtain over a great part of Ireland'. To Tynan, this was caused by a 'savage idea of virtue', but it was also due to the lack of attainable solutions to end marriage.[1] For much of its history, divorce was only available to a minority, and independent Ireland was without any provision for more than eighty years. In consequence, many could only invoke informal means of separation or become relegated to the ranks of the deserted who, by the time of Tynan's writing, were a sizeable but frequently marginalised group in Irish society. Yet, any suggestion that 'owing to the influence of the Roman Church ... [divorce] was never permitted in Ireland' is too sweeping.[2] For much of this history, the Catholic Church shared moral terrain with other faiths. It also rarely spoke with one voice as was apparent in the 1850s divorce debates, in deliberations over Parnell's morality in the early 1890s and when divorce reform began to be sought with increased frequency in the 1960s. By the latter juncture, some of the Irish Catholic hierarchical opposition to the state alone dictating divorce provision was at odds with Vatican II. Given the tradition of independence in Irish clericalism, this was unsurprising, but the 'hierarchy could no longer regard the laity as footsoliders [sic] to be given their orders'. Their influence was further curtailed by the 1983 Code of Canon Law, which, as in Cullen's day, disallowed direct political interjection.[3] The consternation in Irish clerical and legal circles at Pope John Paul II's 2002 call for lawyers to conscientiously object to represent clients seeking to divorce was emblematic of how much Ireland had changed.[4]

---

[1] Katharine Tynan, 'A new Irish novelist', a review of Grace Rhys's Land League novel, *Mary Dominic* in *The Bookman* (January 1899), p. 118.
[2] Montgomery Hyde, *Tangled web*, p. 27.
[3] Perreau-Saussine, *Catholicism and democracy*, p. 118.
[4] The pope was addressing the Tribunal of the Roman Rota, the Catholic Church Court of Appeal and the body which deals with annulments (*Irish Times*, 29 January 2002).

Despite the lack of legislative progress pertaining to Irish divorce from the mid-nineteenth century, the grounds for Irish divorce were not inert. The Westropp precedent, allowing the legal rulings of the divorce court to be applied in both Westminster and the parliament of Northern Ireland, was particularly significant in allowing a broader definition of legal cruelty, lessening the demand for the often harrowing and humiliating criminal conversation suit and eventually equalising the gendered grounds of parliamentary divorce. Northern Ireland's emulation of Westminster reforms as well as the routine application of English case law and test cases taken to the European courts also facilitated legal change. Although there was no sustained campaign to remove the constitutional ban on divorce in independent Ireland until the 1980s, this does not confirm the existence of a consensus of popular opine that 'dissuaded both British and Irish legislators from pressing reform'.[5] Claims that a storm of protest would accompany any reform of Ireland's divorce provision were inflated and only partially realised in the late-twentieth-century referenda campaigns. Until then, with only a few exceptions, those who experienced the hardships of the law at first hand, either as divorce petitioners or legal practitioners, did not seek reform. Such reticence is explained by an unwillingness to face charges of dubious morality and a long acquiescence to the idea that divorce reform was simply unattainable. However, attitudinal changes towards marriage, marital cruelty, husbands' superiority, wifely endurance and a reassessment of the role of church and state in individual lives collectively led to divorce reform.

The proclaimed societal impact of divorce was also exaggerated. There is little evidence of the hasty divorces or the solely Protestant complexion of divorcees so often espoused by anti-divorce campaigners. The forecasted apocalyptic figures of divorces have never been met, providing further testament of the false furore which long encircled the issue of divorce.[6] The moderate rate of divorce can partly be explained by moral conservatism, but a process of customisation to the reality of marriage breakdown also impacted: many had been without a partner for so long that they did not seek legal redress, or did not know the whereabouts of their spouse, when divorce became available. Cost also remained a consideration and, for some, especially if ineligible for legal aid, a deterrent. Although Ireland's self-proclaimed 'most successful divorce agency' advertised divorce for €460 for those in receipt of social welfare

---

[5] Fitzpatrick, 'Divorce and separation', p. 195.
[6] About 20,000–30,000 divorcees were predicted in the first post-reform year in the Republic of Ireland, for example (Hamilton, *The case against divorce*, p. 42).

and some handled their own divorces at a cost of €25,[7] uncontested divorces cost an estimated €2,000–€3,000 in the 2000s. The latter, although ten times less than the equivalent of its earlier parliamentary predecessor in Westminster, was still beyond the means of many. More protracted divorces can be hugely expensive: Seamus S.'s divorce in the Republic of Ireland cost €50,000 in 2012: 'You still love that person and think, What did I do wrong? It's a scar that you carry. ... I lost my kids' time, and three houses and four cars in order to pay the legal fees.'[8]

Divorce was never easy and its cost was rarely solely financial. 'Aoife', recounting her experience of divorce in 2015, described it as 'a massive emotional trauma, and I wouldn't recommend it in any way. The family law courts are humiliating, dreadful'. Her depiction of the court as 'a bullring ... in the full hearing of strangers' was reminiscent of the appeals for compassion made by those calling for divorce to be removed from the parliamentary arena from the nineteenth century onwards. Thus, although the location of hearings changed, the trials of giving evidence on the intricacies and intimacies of married life transcended the centuries. Although 'Aoife' got custody, she received no maintenance and had to sell land to 'pay ... [her spouse] off in a lump sum. He [her former spouse] has since become distant from our child and doesn't turn up for his scheduled visits.'[9]

Despite the emphasis placed on mediation, especially in the Republic of Ireland's legal system, reconciliation was rare. Some adulterous women were disarmingly frank in this regard: Elizabeth Fife-Young's written admission of 1920 to her spouse declared of her paramour: 'I know mother thinks I am all wrong ... am not going to write a lot of sentimental twaddle, but I want to tell you that I love him, and ... admire and respect him more than any man I have ever known.'[10] Mary Doupe was equally irreconcilable in the following year: 'There is no use my brother's trying to deceive you ... a detective caught us in Limerick ... they brought me home ... how could you expect me back? ... He is honourable, and you are mean. I would not give his little toe for your whole carcase [sic].'[11] Family members and friends often mediated between the parties, but not all supported reconciliation. Baroness Jose Carbery's father rebuffed her husband's approach to broker a reconciliation and she subsequently divorced in Westminster in 1920.[12] Some reconciliations were also

---

[7] The main cost of divorce comes at the separation stage when much of the legal settlement is arranged (*Southern Star*, 24 December 2005 and *Irish Independent*, 10 October 2002).
[8] *Irish Times*, 17 January 2015.   [9] Ibid.   [10] 24 June 1920 (PA, HC/CL/CO/BF/2/4).
[11] Ibid., 30 June 1921.
[12] Beaten with a whip, the cruelty in this case was described as 'very distressing ... he seemed to have been brought up without any self-control, and a man of that sort was

short lived. The reconciliatory efforts of Lady Viola Gore's mother lasted just three weeks.[13] Following a reconciliation in which Maurice Boland's wife asked not to be brought 'to the same neighbourhood' for fear of censure in 1918, she left her wedding ring and a letter, noting they 'could not go on any longer ... nothing on earth will get me back. We made a mistake[,] life has been a hell living with you. You can divorce me as you said you would. No need to worry about me.'[14] Little has changed: the Law Reform Commission acknowledged mediation's seemingly minimal effect and judges are sceptical of the level of solicitors' engagement with the issue.[15] This is evidenced by Families, a Limerick-based support group for those who are separated and divorced, which recorded only two to three reconciliations out of a total of 3,000 members in 2015.[16]

The low level of reconciliation conjoined with an increasingly compassionate approach to divorce is promoting reform. The cessation of fault-based and non-consensual divorce is currently under review in Britain, so Northern Ireland may have to again face its divorce demons. The delay required between separation and divorce was also a cause of continued disquiet in the Republic of Ireland: 'When you count the years leading up to the separation and the recovery from the divorce, it's really 10 years of your life swept away.' As John Farrelly, director of Accord, the Catholic marriage guidance council, averred, Ireland was 'draconian still ... with a punishing legal route ... designed over two decades previously'.[17] There was therefore no quick escape from Tynan's loveless unions.[18] However, an Irish divorce referendum to allow the period of separation before divorce to be reduced, mostly likely to two years, and make the recognition of foreign divorces explicit in the Irish constitution was held on 24 May 2019. The lack of rancour this engendered and the 82.07 per cent of votes cast in favour of this change, one of the biggest majorities seen since the vote on the Belfast Agreement in 1998, is indicative of a huge attitudinal shift across the whole of the country.[19] As Minister for Culture Josepha Madigan rightly noted, this, like the

a dangerous companion for a tenderly-reared and delicately nurtured young girl' (*Irish Times*, 13 December 1919). See also 10 June 1920 (PA, HC/CL/CO/BF/2/4).
[13] Ibid., 31 July 1916 (HC/CL/CO/BF/2–3).   [14] Ibid., 6 August 1919.
[15] Report: Alternative Dispute Resolution: Conciliation and Mediation (LRC 98–2010, November 2010), p. 74.
[16] Families also meet in Waterford and Cork (*Irish Times*, 27 January 2015).
[17] Ibid., 17 January 2015.
[18] Many suggested that two years between separation and divorce would be a sufficient delay (ibid., 27 January 2015).
[19] Also known as the Good Friday Agreement, the Belfast Agreement established the basis for devolved government in Northern Ireland on a power-sharing basis. It also created several institutions between Northern Ireland and the Republic of Ireland and the Republic of Ireland and the UK.

earlier votes on same-sex marriage and abortion, showed the 'kindness and understanding' of the Irish electorate.[20]

'Second-bite' divorces, where one party sought to amend the financial agreement, however, remain problematic. This was especially apparent in the Celtic Tiger era where wealth was often quickly accumulated and lost. Sizeable assets led to very substantial divorce settlements; €5 million and 51 per cent of a spousal pension was awarded to a wife in 2001 which is believed to be the largest award by the Irish courts, but other seven-figure settlements were made.[21] The continuation of the *in camera* rule for divorce hearings until 2014 also obscured the nature of divorce suits including the number of uncontested cases. Written judgements in more significant cases heard by the High and Supreme Courts determined legal precedents without identifying the protagonists by name, but circuit court hearings are rarely written up.[22] Even with these limitations, the history of divorce illuminates much about the often-hidden actualities of married life and the brokerage of power in a domestic setting. Divorce ultimately frees people from unhappy, loveless and abusive unions. Its denial in the Republic of Ireland for much of the twentieth century was due to a state balancing act between the common good and the rights of the individual that was often performed to the detriment of the latter.[23] Issues of self-determination, jurisdictional boundaries and state building were regularly deemed of more pressing importance than divorce. Moreover, the frequently unacknowledged system of Irish parliamentary divorce allowed the myth of a morally superior country that had no need for divorce provision to perpetuate. This afforded the opponents of divorce in both the north and south of the country with a moral high ground from which to purport an exceptionalism which did not reflect the complexities of marriage in modern Ireland.[24] That this was erroneous is proven by independent Ireland's ban on divorce, a move

---

[20] A total of 1,384,192 votes were cast in favour and 302,319 votes were cast against the 2019 divorce referendum. No constituency rejected the proposal, but Monaghan was most resistant to the proposed change. The turnout was 50.89 per cent (*Irish Times*, 25 May 2019).

[21] Such cases were often appealed. See, for example, M. K. v. S. K., 2001.

[22] *Irish Times*, 20 January 2015. The inconsistencies that this lack of case law might produce was criticised by members of the legal profession including the 2001 Working Group on a Courts Commission (*Irish Times*, 9 September 1999). Even in reported cases, custody and maintenance arrangements are often not mentioned.

[23] Article 41.2, 1937 Irish constitution.

[24] This idealisation was not solely indigenous; John Arthur Barratt, a member of the US Supreme Court Bar, the New York Bar and the English Bar, inferred that the level of sexual morality was as high in the United States as in any part of northern or western Europe 'except possibly amongst the Roman Catholic peasantry of Ireland' (J. A. Barratt to *Royal Commission on Divorce ... Minutes of Evidence*, vol. 2 [London, 1912], p. 180).

prompted by an apprehension that Irish citizens would divorce and remarry if permitted by the state. However, it ultimately proved impossible to sustain the claim that the constitutional ban prevented marital breakdown. Moral conservatism in Northern Ireland similarly led to reluctance to legislate on divorce to ensure genuine parity of provision with the rest of the UK. Yet, despite being controversial and contested throughout its long history, divorce afforded the only means for a permanent release from the bonds of marriage and a subsequent union, options which were too long denied to many of Ireland's citizens.

Bibliography

Primary sources

Dublin Diocesan Archives

Cullen papers
Walsh papers

Irish College Rome Archive

Hagan papers
Kirby papers

London School of Economics

Full report of the great sensational divorce suit of O'Shea v. O'Shea and Parnell (1890)

National Archives, Ireland

Council of Ireland papers
Department of the Taoiseach papers
Department of Foreign Affairs papers
Divorce – Irish Constitution, Embassy of Ireland to the Holy See papers
New Ireland Forum papers
Office of the Attorney General papers
Tenth amendment to the constitution, 1986 (Divorce)

National Library of Ireland

Bruce Arnold papers
Conyngham papers
Democratic Left papers
Dunalley papers
Irish Countrywomen's Association papers

Irish Labour Party Archive
Irish Queer Archive
James Douglas papers
Leitrim papers
Mervyn Taylor papers
Monteagle papers
Prior-Wandesforde papers
Wicklow papers
Yeats papers

Northern Ireland Assembly Library, Belfast

Divorce Acts (Northern Ireland), 1925–1939 (Belfast, 1939)
Standing Orders of the Parliament of Northern Ireland Senate and the House of Commons relative to the bringing in and proceedings on local bills . . . (Belfast, 1926)

Parliamentary Archives, House of Lords

Irish divorce papers, 1896–1922
Manuscript minutes and booklets of evidence on divorce bills, 1911–21
Minutes of evidence on divorce bills, 1922
Irish divorce papers, 1896–1922
Select Committee on divorce bills (minutes of proceedings and minutes of evidence relating to Irish cases, of the House of Commons Select Committee on divorce bills), 1907–22

Parliamentary/Government Records

Calendar of the Journals of the House of Lords, from 10 May 1768, to 21 January 1808 (n.d.).
Constitution of Ireland (Dublin, 1937).
Dáil Éireann debates
Department of Finance and Personnel Northern Ireland/A consultation from the Office of Law Reform, *Divorce in Northern Ireland. A better way forward* (Belfast, 1999)
Gorell Barnes, H. and De Montmorency, J. E. G., *The Divorce Commission. The majority and minority reports* (London, 1912)
Hansard, House of Commons debates
Hansard, House of Lords debates
Hansard, Northern Ireland House of Commons debates
Hansard, Northern Ireland Senate debates
Journal of the House of Lords
New Ireland Forum Report (Dublin, 1984)
Office of Law Reform, *Divorce – the new law in Northern Ireland. An equality impact assessment of the Matrimonial Proceedings and Family Law Bill 2002* (April 2002)

Report of the Committee on the Constitution (Dublin, 1967)
Report of the Royal Commission on Divorce and Matrimonial Causes (London, 1912)
Report of the Royal Commission on the Laws of Marriage (London, 1868)
Royal Commission on Divorce and Matrimonial Causes. Minutes of evidence taken before the Commission on Divorce and Matrimonial Causes (3 vols, London, 1912)
Seanad Éireann debates
Sessional papers of the House of Lords, *Reports from the Commissioners on the laws of marriage and divorce with minutes of evidence, appendices and indices* (3 vols., Irish University Press Series of British Parliamentary Papers, Shannon, 1969)
Standing Advisory Commission on Human Rights, *Report on the law in Northern Ireland relating to divorce and homosexuality* (London, 1977)

Presbyterian Historical Society, Belfast

A Committee of Ministers of Various Denominations, *Grievances of Protestant Dissenters under the recent Irish Marriages Act, and the immoral tendency of that measure stated and exposed* (Belfast, 1859)
Cooke, Rev. Dr, *Presbyterian Marriages. Authentic report of the Rev. Dr. Cooke's speech, at the special meeting of the Presbyterian Church in Ireland, May Street Church, Belfast, 10 March 1842* (Belfast, 1842).
Minutes of General Assembly of the Presbyterian Church in Ireland, 1850–1860.

Public Record Office of Northern Ireland

Abercorn papers
Annesley papers
Belfast Council for Social Welfare papers
Beresford transcripts
Divorce case papers of Lily Chambers v. Holt Waring Chambers, Co. Down, 1932–40
Divorce case papers of Jane Hanna v. George Hanna, Armagh, 1873
Divorce case papers of Robert McClintock, Londonderry, 1888
Divorce case papers, Magowan v. Magowan, c. 1910–21
Divorce case papers of Walker v. Walker, 1819
Divorce petition of Mary Elizabeth Orr, Belfast, 1902
Divorce suit and bill of 1st Viscount Belmore, 1793
Dufferin and Ava papers
Dunleath papers
Enniskillen papers
Extracts from the *House of Lords' Journal* re. the Abercorn Divorce Bill, 1799
Hely-Hutchinson papers

L'Estrange and Brett Solicitors, Belfast, papers
MacGeough Bond papers
Maxwell papers
Meeting of the Northern Ireland Executive, 1974
Nesbitt papers
Northern Ireland Cabinet papers
Northern Ireland Cabinet Secretariat
Northern Ireland Department of Home Affairs
Northern Ireland Department of Finance
Northern Ireland Prime Minister's Office
Papers re. matrimonial causes in consistorial court concerning divorce
    and alimony in case of Delacherois v. Delacherois, Armagh, 1869 and
    1871
Walker v. Walker, 1819 copy of declaration filed in consistorial court,
    Dublin, 1719

John Rylands, Library, University of Manchester

Minutes of Conference of Methodist Societies in Ireland, 1857

Printed primary sources

Anon., *Authentic report of the crim. con. trial of Joynt v. Jackson in the Exchequer Court, Dublin commencing May 10th, 1880 from shorthand notes by a gentleman in court* (Dublin, 1880).

Crim. con. actions and trials and other legal proceedings relating to marriage before the passing of the present Divorce Act (London, c. 1857).

Crim. con. A full, faithful, and impartial report of the trial wherein Sir John M. Doyle, KCB and KTS was plaintiff: and George Peter Brown, Esq. defendant for criminal conversation with the plaintiff's wife … (Dublin, 1820).

Divorce in 1857: The Talbot case. Letters by 'Cujus', containing full particulars of the case, with observations on the present unsatisfactory state of the law (London, 1857).

(MacHale, John, pseudonym Hierophilos), *The letters of Hierophilos, on the education of the poor of Ireland; together with a letter on Divorce, to the Archbishop of Canterbury: to which are subjoined, the letters of Bibliophilos* (Dublin, 1821).

Reports of some cases in which the Marquess and Marchioness of Westmeath have been litigant parties (London, 1825).

Talbot v. Talbot. A report of the speech of William Keogh, Esq, MP, Solicitor General for Ireland, on behalf of the appellant, before the High Court of Delegates, Jan. 8, 1855 (London and Dublin, 1855).

The most noble George Thomas John, Marquess of Westmeath, appellant, against the most noble Emily Anne Bennett Elizabeth, Marchioness of Westmeath (his wife), respondent: an appeal from the Arches Court of Canterbury (London, 1828).

The Newsman's full and revised report of the extraordinary marriage case, Thelwall v. Yelverton, tried before Lord Chief Justice Monahan, the Court of Common Pleas, Dublin . . . 1861 (London, 1861).

The O'Shea- Parnell divorce case. Full and complete proceedings (Boston, n.d.).

Trials for adultery: or, the history of divorces (7 vols., new impression of London 1779–80 ed., New Jersey, 2006).

Barrington, Shute, *The house of peeresses: or, female oratory. Containing the debates of several Peeresses on the Bishop of Landaff's Bill for the more effectual discouragement of the crime of adultery* (London, 1779).

Chapone, Sarah, *The hardships of the English laws. In relation to wives. With an explanation of the original curse of subjection passed upon the woman. In an humble address to the legislature* (London, 1735).

'Castamore', *Conjugium languens: or, the natural, civil, and religious mischiefs arising from conjugal infidelity and impunity* (London, 1700).

Clark, C. and Finnelly, W. (eds,), *Reports of cases heard and decided in the House of Lords on appeals and writs of error . . . during the sessions 1838 and 1839*, vol. 6 (Boston, 1873).

(E.A.Y), *Annals of fashionable gallantry: a collection of remarkable trials for crim. con., divorce, adultery, seduction, cruelty, and c.; The whole forming a complete history of the private life and amours of many characters in the most ellvated [sic] sphere, interspersed with many curious anecdotes of supreme bon jon* (London, 1830).

Haggard, John, *Reports of cases argued and determined in the English Ecclesiastical Courts at Doctors' Commons and in the High Court of Delegates* (4 vols., London, 1829–32).

Lowry-Corry, Armar (Earl Belmore), *The trial of Viscountess Belmore (formerly Lady Henrietta Hobart, daughter to John Earl of Buckinghamshire) for adultery with the Earl of Ancram* (London, 1793).

Napier, Joseph, *England or Rome, which shall govern Ireland? A reply to the letter of Lord Monteagle* (Dublin, 1851).

Norton, Caroline, *A letter to the Queen on Lord Chancellor Cranworth's Marriage and Divorce Bill* (Cambridge, 2010, reprint of 1855 ed.).

English laws for women in the nineteenth century (n.p., 2009, reprint of 1854 ed.).

Observations on the natural claim of the mother to the custody of her infant children as affected by the Common Law right of the father (London, 1837).

Nugent, George Frederick, *Crim. con. A narrative of a late trial in a cause of crim. con. wherein the Rt. Hon. George, Earl of Westmeath was plaintiff, and the Hon. Augustus Cavendish Bradshaw, defendant* (Dublin, 1796).

Paget, Thomas Tertius, *A letter to his Excellency the Lord Lieutenant of Ireland in the Judgment of the High Court of Delegates in the case of Talbot v. Talbot* (London, 1856).

Philips, Charles, *The speech of Mr. Philips, delivered in the Court of Common Pleas, Dublin, in the case of Guthrie versus Sterne, for Adultery* (London, 1816).

Phillips, Charles (ed.), *The speeches of Charles Phillips, Esq. delivered at the Bar, on various public occasions, in Ireland and England* (London, 1817).

Pilkington, Letitia, *Memoirs of Mrs Letitia Pilkington 1712–50* (London, reprint of first ed., 1748–54, 1928).

Plowden, Francis, *Crim. con. biography: or celebrated trials in the ecclesiastical and civil courts for adultery and other crimes connected with inconsistency, from the period of Henry the eighth to the present time*, vols. 1–2 (London, 1830).

Power Cobbe, Frances, *The duties of women. A course of lectures* (*London, 1881*).

Life of Frances Power Cobbe by herself (vol. II, London, 1894).

Stead, William T., *The discrowned king of Ireland with some opinions of the press on the O'Shea divorce case* (London, 1891).

Westmeath, Marquess of (George Thomas Nugent), *A sketch of Lord Westmeath's case* (Dublin, 1828).

(George Thomas Nugent), *A reply to the 'Narrative of the Marchioness of Westmeath'* (London, 1857).

Westmeath, Marchioness of (Emily Anne Bennett Elizabeth Nugent), *A narrative of the case of the Marchioness of Westmeath* (London, 1857).

Newspapers/Periodicals

Armagh Guardian
Belfast News-Letter
Belfast Telegraph
The Bell
The Bookman
The Catholic Bulletin
Catholic Herald
Catholic Telegraph
Christian Advocate
Church of Ireland Gazette
Contemporary Review
Cork Examiner
Daily Express
Daily Mail
The Eugenic Review
The Examiner
Finns Leinster Journal
Fortnight
Freeman's Journal and Daily Commercial Advertiser
The Furrow
The Globe
Horizon
Illustrated London News
Irish Catholic
The Irish Citizen
Irish Ecclesiastical Gazette
Irish Examiner
Irish Independent
The Irish Jurist and Local Government Review
Irish Law Times Review
The Irish Law Times and Solicitors' Journal

Irish Press
Irish Statesman
Irish Times
Journal of the House of Lords
Kilkenny People
The Leader
Morning Post
The Observer
The Saturday Review
Southern Star
Studies
Sunday Independent
The Tablet
The Times
The Watchman and Wesleyan Advertiser
Weekly Irish Times
Wesleyan-Methodist Magazine
Women's Action
Women's Watch

Printed Secondary Sources

Books

Abels, Jules, *The Parnell tragedy* (New York and London, 1966).
Andrews, David, *Kingstown Republican* (Dublin, 2007).
Atkinson, Diane, *The criminal conversation of Mrs Norton* (London, 2012).
Bailey, Joanne, *Unquiet lives: marriage and marriage breakdown in England, 1660–1800* (Cambridge, 2003).
Ballard, Linda May, *Forgetting frolic. Marriage traditions in Ireland* (Belfast, 1998).
Bartlett, Thomas, *Ireland. A history* (Cambridge, 2010).
Beale, Jenny, *Women in Ireland. Voices of change* (Houndsmills, 1986).
Biggs, John M., *The concept of matrimonial cruelty* (London, 1962).
Binchy, D. A. et al., *Studies in early Irish law* (Dublin, 1936).
Binchy, William, *A casebook on Irish family law* (Abingdon, 1984).
   Is divorce the answer? (Dublin, 1983).
Binchy, William, Doran, Kevin, O'Reilly, John and Lowry, Nick, *Fusion or fission. Ireland's option for the family* (Dun Laoghaire, 1988).
Blanchard, Paul, *The Irish and Catholic power. An American interpretation* (Boston, 1953).
Bland, Lucy, *Modern women on trial. Sexual transgressions in the age of the flapper* (Manchester, 2013).
Blasius, Dirk, *Divorce in Germany, 1794–1945. Historical perspectives on divorce law* (Göttingen, 1987).
Blom-Cooper, Louis, Dickson, Brice and Drewry, Gavin (eds.), *The Judicial House of Lords, 1876–2009* (Oxford, 2009).

Bodichon, Barbara Leigh, *A brief summary, in plain language, of the most important laws concerning women; together with a few observations thereon* (London, 1854).

Bonfield, Lloyd, *Marriage settlements, 1601–1740* (Cambridge, 1983).

Bowen, Desmond, *Paul Cardinal Cullen and the shaping of modern Irish Catholicism* (Dublin, 1983).

Boyce, D. George and O'Day, Alan (eds.), *Parnell in perspective* (London, 1991).

Boyle, C. K. and Greer, D. S., *New Ireland Forum. The legal systems, north and south* (Dublin, 1983).

Breen, Michael J., *The influence of mass media on divorce referenda in Ireland* (Lampeter, 2010).

Brown, Michael and Donlan, Seán Patrick (eds.), *The law and other legalities of Ireland, 1689–1850* (Farnham, 2011).

Browne, Arthur, *A compendious view of the ecclesiastical law of Ireland* ... (2nd ed., Dublin, 1805).

Burke's Peerage (99th ed., London, 1949).

Byrne, Anne and Leonard, Madeleine (eds.), *Women and Irish society. A sociological reader* (Belfast, 1997).

Byrne, James Patrick, *The New Law of Divorce and Matrimonial Causes applicable to Ireland; with the Acts 21 and 22 Vic., c. 85 and 21 and 22 Vic., c. 108 popularly explained* (Dublin, 1859).

Callaghan, Mary Rose, *'Kitty O'Shea'. The story of Katharine Parnell* (London, 1989).

Callanan, Frank, *The Parnell split 1890–91* (Cork, 1992).

Campbell, T. J., *Fifty years of Ulster, 1890–1940* (Belfast, 1941).

Celello, Kristen, *Making marriage work: a history of marriage and divorce in the twentieth-century United States* (Chapel Hill, 2009).

Chester, Robert (ed.), *Divorce in Europe* (Leiden, 1977).

Chused, Richard H., *Private acts in public places: a social history of divorce in the formative era of American family law* (Philadelphia, 1994).

Clifford, Frederick, *A history of private bill legislation* (2 vols., new impression of London 1885–7 ed., London, 1968).

Coakley, John and Gallagher, Michael (eds.), *Politics in the Republic of Ireland* (3rd ed., London and New York, 1999).

Conley, Carolyn A., *Melancholy accidents: the meaning of violence in post-famine Ireland* (Lanham and Oxford, 1999).

Connelly, Alpha (ed.), *Gender and the law in Ireland* (Dublin, 1993).

Connolly, Linda, *The Irish women's movement from revolution to devolution* (Basingstoke, 2002).

Connolly, Linda and O'Toole, Tina, *Documenting Irish feminisms. The second wave* (Dublin, 2005).

Cooney, John, *John Charles McQuaid* (Dublin, 1999).

Copley, Antony, *Sexual moralities in France, 1780–1980: new ideas on the family, divorce and homosexuality* (London, 1989).

Corish, Patrick J. and Sheehy, David, *Records of the Irish Catholic Church* (Dublin, 2001).

Cosgrove, Art (ed.), *Marriage in Ireland* (Dublin, 1985).

Cott, Nancy, *Public vows: a history of marriage and the nation* (Cambridge, MA, 2000).

Cretney, Stephen, *Family law in the twentieth century. A history* (Oxford, 2005).

Crone, John, S., *A concise dictionary of Irish biography* (London, 1928).

Cruise O'Brien, Conor, *States of Ireland* (London, 1972).

Cullen Owens, Rosemary, *A social history of women in Ireland, 1870–1970* (Dublin, 2005).

Dillon, Michelle, *Debating divorce. Moral conflict in Ireland* (Lexington, KY, 1993).

Doggert, Maeve E., *Marriage, wife-beating and the law in Victorian England. 'Sub Virga Viri'* (London, 1992).

Duncan, William, *The case for divorce in the Irish Republic* (Dublin, 1979).

Earner-Byrne, Lindsey, *Letters of the Catholic poor. Poverty in independent Ireland, 1920–40* (Cambridge, 2017).

Edgeworth, Maria, *Castle Rackrent and ennui* (1800, London, 1992 ed.).

Eekelaar, John M. and Katz, Sanford N. (eds.), *Family violence: an international and interdisciplinary study* (Toronto, 1978).

Edwards, Susan M., *Policing 'domestic' violence. Women, the law and the state* (London, 1989).

Engel, Barbara Alpern, *Breaking the ties that bound: the politics of marital strife in late imperial Russia* (Ithaca, NY, 2011).

Ervine, St John, *Parnell* (London, 1928, this ed. London, 1925).

Eska, Charlene M., *Cáin Lánama: An old Irish tract on marriage and divorce law* (Leiden, 2009).

Faloon, Harris W., *The marriage law of Ireland: with an introduction and notes* (Dublin, 1881).

Fanning, Bryan, *The quest for modern Ireland. The battle of ideas, 1912–1986* (Dublin, 2008).

Farrell, Brian (ed.), *De Valera's constitution and ours* (Dublin, 1988).

Feeney, John, *John Charles McQuaid, the man and the mask* (Dublin and Cork, 1974).

Ferriter, Diarmaid, *Occasions of sin. Sex and society in modern Ireland* (London, 2009).

The transformation of Ireland, 1900–2000 (London, 2004).

Fenn, Henry Edwin, *Thirty-five years in the Divorce Court* (London, 1911).

Finlay, Henry, *To have and not to hold: a history of attitudes to marriage and divorce in Australia, 1858–1975* (Sydney, 2005).

Finnegan, Richard B. and Wiles, James L., *Women and public policy in Ireland. A documentary history, 1922–97* (Dublin and Portland, OR, 2005).

Foyster, Elizabeth, *Marital violence: an English family history, 1660–1857* (Cambridge, 2005).

Fremantle, Anne, *The papal encyclicals in their historical context. The teachings of the popes* (New York, 1956).

Fuess, Harald, *Divorce in Japan: family, gender, and the state, 1600–2000* (Stanford, 2004).

Fuller, Louise, *Irish Catholicism since 1950. The undoing of a culture* (Dublin, 2004).

Gemmill, John A., *The practice of the parliament of Canada upon bills of divorce: including an historical sketch of parliamentary divorce and summaries of all the bills resented to parliament from 1867 to 1888, also notes on the provincial divorce courts, and c.* (Toronto, 1889).

Glendon, Mary Ann, *Abortion and divorce in Western law. American failures, European challenges* (Cambridge, MA, 1987).

Goode, William J., *Women in divorce* (New York and London, 1956).

Gordon, John William, *The appellate jurisdiction of the House of Lords and of the full parliament* (London, 1905).

Gorell Barnes, John, *1st Lord Gorell (1848–1913), a memoir* (London, 1920).

Grant, James, *Random recollections of the Lords and Commons* (2 vols., London, 1838).

Hamilton, Mark, *The case against divorce* (rev. ed., Dundalk, 1995).

Hammerton, James A., *Cruelty and companionship: conflict in nineteenth-century married life* (London and New York, 1992).

Hand, G. J., *English law in Ireland, 1290–1324* (Cambridge, 1967).

Harris, Janice Hubbard, *Edwardian stories of divorce* (New Brunswick, NJ, 1996).

Heilmann, Ann, *The late Victorian marriage question: a collection of key new woman texts* (5 vols., Abingdon, 1998).

Hill, Myrtle, *Women in Ireland. A century of change* (Belfast, 2003).

Holmes, Andrew R., *The shaping of Ulster Presbyterian belief and practice, 1770–1840* (Oxford, 2006).

Horstman, Allen, *Victorian divorce* (London, 1985).

Howlin, Niamh and Costello, Kevin (eds.), *Law and the family in Ireland, 1800–1950* (London, 2017).

Humphreys, Alexander J., *New Dubliners. Urbanization and the Irish family* (London, 1966).

Hynes, Samuel, *The Edwardian turn of mind* (Princeton, 1968).

Inglis, Tom, *Moral monopoly. The rise and fall of the Catholic Church in modern Ireland* (2nd ed., Dublin, 1998).

Irish Bishops' Pastoral (Tomás Ó Fiaich, Kevin McNamara, Joseph Cunnarie and Thomas Morris), *Love is for life. A pastoral letter issued on behalf of the Irish hierarchy* (Dublin, 1985).

Jackman, Isaac, *The divorce, a farce: as it is performed at the Theatre Royal, Drury Lane. Written by the author of* All the world's a stage (London, 1781).

Jefferies, Henry, *Priests and prelates of Armagh in the age of the reformations, 1518–58* (Dublin, 1997).

Jeffery, Reginald W. (ed.), *Dyott's diary, 1781–1845: a selection from the journal of William Dyott, sometime general in the British army and aide-de-coup to His Majesty King George III* (2 vols. London, 1907).

Jeffreys, Shelia (ed.), *The sexuality debates* (London and New York, 1978).

Jenkins, Roy, *Gladstone* (London, 1995).

Johnston-Liik, Edith Mary, *History of the Irish parliament, 1682–1800* (6 vols., Belfast, 2002).

Joyce, James, *Ulysses* (London, 1922).

Kearns, Kevin C., *Dublin tenement life. An oral history* (Dublin, 1996).

Kee, Robert, *The laurel and the ivy. The story of Charles Stewart Parnell and Irish nationalism* (London, 1993).

Kehoe, Elizabeth, *Ireland's misfortune. The turbulent life of Kitty O'Shea* (London, 2008).

Kelly, Fergus, *A guide to early Irish law* (Dublin, 1989, reprint of 1988 ed.).

(ed.), *Marriage disputes. A fragmentary Old Irish Law-Text* (Early Irish Law Series, vol. 6, Dublin, 2014).

Kennedy, Finola, *Cottage to crèche. Family change in Ireland* (Dublin, 2001).

Kenny, Gillian, *Anglo-Irish and Gaelic women in Ireland, c.1175–1540* (Dublin, 2007).

Kenny, Mary, *Goodbye to Catholic Ireland* (London, 1997).

Keogh, Dermot, *The Vatican, the bishops and Irish politics, 1919–30* (Cambridge, 1986).

Keogh, Dermot and McCarthy, Andrew J., *The making of the Irish constitution 1937* (Dublin, 2007).

Kiely, Gabriel (ed.), *In and out of marriage. Irish and European experiences* (Dublin, 1992).

Kitchin, S. B., *A history of divorce* (London, 1912).

Korobkin, Laura Hanft, *Criminal conversations. Sentimentality and nineteenth-century legal stories of adultery* (New York, 2014).

Kuch, Peter, *Irish divorce/Joyce's Ulysses* (Basingstoke, 2017).

Lacey, T. A., *Marriage in church and state* (revised ed., London, 1947).

Lee, J. J., *Ireland, 1912–85. Politics and society* (Cambridge, 1989).

Leneman, Leah, *Alienated affections. The Scottish experience of divorce and separation, 1684–1830* (Edinburgh, 1998).

Luddy, Maria, *Women in Ireland, 1800–1918. A documentary history* (Cork, 1995).

Lyons, F. S. L., *Charles Stewart Parnell* (London, 1978).

Macbeth, George, *Anatomy of a divorce* (London, 1988).

MacCuarta, Brian, *Catholic revival in the North of Ireland, 1603–41* (Dublin, 2007).

MacCurtain, Margaret, *Ariadne's thread. Writing women into Irish history* (Galway, 2008).

Macqueen, John Fraser, *A practical treatise on divorce and matrimonial jurisdiction under the act of 1857 and new orders* (London, 1858).

A practical treatise on the appellate jurisdiction of the House of Lords and Privy Council together with the practice on parliamentary divorce (London, 1842).

The rights and liabilities of husband and wife, at law and in equity: as affected by modern statues and decisions (London, 1848).

MacSuibhne, Peadar, *Paul Cullen and his contemporaries with their letters from 1820–1902* (3 vols., Naas, 1961, 1962 and 1965).

McAreavey, John, *The Canon law of marriage and the family* (Dublin, 1997).

McBride, Ian, *Eighteenth century Ireland* (Dublin, 2009).

McClain, Linda C. and Grossman, Joanna L. (eds.), *Gender equality. Dimensions of women's equal citizenship* (Cambridge, 2009).

Malcomson, A. P. W., *The pursuit of the heiress. Aristocratic marriage in Ireland, 1750–1820* (Belfast, 1982).

Marriage and divorce statistics. England and Wales, 1837–1983, series FM2, no. 16 (London, 1990).

Matheson, Robert E., *A digest of the Irish matrimonial law* (Dublin, 1888).

Matthew, H. C. G. (ed.), *The Gladstone diaries, 1887–91,* vol. 6 (10 vols., Oxford, 1994).

Meehan, Ciara, *A just society for Ireland? 1964–87* (Basingstoke, 2013).

Meek, C. E. and Simms, M. K. (eds.), *'The fragility of her sex'? Medieval Irish women in the European context* (Dublin, 1996).

Montgomery, Fiona A., *Women's rights. Struggles and feminism in Britain c. 1770–1970* (Manchester, 2006).

Montgomery Hyde, H., *A tangled web. Sex scandals in British politics and society* (London, 1986).

Mortimer, Robert C., *Putting asunder. A divorce law for contemporary society. The report of a group appointed by the Archbishop of Canterbury in January 1964* (London, 1966).

Murray, Patrick, *Oracles of God. The Roman Catholic Church and Irish politics, 1922–37* (Dublin, 2000).

Musson, Anthony and Stebbings, Chantal (eds.), *Making legal history. Approaches and methodologies* (Cambridge, 2012).

Newark, F. H., Cook, J. I., Harkness, D. A. E., Freer, L. G. P. and Neill, D. G. (eds.), *Devolution of a government: the experiment in Northern Ireland* (London, 1953).

O'Brien, Mags (ed.), *Divorce? Facing the issues of marital breakdown* (Dublin, 1995).

O'Faolain, Sean, *The Irish* (1947, revised edition, London, 1969).

O'Shea, Katharine, *Charles Stewart Parnell. His love story and political life* (London, 1973 ed. of London, 1914 ed.).

O'Sullivan, Donal J., *The Irish Free State and its senate* (London, 1940).

Orgel, Stephen and Goldberg, Jonathan (eds.), *John Milton. The major works* (Oxford, 2003).

Osborough, W. N., *Studies in Irish legal history* (Dublin, 1999).

Outhwaite, R. B., *The rise and fall of the English ecclesiastical courts, 1500–1860* (Cambridge, 2006).

Perreau-Saussine, Emile, *Catholicism and democracy* (Princeton and Oxford, 2011).

Peterson del Mar, David, *What trouble I have seen. A history of violence against wives* (Cambridge, MA and London, 1996).

Phillimore, R. J., *The law of domicil* (London, 1847).

Thoughts on the law of divorce in England (London, 1844).

Phillips, Roderick, *Putting asunder. A history of divorce in western society* (Cambridge, 1988).

Untying the knot. A short history of divorce (Cambridge, 1991).

Family breakdown in late eighteenth-century France: divorces in Rouen, 1792–1803 (Oxford, 1980).

Pindar, Peter, *Lord Auckland's triumph: or the death of crim. con.: a pair of prophetic odes* (London, 1800).

Potter, Matthew, *William Monsell of Tervoe, 1812–94. Catholic unionist, Anglo-Irishman* (Dublin and Portland, OR, 2009).

Power, Patrick C., *Sex and marriage in ancient Ireland* (Cork, 1976).

Prior, Pauline M., *Madness and murder. Gender, crime and mental disorder in nineteenth-century Ireland* (Dublin, 2008).

Probert, Rebecca, *Marriage law and practice in the long eighteenth century. A reassessment* (Cambridge, 2009).

Pulling, Alexander, *Private bill legislation: can anything now be done to improve it?* (London, 1859).

Quilter, Harry (ed.), *Is marriage a failure?* (London and New York, 1984).

Rafferty, Oliver P. (ed.), *Irish Catholic identities* (Manchester, 2013).

Rattigan, Henry A. B., *The law of divorce applicable to Christians in India (The Indian Divorce Act 1869* (London, 1897).

Redmond, Jennifer, Tiernan, Sonja, McAvoy, Sandra and McAuliffe, Mary (eds.), *Sexual politics in modern Irish history* (Dublin, 2015).

Ringrose, Hyacinthe, *Marriage and divorce laws of the world* (London, 1911).

Robb, George and Erber, Nancy (eds.), *Disorder in the court: trials and sexual conflict at the turn of the century* (New York, 1999).

Roberts, James, *Divorce bills in the imperial parliament* (Dublin, 1906).

Rockett, Kevin, *Irish film censorship: a cultural journey from silent film to internet pornography* (Dublin, 2004).

Rohan, Dorine, *Marriage Irish style* (Cork, 1969).

Rowbotham, Judith and Stevenson, Kim (eds.), *Criminal conversations. Victorian crimes, social panic and moral outrage* (Columbus, OH, 2005).

Royle, E., *Modern Britain. A social history, 1750–1997* (2nd ed., London and New York, 1997).

Seymour, Mark, *Debating divorce in Italy; marriage and the making of modern Italians, 1860–1974* (Basingstoke, 2006).

Shanley, Mary Lyndon, *Feminism, marriage and the law in Victorian England* (Princeton, 1989).

Shannon, Geoffrey (ed.), *The divorce act in practice* (Dublin, 1999).

Shatter, Alan Joseph, *Family law in the Republic of Ireland* (Dublin, 1977).

Silverman, M. and Gulliver, P. H. (eds.), *Approaching the past: historical anthropology through Irish case studies* (New York, 1992).

Sinclair, Robert Victor, *The rules and practice before the parliament of Canada upon bills of divorce* (Toronto and London, 1915).

Skinner, Quentin (ed.), *Families and states in Western Europe* (Cambridge, 2011).

Spreng, Jennifer E., *Abortion and divorce law in Ireland* (Jefferson, NC and London, 2004).

Smith, Bonnie G. (ed.), *Women's history in global perspective* (3 vols., Urbana and Chicago, 2004–5).

Snell, James, *In the shadow of the law. Divorce in Canada, 1900–39* (Toronto, 1991).

Steinbach, Susie, *Women in England, 1760–1914. A social history* (London, 2004).

Steuart, A. F. (ed.), *The diary of a lady in waiting*, vol. 2 (2 vols., London, 1908).

Stone, Lawrence, *Broken lives. Separation and divorce in England, 1660–1857* (Oxford, 1993).

   Road to divorce. England, 1530–1987 (Oxford, 1991).

   Uncertain unions. Marriage in England, 1660–1753 (Oxford, 1992).

Thompson, Torri L. (ed.), *Marriage and its dissolution in early modern England* (4 vols., London, 2005).

Tosh, John, *A man's place. Masculinity and the middle-class home in Victorian England* (New Haven and London, 1999).

Trouille, Mary, *Wife abuse in eighteenth-century France* (Oxford, 2009).

Ulster Year Book (Belfast, 1956).

Vaughan, W. E., and Fitzpatrick, A. J. (eds.), *Irish historical statistics. Population, 1821–1971* (Dublin, 1978).

Walls, Muriel and Bergin, David, *The law of divorce in Ireland* (Bristol, 1997).

Ward, Peter, *Divorce in Ireland. Who should bear the cost?* (Cork, 1993).

Westropp, George, *The Westropp. family 1250–2000* (London, 2000).

Whyte, John H., *Church and state in modern Ireland, 1923–79* (Dublin, 1984).

Political problems, 1850–60, vol. 5, no. 2 of Corish, Patrick J. (ed.), *A history of Irish Catholicism* (Dublin, 1967).

Williams, O. C., *Historical development of private bill procedure* (London, 1948).

Wilson, Deborah, *Women, marriage and property in wealthy landed families in Ireland, 1750–1850* (Manchester, 2009).

Wood, J. Carter, *Violence and crime in nineteenth-century England. The shadow of our refinement* (London and New York, 2004).

Wood, Kieron and O'Shea, Paul, *Divorce in Ireland. The options. The issues. The law* (Dublin, 1997).

Articles/Pamphlets

Abbate, L. L., 'What God has joined "let" man put asunder: Ireland's struggle between canon and common law relating to divorce', *Emory International Law Review*, vol. 16, no. 2 (2002), pp. 583–637.

Anderson, Olive, 'Emigration and marriage break-up in mid-Victorian England', *The Economic History Review*, New Series, vol. 50, no. 1 (February 1997), pp. 104–9.

'Hansard's hazards: an illustration from recent interpretations of Married Women's Property Law and the 1857 Divorce Act', *English Historical Review*, vol. 112, no. 449 (November 1997), pp. 1202–15.

Anderson, Stuart, 'Legislative divorce. Law for the aristocracy?', G. R. Rubin and David Sugarman (eds.), *Law, economy and society, 1750–1914* (Abingdon, 1984), pp. 412–44.

Andrew, Donna T., '"Adultery-a-la-Mode": privilege, the law and attitudes to adultery, 1770–1809', *History*, vol. 82, no. 265 (January 1997), pp. 5–23.

Anon., 'Statement from the Church of Ireland Role of the Church Committee', *The Furrow*, vol. 28, no. 4 (April 1977), pp. 255–7.

Beaumont, Catriona, 'Moral dilemmas and women's rights: The attitude of the Mothers' Union and Catholic Women's League to divorce, birth control and abortion in England, 1928-39', *Women's History Review*, vol. 16, no. 4 (2007), pp. 463-85.

Bergin, John, 'Irish private divorce bills and acts of the eighteenth century' in Kelly, James, McCafferty, John and McGrath, Charles Ivan (eds.), *People, politics and power* (Dublin, 2009), pp. 94–121.

Binchy, William, 'Divorce in Ireland: legal and social perspectives', *Journal of Divorce*, vol. 2, no. 1 (Fall, 1978), pp. 99–108.

'Family Law reform in Ireland: some comparative aspects', *International and Comparative Law Quarterly*, vol. 25 (October 1976), pp. 901–9.

Bromage, Arthur W. and Bromage, Mary C., 'The Irish constitution: a discussion of its theoretical aspects', *The Review of Politics*, vol. 2, no. 2 (April 1940), pp. 154–66.

Brooke, William G., 'Report on the differences in the law of England and Ireland as regards the protection of women', *Report to the Council of the Statistical and Social Inquiry of Ireland* (21 January 1873), pp. 202–29.

'Rights of married women in England and Ireland', *The Irish Law Times and Solicitors' Journal* (31 May 1873), pp. 280–3.

Buckley, James, 'A tour of Ireland in 1672-4', *Cork Historical and Archaeological Society*, vol. 10 (1904), pp. 85–100.

Burley, Jenny and Regan, Francis, 'Divorce in Ireland: the fear, the floodgates and the reality', *International Journal of Law, Policy and the Family*, vol. 16, no. 2 (2002), pp. 202–22.

Chester, Robert and Streather, Jane, 'Cruelty in English divorce: some empirical findings', *Journal of Marriage and the Family*, vol. 34, no. 4 (November 1972), pp. 706–12.

Coakley, John, 'Moral conservatism in a secularizing society: the Irish divorce referendum of 1986', *West European Politics*, vol. 10, issue 2 (April 1987), pp. 291–7.

Colgan McCarthy, Imelda, 'Out of the myth into history. A hope for Irish women in the 1900s', *Journal of Feminist Family Therapy*, vol. 4, no. 3/4 (1992), pp. 37–46.

Conley, Carolyn A., 'No pedestals: women and violence in late nineteenth-century Ireland', *Journal of Social History*, vol. 28, no. 4 (summer 1995), pp. 801–18.

Connell, K. H., 'Peasant marriage in Ireland: its structure and development since the famine', *Economic History Review*, new series, vol. 14, no. 3 (1962), pp. 502–23.

Coulter, Carol, '"Hello divorce, goodbye Daddy": women, gender and the divorce debate' in Bradley, Anthony and Valiulis, Maryann Gialanella (eds.), *Gender and sexuality in modern Ireland* (Amherst, MA, 1997), pp. 275–98.

Daly, M. E., 'The Irish family since the Famine: continuity and change', *Irish Journal of Feminist Studies*, vol. 3, no. 2 (1999), pp. 1–21.

Darcy, R. and Laver, Michael, 'Referendum dynamics and the Irish divorce amendment', *The Public Opinion Quarterly*, vol. 54, no. 1 (Spring, 1990), pp. 1–20.

Dillon, Kathleen M., 'Divorce and remarriage as human rights: the Irish constitution and the European Convention on human rights at odds in Johnston v. Ireland', *Cornell International Law Journal*, vol. 22, no. 63 (1989), pp. 63–90.

Duncan, William, 'Desertion and cruelty in Irish matrimonial law', *The Irish Jurist*, vol. 7, new series (1972), pp. 213–40.

'Supporting the institution of marriage in Ireland', *The Irish Jurist*, vol. 2 (1978), pp. 215–32.

Earner-Byrne, Lindsey, 'The family in Ireland, 1800-2015' in *Cambridge History of Ireland*, vol. 4 (4 vols., Cambridge, 2018), pp. 625–56.

Erickson, Avril B. and McCarthy, Fr John R., 'The Yelverton case: civil legislation and marriage', *Victorian Studies*, vol. 14, no. 3 (March 1971), pp. 275–91.

Eska, Charlene, 'Varieties of early Irish legal literature and the Cáin Lánama fragments', *Viator*, no. 1 (2009), pp. 1–16.

Evason, E., 'The ABC of suffering: divorce reform in Northern Ireland', *Fortnight*, no. 148 (27 May 1977), pp. 7–8.

Finlay, Henry, 'Lawmaking in the shadow of Empire: divorce in colonial Australia', *Journal of Family History*, vol. 24, no. 1 (January 1999), pp. 74–109.

Finlay, Peter, 'Divorce in the Irish Free State', *Studies: An Irish Quarterly Review*, vol. 13, no. 51 (September 1925), pp. 353–62.

Fitzpatrick, David, 'A curious middle place: the Irish in Britain, 1871–1921' in Gilley, S. and Swift, R. (eds.), *The Irish in Britain, 1815–1939* (London, 1989), pp. 10–59.

'Divorce and separation in modern Irish history', *Past and Present*, no. 114 (February 1987), pp. 172–96.

'Yeats in the Senate', *Studia Hibernica*, vol. 12 (1972), pp. 7–26.

Garvin, Tom, 'The politics of denial and of cultural deference: the referenda of 1983 and 1986 in context', *The Irish Review*, no. 3 (1988), pp. 1–7.

Griswold, Robert L., 'Sexual cruelty and the case for divorce in Victorian America', *Signs*, vol. 11, no. 3 (1986), pp. 529–41.

Hamilton, Susan, 'Making history with Frances Power Cobbe: Victorian feminism, domestic violence, and the language of imperialism', *Victorian Studies*, vol. 43, no. 3 (Spring, 2001), pp. 437–60.

'The practice of everyday feminism: Frances Power Cobbe, divorce, and the *London Echo*, 1868–1875', *Victorian Periodicals Review*, vol. 35, no. 3 (Fall, 2002), pp. 227–42.

Harding, Maebh, 'Religion and family law in Ireland: from a Catholic protection of marriage to a 'Catholic' approach to nullity' in Orucu, E. and Mair, J. (eds.), *The place of religion in family law: a comparative search* (Antwerp, 2011), pp. 161–85.

Hayden, Mary, 'Women in the Middle Ages', *The Irish Review*, vol. 3, no. 30 (August 1913), pp. 282–95 and 'Conclusion', ibid., vol. 3, no. 31 (September 1913), pp. 344–58.

Hogan, G. W., 'Law and religion: church-state relations in Ireland from independence to the present day', *American Journal of Comparative Law*, vol. 35, no. 1 (Winter 1987), pp. 47–96.

Humphreys, A. J., 'Migration to Dublin: its social effects', *Christus Rex*, 9 (1955), pp. 192–9.

James, Christine P., 'Céad Míle Fáilte? Ireland welcomes divorce: the 1995 Irish divorce referendum and the Family (Divorce) Act of 1996', *Duke Journal of Comparative and International Law*, vol. 8, no. 175 (1997–8), pp. 175–228.

Jones, Cedric, 'The non-recognition of foreign divorces in Ireland', *The Irish Jurist*, vol. 3 (1968), pp. 299–321.

Kaye, J. W., 'Outrages on women', *North British Review*, vol. 25, no. 49 (1856), pp. 233–56.

Keating, Anthony, 'Sexual crime in the Irish Free State, 1922–33: its nature, extent and reporting', *Irish Studies Review*, vol. 20, no. 2 (May 2012), pp. 135–56.

Kelleher Khan, Helena, 'The Yelverton affair: a nineteenth-century sensation', *History Ireland*, vol. 13, no. 1 (January–February 2005), pp. 21–5.

Kelly, Henry Ansgar, 'Rule of thumb and the folklaw of the husband's stick', *Journal of Legal Education*, vol. 44, no. 3 (1994), pp. 341–65.

Kelly, James, 'The private bill legislation of the Irish parliament, 1692–1800', *Parliamentary History*, vol. 33, no. 1 (February 2014), pp. 73–96.

Kenny, Gillian, 'Anglo-Irish and Gaelic laws and traditions in late medieval Ireland', *Journal of Medieval History*, vol. 32, no. 1 (March 2006), pp. 27–42.

Kitchen, Rob and Lysaght, Karen, 'Sexual citizenship in Belfast, Northern Ireland', *Gender, Place and Culture*, vol. 11, no. 1 (2004), pp. 83–103.

Levine, Philippa, "So few prizes and so many blanks': marriage and feminism in late 19th-century England', *Journal of British Studies*, vol. 28, no. 2 (April 1989), pp. 150–74.

Lowenstein, Ludwig F., 'Causes and associated features of divorce as seen by recent research', *Journal of Divorce and Remarriage*, vol. 42, no. 3/4 (2005), pp. 153–71.

McBride, Theresa, 'Public authority and private lives: divorce after the French Revolution', *French Historical Studies*, vol. 17, no. 3 (Spring 1992), pp. 747–68.

McCandless, Peter, '"Liberty and lunacy": the Victorians and wrongful confinement', *Journal of Social History*, vol. 11, no. 3 (1978), pp. 366–86.

Mahon, Evelyn, 'Women's rights and Catholicism in Ireland', *New Left Review* (November–December 1987), pp. 53–77.

Malcomson, A. P. W., 'A lost natural leader: John James, first Marquess of Abercorn (1756–1818)', *Proceedings of the Royal Irish Academy*, vol. 88 (September 1988), pp. 61–86.

Melikan, R. A., 'Pains and penalties procedure: How the House of Lords "tried" Queen Caroline', *Parliamentary History*, vol. 20 (2001), pp. 311–32.

Murphy, Seamus, 'Against divorce', *Studies. An Irish Quarterly Review*, vol. 84, no. 333 (Spring, 1995), pp. 7–16.

Nolan, Michael, 'The influence of Catholic nationalism on the legislature of the Irish Free State', *The Irish Jurist*, vol. 10, new series (1975), pp. 128–69.

O'Callaghan, Edward P., 'Bishop Edward Thomas O'Dwyer and the fall of Parnell: a reassessment', *Journal of the Galway Archaeological and Historical Society*, vol. 36 (1977–8), pp. 5–13.

O'Connor, Frank, 'The future of Irish literature', *Horizon* (January 1942), pp. 55–63.

O'Halloran, Kerry, 'The family and law in a divided land', *Dublin University Law Journal*, vol. 19 (1997), pp. 77–86.

O'Higgins,Kathleen, *Marital desertion in Dublin. An exploratory study* (Economic and Social Research Institute, Broadsheet, no. 9) (May, 1974).

O'Shea, Katharine and Fair, John D., 'Letters of mourning from Katharine O'Shea to Delia Tudor Stewart Parnell', *Irish Historical Studies*, vol. 31, no. 122 (November 1998), pp. 241–6.

Otway-Ruthven, Jocelyn, 'The native Irish and English law in medieval Ireland', *Irish Historical Studies*, vol. 7, no. 25 (March 1950), pp. 1–16.

Queckett, Arthur S., 'Divorce law reform in Northern Ireland', *Journal of Comparative Legislation and International Law*, 3rd series, vol. 22, no. 1 (1940), pp. 32–5.

Rafferty, Deirdre, 'Frances Power Cobbe' in Mary Cullen and Maria Luddy (eds.), *Women, power and consciousness in 19th-century Ireland* (Dublin, 1995), pp. 89–117.

Ralls, Walter, 'The papal aggression of 1850: a study in Victorian anti-Catholicism', *Church History*, vol. 43, no. 2 (1974), pp. 242–56.

Redmayne, Sharon, 'The Matrimonial Causes Act 1937. A lesson in the art of compromise', *Oxford Journal of Legal Studies*, vol. 13, no. 2 (Summer 1993), pp. 183–200.

Rowntree, Griselda and Carrier, Norman H., 'The resort to divorce in England and Wales, 1858-1957', *Population Studies*, vol. 11, no. 3 (March 1958), pp. 188–233.

Ryan, Frederick, 'The latest crusade', *The Irish Review*, vol. 1, no. 11 (January 1912), pp. 521–6.

Ryan, Louise, 'Publicising the private: suffragists' critique of sexual abuse and domestic violence' in Louise Ryan and Margaret Ward (eds.), *Irish women and the vote. Becoming citizens* (Dublin, 2007), pp. 75–89.

Samuels, A. W., 'The law of divorce in Ireland', *Journal of the Statistical and Social Inquiry Society of Ireland*, vol. vi (June 1887), pp. 186–92.

Savage, Gail, 'Erotic stories and public decency: newspaper reporting of divorce proceedings in England', *The Historical Journal*, vol. 41, no. 2 (1998), pp. 511–28.

'The operation of the 1857 Divorce Act, 1860–1910, a research note', *Journal of Social History*, vol. 16, no. 4 (Summer 1983), pp. 103–10.

'"The instrument of an animal function": Marital rape and sexual cruelty in the Divorce Court, 1858–1908'in Lucy Delap, Ben Griffin and Abigail Wills (eds.), *The politics of domestic authority in Britain since 1800* (Basingstoke, 2009), pp. 43–57.

'"They would if they could": Class, gender and popular representation of English divorce litigation, 1858–1908', *Journal of Family History*, vol. 36, no. 2 (2011), pp. 173–90.

Seabourne, Gwen, 'Coke, the statute, wives and lovers: routes to a harsher inter-pretation of the statute of Westminster 11 c.34 on dower and adultery', *Legal Studies*, vol. 34, no. 1 (2014), pp. 123–42.

Seward, Rudy Ray, Strivers, Richard A., Igoe, Donal G., Amin, Iftekhan and Cosimo, Deborah, 'Irish families in the twentieth century: exceptional or converging?', *Journal of Family History*, vol. 30 (2005), pp. 410–30.

Shaw, Helen, 'Untying the knot: the North and divorce', *Fortnight*, no. 241 (23 June–6 July 1986), pp. 5–6.

Simms, Katherine, 'The legal position of Irishwomen in the later middle ages', *The Irish Jurist*, vol. 10, new series (1975), pp. 96–111.

Snell, James, 'Marital cruelty: women and the Nova Scotia divorce court, 1900–39', *Acadiensis*, vol. xviii, no. 1 (Autumn 1988), pp. 3–32.

Staves, Susan, 'Money for honor: damages for criminal conversation', *Studies in Eighteenth Century Culture*, vol. 11 (1982), pp. 279–97.

Steiner-Scott, Elizabeth, '"To bounce a boot off her now and then . . .": Domestic violence in post-famine Ireland' in Maryann Valiulis and Mary O'Dowd (eds.), *Women in Irish history* (Dublin, 1997), pp. 125–43.

Tierney, Mark, 'Dr Croke, the Irish Bishops and the Parnell crisis, 18 November 1890–21 April 1891. Some unpublished correspondence', *Collectanea Hibernica*, no. 11 (1968), pp. 111–48.

Thomas, Keith, 'The double standard', *Journal of the History of Ideas*, vol. 20, no. 2 (April 1959), pp. 195–216.

Urquhart, Diane, 'Ireland's criminal conversations', *Études Irelandaises*, vol. 37, no. 2 (2012), pp. 65–80.

White, Harry Vere, 'Divorce', *Irish Church Quarterly*, vol. 6, no. 22 (April 1913), pp. 89–103.

Williams, Colwyn D., 'Nullity jurisdiction in Northern Ireland', *The Modern Law Review*, vol. 19, no. 6 (November 1956), pp. 669–78.

Wolfram, Sybil, 'Divorce in England, 1700–1857', *Oxford Journal of Legal Studies*, vol. 5 (1985), pp. 155–86.

Theses

Harding, Maebh, 'The definition of marriage in Irish law in the 21st century; a comparative analysis of common law and civil law' (2 vols., unpublished PhD thesis, University College, Dublin, 2008).

Sayers, Abby, 'Publicizing private life: criminal conversation trials in 18th-century Britain' (unpublished MA thesis, Auburn University, Auburn, AL, 2010).

Electronic sources

Dictionary of National Biography: www.oxforddnb.com
Free Presbyterian Church: www.freepress.org
Law Reform Commission: www.lawreform.ie
Irish Catholic: www.irishcatholic.ie
Irish College, Rome: www.irishcollege.org
Northern Ireland Registrar General Annual Reports: www.NISRA.gov.uk
Papal encyclicals: www.papalencyclicals.net
Radio Telefís Éireann: www.rte.ie
Republic of Ireland Central Statistics Office: www.cso.ie

Index